Performance Analysis of Queuing and Computer Networks

CHAPMAN & HALL/CRC
COMPUTER and INFORMATION SCIENCE SERIES

Series Editor: Sartaj Sahni

PUBLISHED TITLES

ADVERSARIAL REASONING: COMPUTATIONAL APPROACHES TO READING THE OPPONENT'S MIND
Alexander Kott and William M. McEneaney

DISTRIBUTED SENSOR NETWORKS
S. Sitharama Iyengar and Richard R. Brooks

DISTRIBUTED SYSTEMS: AN ALGORITHMIC APPROACH
Sukumar Ghosh

FUNDEMENTALS OF NATURAL COMPUTING: BASIC CONCEPTS, ALGORITHMS, AND APPLICATIONS
Leandro Nunes de Castro

HANDBOOK OF ALGORITHMS FOR WIRELESS NETWORKING AND MOBILE COMPUTING
Azzedine Boukerche

HANDBOOK OF APPROXIMATION ALGORITHMS AND METAHEURISTICS
Teofilo F. Gonzalez

HANDBOOK OF BIOINSPIRED ALGORITHMS AND APPLICATIONS
Stephan Olariu and Albert Y. Zomaya

HANDBOOK OF COMPUTATIONAL MOLECULAR BIOLOGY
Srinivas Aluru

HANDBOOK OF DATA STRUCTURES AND APPLICATIONS
Dinesh P. Mehta and Sartaj Sahni

HANDBOOK OF DYNAMIC SYSTEM MODELING
Paul A. Fishwick

HANDBOOK OF PARALLEL COMPUTING: MODELS, ALGORITHMS AND APPLICATIONS
Sanguthevar Rajasekaran and John Reif

HANDBOOK OF REAL-TIME AND EMBEDDED SYSTEMS
Insup Lee, Joseph Y-T. Leung, and Sang H. Son

HANDBOOK OF SCHEDULING: ALGORITHMS, MODELS, AND PERFORMANCE ANALYSIS
Joseph Y.-T. Leung

HIGH PERFORMANCE COMPUTING IN REMOTE SENSING
Antonio J. Plaza and Chein-I Chang

PERFORMANCE ANALYSIS OF QUEUING AND COMPUTER NETWORKS
G. R. Dattatreya

THE PRACTICAL HANDBOOK OF INTERNET COMPUTING
Munindar P. Singh

SCALABLE AND SECURE INTERNET SERVICES AND ARCHITECTURE
Cheng-Zhong Xu

SPECULATIVE EXECUTION IN HIGH PERFORMANCE COMPUTER ARCHITECTURES
David Kaeli and Pen-Chung Yew

Performance Analysis of Queuing and Computer Networks

G. R. Dattatreya
University of Texas at Dallas
U.S.A.

CRC Press
Taylor & Francis Group
Boca Raton London New York

CRC Press is an imprint of the
Taylor & Francis Group, an **informa** business
A CHAPMAN & HALL BOOK

Cover graphic represents the queing network for the contention-free channel access problem in Exercise 20, Chapter 5.

CRC Press
Taylor & Francis Group
6000 Broken Sound Parkway NW, Suite 300
Boca Raton, FL 33487-2742

First issued in paperback 2019

© 2008 by Taylor & Francis Group, LLC
CRC Press is an imprint of Taylor & Francis Group, an Informa business

No claim to original U.S. Government works

ISBN-13: 978-1-58488-986-1 (hbk)
ISBN-13: 978-0-367-38722-8 (pbk)

Library of Congress Cataloging-in-Publication Data

Dattatreya, G. R.
  Performance analysis of queuing and computer networks / author, G.R. Dattatreya.
     p. cm. -- (Chapman & hall/CRC computer and information science series)
  "A CRC title."
  Includes bibliographical references and index.
  ISBN 978-1-58488-986-1 (hardback : alk. paper) 1. Computer
  networks--Evaluation. 2. Network performance (Telecommunication) 3. Queuing
  theory. 4. Telecommunication--Traffic. I. Title.

TK5105.5956D38 2008
004.6--dc22   2008011866

Visit the Taylor & Francis Web site at
http://www.taylorandfrancis.com

and the CRC Press Web site at
http://www.crcpress.com

To my family

Contents

Preface

The principles used in the design, operation, and interconnections of data communication networks have been mature for well over a decade. The technology is very pervasive and upgrades to the equipment are very frequent. Therefore, a first course on the topic of computer networks is very useful for students intending to professionally work with this technology. Indeed, the vast majority of undergraduate students majoring within and bridging the electrical engineering and computer science disciplines study a course on computer networks. Simultaneously, a course on probability theory, required for such students, has generally expanded to include some material on queues, a fundamental topic in performance analysis of data communication networks. Alternatively, many undergraduate degree programs within these disciplines offer a follow up course, after probability theory, covering related topics including queues. However, in both these scenarios, a common observation is that queues are not taught with a systematic development of even the elementary results. Even if the subject has a chapter on Markov chains, the balance equations are written in a hurried fashion and students get a false impression that it is a rigorous development. Two examples of additional pitfalls are the following. Students get the false impression that they have formally derived the result that a stable queue reaches equilibrium. They also find it obvious that the departure process of an M/M/1/∞ queue is Poisson. While many such results are indeed true, there is a dangerous tendency to believe that the results extend to other similar but more general cases of queues and Markov chains.

Books and formal courses on stochastic processes or queuing theory generally dwell on the systematic development of the mathematical principles governing various types of Markov chains to force conclusions on when such desirable results are true and when they are not. This approach appears to be abstract, long-winded, and even graduate students in applied sciences and engineering tend to feel lost in a maze. Also, in such an approach, at the end of an abstract approach to Markov chains, simple queues are trivial examples and are not treated at length. Furthermore, in both the above approaches, only very simple examples from the application area of computer networks are introduced. The typical student completes the course with the frustration that only some formulas were given in the course. Instructors, on the other hand, form the following erroneous opinions about students. (*a*) They are impatient and do not realize the value of the mathematical principles governing even the simplest of queues. (*b*) They don't realize that practical systems are more complicated variations or interconnections of simple systems and that simple systems should be thoroughly understood first. (*c*) They just want some magical formulas not only for simple queues, but also for practical telecommunication systems they will encounter in their job-related activities. (*d*) They don't realize that each practical application system is different, and without a complete specification, it cannot be analyzed, even if such an analysis is feasible with skills available to students.

This book attempts to strike a balance between (*i*) mathematical skills of incoming students, (*ii*) mathematical skills that can be taught as part of this course, (*iii*) generality, (*iv*) rigor, (*v*) focus, (*vi*) details, and (*vii*) model formulation for application systems in computer networks.

Its prerequisites are well specified as follows. College mathematics including differential and integral calculus, elementary matrix theory (but not linear algebra), and a course on elementary probability theory. Principles of stochastic processes and advanced matrices (such as eigenvalue theory) are *not* assumed to be known to students. Throughout the book, the development is motivated and illustrated by examples and exercises in computer systems and networks. Mathematical derivations are part of the material; however, focus is maintained by splitting the development of a sequence of results into smaller tasks and discussing the role of the results in the big picture at every step. Also, final results are prominently restated with the appropriate conditions for their validity. Examples that violate the conditions and hence do not enjoy the corresponding results are included. Therefore, the book is self contained and can also serve as a reference for practicing engineers. As a consequence, only a short bibliography of mostly unreferenced books is included.

An additional advantage of this approach is that instructors and students can opt for detailed coverage of some topics while summarily browsing through the mathematical development of others and quickly moving onto applications. That is, the instructor can choose the level of detail and emphasize on different sets of subtopics. Therefore, even though the material may appear to be too vast for a one semester course, selection of topics is easy.

Many concepts and results of probability theory and stochastic processes are developed with the help of queues as applications. This avoids unnecessary abstractness and allows treating many different types of queues that appear in computer networks over a shorter time. This approach gives students motivation to study the needed principles and results. Every such development uses no more than the stated college mathematics (listed above) and principles thus far developed in the book, except in the final two chapters on advanced material. The book uses alternative and simpler techniques, in many places, to avoid using results from higher (say graduate level) mathematics. This avoids undue generality and keeps the focus on necessary results.

The material in the book begins by describing queues and with fairly extensive descriptions of activities in computer systems and networks resulting in various types of queues to motivate the students. Appendix A is a brief but rigorous and self contained review of elementary probability theory with examples and exercises.

Chapter 2 is devoted to traffic models. Pareto random variable is introduced as a model for either inter-arrival time or for service time in some computer network queues. The development also serves as a warm-up exercise in the use of probability theory. Poisson and exponential random variables are systematically developed from a practical source that emits jobs or electrons at random and with a constant rate. All their properties are developed. Simulation is introduced and the transformations from a uniformly distributed random variable to generate other important random variables are developed. Simple concepts of parameter estimation are also developed. Mean square convergence of a sequence of random variables is introduced as a natural topic in estimation. This finds use later in the analysis of sample functions of Markov chains and in the development of the Little's result. A very simple model for error-prone data channels is developed. The model is fully specified if the bit error rate at any data transmission rate is known. It is demonstrated with a throughput optimization example.

Chapter 3 is on equilibrium $M/M/1/\infty$ queue. Properties of Poisson and exponential random variables developed in Chapter 2 are heavily used. The equilibrium solution is systematically developed (without using any concepts from stochastic processes). To retain interest in equilibrium solution, it is shown that if such a system is in equilibrium at some time instant, it will remain so for all the time to come. To illustrate that we can construct practical models from simple (but not necessarily practical) models, a round robin version of $M/M/1/\infty$ queue with non-vanishing piecemeal service times is introduced and all the results are systematically developed. This also allows for a simple analysis of a data link affected by erroneous packets which are required to be retransmitted. The Poisson nature of the departure stream of an $M/M/1/\infty$ system is proved without using reversibility. This result is important to students for two reasons. It validates the assumption that packet arrivals into a queue can be Poisson even if bits and hence packets arrive over nonzero time intervals. Also, that the output stream can be fed in its entirety or through a probabilistic split to another queue as Poisson inputs. That is, a feed-forward network of $M/M/1/\infty$ queues can be analyzed with the help of results on individual $M/M/1/\infty$ queues. The non-Poisson nature of the merged stream of customers arriving at the waiting line of a round robin scheme is also shown. The probability density function and the Laplace transform of the busy time periods in an $M/M/1/\infty$ queue are systematically developed. All the results on $M/M/1/\infty$ queues are mathematically developed without using (and before introducing) the concept of stochastic processes. Any use of the term " average" of a random variable refers to its expectation and is clear from the context. As a consequence of the use of random variables only (and not random processes), Little's result, which is on time averages, is not introduced or used in this chapter.

Chapter 4 is on continuous time, state dependent single Markovian queues. The definitions and elementary concepts of stochastic processes are easily developed with the help of a queue as an application example. Continuous parameter Markov chains are introduced with the $M/M/1/\infty$ queue as an example. Balance equations for the equilibrium state probabilities of an irreducible chain are derived by first deriving the differential equations, just as is done for the case of $M/M/1/\infty$ queue. This is rigorous, and it also reinforces the concepts developed earlier. The conclusion is that if the balance equations result in a unique solution for the state probabilities, we have a nice Markov chain that can be in equilibrium and whose equilibrium performance figures can be evaluated. The general development of uniqueness of solution for a positive recurrent Markov chain is deferred to a later chapter. This decision is motivated by the desirability of an early introduction of a rich class of application systems in the computer networks area. An intuitive approach to develop the results for long-term time averages is followed by a thorough and rigorous development. Little's result is proved for FIFO and non-FIFO systems. In addition to the usual state dependent application examples with finite buffers and multiple servers, a very simple model of analysis of a heavily loaded Carrier Sense Multiple Access with Collision Detection (CSMA/CD) system is developed. Justification for the heavily loaded assumption is made by arguing that the individual stations attempt to transmit control packets when payload packets are absent in the buffer. The model and its utility from this example are comparable to the simplistic analysis of continuous time ALOHA to derive the maximum possible throughput, taught in a first course on computer networks. A similar system for CSMA/CA wireless LANs is completely described in exercises for students to analyze. A contention-free CSMA LAN performance analysis problem with a finite number of transmitting stations and heterogeneous arrival rates is similarly formulated. Its analysis and performance optimization is carried out. Other interesting examples in computer systems and networks are also included. Illustrative exercises on computer network performance analysis are listed.

Chapter 5 is on the M/G/1 queue. The recurrence equations for the state sequence of the imbedded (embedded) Markov chain of an M/G/1/∞ queue are developed. The uniqueness of solution to the resulting equilibrium balance equations is easily shown. The equilibrium state probabilities at departure time instants being the same as the expected long-term time averages of state occupancies is shown with the help of the PASTA property, which is also developed. The Pollackzec-Khinchin mean value formula is completely derived without developing or using the corresponding transform formula. The expected time averages of state occupancies for a finite buffer M/G/1 queue are also developed. The contention-free LAN performance analysis problem with heterogeneous arrival rates, first studied in Chapter 4, is generalized in the exercises here, to allow for heterogeneous packet sizes. This is a useful feature in Voice Over IP (VOIP) application.

Chapter 6 is on discrete time queues. A detailed analysis of timing within and across slots is very important to understand the various possible and impossible events concerning arrivals to and departures from empty and full systems. The analysis leads two different Markov chains, for the states, at slot centers and slot edges, respectively. State classification is developed with practical examples from computer systems. Existence and uniqueness of the solution of equations for equilibrium state probabilities is shown without using advanced linear algebra or advanced matrix theory. Interrelationships between these Markov chains are developed for students to clearly identify the correct quantities to be used to obtain the performance figures. Interesting examples from synchronous digital systems are used to illustrate the topic. Examples and exercises on the topic of slotted networks and sensor networks are also included.

Chapter 7 is on continuous time Markovian queuing networks. The case of open queuing networks is studied first. The Markovian nature of such systems is pointed out. Balance equations and traffic equations are developed. The product form solution is verified to hold. Illustrative properties and examples are included. For closed queuing networks, in addition to the verification of the product form solution, convolution algorithm, performance figures, and mean value analysis are developed with the necessary details. Illustrative properties and application problems are included.

Chapter 8 is on G/M/1 queues. The imbedded Markov chain of the G/M/1/∞ queue is analyzed. Results are specialized to Pareto interarrival times (IAT). The effective load as a function of normalized load and the Hurst parameter of the Pareto IAT are very illustrative; the average buffer occupancies are considerably worse than those in M/M/1/∞ queues for the same load. Furthermore, these averages steeply increase as the Hurst parameter increases towards 1. These results bring out the bursty nature of data traffic with Pareto IAT. The derivations use no results from outside and are fairly easy to follow, although obtaining the Laplace transform for a Pareto IAT is somewhat lengthy. Evaluation of equilibrium state probabilities at arrival time instants in a finite buffer G/M/1 queue is straightforward and included. From these, packet drop rates (due to the finite buffer), expected response time, and average queue size are easy to evaluate.

Chapter 9 introduces and analyzes a few bursty traffic models and their effects on queues. Chapter 10 introduces fluid-flow models and their analyses. These topics are considered somewhat advanced and the treatment here does use matrix theory and systems of ordinary differential equations. The motivation, model development, and relations to other models are nevertheless simple to follow, as are the final developed results. A conscious attempt is made to develop the advanced mathematical results as and when needed. Only very occasionally is a reference made to a specific advanced result in the literature, listed in the short bibliography.

Chapter 9 is devoted to bursty traffic and corresponding queues. Principles of smooth and bursty traffic are introduced with the help of simple probability theoretic principles. In the literature, exact results on queues input with some models of bursty traffic have been elusive even with sophisticated mathematical tools. A tractable approximation to self-similar traffic is developed as follows. Merging numerous (theoretically, unbounded number of) streams of traffic with heavy-tailed IAT is known to result in a self-similar data source. In this chapter, the heavy-tailed Pareto random variable is approximated by a hyperexponential random variable. Merging several such data packet streams (each with a hyperexponential IAT) results in a Markovian Arrival Process (MAP) with a very large number of states. This Markov chain is shown to sport a product form solution which is evaluated with the help of an efficient algorithm. This also introduces state dependent closed queuing networks. A queue fed by such a packet source is analyzed. The complexity of the solution for the queue depends only on the number of states in the Markov chain of the data source. Matrix inversion is not required here. The complete analysis of such a queue is based on the original work of Marcel Neuts which deals with a more general system. Queues fed by data packet streams generated by a Markov modulated Poisson process (MMPP) are similarly but briefly analyzed. Evaluation of results on a queue input by an MMPP requires inversion of a square matrix with the number of rows equal to the number of states in the MMPP. Some results are left for students to develop and are listed in exercises. The product form solution developed here for closed networks with stations that offer immediate service expands the applicability of closed networks. Some interesting application problems on the topic of cognitive radio networks are formulated in exercises.

The final chapter, Chapter 10, is on fluid flow models. Data packets are considered to flow into a buffer at a rate that can switch from one value to another over a countable set of rates. The output from the buffer has similar features. These rates change in a continuous time Markov chain fashion. The analysis technique is first introduced with a two state ON-OFF Markov chain model of a packet train feeding into a leaky-bucket with a constant draining rate. An illustrative example demonstrates all the aspects of solution development for this two state Markov chain fluid input problem. Differential equations for the cumulative distributions of the buffer content in the general case of multistate Markov chain controlling the input and draining rates are formally developed. Solution follows the earlier developed eigenvalue-eigenvector approach. Little's result for the general case of a stable fluid flow system is systematically developed. If the number of states of the Markov chain controlling the flow rates is infinity, a matrix-method solution is not possible, in general. The simplest case of an infinite state Markov chain controlling the flow rates is the output of an $M/M/1/\infty$ queue feeding a constant rate leaky bucket. This is analyzed and illustrated with a variation of the first example. Comparison of the two different but similar systems is very illustrative.

I would like to express my appreciation and gratitude to many people who have directly and indirectly helped me through the development and preparation of this book. My wife Manorama has been very supportive and freed me from the many day-to-day concerns that would otherwise have impeded progress. She has willingly endured my unpredictable hours of work day and night. I thank her from the depths of my heart. My son Madhur's eagerness to see this book published provided additional motivation. Growing up, my parents, brothers, and sisters instilled in me a deep appreciation for education and critical thinking. I am indebted to all of them.

I have taught several sections from the first seven chapters to numerous students at the University of Texas at Dallas. Discussions with them and their questions and feedback have contributed to the way I treat the topics in this book. I have used some material from the research publications of my former Ph.D. students Sarvesh Kulkarni and Larry Singh. They were my teaching assistants for a few semesters each and have helped me in other ways with this book. Early versions of sections from some of the chapters were prepared as notes for an online course through a grant from the Telecampus program of the University of Texas System. Larry Singh prepared those electronic notes. R. Chandrasekaran and Shun-Chen Niu have spent a lot of time with me answering my questions on mathematics in general and on queues and Markov chains in particular. I am very thankful to them.

I thank Marwan Krunz of the University of Arizona, Sartaj Sahni of the University of Florida, and Medy Sanadidi of the University of California at Los Angeles for their early reviews on a few chapters. I thank Sartaj Sahni, the series editor, additionally, for including this book in the Series on Computer and Information Science. Finally, I thank the editorial and publishing staff of Taylor & Francis, in particular, Theresa

Delforn, Shashi Kumar, Amy Rodriguez, and Bob Stern, for their timely assistance and cooperation.

I am solely responsible for errors and omissions in this book. A publisher's website is planned to receive and announce errata. I will be grateful for any criticism and suggestions for corrections I receive.

G. R. Dattatreya

Short Bibliography

1. D. Gross and C. M. Harris, *Fundamentals of Queueing Theory*. Wiley Series in Probability and Statistics, 1998.

2. F. P. Kelly, *Reversibility and Stochastic Networks*. John Wiley, 1979.

3. L. Kleinrock, *Queueing Systems. Volume I: Theory*. Wiley Interscience, 1975.

4. L. Kleinrock, *Queueing Systems. Volume II: Computer Applications*. Wiley Interscience, 1976.

5. M. F. Neuts, *Matrix-Geometric Solutions in Stochastic Models: An Algorithmic Approach*. Baltimore, MD: Johns Hopkins University Press, 1981.

6. A. Papoulis and S. U. Pillai, *Probability, Random Variables and Stochastic Processes*. NY: McGraw Hill Higher Education, 2002.

7. K. S. Trivedi, *Probability and Statistics with Reliability, Queueing, and Computer Science Applications*. Wiley-Interscience, 2001.

8. R. W. Wolff, *Stochastic Modeling and the Theory of Queues*. Prentice Hall, 1989.

Chapter 1

Introduction

1.1 Background

A queue is an arrangement for the members of a set to appear for an activity, complete it, and leave. Such appearances are called *arrivals*. The activity is called *service*. The members arriving for service are called *customers*, even though they may not be humans in every case. Customers may be physical devices, or even abstract entities such as electromagnetic signals representing a data packet. The arrangement is also called a *queueing system*. The word queueing is also spelled *queuing*, now-a-days. Queues occur extensively in all walks of life and in many technological systems. They gained importance in machine shops with a demand for quick repair turn around during World War II. The simplest examples of queues are those in banks with customers being served by tellers, calls appearing at telephone exchanges, and population dynamics of, say, rabbits and foxes in a forest.

The following are some common features in a queuing system. Arrival time instants are usually uncertain, with a statistically steady behavior of the time intervals between successive arrivals. Similarly, the service times are also usually uncertain with a statistically steady behavior. Customers may wait in a *waiting line* to receive service. In the simplest arrangement, service is provided in a *first-in, first-out* (FIFO) order. In such a system, the customer receiving service is said to be at the *head* of the queue and a fresh arrival joins the *tail* of the queue. A customer *departs* from a queue after receiving service. In another type of arrangement, service is provided in parts or *piecemeal* with a customer typically alternating between the waiting mode and the service mode, returning to the tail of the waiting line after a piece of service. The customer leaves the entire system at the end of the complete service, possibly after many time intervals of piecemeal service, separated by time intervals of waiting. Queues with *last-in, first-out* (LIFO) service, and service in *random order* are also found in practice. An LIFO arrangement is commonly referred to as a stack (instead of being called a queue). In some applications, multiple customers may receive service simultaneously, with the help of multiple servers in the system. There may also be multiple waiting lines with customers moving from one queue to another. Such systems with interacting queues are called *queuing networks*. In such queuing networks, customers may move from the departing point of one queue to the tail of another. A customer may return to the tail of the departing queue itself. A customer may also arrive at the tail of an earlier visited queue for additional service. After possibly many such visits to multiple queues, a customer finally leaves the entire network.

Individual computers and computer networks abound with queues. Statistical averages of various quantitative criteria governing such queues are useful to assess the acceptability of the performance. Their evaluations are also useful to optimize the performance by tuning control parameters and to determine the number and qualities of processors and other servers required to achieve an acceptable degree of performance, in applications. Several examples of queuing in computers and their networks are described in the following section, to motivate a detailed study of the subject.

1.2   Queues in Computers and Computer Networks

1.2.1   Single processor systems

A computer processes jobs submitted to it by a user. Many of these jobs are ready-made computer programs that a user initiates through a keyboard command or by pointing the computer mouse pointer at a representative icon and clicking it. Internally, the main monitor program, called the *operating system* (OS) itself keeps the computer busy to a certain extent with housekeeping operations, even when there is no external job to process. For example, checking to see if any program is initiated by a user is a house-keeping operation. If a user strikes a key on the keyboard, that information stays in a memory buffer; the fact that the computer's attention has been called to the data-input device (keyboard) is stored in another buffer. The OS lets the computer to frequently check these buffers called the input ports. Input and output (I/O) between the computer and the external devices are through organized handshake procedures with the computer and the I/O device having a full knowledge of whose turn it is to respond and how, for every step of the process. When an external input device has submitted a request, the OS invokes one or more programs to examine the request and processes the same.

Most individual computer systems are built around a single processor each. Such a processor is called the Central Processing Unit (CPU). Even if the processor has pipelined or vector processing hardware, machine instruction executions are completed one by one in such machines. However, the CPU gives attention to segments of many different programs, in sequence. That is, whereas the machine instructions are executed one after another, the execution of program jumps from one subsequence of instructions in a program to another subsequence of a *different* program. The scheduling algorithm for such jumps between different programs is influenced by a variety of factors such as which Input/Output (I/O) device becomes active during an execution period. Even when there is no such external stimuli during a time period, the OS changes the CPU's attention from one program to another, with the help of internal timers. This feature is deliberately incorporated so that the execution of a short program is not completely held up while the CPU completes the execution of a very long program.

The machine instruction execution is relatively very fast in comparison with the usual speed at which the external requests draw the attention of the computer. Therefore, many times, the user feels that the computer is processing all the requests simultaneously, and hence the terms "multiprogramming" and "time sharing" are used to describe the operation of such a single computer system.

The queue in such a single computer system consists of arrivals of external jobs or requests submitted by the user. The server is the CPU giving piecemeal attention to the requests. Partially processed requests are sent back to the tail of the queue, whenever the CPU decides to change its attention to the next job in the queue. Such processing and queuing systems are referred to by the name *round robin*. More complicated queuing systems can be formulated by accounting for the interaction of the I/O devices and the CPU.

1.2.2 Synchronous multi-processor systems

Multiple computers are synchronously interconnected in some specialized systems to allow parallel processing. In such systems, all activities and data movement are controlled by a single master-clock that ticks at a constant rate. There may be other clocks synchronized with the master-clock. There may be a single or multiple service points. The number of master clock cycles, also known as *slots*, can vary from one invocation of a program to another. Statistical averaging of the performance metrics are useful to assess the overall systems. In such a system, a sequence of programs arrives and processing is FIFO, leading to a simple queue. However, the slotted operation requires the quantity "time" to be treated as a discrete variable.

1.2.3 Distributed operating system

In many other applications, several computers, terminals, and workstations, all generally referred to as *clients*, are connected to one or a few high performance computers called the servers. Client machines may process many jobs themselves. They may also ship jobs to the servers when deemed necessary. All the activities are controlled by a loosely coupled *distributed operating system* (DOS). There is no master-clock controlling the movement of customers; hence the time variable is a continuous one. In this configuration, jobs or requests may wait for various types of service at multiple locations. Therefore, there are several queues in such a system. Jobs may also visit service points repeatedly, due to the time sharing organization mentioned earlier. The overall organization is a network of queues.

1.2.4 Data communication networks

1.2.4.1 Data transfer in communication networks

In data communication networks, computers, called host machines are interconnected by a system of communication links. The interconnected system of links, not including the host machines, is known as the subnet. The host machines run application programs that require movement of data between different computers. All the computers are independent devices and there is no single DOS controlling the computers. The primary purpose is data transfer between computers which are possibly geographically separated by hundreds or thousands of kilometers. The process of data transfer requires running computer programs such as format conversion, proper I/O, etc., but the applications themselves are not generally computation-intensive. The level of cooperation is at a higher level in the sense that data transfer of every single item is not a tightly controlled handshake procedure. The following example illustrates the above situation. In an ongoing data transfer, the computer receiving data from an incoming data link is generally ready for the task. However, over a particular short time interval, it may not have processed all the received data available on its input ports. Several bytes of additional data may arrive in a quick sequence. In such a case, the newly arrived data may write over existing data in the input ports. If the recipient computer is configured not to accept data on input ports until existing data are processed, the newly arriving data will simply not be entered into any input ports and vanish! This demonstrates that such a computer network is less reliable than a tightly controlled interconnection between a single computer and its I/O devices. Another source of lack of reliability is the bit errors possibly introduced due to noise over long data links, especially over wireless networks. Such lack of reliability is taken into consideration and programs running on the computers attempt to compensate for the same through the use of error detection, acknowledgments, and retransmissions. These slow down the overall data transfer processes creating the necessity of queuing. If the overall data movement is not efficient enough, queuing delays will accumulate. The long queues necessitate very large buffers in which to hold waiting data. This becomes impractical, even if we resign ourselves to tolerate longer overall delays. Therefore, data transfer in practical computer networks is required to be very efficient.

1.2.4.2 Organization of a computer network

The overall network has a hierarchical structure with a backbone subnet made of a small number of high data rate links. A data link connects two routers. A router is a high speed special purpose computer, but it is not a host machine. A router can support multiple links, going in different directions. Each link is usually bidirectional, and can be equivalently considered to be two unidirectional links in opposite directions. Each router in the backbone subnet in turn feeds into different portions of the network. Each such portion itself is an interconnection of routers realized with the help of data links. Each of these routers feeds into one or more *local area networks* (LANs). A LAN uses a single broadcast medium through which several host computers communicate among themselves. One single computer on the LAN also functions as a LAN server to facilitate communication between the other host computers on the LAN and the rest of the world.

In data networks, communication between host machines is not in a contiguous stream of bits. An overall communication of a large file is accomplished by splitting the file into individual *data items*, with each data item consisting of a stream of several bits. The number of bits in a data item can range from hundreds to several thousands. Data items are *transmitted* from one point to the next over links. All the data items belonging to a file to be transferred do not necessarily go through the same sequence of links and do not appear at the eventual destination in the exact same order of transmission at the original source. Software in the original source host and the eventual destination host cooperate to reassemble data items to reconstruct the original file. Such software at each of the hosts of the origin of the file and the destination are called *transport layer* software. Thus, even the software for the data communication over a computer network is organized in a hierarchical way with different software modules responsible for different activities. Each *layer* of the overall software appends additional bits called *headers* to a data item to manage the transfer of a data file to the eventual destination. Several headers are added and removed in the course of the overall transfer of a data item. At the transport layer, a data item including its header is called a *transport data unit* or TPDU. The network layer is responsible for decisions on which data link a data item should be transmitted. At the network layer, a data item is called a *packet*. Between the end points of a single link, the *datalink layer* (DLL) software manages error correction, verification of successful transfer, etc. The data items in this layer are called *data frames*. The *medium access control layer* (MAC) manages data transfer over a broadcast link such as a LAN. The primary problems encountered by the MAC layer are cooperative access of the common communication channel, managing *collisions* which are unintended destructive overlapping transmission by multiple hosts, etc.

1.2.5   Queues in data communication networks

The total number of data links in such a vast network is very small in comparison with the number of host computers. In the case of a LAN, only one of the many host computer can successfully transmit data over the broadcast medium at any time. Therefore data communication over such an enormous and complicated network is required to be very efficient. Let us now understand some of the queuing that occurs in computer networks. A router receives data frames on incoming links, from another router. The network layer processes each packet very minimally and gives it to the DLL corresponding to another link over which the packet should be retransmitted. Following are some details. The DLL at the receiving router performs error detection and keeps track of whether or not all transmitted frames from the preceding router are received. The DLL strips the frame header and gives the packet to the network layer. The network layer examines the packet header. It determines the link over which the packet should be retransmitted (forwarded) towards the eventual destination. A few fields of the packet header, such as the number of hops may be updated and the packet is passed onto the DLL. The DLL introduces

- redundancy bits for error detection,

- serial number to track whether or not all the packets are successfully received by the router on the other side of the forward link, and

- frame boundary bits to determine the start and end of a frame.

The resulting data frame is transmitted on the forward link. The entire process at the router can be approximated to be a single FIFO queuing system. The real situation is a little more complicated. A router uses a more involved *data link protocol* over each of its links. As mentioned above, the activity includes using (a finite field) serial numbering of the data frames, acknowledgments, and retransmissions if necessary. Therefore, after transmitting a data frame, the router needs to hold it in another queue. It can be deleted only after the router receives an explicit or implicit acknowledgment from the frame receiving router. Thus, a better approximation uses two *interacting queues*.

A host computer connected to a common LAN maintains data frames for transmission in a queued buffer. When transmitted, a packet can collide with another, if a different host computer also starts transmitting a packet, in an overlapping time interval. Thus we have multiple queues with *interacting servers*, in a LAN.

1.3   Queuing Models

A model of a physical system is a mathematically precise representation of the interaction of several variables and functions governing the original system. The spirit behind the mathematical representation is two-fold as follows. We would like the representation to duplicate the functioning of the original system as closely as our knowledge of the system and our knowledge of mathematics allow us to do. We would also like the mathematical representation to be simple enough for us to analyze the same, with our limited knowledge of mathematics, and evaluate the required performance characteristics. Therefore, in most cases, these precise mathematical models are approximations of the real characteristics of the systems being modeled. These desirable features are often contradictory and therefore lead to multiple models with a simple model on the one hand and a more accurate but complicated one on the other, for the same physical system. A simple queuing model is a single FIFO queue. Such a model may be an adequate representation for a single database server and an acceptable approximate representation of a network router. Figure 1.1 shows a usual pictorial representation of a single FIFO queue. The circle at the right is the service area. At most one customer can be in the service area at any time. The server is required to be busy, serving, if there is at least one customer in the system. Customers are represented by short vertical lines. Waiting customers are in the buffer to the left of the service area. The mathematical behaviors of the *arrival time instants* and *service time* intervals for different customers are parts of the model. The arrival time instants are equivalently represented by *inter-arrival times* (IATs) and the time instant of the first arrival. The amount of time a customer spends in the entire system is called the *response time* which is the sum of the *waiting time* and the service time. Response time is also called sojourn time. Typical performance characteristics

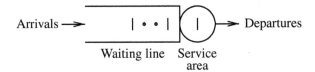

FIGURE 1.1: FIFO queue representation

of interest in such a simple queue include the following. The *average number of customers* found in the system. This is defined as follows. The number of customers in the system is a function of the continuous time variable. The average of this time varying function, over a long time interval, is the required performance figure. The average response time is the average of the response time intervals experienced by all the customers over the long time interval. The average waiting time and the average service time are similarly defined. The *fraction of time* the server is busy is also an important performance criterion. It corresponds to the total of the time intervals that the server is busy, divided by the total time of the queue operation. This fraction is known as the *utilization* of the server. The number of customer positions in a waiting line may be finite in some application systems. In such cases, a customer attempting to arrive is not allowed to wait in the waiting line. Such queues are known as finite buffer queues.

David George Kendall (1918–2007) introduced a notation to represent different classes of single waiting line queues in the year 1953. The $A/B/m/k/n$ queue has interarrival times of type A and service times of type B. The parameter m is the number of servers, k is the maximum number of customers allowed to be in the queue (including any being serviced) at any time, and n is the size of the population from which customers arrive. Classes of A and B are distinguished by their statistical properties.

The behavior of a queue is cumulative, in the sense that the number of customers found at any time instant is affected by previous activity. Clearly, the future behavior of the queue is affected by the the number of customers found at the current time instant. In general, the time instant of the next arrival may depend on the past, for example, on the time instant of the most recent arrival. Similarly, time instant at which the customer being currently served will depart may depend on when the time instant the previous customer departed after service. However, it turns out we can construct simple mathematical models of IATs and service times wherein the statistics of the future behavior of a queue depends only on the number of customers in the system at the present time instant and not even on the time instants of the most recent arrival and departure. These are developed in the chapters to follow.

Many complicated queuing systems can be modeled with the help of modifications of simple models, or with interconnections of simple models or with both. Therefore, it is very important to study very simple models in the beginning, even if they appear to be unrealistically ideal. A study of a variety of simple models and some of their modifications and interconnections also helps us to develop more realistic models for physical systems. Such a study also enhances the level of our mathematical knowledge and helps us to attempt analysis of more realistic, complicated models. Occasionally, it turns out that some performance characteristics of a more involved

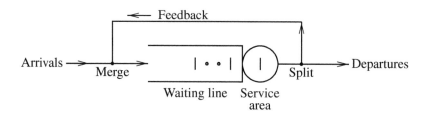

FIGURE 1.2:   Round robin queue

model are the same as the corresponding ones for a simple model. For example, consider a round robin scheme, the model for which is obtained by using a feedback path in the simple FIFO model. A pictorial representation is shown in Figure 1.2. The wperating system's timer decides when to pause the service for a job and feed it back to the queue's tail. The time for feedback is usually negligible in comparison with each continuous service time intervals. Therefore, the number of customers in the FIFO and in the corresponding round robin models are identical, all the time. This implies that the two models have the same average number of customers and server utilization. The following describes a few examples of models for queues for different systems constructed by making modifications to simple models. A model for the queue for multiple servers in a DOS with a few computation intensive servers is shown in Figure 1.3. Job arrivals are those submitted by many client computers. They queue up for FIFO service. Each server has its own service area. There can be at most one customer in each service area. The DOS must use a scheduling policy on which server to send an arriving job to, if there are multiple servers free to serve, when an arrival comes in. In some client server systems, a client may be allowed to submit only one job to the server and is not allowed to submit another job until the previously submitted job is complete. In such a system, the arrivals are functions of the number of jobs in the servers' queue. In a more general system of multiple processors, jobs queue up in front of all servers. The DOS may ship jobs from the output of one queue to the tail of another or to the tail of the original

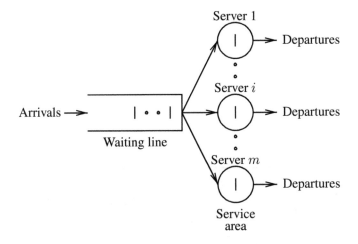

FIGURE 1.3: A queue with multiple servers

queues. At some time, possibly after visiting several queues multiple times, a job finally departs. Such a system is called an *open queuing network* and is depicted in Figure 1.4. Alternatively, in a DOS, we can model all the processes of the DOS as customers that move from one queue to another depending on the data received. External programs now function as data to the DOS. In such a case, the number of customers in the queuing network is a constant all the time. Such systems are called *closed queuing systems.* The model for a queuing system is not complete without a precise mathematical specification of the behavior of interarrival times and service times. The model may also require a scheduling policy for system operation. The interarrival times and service times are usually uncertain quantities; they vary from one job to another. But they also usually possess statistically steady behavior over a long time of operation. Therefore, we use probability theoretic models for these. In some cases, the scheduling policy can be varied to optimize some performance criterion of the system.

1.4 Conclusion

Many real computer networks' queuing models are very complicated. However, in many cases, approximate models can be developed with the help of either the variations of simple models or some interconnections of simple models. Examples

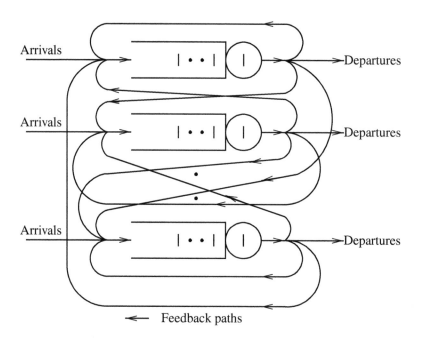

FIGURE 1.4:   Open queuing network

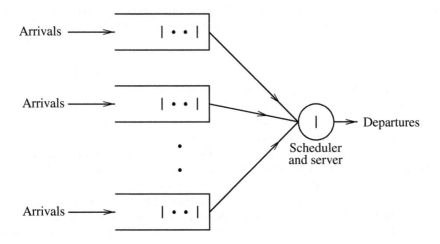

FIGURE 1.5: Multiple queues with a single scheduler and server

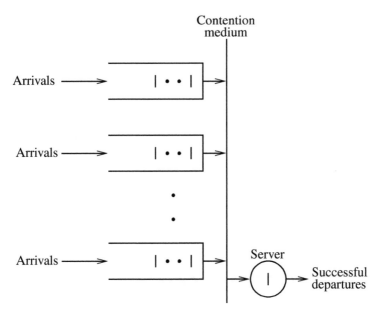

FIGURE 1.6: Multiple queues with contention based service

of these were included at the beginning of this chapter to motivate a detailed study of queuing models starting from very simple models. The next chapter deals with the introduction and detailed analysis of simple traffic models. Simulation of these traffic patterns is also a topic there. In addition, simple principles and procedures of parameter estimation are included. They are very useful in the analysis of real or simulated traffic patterns.

Many of computer networks' diverse performance metrics are statistical averages. therefore, by and large, analyses of queues are applications of probability theory and stochastic processes. These are functions of the behavior of time periods of internal activities and external load or request patterns. Typically, requests for service wait in queues. Therefore, queuing theoretic principles are the main set of tools in our performance analysis. Statistical averaging of the quantities affecting the performance requires the study of the variations of those quantities as they occur repeatedly. Evaluation of such statistical averages is facilitated by the extensive use of Probability Theory and Random Processes, in queuing theory. Many advanced principles of probability theory and elementary principles of random processes are easier to grasp with the help of the applications in which they find use. They are introduced and covered in the necessary detail, as needed, in the following chapters. A review of Probability Theory appears in the Appendix at the end of the book.

Chapter 2

Characterization of Data Traffic

2.1 Introduction

Data traffic is the sequence of movement of data items through a point or a physical device. A typical data item is a contiguous sequence of bits forming a data packet. When these data items pass through a physical device, there is usually some impediment in the form of reception, processing, and forwarding. Such an impediment results in queuing and causes time delays. In general, queues have successive arrivals of customers as inputs. These arrivals experience possible waiting and service before being output as successive departures. This chapter introduces important random variables that constitute models for arrival and service disciplines. The statistical nature of arrivals can be expressed in different ways. For example, if successive interarrival times (IATs) are independent, a specification of the initial condition in the form of the time instant at which the operation of the queue starts and the probability density function (pdf) of IATs are sufficient to completely describe the nature of arrivals. The Pareto random variable for IATs is one such model. This random variable exhibits some important variations in its characteristics, based on the values of the parameters of its pdf. Its variance can be finite or infinite. Infinite variance random variables find applications in characterizing bursty data traffic. Therefore Pareto random variables are studied in this chapter. Since its study is a valuable review of elements of probability theory, it is introduced first.

The number of arrivals over a time interval is another important way of characterizing the nature of arrivals. In general, this requires the specification of the initial condition and the time instants of the start and end of the interval over which the random variable number of arrivals is characterized. There is an important class of arrival disciplines for which this specification can be considerably simplified; the initial condition of the starting time and the exact time instants constituting the time interval over which the number of arrivals is being characterized are not important. The only important quantity influencing the number of arrivals is the amount of time in the time interval. This class of arrivals is known as Poisson arrivals, named in honor of Simeon Denis Poisson (1781–1840), a French scientist. The IATs in a stream of Poisson arrivals are independent and identically distributed (iid) exponential random variables. This class of random variables possess a very interesting property known as "memorylessness." The exponential random variable is a very useful model for service times since the memoryless property greatly simplifies the analysis of queues. Poisson and exponential random variables are studied in detail, following a study of the Pareto random variable.

One of the practical problems encountered in data communication networks is the errors in received data packets. Errors are caused by noise in physical links. A simple model of noise and its effects on bit errors and data packet errors is introduced. A particular advantage of this model is that if the packet error rate at a particular data transmission rate is given, the corresponding packet error rate at a different data transmission rate can be evaluated. This helps in optimizing the data transmission rate.

The basic approach to simulation of a queue is to generate outcomes of random variables corresponding to data traffic and use them in the way the queue operates. Therefore, simulation of random variables corresponding to data traffic is fundamental to the simulation of queues. Computer simulation of random variables is most commonly implemented by attempting to repeatedly generate iid outcomes of a very simple random variable and subjecting them to the needed transformations. Unfortunately, computers execute algorithms in a deterministic way. Therefore, if a simulation algorithm is run repeatedly with identical external data input, it produces identical results for every run. There is nothing random about this. If the external inputs themselves form all of the extensive random data, we are not using the computer to simulate; we would only be using it to operate a system, possibly a queue, to which random data from elsewhere are input. The best we can hope to achieve is to use the computer to generate a long sequence of numbers that "appear" to have the properties of the outcome of a sequence of iid random variables. There are excellent algorithms for this purpose. Typically they approximate the generation of iid uniformly distributed random variables. The length of the sequence of such generated numbers is typically $2^k - 1$ where k is the number of bits in the computer word the the algorithm uses. If the algorithm is run to generate more than $2^k - 1$ random numbers, the sequence repeats. The algorithms also accept an external input called the seed that determines the starting point in the cyclic sequence of generated numbers. Thus, by giving different seeds, practically different simulation trials are realized.

The next step in simulation of queues is to generate outcomes of random variables for different data traffic models. This is usually accomplished by using mathematical transformations of a uniformly distributed random variable (that can be simulated) to the desired random variables. This is also a topic studied in this chapter.

Finally, analysis of simulation results require an understanding of the basic principles of parameter estimation from random samples. Only some very elementary principles of parameter estimation are included in this chapter.

2.2   The Pareto Random Variable

The Pareto random variable is named in honor of Vilfredo Federico Damaso Pareto (1848–1923), a French-Italian scientist. It is characterized by a pdf which varies as a negative power of the outcome and a value of zero for pdf for small values of the outcome. That is, if X is Pareto, its pdf

$$f_X(x) = \begin{cases} v\,x^{-u}, \; x \geq w \\[2mm] 0, \qquad x < w. \end{cases}$$
(2.1)

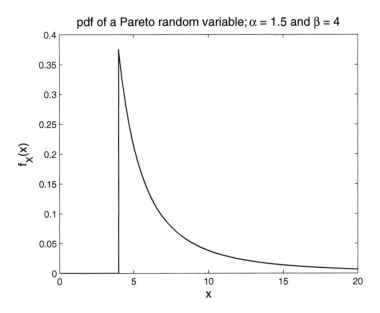

FIGURE 2.1:   Density function of a Pareto random variable; $\alpha = 1.5, \beta = 4$

To make this a valid pdf, we need

$$\int_{-\infty}^{\infty} f_X(x) \, dx = 1. \tag{2.2}$$

Now,

$$\int_{-\infty}^{\infty} f_X(x) \, dx = v \int_{w}^{\infty} x^{-u} \, dx \tag{2.3}$$

$$= \frac{v}{1-u} \left[x^{-u+1} \right]_{w}^{\infty}. \tag{2.4}$$

We need $u > 1$ and $w > 0$ for this integral to be finite. Then,

$$\int_{-\infty}^{\infty} f_X(x) \, dx = \frac{v}{u-1} \, w^{-(u-1)} = 1. \tag{2.5}$$

Therefore,

$$v = (u-1) \, w^{u-1} \tag{2.6}$$

and

$$f_X(x) = (u-1) \, w^{u-1} \, x^{-u} \tag{2.7}$$

$$= \frac{u-1}{w} \left(\frac{w}{x} \right)^{u}. \tag{2.8}$$

We introduce new constants, $\alpha = u - 1 > 0$ and $\beta = w > 0$ in order to express the density function in a commonly represented form. We have

$$f_X(x) = \begin{cases} \frac{\alpha}{\beta} \left(\frac{\beta}{x} \right)^{\alpha+1}, & x \geq \beta \\ 0, & x < \beta. \end{cases} \tag{2.9}$$

An alternative common form of representation uses the Hurst parameter H instead of α. Harold Edwin Hurst (1880–1978) was a British hydrologist. He studied long term storage capacities of reservoirs based on empirical observations on the river Nile. The Hurst parameter for a Pareto random variable is given by

$$H = \frac{3-\alpha}{2}. \tag{2.10}$$

Let us evaluate the properties of the above valid density function. The cumulative distribution function (cdf) is

$$P[X \leq x] = \int_{\beta}^{x} f_X(x)dx, \quad x \geq \beta \tag{2.11}$$

$$= 1 - \left(\frac{\beta}{x}\right)^{\alpha}, \quad x \geq \beta \tag{2.12}$$

$$= 0, \quad x < \beta. \tag{2.13}$$

The expectation

$$E[X] = \int_{-\infty}^{\infty} x\, f_X(x)\, dx \tag{2.14}$$

$$= \int_{\beta}^{\infty} \frac{\alpha}{\beta} x \left(\frac{\beta}{x}\right)^{\alpha+1} dx \tag{2.15}$$

$$= \alpha\, \beta^{\alpha} \int_{\beta}^{\infty} x^{-\alpha}\, dx \tag{2.16}$$

$$= \alpha\, \beta^{\alpha} \left[\frac{x^{-\alpha+1}}{-\alpha+1}\right]_{\beta}^{\infty}. \tag{2.17}$$

Now, α needs to be larger than 1 for finite $E[X]$. Therefore, for $\alpha > 1$

$$E[X] = \frac{\alpha\, \beta^{\alpha}}{\alpha - 1} \beta^{-\alpha+1}$$

and finally, we have

$$E[X] = \begin{cases} \frac{\alpha \beta}{\alpha-1}, & \text{if } \alpha > 1 \\ \infty, & \text{if } \alpha \leq 1. \end{cases} \tag{2.18}$$

The variance Pareto random variable is evaluated as

$$\text{var}[X] = \int_{-\infty}^{\infty} (x - E[X])^2 \, f_X(x) \, dx \tag{2.19}$$

$$= E[X^2] - E^2[X]. \tag{2.20}$$

Equation (2.20) follows by expanding the square in equation (2.19).

$$E[X^2] = \int_{-\infty}^{\infty} x^2 \, f_X(x) \, dx \tag{2.21}$$

$$= \alpha \, \beta^\alpha \int_{\beta}^{\infty} x^{-\alpha+1} \, dx \tag{2.22}$$

$$= \alpha \, \beta^\alpha \left[\frac{x^{-\alpha+2}}{-\alpha+2} \right]_{\beta}^{\infty}. \tag{2.23}$$

For $E[X^2]$ to be finite, we need $\alpha > 2$. If $\alpha > 2$,

$$E[X^2] = \frac{\alpha\beta^\alpha \beta^{-\alpha+2}}{\alpha - 2} = \frac{\alpha\beta^2}{\alpha - 2}. \tag{2.24}$$

Summary
The Pareto random variable X can have any physical dimension, such as length, mass, time, or bits (approximating number of bits by a real number). The parameter α is dimensionless, and β has the same dimension as X.

$$f_X(x) = \begin{cases} \frac{\alpha}{\beta} \left(\frac{\beta}{x} \right)^{\alpha+1}, & \text{if } x \geq \beta \\ 0, & \text{if } x < \beta, \end{cases} \tag{2.25}$$

$$F_X(x) = \begin{cases} P[X \leq x] = 1 - \left(\frac{\beta}{x} \right)^{\alpha}, & \text{if } x \geq \beta \\ 0, & \text{if } x < \beta, \end{cases} \tag{2.26}$$

$$E[X] = \begin{cases} \frac{\alpha\beta}{\alpha-1}, & \text{if } \alpha > 1 \\[2ex] \infty, & \text{if } \alpha \leq 1, \end{cases} \tag{2.27}$$

$$\text{var}[X] = \begin{cases} \frac{\alpha\beta^2}{\alpha-2} - \left(\frac{\alpha\beta}{\alpha-1}\right)^2, & \text{if } \alpha > 2 \\[2ex] \infty, & \text{if } \alpha \leq 2. \end{cases} \tag{2.28}$$

The range $\alpha \in (1, 2]$ is of interest to us. In this range, the mean is finite but the variance is infinity. Data traffic in present day LANs is very bursty, despite having an overall finite average value. Modeling interarrival times between successive data packets by a Pareto random variable with $\alpha \in (1, 2]$ is gaining popularity. It turns out that we can easily simulate Pareto random numbers, as discussed later in this Chapter.

Example 2.1
 In an Ethernet, successful packets (those that are transmitted without collisions) appear as the presence or absence of a successful packet, over a time interval. An example of such a trace is shown in Figure 2.2. Extensive experiments with Ethernet traffic have led to a model in which the time intervals between the end of one packet and the beginning of the next are Pareto with $\alpha = 1.2$ as an estimate. Let the average of such OFF times in the data packet train be 1 millisecond (msec and ms are also used to denote millisecond). Find the minimum time interval between successive packets. Find $P[X > 10\,\text{msec}]$, i.e., the probability of finding no arrival in 10 msec since the end of the previous packet. ⬜

Solution

$$E[X] = \frac{\alpha\beta}{\alpha - 1} \tag{2.29}$$

$$\beta = \frac{E[X](\alpha - 1)}{\alpha} = \frac{1\,\text{msec}\,(1.2 - 1)}{1.2} \tag{2.30}$$

$$= \frac{1}{6}\,\text{msec.} \tag{2.31}$$

Since $f_X(x) = 0$, for $x < \beta$, the OFF time is always $\frac{1}{6}$ msec or higher. Note the

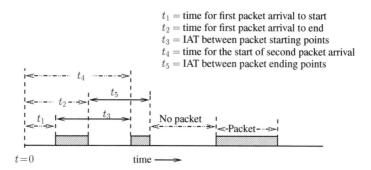

t_1 = time for first packet arrival to start
t_2 = time for first packet arrival to end
t_3 = IAT between packet starting points
t_4 = time for the start of second packet arrival
t_5 = IAT between packet ending points

FIGURE 2.2:   ON-OFF model of a packet train.

difference between two random variables associated with the stream of packets, the OFF times and the IATs.

$$P[X > 10\,\text{msec}] = 1 - F_X(10) \tag{2.32}$$

$$= 1 - \left[1 - \left(\frac{1}{60} \right)^{1.2} \right] \tag{2.33}$$

$$= \left(\frac{1}{60} \right)^{1.2} \approx 0.007. \tag{2.34}$$

The probability of OFF time to be larger than or equal to 10 times the mean is still not too small! This is the heavy-tailed property of this random variable. Later on, we will compare this with the probability of the same event for an exponential random variable with the same mean.   ☐

Example 2.2
The probability density function of the time for the next bus arrival starting at 8 AM as zero time is Pareto with $\alpha = 1.7$ and $\beta = 1$. Time is measured in minutes. At 8:05 AM, the bus had not arrived. Determine the probability that the bus will not arrive for at least t more minutes after 8:05 AM.   ☐

Solution
Starting from equation (2.13) for $P[X \leq x]$ of a Pareto random variable, we have

$$P[X > x] = \left(\frac{\beta}{x}\right)^{\alpha}, x > \beta. \qquad (2.35)$$

Let T be the absolute arrival (random) time

$$P[T > 8:05 + t | T > 8:05] = \frac{P[T > 8:05 + t]}{P[T > 8:05]} = \frac{P[X > 5 + t]}{P[X > 5]} \qquad (2.36)$$

$$= \left(\frac{5}{5+t}\right)^{1.7}. \qquad (2.37)$$

▯

Example 2.3
An agent in a train A is required to give a key to another agent in train B. It is known that Train B will be parked at a station S between 3:00 PM and 4:00 PM. Train A starts from a distant point at 1 PM the same day. Its travel time to reach station S is a Pareto random variable with $\alpha = 3$ and $\beta = 1$ hour. It will stop next to where train B would be in station S for a negligible amount of time and proceed. What is the probability that the hand-over of the key will be successful? Ignore the time for agents to walk to each other if and the two trains stop next to each other. ▯

Solution
Let X be the random variable of the time in hours it takes for train A to travel to station S. We need

$$P[2 < X < 3] = \int_{2}^{3} \frac{\alpha}{\beta}\left(\frac{\beta}{x}\right)^{\alpha+1} dx. \qquad (2.38)$$

This evaluates to $\frac{1}{8} - \frac{1}{27} = \frac{19}{216} = 0.088$. ▯

Example 2.4
A Pareto random variable X has $\alpha = 1.5$ and $\beta = 2$. We would like to construct a new random variable for IATs in the form of the random variable $Y = X - a$, with a constant a such that Y is nonnegative but its density is nonzero starting from the outcome 0 itself. Determine a and completely specify the probability density function of Y, its mean and variance. ▯

Solution
If we draw a rough figure (or even imagine one) with the density function pushed so that it starts to be nonzero from the 0 point itself, we find that $a = 2$. Substitute $x = y + 2$ in the expression for the density function. The density of Y is zero for $y < 0$. More systematically,

$$P[y \leq Y < y + dy] = P[y + 2 \leq X < y + 2 + dx], \quad y \geq 0 \quad \text{and } dy = dx.$$
$$(2.39)$$

Therefore, $f_Y(y) = f_X(y + 2)$, $-\infty < y < \infty$. That is,

$$f_Y(y) = 0.75 \left(\frac{2}{y+2} \right)^{2.5}, \quad y \geq 0 \qquad (2.40)$$

$$= 0, \quad y < 0. \qquad (2.41)$$

$$E[Y] = E[X] - 2 = \frac{1.5 \times 2}{1.5 - 1} - 2 = 4. \qquad (2.42)$$

Variance of a random variable does not change with translation. Therefore,

$$\text{var}[Y] = \text{var}[X] = \infty. \qquad (2.43)$$

$\square$

2.3   The Poisson Random Variable

Let us study the traditional and "smooth" interarrival times model. The properties of this random variable can be formally derived by three simple and appealing assumptions. Consider an electron gun shooting out electrons in a narrow beam. This is a random phenomenon. Let us assume that the electrons' arrival times at a particular point follow the three randomness properties below.

1. In a narrow time interval, the probability of an arrival is proportional to the time interval.

2. In a narrow time interval, the probability of two or more arrivals is negligible in comparison with the probability of one arrival.

3. Numbers of arrivals in nonoverlapping time intervals are mutually independent of one another.

Note that $(0, t_1]$ and $(t_1, t_2]$ are nonoverlapping. As an example, if firing times of electrons are independent and statistically steady, then these assumptions are intuitively appealing. Mathematically, the assumptions imply the following.

1.

$$\lim_{\delta t \to 0} \frac{P[\text{one arrival in } \delta t]}{\delta t} = \lambda, \text{ a constant} \tag{2.44}$$

2.

$$\lim_{\delta t \to 0} \frac{P[\text{two or more arrivals in } \delta t]}{P[\text{one arrival in } \delta t]} = 0 \tag{2.45}$$

3.

$$P[k_1 \text{ arrivals in } (t_1, t_2] \text{ and } k_2 \text{ in } (t_2, t_3]]$$

$$= P[k_1 \text{ arrivals in } (t_1, t_2]] \cdot P[k_2 \text{ arrivals in } (t_2, t_3]]. \tag{2.46}$$

From these three defining assumptions, we can derive the probability mass function (pmf), $P[k \text{ arrivals in } (0, T]]$. The pmf will be a function of only one parameter value λ, which is found in the defining assumptions (and the time interval T).

2.3.1 Derivation of the Poisson pmf

Consider a time interval $(0, T]$. Divide this interval into n equal parts. As n increases and tends to ∞, $\frac{T}{n} \to 0$ and we have a narrow sub-interval tending to 0. Therefore, in each such sub-interval, we have one arrival with probability $\frac{\lambda T}{n}$ and zero arrivals with probability $1 - \frac{\lambda T}{n}$. Two or more arrivals occur with zero probability. These arguments are accurate in the limit, as $n \to \infty$. The number k of sub-intervals with arrivals in a total of n sub-intervals is binomially distributed.

$$P[k \text{ arrivals in } (0, T]] = P[k \text{ in } T], \text{ for brevity} \tag{2.47}$$

$$= \lim_{n \to \infty} \frac{n!}{k!(n-k)!} \left(\frac{\lambda T}{n}\right)^k \left[1 - \frac{\lambda T}{n}\right]^{n-k}. \qquad (2.48)$$

We just need to evaluate the above limit.

$$P[k \text{ in } T] = \lim_{n \to \infty} \frac{(\lambda T)^k}{k!} \left[1 - \frac{\lambda T}{n}\right]^{-k} \left[1 - \frac{\lambda T}{n}\right]^n \frac{n!}{n^k(n-k)!}. \qquad (2.49)$$

The quantity

$$\left[1 - \frac{\lambda T}{n}\right]^{-k} \to 1 \text{ as } n \to \infty. \qquad (2.50)$$

Therefore,

$$P[k \text{ in } T] = \lim_{n \to \infty} \frac{(\lambda T)^k}{k!} \left(1 - \frac{\lambda T}{n}\right)^n \times$$
$$\left[\frac{n \cdot (n-1) \cdot (n-2) \cdots (n-k+1)}{n^k}\right]. \qquad (2.51)$$

In the last fraction, each $(n - i)$ in the numerator cancels with an n in the denominator, as $n \to \infty$, for any finite k. Therefore,

$$P[k \text{ in } T] = \frac{(\lambda T)^k}{k!} \lim_{n \to \infty} \left(1 - \frac{\lambda T}{n}\right)^n. \qquad (2.52)$$

Concentrate on

$$\lim_{n \to \infty} \left(1 - \frac{\lambda T}{n}\right)^n = \lim_{n \to \infty} \left[\left(1 - \frac{\lambda T}{n}\right)^{\frac{n}{-\lambda T}}\right]^{-\lambda T} \qquad (2.53)$$

$$= \left[\lim_{a \to 0} (1 + a)^{\frac{1}{a}}\right]^{-\lambda T}. \qquad (2.54)$$

$$= \left[e^{\left\{ \lim_{a \to 0} \frac{1}{a} \ln(1+a) \right\}} \right]^{-\lambda T}. \tag{2.55}$$

Consider

$$\lim_{a \to 0} \frac{\ln(1+a)}{a}.$$

Apply L'Hospital's rule. This rule is named in honor of Guillaume Francois Antoine de L'Hospital, a French mathematician (1661–1704).

$$\lim_{a \to 0} \frac{\ln(1+a)}{a} = \lim_{a \to 0} \frac{1}{(1+a) \cdot 1} \tag{2.56}$$

$$= 1. \tag{2.57}$$

Therefore,

$$\exp\left[\left\{ \lim_{a \to 0} (1+a)^{\frac{1}{a}} \right\} \right] = e \tag{2.58}$$

and,

$$\lim_{n \to \infty} \left[1 - \frac{\lambda T}{n} \right]^n = e^{-\lambda T}. \tag{2.59}$$

Finally,

$$P[k \text{ in } T] = \frac{(\lambda T)^k}{k!} e^{-\lambda T}. \tag{2.60}$$

This is the Poisson pmf. This pmf gives the probabilities of finding various numbers of possible arrivals in a given time interval, if the arrival scheme satisfies the previously mentioned three properties.

2.3.2 Interarrival times in a Poisson sequence of arrivals

Let X be the random variable corresponding to the time for the next arrival, soon after one arrival. Such a random variable is appropriately called the interarrival time.

$$P[X > t] = P[\text{no arrivals in } (0, t]] \tag{2.61}$$

$$= P[0 \text{ in } t] = \frac{(\lambda t)^0}{0!} e^{-\lambda t} \tag{2.62}$$

$$= e^{-\lambda t}. \tag{2.63}$$

$$P[X \leq t] = 1 - e^{-\lambda t} = F_X(t). \tag{2.64}$$

$$f_X(t) = \frac{dF_X(t)}{dt} \tag{2.65}$$

$$= \begin{cases} \lambda e^{-\lambda t}, \, t \geq 0 \\ \\ 0, \quad\quad t < 0, \text{ since interarrival times are nonnegative.} \end{cases} \tag{2.66}$$

$$f_X(t) = \begin{cases} \lambda e^{-\lambda t}, \, t \geq 0 \\ \\ 0, \quad\quad t < 0. \end{cases} \tag{2.67}$$

This is called the *exponential density function*. Therefore, we have that the inter-arrival times are exponential random variables if the number of arrivals in a time interval is Poisson. The Laplace transform of the exponential random variable is derived in Appendix A; if X is exponential with the parameter λ,

$$\mathcal{L}_X(s) = \frac{\lambda}{\lambda + s}. \tag{2.68}$$

2.3.3   Properties of Poisson streams of arrivals

2.3.3.1   Mean of exponential random variable

$$f_X(t) = \begin{cases} \lambda e^{-\lambda t}, \, t \geq 0 \\ \\ 0, \quad\quad t < 0. \end{cases} \tag{2.69}$$

$$E[X] = \int_{-\infty}^{\infty} t \, f_X(t) \, dt = \int_{0}^{\infty} \lambda t \, e^{-\lambda t} \, dt \tag{2.70}$$

$$= \frac{1}{\lambda} \int\limits_{0}^{\infty} (\lambda t)\, e^{-(\lambda t)}\, d(\lambda t) \tag{2.71}$$

$$= \frac{1}{\lambda} \int\limits_{0}^{\infty} y\, e^{-y}\, dy. \tag{2.72}$$

Integrate by parts to obtain

$$E[X] = \frac{1}{\lambda} \left[-y\, e^{-y} - \int (-e^{-y})\, dy \right]_{0}^{\infty} \tag{2.73}$$

$$= \frac{1}{\lambda} \left[-e^{-y} \right]_{0}^{\infty} = -\frac{1}{\lambda} \left[0 - 1 \right] \tag{2.74}$$

$$= \frac{1}{\lambda}. \tag{2.75}$$

2.3.3.2   Mean of the Poisson random variable

If the random variable K is the number of Poisson arrivals with parameter λ, over a time interval t, the expected number of arrivals is

$$E[K] = \sum_{k=0}^{\infty} k \frac{\exp{(-\lambda t)}(\lambda t)^{k}}{k!} \tag{2.76}$$

$$= \sum_{k=1}^{\infty} \frac{\exp{(-\lambda t)}(\lambda t)^{k}}{(k-1)!} \tag{2.77}$$

$$= \lambda t \sum_{k=1}^{\infty} \frac{\exp{(-\lambda t)}(\lambda t)^{(k-1)}}{(k-1)!}. \tag{2.78}$$

Using $j = k - 1$, we have

$$E[K] = \lambda t \sum_{j=0}^{\infty} \frac{\exp{(-\lambda t)}(\lambda t)^{j}}{j!}. \tag{2.79}$$

The sum in the above equation is the sum of all the probabilities of a Poisson random variables and evaluates to 1. Therefore, we have

$$E[K] = \lambda t. \tag{2.80}$$

If t, over which the number of arrivals are considered is a unit time, the expected number of arrivals is λ per unit time. Therefore, the parameter λ is also called the rate of arrivals. Let us compare the means of the exponential and Poisson random variables. From the Poisson mean, the average number of arrivals in a unit amount of time is λ. From the exponential mean, the average time between arrivals is $\frac{1}{\lambda}$. The two are consistent with each other.

2.3.3.3   Variance of the exponential random variable

$$E[X^2] = \int_0^\infty \lambda t^2 e^{-\lambda t}\, dt \tag{2.81}$$

$$= \frac{1}{\lambda^2} \int_0^\infty (\lambda t)^2 e^{-\lambda t}\, d(\lambda t) \tag{2.82}$$

$$= \frac{1}{\lambda^2} \int_0^\infty y^2 e^{-y}\, dy \tag{2.83}$$

$$= \frac{1}{\lambda^2} \left[-y^2 e^{-y} - \int 2y(-e^{-y})\, dy \right]_0^\infty. \tag{2.84}$$

$y^2 e^{-y}$ is 0 for $y = 0$ and for $y = \infty$. So we have,

$$E[X^2] = \frac{2}{\lambda^2} \int_0^\infty y e^{-y}\, dy \tag{2.85}$$

$$= \frac{2}{\lambda^2} \tag{2.86}$$

from the earlier evaluation of $\int_0^\infty y e^{-y}$, when we evaluated $E[X]$.

$$\text{var}[X] = E[X^2] - E^2[X] \tag{2.87}$$

$$= \frac{2}{\lambda^2} - \frac{1}{\lambda^2} = \frac{1}{\lambda^2}. \tag{2.88}$$

If X is exponential with parameter λ, $\text{var}[X] = \frac{1}{\lambda^2}$.

Example 2.5

Let the average of the OFF time random variable (X) be 1 msec (as in the earlier Example 2.1 that used a Pareto random variable), and let X be distributed exponentially. Therefore,

$$P[X > 10\,\text{msec}] = e^{-10} = 4.54 \times 10^{-5}. \tag{2.89}$$

This is much smaller than the corresponding probability (0.007) obtained by using the Pareto distribution we considered earlier. ▯

2.3.3.4 Variance of Poisson random variable

Let N_A be the number of arrivals in time T. Instead of evaluation $E[N_A^2]$ to find var$[N_A]$, it is easier to find $E[N_A(N_A - 1)]$ first, since we have $k!$ in the expression for $P[N_A = k]$. We have

$$E[N_A(N_A - 1)] = \sum_{k=0}^{\infty} k(k-1)\frac{(\lambda T)^k}{k!}\,e^{-\lambda T}.$$

The argument of summation is 0 for $k = 0$ and for $k = 1$. Therefore,

$$E[N_A(N_A - 1)] = (\lambda T)^2\, e^{-\lambda T} \sum_{k=2}^{\infty} \frac{(\lambda T)^{k-2}}{(k-2)!} = (\lambda T)^2. \tag{2.90}$$

$$E[N_A^2] - E[N_A] = (\lambda T)^2. \tag{2.91}$$

$$E[N_A^2] = (\lambda T)^2 + \lambda T. \tag{2.92}$$

$$\text{var}[N_A] = E[N_A^2] - E^2[N_A] \tag{2.93}$$

$$= (\lambda T)^2 + \lambda T - (\lambda T)^2 \tag{2.94}$$

$$= \lambda T. \tag{2.95}$$

For the Poisson random variable, we see that $E[N_A] = \text{var}[N_A] = \lambda T$.

2.3.3.5 The $\mathcal{Z}$ transform of a Poisson random variable

If N is the Poisson number of arrivals over a time interval t and with a rate λ,

$$\mathcal{Z}_N(z) = \sum_{j=0}^{\infty} \frac{\exp{(-\lambda t)}(\lambda t)^j}{j!}\,z^j \tag{2.96}$$

$$= \frac{\exp{(-\lambda t)}}{\exp{(-\lambda tz)}} \sum_{j=0}^{\infty} \frac{\exp{(-\lambda tz)}(\lambda tz)^j}{j!} \qquad (2.97)$$

$$= \exp[-\lambda t(1 - z)]. \qquad (2.98)$$

2.3.3.6 Memoryless property of the exponential random variable

Suppose we observed an arrival at $t = 0$, and we are waiting for the next arrival in a Poisson stream. We have that the time for the next arrival, X, is exponential. Let the arrival rate be λ. Suppose that at $t = t_1$, we still have not seen the next arrival, and we wonder "how much longer" we might have to wait. Of course, "how much longer" is also a random variable. The distribution of this random variable may be influenced by the fact that we have waited for t_1 amount of time, without success. Let us evaluate the conditional probability $P[X > t_1 + t | X > t_1]$. The quantity t is the real variable corresponding to the additional wait period beyond t_1. This gives,

$$P[X > t_1 + t | X > t_1] = \frac{P[(X > t_1 + t) \text{ and } (X > t_1)]}{P[X > t_1]}, \quad t_1, t > 0$$

$$(2.99)$$

$$= \frac{P[X > t_1 + t]}{P[X > t_1]} \qquad (2.100)$$

$$= \frac{1 - F_X(t_1 + t)}{1 - F_X(t_1)} \qquad (2.101)$$

$$= \frac{e^{-\lambda(t_1 + t)}}{e^{-\lambda t_1}} \qquad (2.102)$$

$$= e^{-\lambda t} \qquad (2.103)$$

which is also the same as $P[X > t]$. Thus, we see that $P[X > t_1 + t | X > t_1] = P[X > t]$. That is, "how much longer" we need to wait is independent of how long we have already waited! In other words, this scheme "forgets" how long an arrival has not occurred. We refer to this as the *memoryless property* of the Poisson stream of arrivals. This property actually helps in simplifying analysis.

2.3.3.7 Time for the next arrival

An important use of the memoryless property is that in studying a sequence of Poisson arrivals, we do not have to be careful to verify that an arrival occurred at $t = 0$, in order to claim that time for the next arrival is exponential. At any point in time, since how long ago the most recent arrival occurred is irrelevant, the "time for next arrival" is always exponential with the same parameter λ.

2.3.3.8 Nonnegative, continuous, memoryless random variables

Note that in order for the variable t_1 to cancel in the numerator and denominator of

$$\frac{P[X > t_1 + t]}{P[X > t_1]},$$

$P[X > t_1]$ must be of the form of an exponential, i.e., a^{bt_1}. Normalizing the random variable to make it a valid, continuous, nonnegative random variable, we find that X must be an exponential random variable.

2.3.3.9 Succession of iid exponential interarrival times

We found that a Poisson stream implies exponential interarrival time. Now, let us argue the converse. Let the interarrival times be iid exponential. At any time instant t, irrespective of when the most recent arrival occurred,

a)

$$P[\text{an arrival in } (t, t + \delta t]] = f_X(t| \text{ start observing at } t)\delta t \quad (2.104)$$

$$= f_X(0)\delta t \quad (2.105)$$

$$= \lambda \delta t. \quad (2.106)$$

Next, note that successive interarrival times are independent.

$$P[\text{two or more arrivals in } (0, \delta t]]$$

$$= P[\text{one arrival in } (0, \delta t]] \times$$

$$P[\text{more arrivals in } (0, \delta t], \text{ after first arrival}]$$

$$\leq (P[\text{one arrival in } (0, \delta t])^2 \quad (2.107)$$

$$\leq (\lambda \delta t)(\lambda \delta t), \quad (2.108)$$

since the second arrival has even less time than δt. Therefore,

$$\frac{P[\text{more than one arrival in } \delta t]}{P[\text{one arrival in } \delta t]} \leq \lambda \delta t. \qquad (2.109)$$

b) In the limit,

$$\lim_{\delta t \to 0} \frac{P[\text{more than one arrival in } \delta t]}{P[\text{one arrival in } \delta t]} = 0. \qquad (2.110)$$

c) Now consider nonoverlapping intervals, The number of arrivals in $(t_1, t_2]$ is independent of those in $(0, t_1]$, due to the following.

    i) interarrival times are independent, and

    ii) time for next arrival from t_1 is independent of when the previous arrival occurred.

Thus a sequence of arrivals with iid exponential interarrival times satisfy all defining assumptions of a Poisson stream of arrivals. Finally, we refer to the defining assumptions as "constant rate" random arrivals, and we have the equivalence between the three types of arrival schemes depicted in Figure 2.3.

2.3.3.10   Merging two independent Poisson streams

The following derivation shows that merging two independent Poisson streams with rates λ_1 and λ_2 results in a Poisson stream with the added arrival rate $\lambda_1 + \lambda_2$. Let the observation point in Figure 2.4 be C. We are interested in

$$P[n \text{ arrivals in stream at } C \text{ over time interval } T]. \qquad (2.111)$$

In order to have n arrivals, we can have j arrivals from the top input stream (with rate λ_1) and $n - j$ arrivals from the bottom input stream (the one with rate λ_2). Of course, $0 \leq j \leq n$. Write the probability of the joint event of j arrivals from the top input stream and and $n - j$ arrivals from the bottom input stream. Use the fact that the two input streams are independent. Sum this joint probability over $0 \leq j \leq n$. Simplify and evaluate the sum to obtain the required probability. Hence, show that the arrival stream at C is Poisson with rate $\lambda_1 + \lambda_2$. The required probability is

$$P[n \text{ at } C \text{ over } T] = \sum_{j=0}^{n} \frac{e^{-\lambda_1 T} (\lambda_1 T)^j}{j!} \frac{e^{-\lambda_2 T} (\lambda_2 T)^{n-j}}{(n-j)!}$$

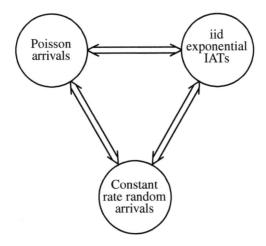

FIGURE 2.3: Equivalence of three types of arrival streams

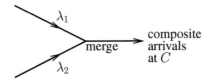

FIGURE 2.4: Merging two Poisson streams

$$= e^{-(\lambda_1+\lambda_2)T} T^n \sum_{j=0}^{n} \frac{\lambda_1^j \lambda_2^{n-j}}{j!\,(n-j)!}. \qquad (2.112)$$

Anticipating $\frac{(\lambda_1+\lambda_2)^n}{n!}$ as a factor in the final result, multiply and divide by this quantity.

$$P[n \text{ at } C \text{ over } T] = \frac{e^{-(\lambda_1+\lambda_2)T}\left[(\lambda_1+\lambda_2)T\right]^n}{n!} \sum_{j=0}^{n} \frac{n!}{j!\,(n-j)!} \frac{\lambda_1^j \lambda_2^{n-j}}{(\lambda_1+\lambda_2)^n}$$

$$= \frac{e^{-(\lambda_1+\lambda_2)T}\left[(\lambda_1+\lambda_2)T\right]^n}{n!} \times$$

$$\sum_{j=0}^{n} \frac{n!}{j!\,(n-j)!} \left(\frac{\lambda_1}{\lambda_1+\lambda_2}\right)^j \left(\frac{\lambda_2}{\lambda_1+\lambda_2}\right)^{n-j}. \qquad (2.113)$$

In the above, $\frac{\lambda_1}{\lambda_1+\lambda_2}$ and $\frac{\lambda_2}{\lambda_1+\lambda_2}$ can be considered to be probability values summing to 1. With this interpretation, the sum in the above equation is the sum of all probabilities of a fictitious binomial random variable. Therefore this sum must evaluate to 1, giving us

$$P[n \text{ at } C \text{ over } T] = \frac{e^{-(\lambda_1+\lambda_2)T}\left[(\lambda_1+\lambda_2)T\right]^n}{n!}$$

showing that the resulting stream at C is Poisson with rate $\lambda_1 + \lambda_2$.

An alternative proof, based on the $\mathcal{Z}$ transform is much simpler. Over a time interval t, let M and N be the random variable number of arrivals in the original streams being merged. Let K be the number of arrivals in the merged stream. Clearly, $K = M + N$. Therefore,

$$\mathcal{Z}_K(z) = \mathcal{Z}_M(z)\mathcal{Z}_N(z) \qquad (2.114)$$

$$= \exp[-\lambda_1 t(1-z)]\exp[-\lambda_2 t(1-z)] \qquad (2.115)$$

$$= \exp[-(\lambda_1+\lambda_2)t(1-z)]. \qquad (2.116)$$

The final expression corresponds to a Poisson random variable with rate $\lambda_1 + \lambda_2$. As an even simpler approach to show the same result, consider the probability of no arrival at C from the time instant zero until t. Due to the memorylessness of both the streams and due to their independence,

$$P[\text{no arrival at } C \text{ in } (0,t]] = \exp(-\lambda_1 t)\exp(-\lambda_2 t) \qquad (2.117)$$

$$= \exp[-(\lambda_1 + \lambda_2)t] \qquad (2.118)$$

from which it follows that the time for the next arrival at C is exponential with rate $\lambda_1 + \lambda_2$.

2.3.3.11 iid probabilistic routing into a fork

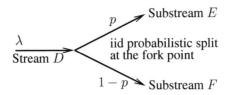

FIGURE 2.5: Probabilistic splitting of a Poisson stream

Let a Poisson stream of arrivals D with rate λ be split iid probabilistically into substream E with probability p and substream F with probability $1 - p$. We are interested in

$$P[n \text{ arrivals in substream } E \text{ over time interval } T]. \qquad (2.119)$$

In order for us to have n arrivals in E, there must be $k \geq n$ arrivals in D, before splitting. Write the probability of observing "$k \geq n$ in the original stream AND only n of these k being chosen to be routed to substream E." That is, determine

$$P[(k \text{ in } D \text{ over } T) \text{ AND } (n \leq k \text{ chosen for } E)]. \qquad (2.120)$$

Then, sum the above probabilities over $n \leq k \leq \infty$ to obtain

$$P[n \text{ in substream } E \text{ over } T] = \sum_{k=n}^{\infty} \frac{e^{-\lambda T} (\lambda T)^k}{k!} \frac{k!}{n! \, (k-n)!} p^n \, (1-p)^{k-n} .$$

Again, anticipate the expression $\frac{e^{-p\lambda T} (p\lambda T)^n}{n!}$ and take everything else inside the sum.

$$P[n \text{ in substream } E \text{ over } T]$$

$$= \frac{e^{-p\lambda T}\,(p\lambda T)^n}{n!} \sum_{k=n}^{\infty} \frac{e^{-(1-p)\lambda T}\,(\lambda T)^{k-n}\,(1-p)^{k-n}}{(k-n)!}. \qquad (2.121)$$

Use $j = k - n$.

$$P[n \text{ in substream } E \text{ over } T] = \frac{e^{-p\lambda T}\,(p\lambda T)^n}{n!} \sum_{j=0}^{\infty} \frac{e^{-(1-p)\lambda T}\,[(1-p)\,\lambda T]^j}{j!}.$$

The sum is the sum of all possible probabilities of a fictitious random variable and hence evaluates to, leaving us with the Poisson pmf expression. Note that if a Poisson stream with rate λ is split with alternate arrivals branching into two substreams, the resulting stream is not Poisson, as shown below. The IAT Y in each substream is the sum of two iid exponential random variables each with parameter λ.

$$f_Y(y) = \int_0^y \lambda e^{-\lambda(y-w)} \lambda e^{-\lambda w}\, dw \qquad (2.122)$$

$$= \int_0^y \lambda^2 e^{-\lambda y}\, dw \qquad (2.123)$$

$$= \lambda^2 y e^{-\lambda y}. \qquad (2.124)$$

Obviously, this can never be expressed as $\alpha e^{-\alpha y}$ for any constant α. Hence Y is not exponential.

Example 2.6
At a train station ticket counter, service time is exponentially distributed with a rate of 1 customer per minute. A customer A comes to the ticket counter at 9:58 AM and finds only one customer in the ticket counter; he was being served. The train is scheduled to leave at 10:00 AM. What is the probability that A will catch the train? Ignore the time that A needs to run to the train after purchasing the ticket.   ☐

Solution
IDTs are iid exponential with an average of 1 minute. If two IDTs take place in 2 minutes, the customer A would have purchased the ticket before 10:00 AM. This is identical to having *at least* two Poisson arrivals with rate one per minute in the two minute time interval.

$$P[N \geq 2] = 1 - P[N = 0] - P[N = 1] \qquad (2.125)$$

$$= 1 - \exp(-2) - 2\exp(-2) \qquad (2.126)$$

$$\approx 0.6. \qquad (2.127)$$

$\Box$

2.4 Simulation

We would like to simulate the operation of various configurations of queuing networks on the computer. These activities require generating the following types of random numbers.

1. Generalized Bernoulli random number.

2. Geometric and modified geometric random numbers.

3. Exponentially distributed random number.

4. Pareto distributed random number.

Generating a generalized Bernoulli random number allows us to switch over several possible output links at a router. It also allows us to generate arrivals and service completions in discrete time queuing systems. Generating an exponential random variable allows us to generate Poisson traffic by generating a sequence of interarrival times. It also allows us to generate the popular exponentially distributed service times. Generating a Pareto random variable allows us to simulate wildly fluctuating interarrival times and service times that are observed in bursty traffic.

2.4.1 Technique for simulation

A common technique in computer simulation is to generate a sequence of iid random numbers uniformly distributed over the real interval $[0, 1)$ and use mathematical transformations. Most computers have such routines that generate very good approximations of iid uniformly distributed random numbers. Let us study the mathematical transformations of U, the uniform random variable distributed over the real segment $[0, 1)$, to realize simulation of important distributions.

2.4.2 Generalized Bernoulli random number

A generalized Bernoulli random variable has a finite number of outcomes, each with a nonzero probability. Let the sample space of the random experiment be B be $S_B = \{b_1, \cdots, b_m\}$, with real valued b_i Let the probabilities of these outcomes be $p_1, \cdots, p_m$, respectively. Divide the unit interval into m parts with each part corresponding to the required probabilities. That is, let $a_0 = 0$, $a_i = a_{i-1} + p_{i-1}$, $i = 1, \cdots, m$. Generate a U. Let the outcome be u. The outcome of the corresponding generalized Bernoulli simulation is b_i, if $a_{i-1} \leq u < a_i$. Figure 2.6 shows the transformations from $\{p_i\}$ to $\{a_i\}$ and then to $\{b_i\}$.

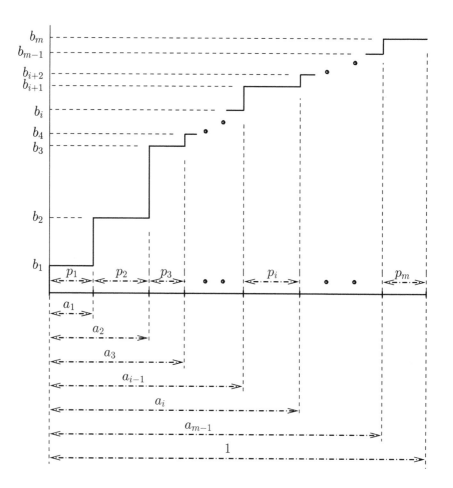

FIGURE 2.6:   Transformation to generate a generalized Bernoulli random number

2.4.3 Geometric and modified geometric random numbers

The modified geometric random variable K is nonnegative discrete and has a pmf given by

$$P[K = k] = p^k(1 - p), \quad k = 0, 1, \cdots. \tag{2.128}$$

We use a Bernoulli random number generator whose successes are iid with

$$P[\text{success}] = p \quad \text{and} \tag{2.129}$$

$$P[\text{failure}] = 1 - p. \tag{2.130}$$

Generate iid Bernoulli random numbers repeatedly until we get the first failure. Count the number of successes observed. This is the required modified geometric random number. The geometric random number is simply the number of Bernoulli trials up to and including the first failure in the above approach.

2.4.4 Exponential random number

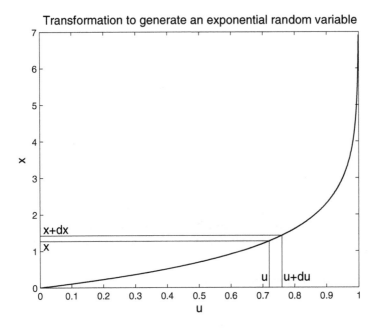

FIGURE 2.7: Transformation to generate exponential random number; $\lambda = 1$

Let

$$X = \begin{cases} -\frac{1}{\lambda}\ln(1-U), & 0 \le U < 1 \\ 0, & \text{otherwise} \end{cases} \tag{2.131}$$

This is a deterministic function of the random variable U and results in random variable X. The outcome u translates to the outcome of X as

$$x = \begin{cases} -\frac{1}{\lambda}\ln(1-u), & 0 \le u < 1 \\ 0, & \text{otherwise.} \end{cases} \tag{2.132}$$

as depicted in Figure 2.7. The inverse function is

$$u = \begin{cases} 1 - e^{-\lambda x}, & 0 \le x < \infty \\ \text{undefined, otherwise.} \end{cases} \tag{2.133}$$

$$\frac{du}{dx} = \lambda e^{-\lambda x} \text{ in the defined region.} \tag{2.134}$$

$$P[u < U \le u + du] = P[x < X \le x + dx]. \tag{2.135}$$

Equivalently,

$$f_U(u)du = f_X(x)\,dx \tag{2.136}$$

$$f_X(x) = f_U(u)\frac{du}{dx} \text{ expressed as a function of } x. \tag{2.137}$$

Thus,

$$f_X(x) = \begin{cases} \lambda e^{-\lambda x}, & x \ge 0 \\ 0, & x < 0. \end{cases} \tag{2.138}$$

We have the needed result, i.e., if U is distributed uniformly over the real segment $[0, 1)$, $X = -\frac{1}{\lambda}\ln(1 - U)$ is exponentially distributed with parameter λ. Therefore, to generate an exponentially distributed random number, generate a uniformly distributed random number u and subject it to the transformation $-\frac{1}{\lambda}\ln(1 - u)$.

2.4.5 Pareto random number

$$f_X(x) = \begin{cases} \frac{\alpha}{\beta}\left(\frac{\beta}{x}\right)^{\alpha+1}, & x \ge \beta \\ 0, & x < \beta. \end{cases} \tag{2.139}$$

We want a function $x = g(u)$ such that when $u = 0$, $x = \beta$ and when $u \to 1$, $x \to \infty$ and with $f_X(x) = f_U(u) \frac{du}{dx}$. We know that $f_U(u) = 1$ in the range of interest. Therefore,

$$f_X(x) = \frac{du}{dx} = \frac{\alpha}{\beta} \left(\frac{\beta}{x}\right)^{\alpha+1}. \tag{2.140}$$

We can formally derive the required function.

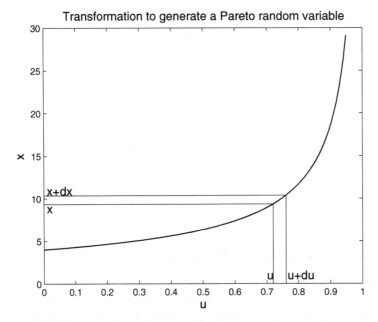

FIGURE 2.8: Transformation for Pareto random number generation; $\alpha = 1.5$ and $\beta = 4$

$$\frac{du}{dx} = \frac{\alpha}{\beta} \left(\frac{\beta}{x}\right)^{\alpha+1} \tag{2.141}$$

$$u = \int \frac{\alpha}{\beta} \left(\frac{\beta}{x}\right)^{\alpha+1} dx \tag{2.142}$$

$$= \alpha\beta^\alpha \int x^{-\alpha-1} dx \tag{2.143}$$

$$= -\left(\frac{\beta}{x}\right)^\alpha + c. \tag{2.144}$$

Set $c = 1$ to satisfy $x = \beta$ when $u = 0$. Therefore,

$$\left(\frac{\beta}{x}\right)^\alpha = 1 - u \tag{2.145}$$

$$x^{-\alpha} = \beta^{-\alpha}(1 - u) \tag{2.146}$$

$$x = \beta(1 - u)^{-\frac{1}{\alpha}}. \tag{2.147}$$

$x = \infty$ when $u = 1$ is easily verified. See Figure 2.8 for the shape of the function. Therefore, to simulate a Pareto random number with parameters α and β, generate a u and subject it to the transformation $\beta(1 - u)^{-\frac{1}{\alpha}}$.

2.5   Elements of Parameter Estimation

Analysis of data collected during real or simulated experiments is important. In some situations, summary parameter values representing a data set is useful to control a queuing system or a network. A statistic is a mathematical transformation from a sequence of observations of outcomes of one or more random variables to a single value. Such a statistic is usually developed with the hope that the value represents a useful parameter of the family of random variables. Such a transformation is known as an estimator and the resulting value, the estimate. Even though the final value is usually never exactly equal to the parameter it is supposed to be representing, the transformation may satisfy some desirable properties. Study of such transformations and their properties is known as mathematical statistics. A more focused topic that deals with the development and study of transformations to represent particular parameters of random phenomena is also known as estimation theory. Estimating a value to represent an unknown parameter is called "point estimation." An alternative approach is to estimate a lower and an upper bound for the unknown parameter and a probability (also called confidence limit) with which the interval contains the unknown parameter. This is known as an interval estimate and is more applicable for human beings to understand the quality of the estimate. Only the simplest of principles of point estimation are introduced in this section.

2.5.1 Parameters of Pareto random variable

Consider a sequence of exponential interarrival time observations $x_1, x_2, \cdots, x_n$, obtained as outcomes of iid trials of X. We expect the sample average

$$\frac{1}{n} \sum_{j=1}^{n} x_j \qquad (2.148)$$

to be close to $\frac{1}{\lambda}$. We refer to the above expression (2.148) as an *estimate* for the mean $\frac{1}{\lambda}$. Likewise,

$$\frac{1}{n} \sum_{j=1}^{n} \left(x_j - \frac{1}{n} \sum x_i \right)^2 \qquad (2.149)$$

is an estimate of the variance of X. If X is Pareto, how can we estimate the corresponding parameters α and β? Note the additional difficulty if the variance is infinity. Using ideas developed in simulation, we can transform the random variable to be of finite variance and try to estimate α and β with the help of the sample mean and sample variance of the transformed data. Let X be a Pareto random variable with parameters α and β, so that

$$f_X(x) = \begin{cases} \frac{\alpha}{\beta} \left(\frac{\beta}{x} \right)^{\alpha+1}, & x \geq \beta \\ 0, & x < 0. \end{cases} \qquad (2.150)$$

Let

$$y = \begin{cases} \ln x, & x \geq \beta \\ \text{undefined}, & x < \beta, \end{cases} \qquad (2.151)$$

as in Figure 2.9. This severely reduces from higher values of x to lower values of y.

$$x = e^y \text{ in the region.} \qquad (2.152)$$

$$\frac{dx}{dy} = e^y. \qquad (2.153)$$

The transformation is monotonically increasing. Therefore,

$$f_X(x)dx = f_Y(y)dy. \qquad (2.154)$$

$$f_Y(y) = f_X(x)\frac{dx}{dy}, y \geq \ln \beta \qquad (2.155)$$

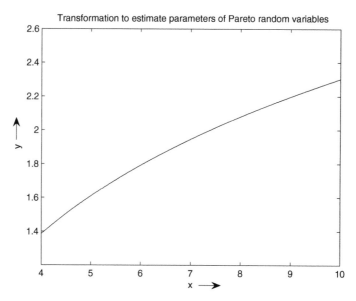

FIGURE 2.9: Transformation $y = \ln x$ to estimate parameters of Pareto random variable

$$= f_X(x = e^y)e^y \tag{2.156}$$

$$= \frac{\alpha}{\beta}\frac{\beta^{\alpha+1}}{(e^y)^{\alpha+1}}e^y. \tag{2.157}$$

$$f_Y(y) = \begin{cases} \alpha\beta^\alpha e^{-\alpha y}, & y \geq \ln\beta \\ 0, & y < \ln\beta. \end{cases} \tag{2.158}$$

We can evaluate the mean and variance of Y and try to express α and β as functions of $E[Y]$ and $\text{var}[Y]$. However, this turns out to be complicated for an algebraic solution. Note also that this method works even for $1 < \alpha \leq 2$ for which $\text{var}[X] = \infty$. There is an easier technique. Let X be Pareto, and so

$$f_X(x) = \begin{cases} \frac{\alpha}{\beta}\left(\frac{\beta}{x}\right)^{\alpha+1}, & x \geq \beta \\ 0, & x < 0. \end{cases} \tag{2.159}$$

Let $y = \frac{1}{x}$. We know from probability theory,

$$E[Y] = \int_{-\infty}^{\infty} y f_X(x) dx, \tag{2.160}$$

with y expressed as a function of x. We have,

$$E\left[\frac{1}{X}\right] = \int_{\beta}^{\infty} \frac{\alpha}{\beta} \left(\frac{\beta}{x}\right)^{\alpha+1} \frac{1}{x} dx \quad \text{for Pareto random variable} \tag{2.161}$$

$$= \alpha \beta^{\alpha} \int_{\beta}^{\infty} x^{-\alpha-2} dx \tag{2.162}$$

$$= \frac{\alpha \beta^{\alpha}}{-\alpha - 1} \left[x^{-\alpha-1} \right]_{\beta}^{\infty} \tag{2.163}$$

$$= \frac{\alpha \beta^{\alpha} \beta^{-\alpha-1}}{\alpha + 1} \tag{2.164}$$

$$= \frac{\alpha}{\beta(\alpha + 1)} \tag{2.165}$$

$$= \frac{\alpha}{\beta(\alpha + 1)}, \quad \text{for } \alpha > 1. \tag{2.166}$$

Note that this has the dimensions of $\frac{1}{x}$. With the help of $E[X] = \frac{\alpha \beta}{\alpha-1}$ and $E[\frac{1}{X}] = \frac{\alpha}{\beta(\alpha+1)}$, we can solve for α and β. If we use estimates of $E[X]$ and $E[\frac{1}{X}]$ in place of true moments, we get estimates of α and β, as follows. Let the estimate of $E[X] = \hat{\mu} = \frac{\hat{\alpha}\hat{\beta}}{\hat{\alpha}-1}$. Let the estimate of $E[\frac{1}{X}] = \hat{\eta} = \frac{\hat{\alpha}}{\hat{\beta}(\hat{\alpha}+1)}$.

$$\hat{\mu}\hat{\eta} = \frac{\hat{\alpha}^2}{\hat{\alpha}^2 - 1}; \quad \hat{\alpha}^2 \hat{\mu}\hat{\eta} - \hat{\mu}\hat{\eta} - \hat{\alpha}^2 = 0 \tag{2.167}$$

$$\hat{\alpha}^2 (\hat{\mu}\hat{\eta} - 1) = \hat{\mu}\hat{\eta} \tag{2.168}$$

$$\hat{\alpha} = \sqrt{\frac{\hat{\mu}\hat{\eta}}{\hat{\mu}\hat{\eta} - 1}}. \tag{2.169}$$

$$\hat{\beta} = \frac{\hat{\mu}(\hat{\alpha} - 1)}{\hat{\alpha}}. \tag{2.170}$$

2.5.2 Properties of estimators

Consider a sequence of iid random variables $X_1, \cdots, X_n$, each having the same distribution as that of X. The mean of X is estimated as the sample average

$$\hat{\mu} = \frac{1}{n} \sum_{i=1}^{n} X_i. \tag{2.171}$$

Note that if we use the outcomes x_i in the above equation, we get the numerical value of the estimate. But if we use the upper case X_i, then $\hat{\mu}$ is a random variable called the "estimator" with its own distribution and properties. This is useful in developing the properties of the estimators. Taking expectation on both sides of the above equations, we have

$$E[\hat{\mu}] = E[X]. \tag{2.172}$$

This is referred to as the "unbiased" property of the sample mean estimator. By definition of the variance,

$$\text{var}[\hat{\mu}] = E\left[(\hat{\mu})^2\right] - (E[\hat{\mu}])^2 \tag{2.173}$$

$$= E\left[\left(\frac{1}{n}\sum_{i=1}^{n} X_i\right)^2\right] - (E[X])^2 \tag{2.174}$$

$$= E\left[\left(\frac{1}{n}\sum_{i=1}^{n} X_i\right)\left(\frac{1}{n}\sum_{j=1}^{n} X_j\right)\right] - (E[X])^2 \tag{2.175}$$

$$= E\left[\left(\frac{1}{n^2}\sum_{i=1}^{n}\sum_{j=1}^{n} X_i X_j\right)\right] - (E[X])^2 \tag{2.176}$$

$$= \frac{1}{n^2}\left(\sum_{i=1}^{n}\sum_{j=1,j\neq i}^{n} E[X_i X_j] + \sum_{i=1}^{n} E[X_i^2]\right) - (E[X])^2. \tag{2.177}$$

In the above, the double summation is split up into two parts. In the first part $j \neq i$. Under this condition, X_i and X_j are independent, so that $E[X_iX_j] = E[X_i]E[X_j] = (E[X])^2$. In the second part, $j = i$ and $E[X_iX_j]$ becomes $E[X_i^2] = E[X^2]$. Therefore,

$$\text{var}[\hat{\mu}] = \frac{1}{n^2}\sum_{i=1}^{n}\sum_{j=1,j\neq i}^{n}(E[X])^2 + \frac{1}{n^2}\sum_{i=1}^{n}E[X^2] - (E[X])^2 \quad (2.178)$$

$$= \frac{n(n-1)}{n^2}(E[X])^2 + \frac{E[X^2]}{n} - (E[X])^2 \quad (2.179)$$

$$= \frac{n-1}{n}(E[X])^2 - \frac{n}{n}(E[X])^2 + \frac{E[X^2]}{n} \quad (2.180)$$

$$= \frac{E[X^2] - (E[X])^2}{n} \quad (2.181)$$

$$= \frac{\text{var}[X]}{n}. \quad (2.182)$$

That is,

$$\text{var}[\hat{\mu}] = \frac{\sigma^2}{n} \quad (2.183)$$

where σ^2 is the variance of X. As we have seen, the variance is a measure of variation around the mean. Therefore, the estimate of the sample mean improves as more samples are used, since the variance decreases as $\frac{1}{n}$. This is another appealing property of the sample mean.

2.6 Sequences of Random Variables

Properties of sequences of random variables are important for parameter estimation. They are also very useful in the study of long-term behavior of queues. This section is an introduction to the topic.

DEFINITION 2.1 *If a sequence of random variables Y_n is such that the sequence of expected values $\{E[Y_n]\}$ converges to some constant a and the* *sequence of variances $\{var[Y_n]\}$ converges to zero as n tends to infinity, we say that the sequence Y_n converges to a in the mean square sense.*   ☐

By this definition, the sample mean sequence $\hat{\mu}(n)$ converges to μ in the mean square sense. The topic of parameter estimation is intimately related to the topic of infinite sequences of random variables, since we are interested in the behavior of estimators with large data sets. The above property is important and is stated as a theorem below.

THEOREM 2.1

The sample average of a sequence of $n > 0$ iid random variables has the same expectation as each of the original random variables. The variance of the sample average is the variance of the original random variable divided by n. If the variance of the iid random variables is finite, the variance of the sample average tends to 0 as $n \to \infty$.   ☐

The following theorem can also be similarly proved and the proof is suggested as an exercise.

THEOREM 2.2

Let $\{Y_1, Y_2 \cdots ,\}$ be an infinite sequence of independent but not necessarily identical random variables. Let the expectation and variance of each Y_i be finite. Let $E[Y_i] = \eta_i$ and let $var[Y_i] = \sigma_i^2$. Form the infinite sequence of the cumulative average of the original sequence of the random variables defined by

$$Z_n = \frac{1}{n} \sum_{j=1}^{n} Y_j. \tag{2.184}$$

Let b be an upper bound on the variances of all Y_i. That is, $\sigma_i^2 \leq b$ for all i. Then, we have the following.

$$\lim_{n \to \infty} E[Z_n] = \lim_{n \to \infty} \frac{1}{n} \sum_{j=1}^{n} \eta_j \tag{2.185}$$

$$\lim_{n \to \infty} var[Z_n] = \lim_{n \to \infty} \frac{1}{n^2} \sum_{j=1}^{n} \sigma_j^2 \tag{2.186}$$

$$\leq \lim_{n \to \infty} \frac{nb}{n^2} \tag{2.187}$$

$$= 0. \tag{2.188}$$

☐

In some cases, the number of trials, n, itself may be the outcome of a random variable. This is illustrated by the following. We observe a sequence of Poisson arrivals with a rate λ. Let T_n be the random variable for the total time of observation up to and including exactly at the n arrival. Let t be the independent time variable. Let t_n be the outcome of T_n. The time for the first arrival and all interarrival times are iid. Let X be the random variable corresponding to the IAT. A good estimate for the average IAT

$$\overline{X}_n = \frac{t_n}{n}. \tag{2.189}$$

From Theorem 2.1, the above estimate is unbiased for any n and the variance of the estimate tends to zero as n tends to infinity. But do we know that n will tend to infinity if we let the time of observation t tend to infinity. We certainly anticipate that we will receive an unlimited number of arrivals if we observe for an unbounded amount of time. But there is no certainty about this event occurring. The following analyzes such random experiments.

2.6.1   Certain and almost certain events

As an additional simple example, consider an iid sequence of tossing an unbiased coin (with equal probability of head and tail). What is the probability of observing a sequence of 100 heads? It is 2^{-100}. The probability is very small, but the event is not impossible. Likewise, if we imagine an infinite sequence of tosses and consider the probability of *all* heads, the probability tends to zero. However, the event of observing all heads in a sequence of heads is not impossible; such an event occurs with zero probability. If we imagine a sample space of innumerable people, each tossing such an independent iid coin, a finite number of those infinite sequences of tossing may indeed produce all heads. This is consistent with the axioms of probability. What is the probability of *not* finding every one of the tosses in the infinite sequence to be heads? This is not a certain event. But its probability is one.

DEFINITION 2.2   *An event that is not certain but occurs with a probability of 1 is known as an "almost certain" or "almost sure" event.*   ▯

An important event that is almost certain is the number of Poisson arrivals over an unbounded amount of time tending to infinity. The following theorem states the necessary conditions and proves it.

THEOREM 2.3
Let X_1, X_2,... be an infinite sequence of independent nonnegative random variables representing the sequence of interarrival times in a sequence of possibly infinite number of arrivals over a time interval $[0, \infty)$. Let

$$P[X_i \rightarrow \infty] = 0, \ i = 1, 2, \ldots \tag{2.190}$$

Then the probability of the number of arrivals being unbounded over the un-bounded time interval is 1.

Proof

Note that equation (2.190) is satisfied for a Pareto random variable with infinite variance also. The infinite additivity extension of the axioms of probability stated in equation A.1 is useful and repeated below. If an infinite sequence of events e_1, e_2, ... are mutually exclusive,

$$P[e_1 \cup e_2 \cup \cdots] = P[e_1] + P[e_2] + \cdots \qquad (2.191)$$

This in turn implies that if the infinite sequence of events e_1, e_2, ... are not mutually exclusive,

$$P[e_1 \cup e_2 \cup \cdots] \le P[e_1] + P[e_2] + \cdots . \qquad (2.192)$$

Since each of the infinite sequence of random variables X_1, X_2, ... satisfies

$$P[X_i \to \infty] = 0, \qquad (2.193)$$

the following is true.

$$P[\text{at least one } X_i \to \infty] = 0 + 0 + \cdots \qquad (2.194)$$

$$= 0. \qquad (2.195)$$

That is, in the cumulative sum of interarrival times (or the total time of arrivals) for every finite number of arrivals is finite with probability one. Therefore, as the time interval tends to infinity, the number of arrivals increases without bounds, with probability one. That is such an event is almost certain but not completely certain. ☐

Returning to our discussion on observing a sequence of Poisson arrivals, the event of an IAT X being infinity is not impossible. The probability density of the exponential IAT tends to zero as the observation variable x tends to zero.

$$P[X > x] = \exp(-\lambda x) \qquad (2.196)$$

$$\lim_{x \to \infty} P[X > x] = 0. \qquad (2.197)$$

That is, the probability of that IAT being infinity is zero. Therefore, in our earlier problem of estimating the expected IAT by observing a sequence of arrivals through unlimited amount of time, the event of observing infinite number of arrivals occurs with probability 1, but is not a certain event. What is the expectation of a random variable which has one almost certain event? This question is important especially for the limiting random variable of a sequence of random variables. For example, consider the number of Poisson arrivals $N(t)$ of rate λ observed over an unbounded interval of time starting from $t = 0$. What is the expectation of the limiting random variable $\lim\limits_{t \to \infty} \frac{N(t)}{t}$? Use the theorem of total expectation.

$$\lim_{t \to \infty} E[\frac{N(t)}{t}] \tag{2.198}$$

$$= E[\lim_{t \to \infty} \frac{N(t)}{t} | \lim_{t \to \infty} N(t) = \infty] P[\lim_{t \to \infty} N(t) = \infty]$$

$$+ E[\lim_{t \to \infty} \frac{N(t)}{t} | N(t) \text{ does not tend to } \infty \text{ as } t \to \infty]$$

$$\times P[N(t) \text{ does not tend to } \infty \text{ as } t \to \infty] \tag{2.199}$$

$$= E[\lim_{t \to \infty} \frac{N(t)}{t} | \lim_{t \to \infty} N(t) = \infty] \times 1$$

$$+ E[\lim_{t \to \infty} \frac{N(t)}{t} | N(t) \text{ does not tend to } \infty \text{ as } t \to \infty] \times 0 \tag{2.200}$$

$$= E[\lim_{t \to \infty} \frac{N(t)}{t} | \lim_{t \to \infty} N(t) = \infty] \tag{2.201}$$

$$= \lim_{t \to \infty} \frac{1}{t} E[N(t)] \tag{2.202}$$

$$= \lim_{t \to \infty} \frac{1}{t} \lambda t \tag{2.203}$$

$$= \lambda \tag{2.204}$$

We are also interested in evaluating the variance of the estimate as $t \to \infty$. We know that

$$\lim_{t \to \infty} \text{var}[\overline{X(n_t)}] = \lim_{t \to \infty} \sum_{k=0}^{\infty} E[\overline{X}^2 | n(t)] P[n(t) \to \infty] - (E[\overline{X}])^2 . \tag{2.205}$$

Since

$$\lim_{t \to \infty} P[n(t) \to \infty] = 1, \tag{2.206}$$

the limiting variance as t tends to infinity is the same as the limiting variance as $n(t)$ tends to infinity which is known to be zero.

2.7   Elements of Digital Communication and Data Link Performance

A simple method of digital communication is through the use of two different electromagnetic signals to represent the two bits 0 and 1. Each signal lasts for a specific fixed time width. The types of signals can be steady voltages of opposite polarity for the bits 0 and 1, sine waves of opposite phase, etc. Let us denote this time width for each bit by τ. The receiving station receives an attenuated and a slightly corrupted form of the transmitted signal. The function of the first subsystem in the receiver equipment is to decide whether the transmitted signal segment was a 0 or a 1. This function is known as detection. The accuracy of detection may be close to but does not reach the perfect 100%. The bit error rate (BER) is the expected fraction of the bits that will be assigned the wrong bit value due to noise. It is an important performance figure of the communication link. Keeping track of the correct beginning of the time width for a bit and ensuring that the attenuation does not differentially affect the bits 0 and 1 are important aspects of the design of the overall communication system. In this Section, our interest is only to develop a simple model for the variation of the BER as a function of the data transmission rate.

2.7.1   The Gaussian noise model

The receiver calculates a single numerical value for each received signal over the time period τ. If there is no noise, the numerical values calculated by the receiver for the two bits 0 and 1 are design parameters known at the receiver and the BER is zero. The effect of noise is an added value to the ideal received value for the bit. Additive noise is the result of undesirable electromagnetic activity in the communication channel as well as thermal activity in the electronic components of the communication systems. A very good and widely applicable mathematical model for the effect of such noise is the Gaussian noise model, named after the German mathematician Carl Friedrich Gauss (1777–1855). The pdf of a Gaussian random variable is given by

$$f_X(x) = \frac{1}{\sqrt{2\pi\sigma^2}} \exp\left(-\frac{(x-\eta)^2}{2\sigma^2}\right). \tag{2.207}$$

The mean of X evaluates to η and the variance, to σ^2. The nature of the Gaussian random variable has its origin in the averaging effects of numerous independent contributions, in much the same way that the Poisson random variable is a consequence of numerous independent emissions. This comparison is only subjective and no attempt to derive the pdf of a Gaussian random variable from fundamental assumptions is made here. The random variable evaluated by the receiver corresponds to the ideal value for the transmitted bit plus the zero mean additive noise value. In a commonly used *Symmetric Binary Communication* system, these mean values for the bits 0 and 1 are of opposite signs and equal absolute value. For convenience, let the mean value of the bit 0 be $-\eta$ and that for bit 1 be $+\eta$, where η is a positive value. Physically, η^2 is proportional to the power in the received signal and σ^2 is proportional to the noise power in the received signal. The signals for both the bits transmit the same power for the same time width τ and hence the same energy. Therefore, the pdf of the received random variable X under the two different conditions of bit transmissions 0 and 1 are given by

$$f_Y(y|0) = \frac{1}{\sqrt{2\pi\sigma^2}} \exp\left(-\frac{(y+\eta)^2}{2\sigma^2}\right) \quad \text{and} \tag{2.208}$$

$$f_Y(y|1) = \frac{1}{\sqrt{2\pi\sigma^2}} \exp\left(-\frac{(y-\eta)^2}{2\sigma^2}\right). \tag{2.209}$$

The time varying value of the actual noise over τ (as opposed to its power) averages to zero over a long time. Therefore, the longer the bit time τ for transmission, the less effective the noise is in causing bit errors. This is similar to the variance of the sample average estimator being inversely proportional to the the number of samples used in averaging, illustrated in Section 2.5.2. The physical dimensions of the random variables can also be scaled to let the value of η to be 1. The equivalent noise variance, as a function of τ then translates to $\frac{\alpha^2}{\tau}$ for some α implicitly determined by the transmitted signal power and noise power. The transmitted bit is a random variable B with outcome b and a sample space of $b \in \{0, 1\}$. Therefore, we have the pdf of the received random variable conditioned on transmitted bit b given by

$$f_Y(y|b) = \frac{1}{\sqrt{2\pi\frac{\alpha^2}{\tau}}} \exp\left(-\frac{(y+(-1)^b))^2\tau}{2\alpha^2}\right). \tag{2.210}$$

How should the receiver decide on the transmitted bit for a received value y? The approach is to maximize the probability of the decision being correct. Let p_0 and $p_1 = 1 - p_0$ be the probabilities with which the transmitter emits bits 0 and 1, respectively. Assume that the sequence of emitted bits are iid. Then, if the receiver receives y, we should maximize the *a posteriori* probability of $b \in \{0, 1\}$ given by the Bayes' theorem. The *a posteriori* probability of b is

$$P[B = b|y] = \frac{p_b f_Y(y|b)}{p_0 f_Y(y|1) + p_1 f_Y(y|1)} \tag{2.211}$$

which is equivalent to maximizing the joint probability density

$$f_Y(y, B = b) = p_b f_Y(y|b) \tag{2.212}$$

over $b \in \{0, 1\}$. In a long stream of transmission, we anticipate that the numbers of bits with values 0 and 1 are approximately equal. This is equivalent to assuming

$p_0 = p_1 = \frac{1}{2}$. Therefore the detection algorithm at the receiver simplifies to deciding $b = 0$, if $y \leq 0$ and that $b = 1$ if $y > 0$. This is illustrated by plotting the two conditional densities $f_Y(y|b)$ in Figure 2.10.

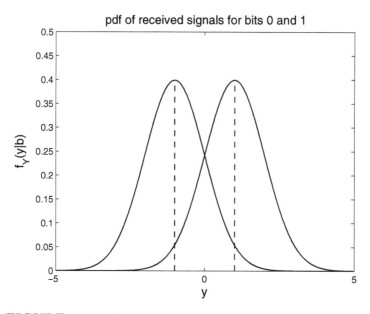

FIGURE 2.10: Gaussian densities of received signals for bits 0 and 1 with a unit noise variance

2.7.2 Bit error rate evaluation

The BER calculation is important to assess the performance of the data link. The receiver makes an error if bit 0 was transmitted and $y > 0$ and if bit 1 was transmitted and $y \leq 0$. Let e_b be the probability of error. This is also the BER we are interested in evaluating.

$$e_b = \int\limits_{y=0}^{\infty} \frac{1}{2} f_Y(y|0)dy + \int\limits_{y=-\infty}^{0} \frac{1}{2} f_Y(y|1)dy. \qquad (2.213)$$

Both the above integrals are equal, due to symmetry. Therefore,

$$e_b = \int\limits_{y=o}^{\infty} f_Y(y|0)dy \qquad (2.214)$$

$$= \int_{y=0}^{\infty} \frac{1}{\sqrt{2\pi \frac{\alpha^2}{\tau}}} \exp\left(-\frac{(y+1)^2 \tau}{2\alpha^2}\right) dy. \qquad (2.215)$$

Substitute

$$v = (y+1)\sqrt{\frac{\tau}{2\alpha^2}} \qquad (2.216)$$

in the above integral. When $y = 0$, v evaluates to $\sqrt{\frac{\tau}{2\alpha^2}}$.

$$dv = dy\sqrt{\frac{\tau}{2\alpha^2}}. \qquad (2.217)$$

Therefore,

$$e_b = \frac{1}{\sqrt{\pi}} \int_{\sqrt{\frac{\tau}{2\alpha^2}}}^{\infty} \exp(-v^2)dv. \qquad (2.218)$$

A standard integral function similar to the above is popularly used. It is defined as the *error function*

$$\text{erf}(x) = \frac{2}{\sqrt{\pi}} \int_{v=0}^{x} \exp(-v^2)dv. \qquad (2.219)$$

For a positive x, the above can be interpreted as the probability of a Gaussian random variable W with zero mean and a variance of $\frac{1}{2}$ falling in a region as follows.

$$\text{erf}(x) = 2\frac{1}{\sqrt{2\pi \times \frac{1}{2}}} \int_{v=0}^{x} \exp\left(-\frac{v^2}{2 \times \frac{1}{2}}\right) dv \qquad (2.220)$$

$$= 2P[0 < W \le x]. \qquad (2.221)$$

We know that $P[0 < W \le \infty] = \frac{1}{2}$. Therefore, we have

$$\text{erf}(0) = 0 \quad \text{and} \qquad (2.222)$$

$$\text{erf}(\infty) = 1. \qquad (2.223)$$

$$\frac{2}{\sqrt{\pi}} \int_{v=x}^{\infty} \exp(-v^2)dv = 1 - \text{erf}(x) \text{ and} \qquad (2.224)$$

$$\frac{1}{\sqrt{\pi}} \int_{v=x}^{\infty} \exp(-v^2)dv = \frac{1}{2} - \frac{1}{2}\text{erf}(x). \qquad (2.225)$$

Returning to the bit error rate, we therefore have

$$e_b = \frac{1}{\sqrt{\pi}} \int_{\sqrt{\frac{\tau}{2\alpha^2}}}^{\infty} \exp(-v^2)dv \qquad (2.226)$$

$$= \frac{1}{2} - \frac{1}{2}\text{erf}\left(\sqrt{\frac{\tau}{2\alpha^2}}\right). \qquad (2.227)$$

We finally have the expression to assess the performance of the channel as a function of τ which is the inverse of the data rate. In reality, the probabilities of the bits 0 and 1 may not be equal, the data bits may not be iid, and there may be other inaccuracies in our simplification. However, that the argument that noise is Gaussian and the effect of the variance of the noise is inversely proportional to τ is a very good approximation. Design approaches to combat noise influences the value of α^2. Since this α^2 represents the effect of noise and plays a central role in using errors in performance, let us rename it as σ_b^2. The physical dimension of σ_b^2 is the reciprocal of time. The final expression for BER that we shall use later is

$$e_b = \frac{1}{2} - \frac{1}{2}\text{erf}\left(\sqrt{\frac{\tau}{2\sigma_b^2}}\right). \qquad (2.228)$$

A useful result from this treatment of digital communication is that if the BER at a particular data rate is given to us, that determines the effective σ_b^2 so that we can evaluate the BER if the data rate is varied. The following example illustrates it well. Alternatively, if we use $s = \frac{1}{\tau}$ as the data transmission (s for sending) rate in bps,

$$e_b = \frac{1}{2} - \frac{1}{2}\text{erf}\left(\sqrt{\frac{1}{2\sigma_b^2 s}}\right). \qquad (2.229)$$

and σ_b^2 can be interpreted as the equivalent noise variance per unit transmission rate of 1 bps.

2.7.3   Frame error rate evaluation

In the data link, the frame error rate (FER), denoted by e_f can be evaluated if we know the distribution of the number of bits in the frames and if we continue to assume the above model of the nature of bit sequence and the effects of noise. A good model for the frame size is an exponential random variable, which is an approximation of the geometric random variable. Let the data frame size K be a geometric random variable with a pmf

$$P[K = k] = q(1 - q)^{k-1}, \quad k = 1, 2, \cdots . \tag{2.230}$$

The average frame size is $E[K] = \frac{1}{q}$. A frame is erroneous if even one bit in the packet is erroneous. Therefore, error rate is given by

$$e_f = \text{FER} = 1 - \sum_{k=1}^{\infty} (1 - e_b)^k q(1 - q)^{k-1} \tag{2.231}$$

$$= 1 - q(1 - e_b) \sum_{k=0}^{\infty} [(1 - e_b)(1 - q)]^k \tag{2.232}$$

$$= 1 - \frac{q(1 - e_b)}{1 - (1 - e_b)(1 - q)} \tag{2.233}$$

$$= \frac{e_b}{1 - (1 - q)(1 - e_b)}. \tag{2.234}$$

Clearly, the FER, or e_f, is a little higher than the BER e_b. Thus, if the average frame size is known and either the BER or FER is known at one data rate, the BER and FER can be evaluated at other data rates.

2.7.4 Data rate optimization

Example 2.7
The BER of a wireless data link operating at 1 Mbps is known to be 10^{-3}. The throughput is defined as the overall bit rate calculated using all the bits in the correctly received packets only. The average packet size is 1000 bits per packet.

1. Determine the equivalent noise parameter, σ_b^2 of this datalink.

2. Plot the throughput, that is, the rate of correctly received bits as the data rate is varied from $\frac{1}{2}$ Mbps to 2 Mbps. What is the data transmission rate (in bps) that maximizes this throughput?

3. The energy consumed per bit is the expected energy expended by the transmitter in order for the receiver to receive a bit correctly, without errors. Energy of a bit transmission is proportional to the bit width. Determine the optimal bit width to minimize the expected energy per correctly received bit.

◻

Solution

1. The error function is strictly monotonically increasing. Define the inverse error function as follows. For a positive u, if $v = \text{erf}(u)$, the inverse function $u = \text{erf}^{-1}(v)$. The domain of v for the inverse function is $[0, 1]$, and the range of u is $[0, \infty)$. For a bit-width of τ and a noise parameter σ_b^2, we have the BER

$$e_b = \frac{1}{2} - \frac{1}{2}\text{erf}\left(\sqrt{\frac{\tau}{2\sigma_b^2}}\right). \qquad (2.235)$$

Rearranging,

$$\sigma_b^2 = \frac{\tau}{2[\text{erf}^{-1}(1-2e_b)]^2}. \qquad (2.236)$$

Due to the monotonicity of the error function, given a value for e_b at a τ, the value of σ_b^2 is easy to evaluate numerically. Indeed, the Matlab software has a built-in function for the inverse of the error function. For $\tau = 10^{-6}$ second and $e_b = 10^{-3}$, σ_b^2 evaluates to 0.10472×10^{-6} second or 0.1047 per Mbps.

2. The expected fraction of a bit correctly received for every transmitted bit is simply the probability that the transmitted bit is in a correctly received data frame. Therefore, the throughput, $E[Y]$, in correctly received bits per second ("sec" is also used to denote a second of time) is the product of the transmitted bit rate (say s for the rate of sending bits) and the probability of correctly receiving a data frame at the receiver.

$$E[Y] = s(1 - e_f) \qquad (2.237)$$

where e_f is the frame error rate FER given by equation (2.234) in Section 2.7.

$$e_f = \frac{e_b}{1 - (1-q)(1-e_b)}, \qquad (2.238)$$

$$e_b = \frac{1}{2} - \frac{1}{2}\text{erf}\left(\sqrt{\frac{1}{2\sigma_b^2 s}}\right) \qquad (2.239)$$

with $\frac{1}{q}$ being the average packet size in bits. We know e_b from above. Figure 2.11 illustrates the variation of the throughput as a function of the data rate s. The throughput reaches a maximum of 0.6358 Mbps at the data rate 0.7445 Mbps.

3. The expected number of bits transmitted for a correctly received bit is $\frac{1}{1-e_f}$. Since energy transmitted per bit is proportional to the bit-width, the expected energy transmitted for every correctly received bit is proportional to

$$E[Z] = \frac{1}{s(1 - e_f)}. \qquad (2.240)$$

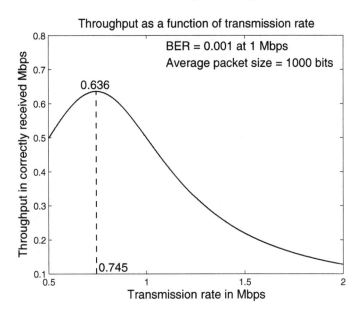

FIGURE 2.11: Throughput of an unreliable link as a function of the data rate

Clearly, the expected energy per correctly received bit is minimized at the same data rate that maximizes the throughput. □

2.8 Exercises

1. Let μ be the finite mean and σ^2 be the finite variance of a Pareto random variable. Express each of α and β as functions of the mean and the variance only. For a mean of 1.5 msec and a variance of 0.75 msec^2, find α and β.

2. In Pareto random variables, β is just a scale factor and, by using different time units, β can always be normalized to 1. So, only α affects the behavior of the Pareto random variable. Let β be 1 msec. Plot the variation of the variance as a function of α, starting from close to 2, up to 10.

3. Consider a *shifted Pareto* random variable Y whose density function is nonzero for $y \geq 0$. The density is given by

$$f_Y(y) = \frac{\alpha}{\beta}\left(\frac{\beta}{y+\beta}\right)^{\alpha+1}, \quad y \geq 0. \tag{2.241}$$

Let its mean and variance be finite and given by μ and σ^2 respectively. Express α as a function of μ and σ^2 only. Express β as a function of μ and σ^2 only.

4. Consider Poisson arrivals with a rate of 1 job per second. Now approximate the arrival process so that there can be at most one arrival in each of successive nonoverlapping narrow intervals of 0.1 sec per interval. What is the probability of exactly one arrival in a 0.2 second time interval (in this approximated model)?

5. A computer is processing a job whose total time requirement is exponentially distributed with parameter μ. The operating system (OS) has started a timer which is also exponentially distributed but with parameter α. If the job is not completely processed by time the OS timer signals its completion, the job is preempted for a later resumption. Let the start of the job's processing and the OS timer be both at time instant 0 (that is, they are started simultaneously and a race ensues). Determine the pdf of the time instant at which the processor will be relieved of the job, either due to completion or due to preemption by the OS.

6. In the above physical system, what is the probability that the OS wins the race? That is, what is the probability of that the OS timer rings before the job's processing is complete?

7. Consider a Poisson stream of arrivals with a rate of one arrival per 3 seconds of time. During a time interval lasting from 0 to 1 second, exactly one arrival occurred, at some unknown time instant $t \in (0, 1]$. Develop the probability density function of the above arrival time instant. That is, determine the probability density function $f(t|$ exactly one arrival in $(0, 1]$).

8. The mean and variance of a continuous, uniformly distributed random variable have been estimated to be 12 and 64, respectively. Estimate the parameters of the distribution.

9. In a computer center, training sessions are offered to groups of three persons at a time. There are enough computers and enough staff to begin a training session as soon as three persons have gathered. People arrive for training in a Poisson process with a rate of 10 per hour. The computer center has been operating for a long time, and it can be shown that the probabilities that $3k$, $3k + 1$, and $3k + 2$ persons have so far arrived are all equal at the time a person arrives (this is taken for granted here). Determine the expected time an arriving person needs to wait before the training can start.

10. A stream of Poisson arrivals is split into two substreams with alternate arrivals being routed to each of the two substreams. Prove that the arrival scheme in each of the substreams is NOT Poisson, with the help of Laplace transforms.

11. A computer system consists of a CPU and an I/O. Each of these components is known to be an exponential server; each job goes through both the components. A frequent user estimated the mean and variance of the total time a job takes to be 10 second and 82 second^2, respectively. CPU and I/O times are independent. Estimate the service rates of the CPU and the I/O.

12. $x_1, ..., x_n$ are the observed outcomes of a random sample from the following uniform density function.

$$f_X(x) = \frac{1}{b-a}, \quad a \leq x \leq b \qquad (2.242)$$

$$= 0, \quad \text{otherwise.} \qquad (2.243)$$

The parameters a and b are unknown. Determine estimates of a and b as functions of $x_1, ..., x_n$.

13. Let X be a Pareto random variable with parameters $1 < \alpha \leq 2$ and $\beta > 0$. Let Y be $\ln(X)$. Determine the density function of Y.

14. Express each of α and β in the above problem as functions of $E[X]$ and $E[\frac{1}{X}]$.

15. Write an algorithm for generating the time instants of a sequence of arrivals starting from 0 and ending T. The IATs are iid Pareto random variables with parameters α and β.

16. Add a segment of algorithm to the above to determine the sample mean and sample variance of the generated IATs.

17. Over many independent and identical trials of a binomial random variable X, the mean was estimated to be 5.5 and the variance was estimated to be 1.7. Estimate the parameters of this binomial random variable X.

18. A Poisson sequence of jobs with rate 1 per second arrive in front of a server. The service requirements of jobs are independent, identical, and exponential with an average time of $\frac{1}{2}$ second. Consider the first k jobs arriving over a time period starting from time $t = 0$. The server is free to start serving at time $t = 0$. What is the probability that ALL k of them get service without any of them having to wait for previous arrivals to complete service? Note that this question does not require queuing theory. This can be solved with properties of Poisson and exponential random variables.

19. A TCP connection lasts for a random amount of time X which is uniformly distributed between 0 and a. The data packets in this connection arrive as a Poisson stream with rate λ. Determine the probability of receiving at least one data packet in such a TCP connection.

20. A TCP connection lasts for a random amount of time X with a probability density $f_X(x)$. The data packets in this connection arrive as a Poisson stream with rate λ. Prove that the expected number of data packets arriving during such a TCP connection is $\lambda E[X]$.

21. In a digital communication system, a sequence of two bits is transmitted as a single symbol. Obviously, there are four different values for the symbols. They are transmitted as the equivalents of the numerical values -1.5, -0.5, 0.5, and 1.5, respectively. After preprocessing at the receiver, the received numerical value corresponds to the transmitted value plus the outcome of a Gaussian random variable X which has a mean $\eta = 0$ and a variance of $\sigma^2 = 0.0169$. Develop the decision algorithm that the receiver should use. Evaluate the numerical value of the probability of error that a symbol experiences through this communication system.

Chapter 3

The $M/M/1/\infty$ Queue

3.1 Introduction

Packet data communication progresses in a sequence of stages. Each stage consists of a subset of the following steps: arrive, wait, process, forward, and travel a physical distance. From the point of view of evaluation of the overall performance, each such stage is a queuing system. This is the case, for example, in a network wherein a data frame over a long distance link starts to appear at the input of a system. In many such systems, arrivals can take place at arbitrary time instants so that interarrival times (IATs) are considered to be real variables as opposed to discrete variables. It is common for a data packet to be referred to as a data frame in the datalink layer of the data communication protocol hierarchy.

The processing system is digital and synchronizes the forwarding activity with its own clock. In such systems the processing time is discrete, since a digital system processes in an integer number of bits. However, due to the very large number of possibilities in the number of bits processed, the processing time is justifiably approximated as a real variable. Hence, such systems are modeled and analyzed as continuous-time queuing systems.

This chapter deals with the simplest queue that is amenable for analysis. In the process, it introduces several key aspects of queuing theory. The basic model of the queue is as follows. Interarrival times are memoryless with rate λ. Equivalently, the sequence of arrival time instants is Poisson. Service times are memoryless with rate μ. There is one server and unlimited waiting room capacity, i.e., an infinite buffer. Service order is FIFO. Figure 3.1 shows the queuing model. Figure 3.2 shows a time plot of numbers of arrivals and departures. Figure 3.3 shows the corresponding number of customers as a function of time $A(t)$ is the number of arrivals as a function of time with $t = 0$ being the starting time, and $D(t)$ is the number of customers that have departed as of t. $N(t) = A(t) - D(t)$ is the number of customers in the system as a function of time. We are interested in performance figures like the average number of customers in the system, average delay in the system (experienced by a customer), and what fraction of time the server is busy. The first task is to find the probability function of $N(t)$ under the condition that the pmf is independent of time t.

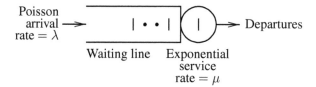

FIGURE 3.1:   The M/M/1/∞ queuing model

3.2   Derivation of Equilibrium State Probabilities

At any instant of time τ, given that the number of customers in the system is $n(\tau)$, the future behavior of the system, that is, at all time instants $t > \tau$, is dependent on $n(t)$ only. This is due to the memorylessness of the interarrival times and also of service times. Following the time instant t, the behavior of the system is a function of the number $n(t)$ and any arrivals and departures after t. The time instants of arrivals and departures after t are independent of the time instants when the most recent arrival or the most recent departure took place, prior to t. This may not be true of other systems studied in later chapters.

DEFINITION 3.1   *The number of customers in the M/M/1/∞ queuing system is referred to as the* **state** *of the system.* ▯

The arrival rate is denoted by λ, and the service rate, by μ. Let

$$P_{ij}(\delta_t) = P[\text{number in system changes from } i \text{ to } j \text{ in } \delta_t] \quad \text{and} \quad (3.1)$$

$$P_n(t) = P[\text{number in system is } n \text{ at time } t]. \quad (3.2)$$

We will be taking limits as $\delta_t \to 0$, so we need to consider at most one arrival in a time interval δ_t, or one departure in δ_t, but not both, since in any time interval, the number of arrivals and the number of service completions are both independent and memoryless. $P[\text{one arrival}]$ is $\lambda\delta_t$, $P[\text{no arrival}]$ is $(1 - \lambda\delta_t)$. Similar relations hold for departures. If $n - 1 \geq 0$,

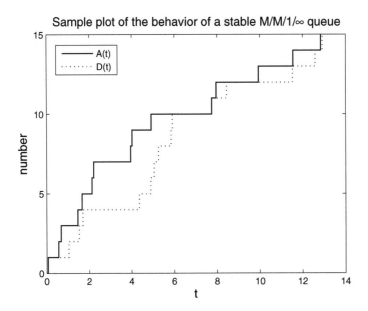

FIGURE 3.2:   Sample plots of cumulative numbers of arrivals and departures as a function of time

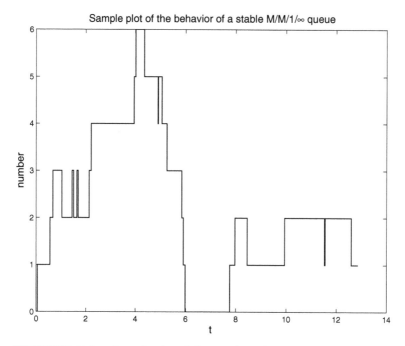

FIGURE 3.3:   Sample plot of the number of customers remaining in the system as a function of time

$$P_n(t + \delta_t)$$

$$= P_n(t)(1 - \lambda\delta_t)(1 - \mu\delta_t) + P_{n-1}(t)\lambda\delta_t(1 - \mu\delta_t) + P_{n+1}(t)(1 - \lambda\delta_t)(\mu\delta_t). \tag{3.3}$$

For $n = 0$,

$$P_0(t + \delta_t) = P_0(t)(1 - \lambda\delta_t) + P_1(t)(1 - \lambda\delta_t)\mu\delta_t. \tag{3.4}$$

Simplifying and ignoring terms containing $(\delta_t)^2$, we have

$$P_n(t + \delta_t) = P_n(t)[1 - (\lambda + \mu)\delta_t] + P_{n-1}(t)\lambda\delta_t + P_{n+1}(t)\mu\delta_t,$$
$$\text{for } n \geq 1 \tag{3.5}$$

$$P_0(t + \delta_t) = P_0(t)[1 - \lambda\delta_t] + P_1(t)\delta_t\mu. \tag{3.6}$$

$$\lim_{\delta_t \to 0} \frac{P_n(t + \delta_t) - P_n(t)}{\delta_t} = -P_n(t)(\lambda + \mu) + P_{n-1}(t)\lambda + P_{n+1}(t)\mu,$$
$$\text{for } n \geq 1. \tag{3.7}$$

$$\frac{dP_n(t)}{dt} = -P_n(t)(\lambda + \mu) + P_{n-1}(t)\lambda + P_{n+1}(t)\mu,$$
$$\text{for } n \geq 1. \tag{3.8}$$

$$\lim_{\delta_t \to 0} \frac{P_0(t + \delta_t) - P_0(t)}{\delta_t} = -\lambda P_0(t) + \mu P_1(t). \tag{3.9}$$

$$\frac{dP_0(t)}{dt} = -\lambda P_0(t) + \mu P_1(t). \tag{3.10}$$

So, we have an unlimited number of simultaneous linear differential equations with constant coefficients. In computer systems and networks, if the arrival and service rates are constants, within a few seconds, several thousands of jobs would have passed through. We subjectively anticipate that the derivatives will reduce in magnitude as time progresses and that the probabilities will settle down to their respective constants and not vary with time. Therefore, we consider the steady state solution to the set of differential equations.

DEFINITION 3.2 *If $\frac{dP_i(t)}{dt} = 0$, for all i in an M/M/1/∞ system at some time t, we say that the system is in equilibrium. at that time t.* □

Let us see if such an equilibrium is possible in our M/M/1 system, derive a "solution" for $P_i(t) = p_i$, for all $i \geq 0$, under such assumptions, and the condition for the assumption to be valid. Let

$$p_i = \lim_{t \to \infty} P_i(t), \ i \geq 0. \tag{3.11}$$

We have

$$-p_0 \lambda + p_1 \mu = 0 \tag{3.12}$$

$$-p_n(\lambda + \mu) + \lambda p_{n-1} + \mu p_{n+1} = 0 \tag{3.13}$$

$$p_1 = \frac{\lambda}{\mu} p_0 \tag{3.14}$$

$$p_0 = \frac{\mu}{\lambda} p_1. \tag{3.15}$$

Using this and with $n + 1 = 2$, we get,

$$-p_1(\lambda + \mu) + \lambda\left(\frac{\mu}{\lambda} p_1\right) + \mu p_2 = 0 \tag{3.16}$$

$$-p_1 \lambda + \mu p_2 = 0 \tag{3.17}$$

$$p_2 = \frac{\lambda}{\mu} p_1. \tag{3.18}$$

Let us check if $p_{i+1} = \frac{\lambda}{\mu} p_i$, by induction. Let $p_k = \frac{\lambda}{\mu} p_{k-1}$ for $k = i$. For $k = i + 1$, we have

$$-p_k(\lambda + \mu) + \lambda p_{k-1} + \mu p_{k+1} = 0. \tag{3.19}$$

Using $p_k = \frac{\lambda}{\mu} p_{k-1}$, we have

$$-p_k(\lambda + \mu) + \lambda\left(\frac{\mu}{\lambda} p_k\right) + \mu p_{k+1} = 0 \tag{3.20}$$

$$-p_k \lambda + \mu p_{k+1} = 0 \tag{3.21}$$

$$p_{k+1} = \frac{\lambda}{\mu} p_k. \tag{3.22}$$

By induction, it follows that

$$p_{n+1} = \frac{\lambda}{\mu} p_n, \; n = 0, 1, 2, \ldots \tag{3.23}$$

$$p_{n+1} = \left(\frac{\lambda}{\mu}\right)^2 p_{n-1} = \left(\frac{\lambda}{\mu}\right)^3 p_{n-2} \cdots \left(\frac{\lambda}{\mu}\right)^{n+1} p_0 \tag{3.24}$$

$$p_n = \left(\frac{\lambda}{\mu}\right)^n p_0. \tag{3.25}$$

Under what conditions will these equilibrium probabilities exist? Sum all these probabilities,

$$\sum_{n=0}^{\infty} p_n = p_0 \sum_{n=0}^{\infty} \left(\frac{\lambda}{\mu}\right)^n. \tag{3.26}$$

This sum is required to be 1. This sum exists only if $\lambda < \mu$. Therefore, under $\lambda < \mu$, the system "can be" in equilibrium with

$$p_0 = \frac{1}{\sum_{n=0}^{\infty} \left(\frac{\lambda}{\mu}\right)^n} = 1 - \frac{\lambda}{\mu}. \tag{3.27}$$

We have the following result.

THEOREM 3.1
Let $\rho = \frac{\lambda}{\mu}$ for an M/M/1/∞ queue with λ being the arrival rate and μ, the service rate. The equilibrium probabilities exist only if $\rho < 1$ or equivalently, if $\lambda < \mu$ and are given by

$$p_n = (1 - \rho)\rho^n, \; n = 0, 1, 2, \ldots. \tag{3.28}$$

□

Conversely, if $p_n = (1 - \rho)\rho^n$, for all $n = 0, 1, \cdots$, then, $\frac{dP_n(t)}{dt} = 0$, for all n, as can be verified by substituting in equation (3.8). The quantity ρ is known by other names "normalized load" and "utilization." on the server. Figure 3.4 shows a plot of p_n as a function of n, for a few different values of ρ. The ordinate at $n = 0$ gives $1 - \rho$ for each plot.

DEFINITION 3.3 Stability   *An M/M/1/∞ queue is said to be stable if the arrival rate λ is strictly less than the service rate μ.*   □

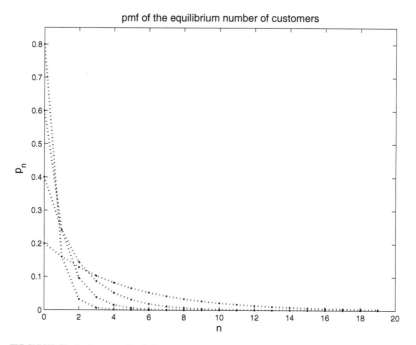

FIGURE 3.4:   pmf of the state of an M/M/1/∞ queue

Whether a system is stable or not depends only on the parameters of the system and not on whether it is currently operating under equilibrium. Steady-state is another name for equilibrium. Steady-state state probabilities is another name for the set $\{p_0, p_1, \dots\}$. Why should $\lambda < \mu$ for stability? λ is the arrival rate, the single parameter representing the load offered to the server. μ is the service rate, the single parameter representing the capacity of service offered to the environment. Obviously, the load cannot exceed the capacity. If it does, the server cannot serve all the arrivals, the queue builds up, and the number of customers will not reach statistical steady-state. Why can λ not equal μ and expect to reach steady-state? The answer is that the interarrival times and service times are random. If $\lambda = \mu$, the server must be attending to one of another customer constantly, with no hope for a free moment. Unfortunately, in the beginning of operation, it is very likely that there are zero customers for some, may be short, periods of time. The server loses these times from logging service and can never recover from such losses. Therefore, the queue eventually builds up even if $\lambda = \mu$.

3.2.1   Operation in equilibrium

Steady state operation is an alternative expression for equilibrium operation. The following theorem shows that if a stable M/M/1/∞ system is in equilibrium at any time instant, it will remain so indefinitely.

THEOREM 3.2
If an M/M/1/∞ queue is in equilibrium at a time instant t = 0, it will continue to be in equilibrium for all t > 0 as well.

Proof
The differential equations governing the behavior of $P_i(t)$, $i = 0, 1, \cdots$, are

$$\frac{dP_0(t)}{dt} = -\lambda P_0(t) + \mu P_1(t) \tag{3.29}$$

$$\frac{dP_n(t)}{dt} = -P_n(t)(\lambda + \mu) + P_{n-1}(t)\lambda + P_{n+1}(t)\mu, \ n \geq 1. \tag{3.30}$$

Differentiating both sides of equations (3.29) and (3.30) with respect to (wrt) t, we find that the LHS is the second derivative $\frac{d^2 P_i(t)}{dt^2}$. The RHS is a linear combination of the first derivatives. All the first derivatives are known to be zero at $t = 0$. Using these in the RHS of the equation with the LHS being the second derivative, we find that all the second derivatives are also zero at $t = 0$. Differentiating equation (3.30) repeatedly, we find that the derivatives of all the state probabilities of *all* higher orders are also zero at $t = 0$.

Now, $0 \leq P_i \leq 1$, for all $i = 0, 1, \cdots$, and $\sum_{i=0}^{\infty} P_i(t) = 1$ ensure that

$$\sum_{i=0}^{\infty} a_i P_i < B \tag{3.31}$$

where a_i, $i = 0, 1, \cdots$ are all finite-bounded, and B is a finite bound. This implies that the RHS of the differential equation (4.16) is finite and bounded for every i which in turn implies that the first derivative of every state probability is finite and bounded at every $t > 0$. Using similar arguments over successively differentiated versions of the differential equations show that the time functions of all state probabilities are continuous with continuous derivatives of all orders. This allows the Taylor series representation for every $P_i(t)$ for every $t > 0$ as

$$P_i(t) = P_i(0) + \sum_{j=1}^{\infty} \frac{1}{j!} \frac{d^j P_i(\tau)}{d\tau^j}\Big|_{\tau=0}, \ i = 0, 1, \cdots . \tag{3.32}$$

Brook Taylor (1685–1731) was an English mathematician. In the above Taylor series, the derivatives are all evaluated at time zero. From the argument above, the derivatives are all zero at time $t = 0$ showing that $P_i(t) = P_i(0)$ for all $i = 0, 1, \cdots$ and for all $t > 0$. ∐

3.2.2 Setting the system to start in equilibrium

A clever way to start the system to be equilibrium right from the starting time instant t_0 is to randomly choose a number of customers in the queue at t_0 by the steady state distribution of equation (3.28). How is this different from starting a queue with a known, constant number (say, zero) of customers at $t = 0$? The difference is explained by considering (imagining) the sample space of an unlimited number of such queues. Let an innumerable number of queues be started at $t = 0$, each with an iid number of customers generated from an ideal random number generation algorithm with the equilibrium state distribution. We do not look at any actual number of customers obtained by the random number generation algorithm. Then, at any later point in time, at $\tau > 0$, the state of all the queues correspond to iid equilibrium state pmf.

On the other hand if all the queues are started with a constant number of customers (say k) at time $t = 0$, then, at a time $\tau > t$, the pmf of the state of the queues is given by the probability values dictated by the differential equations (3.29) and (3.30) at $t = \tau$, and not by the equilibrium state probabilities.

3.3   Simple Performance Figures

The equilibrium state probabilities are

$$p_n = (1 - \rho)\rho^n, \ n \geq 0, \text{ for } \rho < 1. \tag{3.33}$$

$p_0 = (1 - \rho)$ itself is a performance figure, as is $1 - p_0 = \rho$. This condition of no customers in the system is also known by other expressions as "idle," "system is empty," and "server is free."

$$p_0 = P[\text{server is free}] = P[\text{empty}] \tag{3.34}$$

$$1 - p_0 = P[\text{server is busy}]. \tag{3.35}$$

Note that p_0 is the highest of any steady state probability! However, $P[N > 0]$ can be larger than p_0.

$$p_n = (1 - \rho)\rho^n, \ n \geq 0, \tag{3.36}$$

is called a modified geometric pmf and the random variable N, a modified geometric random variable.

Expected Number in the System
The most important visible quantity is the number of customers in a system. The average of which constitutes an equally important performance figure.

$$E[N] = \text{steady state (or equilibrium) expectation of the state} \tag{3.37}$$

$$= \sum_{n=0}^{\infty} n p_n \tag{3.38}$$

$$= \sum_{n=0}^{\infty} n(1 - \rho)\rho^n \tag{3.39}$$

$$= (1 - \rho)\rho \sum_{n=1}^{\infty} n\rho^{n-1}, \text{ since the argument of sum is 0 for } n = 0$$

$$= (1 - \rho)\rho \sum_{n=1}^{\infty} \frac{d}{d\rho}\rho^n. \tag{3.40}$$

Derivative and sum operators can be interchanged, if both exist. We will interchange and verify this to be true (for $\rho < 1$).

$$E[N] = (1 - \rho)\rho \frac{d}{d\rho}\left\{\sum_{n=1}^{\infty} \rho^n\right\} \tag{3.41}$$

$$= (1 - \rho)\rho \frac{d}{d\rho}\left\{\sum_{n=0}^{\infty} \rho^n - \rho^0\right\} \tag{3.42}$$

$$= (1 - \rho)\rho \frac{d}{d\rho}\left\{\frac{1}{1 - \rho} - 1\right\} \tag{3.43}$$

$$= (1 - \rho)\rho \frac{d}{d\rho}\left(\frac{\rho}{1 - \rho}\right) \tag{3.44}$$

$$= (1 - \rho)\rho \frac{(1 - \rho) - \rho(-1)}{(1 - \rho)^2} \tag{3.45}$$

$$= \frac{\rho}{1 - \rho} \tag{3.46}$$

Note that we could have simplified the steps above by noting $\frac{d}{d\rho}1 = 0$.

$$E[N] = \frac{\rho}{(1 - \rho)}. \tag{3.47}$$

This quantity is also known as the average buffer occupancy. We see that as ρ approaches 1, the average number of customers in the system rises very steeply. Therefore, it does not help to try to make the capacity μ close to the load. Even though doing this would reduce the fraction of time the server is free, it severely contributes to increasing $E[N]$. Figure 3.5 shows a plot of $E[N]$.

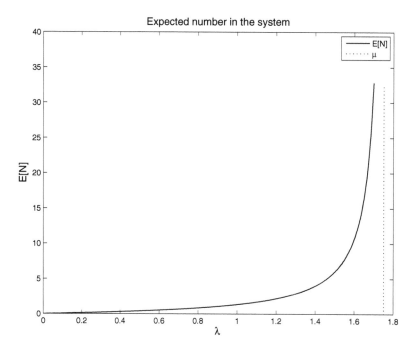

FIGURE 3.5:   Average number in an M/M/1/∞ queue as a function of arrival rate

Variance of the Number in the System

Let us first evaluate

$$E[N(N-1)] = \sum_{n=0}^{\infty} n(n-1)p_n \qquad (3.48)$$

$$= \sum_{n=0}^{\infty} n(n-1)(1-\rho)\rho^n \qquad (3.49)$$

$$= \sum_{n=2}^{\infty} (1-\rho)(n)(n-1)\rho^n \qquad (3.50)$$

$$= (1-\rho)\rho^2 \sum_{n=2}^{\infty} n(n-1)\rho^{n-2} \qquad (3.51)$$

$$= (1-\rho)\rho^2 \sum_{n=2}^{\infty} \frac{d^2}{d\rho^2}\rho^n \qquad (3.52)$$

$$= (1-\rho)\rho^2 \frac{d^2}{d\rho^2} \sum_{n=2}^{\infty} \rho^n \qquad (3.53)$$

$$= (1-\rho)\rho^2 \frac{d^2}{d\rho^2} \sum_{n=0}^{\infty} \rho^n \qquad (3.54)$$

$$= (1-\rho)\rho^2 \frac{d^2}{d\rho^2} \frac{1}{1-\rho} \qquad (3.55)$$

$$= (1-\rho)\rho^2 \frac{d}{d\rho} \frac{1}{(1-\rho)^2} \qquad (3.56)$$

$$= (1-\rho)\rho^2 \frac{2}{(1-\rho)^3} \qquad (3.57)$$

$$= \frac{2\rho^2}{(1-\rho)^2} \qquad (3.58)$$

$$= E[N^2] - E[N]. \qquad (3.59)$$

Equation (3.50) follows since the argument of the summation is zero for $n = 1$ and $n = 2$. Equation (3.54) follows because the second derivatives of the argument for $n = 0$ and 1 are zero anyway.

$$E[N^2] = \frac{2\rho^2}{(1-\rho)^2} + \frac{\rho}{1-\rho} \qquad (3.60)$$

$$= \frac{2\rho^2 + \rho(1-\rho)}{(1-\rho)^2}. \tag{3.61}$$

$$\text{var}[N] = \frac{2\rho^2}{(1-\rho)} + \frac{\rho(1-\rho)}{(1-\rho)^2} - \frac{\rho^2}{(1-\rho)^2} \tag{3.62}$$

$$= \frac{2\rho^2 + \rho - \rho^2 - \rho^2}{(1-\rho)^2} \tag{3.63}$$

$$= \frac{\rho}{(1-\rho)^2}. \tag{3.64}$$

3.4 Response Time and its Distribution

The total time spent by a customer in the system is called the delay or the *response time*. Response time is the sum of service time and any possible waiting time. We will develop the probability density function for the response time with the help of Laplace transforms.

Let R be the random variable for response time and r, its outcome. Under steady state, let a customer enter the system and find n customers already in the system. The remaining service time of any customer under service is exponential with parameter μ, irrespective of any amount of service time already received by that customer, due to the memorylessness of exponential service times. Therefore, the newly entering customer needs to wait for an addition of n iid exponential times before getting into service. Adding the service time of the entering customer, we see the following. The response time of a customer who enters when there are n customers in the system is the sum of $n + 1$ iid exponential service times. Therefore, the conditional transformation,

$$\mathcal{L}_R(s|n) = \left(\frac{\mu}{\mu + s}\right)^{n+1}. \tag{3.65}$$

Using the theorem of total expectation, we have

$$\mathcal{L}_R(s) = \sum_{n=0}^{\infty} \mathcal{L}_R(s|n) p_n \tag{3.66}$$

$$= \sum_{n=0}^{\infty} \left(\frac{\mu}{\mu + s}\right)^{n+1} (1-\rho)\rho^n \tag{3.67}$$

$$= \frac{(1-\rho)\mu}{\mu + s} \sum_{n=0}^{\infty} \left(\frac{\mu\rho}{\mu + s}\right)^n \tag{3.68}$$

$$= \frac{\mu - \lambda}{\mu + s} \frac{1}{1 - \frac{\lambda}{\mu + s}} \qquad (3.69)$$

$$= \frac{\mu - \lambda}{\mu - \lambda + s}. \qquad (3.70)$$

Recognize this as the transform of an exponential random variable. Hence, we have the following result.

THEOREM 3.3
The response time in an equilibrium M/M/1/∞ system, R is an exponential random variable with parameter (or rate) $\mu - \lambda$. That is,

$$f_R(r) = \begin{cases} (\mu - \lambda)e^{-(\mu - \lambda)r}, & r \geq 0 \\ 0, & r < 0. \end{cases}$$

$\square$

Finally, the performance figure expected response time is given by

$$E[R] = \frac{1}{\mu - \lambda}. \qquad (3.71)$$

Figure 3.6 shows a plot of $E[R]$. For the equilibrium M/M/1/$infty$ system,

$$E[N] = \frac{\lambda}{\mu - \lambda}. \qquad (3.72)$$

$$E[R] = \frac{1}{\mu - \lambda}. \qquad (3.73)$$

Therefore,

$$E[N] = \lambda E[R]. \qquad (3.74)$$

3.5   More Performance Figures for M/M/1/∞ System

$E[N_s]$ = Expected number of customers in service. If the server is free, no customer is being served. If the server is busy, exactly one is under service.

$$E[N_s] = E[N_s|\text{busy}]P[\text{busy}] + E[N_s|\text{empty}]P[\text{empty}] \qquad (3.75)$$

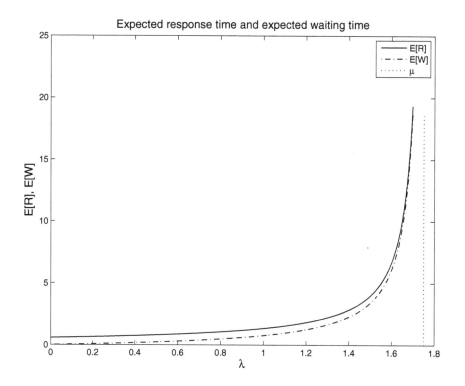

FIGURE 3.6: Expected response time for an M/M/1/∞ queue as a function of arrival rate

$$= 1 \cdot \rho + 0 \cdot (1 - \rho) \tag{3.76}$$

$$= \rho. \tag{3.77}$$

Let the number of customers in waiting be N_w under equilibrium.

$$N(t) = N_w(t) + N_s(t). \tag{3.78}$$

The above formula is always true. Under steady state (we drop t),

$$E[N] = E[N_w] + E[N_s] \tag{3.79}$$

$$E[N_w] = E[N] - E[N_s] \tag{3.80}$$

$$= \frac{\rho}{1 - \rho} - \rho \tag{3.81}$$

$$= \frac{\rho^2}{1 - \rho}. \tag{3.82}$$

$$E[N_w] = \frac{\rho^2}{1 - \rho}. \tag{3.83}$$

Let T_s be the service time random variable and T_w the waiting time. We have the following expression which is always true,

$$R = T_w + T_s, \tag{3.84}$$

and so,

$$E[R] = E[T_w] + E[T_s] \tag{3.85}$$

$$\Rightarrow \frac{1}{\mu - \lambda} = E[T_w] + \frac{1}{\mu} \tag{3.86}$$

$$\Rightarrow E[T_w] = \frac{\lambda}{\mu(\mu - \lambda)}. \tag{3.87}$$

The plots in Figure 3.6 include the expected waiting time, denoted by $E[W]$.

3.6 Waiting Time Distribution

The waiting time in an M/M/1 queue is a mixed random variable. We know that $P[T_w = 0] > 0$, and we have a density function for $f_{T_w}(t|T_w > 0)$. So, the random variable has a continuous component and a discrete component.

$$P[T_w = 0] = P[\text{empty}] = 1 - \rho \qquad (3.88)$$

$$P[T_w > 0] = \rho. \qquad (3.89)$$

The condition $T_w > 0$ implies $N > 0$. The conditional transform of waiting time, under the condition that it is larger than zero is,

$$\mathcal{L}_{T_w}(s|T_w > 0) = \sum_{n=0}^{\infty} \mathcal{L}_{T_w}(s|N = n, N > 0)P[N = n|N > 0] \qquad (3.90)$$

$$= \sum_{n=1}^{\infty} \mathcal{L}_{T_w}(s|n)\frac{P[N = n, N > 0]}{P[N > 0]} \qquad (3.91)$$

$$= \sum_{n=1}^{\infty} \mathcal{L}_{T_w}(s|n)\frac{(1 - \rho)\rho^n}{\rho}. \qquad (3.92)$$

When there is at least one customer at the time a new customer enters, the waiting time for the new customer is the sum of service times of all the n customers. Therefore,

$$\mathcal{L}_{T_w}(s|n) = \left(\frac{\mu}{\mu + s}\right)^n, \; n \geq 1 \qquad (3.93)$$

$$\mathcal{L}_{T_w}(s|T_w > 0) = \frac{1 - \rho}{\rho} \sum_{n=1}^{\infty} \left(\frac{\mu\rho}{\mu + s}\right)^{n-1} \qquad (3.94)$$

$$= \frac{(1 - \rho)\mu}{\mu + s} \frac{1}{1 - \frac{\mu\rho}{\mu+s}} \qquad (3.95)$$

$$= \frac{\mu - \lambda}{\mu - \lambda + s}. \qquad (3.96)$$

Thus, under the condition that a customer waits, the waiting time is distributed exponentially with rate $\mu - \lambda$. The mixed density function of the waiting time is

$$f_w(t) = \begin{cases} (1 - \rho)\delta(t) + \rho(\mu - \lambda)e^{-(\mu-\lambda)t}, & t \geq 0 \\ 0, & t < 0. \end{cases} \qquad (3.97)$$

The function $\delta(t)$ is the *Dirac delta function*, named in honor of Paul Dirac (1902–1984), a British scientist. It is defined by

$$\delta(t) = \begin{cases} 0, t > 0 \\ 0, t < 0 \end{cases} \quad \text{and} \tag{3.98}$$

$$\int_{-\infty}^{\infty} \delta(t)dt = 1. \tag{3.99}$$

The cumulative distribution function is simpler to represent;

$$F_{T_w}(t) = \begin{cases} 1 - \rho e^{-(\mu-\lambda)t}, t \geq 0 \\ 0, \qquad\qquad t < 0. \end{cases} \tag{3.100}$$

3.7 Departures from Equilibrium M/M/1/∞ System

The properties of the stream of departing customers from an equilibrium M/M/1/∞ system are interesting to study. If such output stream is Poisson, it simplifies the analysis of a follow-up queue fed by the departures of the first queue. P. J. Burke showed in 1966 that the output of a class of queues, including the M/M/1/∞ queue, to be Poisson, using the principle of reversibility of Markov processes. A derivation based on simpler principles is developed below. Let us first obtain the nature of the random variable T, the time for the next departure from an equilibrium M/M/1/∞ queue observed from time $t = 0$.

THEOREM 3.4
Let an M/M/1/∞ system be known to be in equilibrium at time $t = 0$. Let T be the random variable time interval for the next departure. If T is observed (without observing any other quantity such as the number in the system), the probability density function of T is exponential with parameter λ, the arrival rate.

Proof
At $t = 0$, the random variable number of customers N has the known modified geometric pmf $p_n = \left(1 - \frac{\lambda}{\mu}\right)\left(\frac{\lambda}{\mu}\right)^n$, $n = 0, 1, \cdots$. The Laplace transform of T is given by

$$\mathcal{L}_T(s) = \sum_{n=0}^{\infty} p_n \mathcal{L}_T(s|N = n). \tag{3.101}$$

If the system is busy at $t = 0$, the time for the next departure is the remaining service time of the customer being served, which is exponentially distributed with parameter

μ. If the system is empty at $t = 0$, the time for the next departure is the sum of the time for the next arrival and its service time. Therefore,

$$\mathcal{L}_T(s|N > 0) = \frac{\mu}{\mu + s} \quad \text{and} \tag{3.102}$$

$$\mathcal{L}_T(s|N = 0) = \frac{\mu}{\mu + s} \frac{\lambda}{\lambda + s}. \tag{3.103}$$

Using these in equation (3.101), we have

$$\mathcal{L}_T(s) = \left(1 - \frac{\lambda}{\mu}\right) \left(\frac{\mu}{\mu + s} \frac{\lambda}{\lambda + s}\right) + \frac{\lambda}{\mu} \frac{\mu}{\mu + s} \tag{3.104}$$

which simplifies to

$$\mathcal{L}_T(s) = \frac{\lambda}{\lambda + s}. \tag{3.105}$$

That is, the time for the next departure starting from any time instant at which the system is known to be in equilibrium (and not conditioned on any other observation about the system) is exponentially distributed with parameter λ. □

The above theorem can also be proved without the use of Laplace transform and with the use of the pdf of the sum of two independent exponential random variables with parameters λ and μ. This is encouraging but not sufficient to conclude that the departure stream is Poisson, since we need successive interdeparture times to be mutually independent for the departure stream to be Poisson. That is, after we observe the time for the first departure, could the next IDT be dependent on the observed time for the first departure? One way to show that successive IDTs are iid is to show that the system will be found to be in equilibrium the time instant after a departure. A simple algebraic proof follows.

LEMMA 3.1
The pmf of the number of Poisson arrivals with rate λ during a time period that is exponentially distributed with parameter μ is modified geometric with a success probability of $\frac{\lambda}{\lambda + \mu}$.

Proof
As usual, $\rho = \frac{\lambda}{\mu}$. At any time instant that the system is busy, the time for the next arrival Y and the time for the next departure X are independent exponential random variables with rates λ and μ respectively, each competing to occur before the other.

$$P[X \leq Y] = \int_{y=0}^{\infty} \int_{x=0}^{y} f_{xy}(x, y) dx dy \tag{3.106}$$

$$= \int_{y=0}^{\infty} \int_{x=0}^{y} \mu e^{-\mu x} \lambda e^{-\lambda y} dx dy \tag{3.107}$$

$$= \int_{y=0}^{\infty} \lambda e^{-\lambda y} \int_{x=0}^{y} \mu e^{-\mu x}\, dx\, dy \tag{3.108}$$

$$= \int_{y=0}^{\infty} \lambda e^{-\lambda y} [-e^{-\mu x}]_0^y\, dy \tag{3.109}$$

$$= \int_{y=0}^{\infty} \lambda e^{-\lambda y} (1 - e^{-\mu y})\, dy \tag{3.110}$$

$$= \int_{y=0}^{\infty} \lambda e^{-\lambda y}\, dy - \int_{y=0}^{\infty} \lambda e^{-(\lambda+\mu)y}\, dy \tag{3.111}$$

$$= 1 - \frac{\lambda}{-(\lambda+\mu)} \left[e^{-(\lambda+\mu)y} \right]_0^{\infty} \tag{3.112}$$

$$= 1 - \frac{\lambda}{\lambda+\mu} \tag{3.113}$$

$$= \frac{\mu}{\lambda+\mu} \tag{3.114}$$

We will use the above property between two independent and competing exponential random variables in other applications also. At any time instant the system is busy, the probability that the next change is an arrival and not a departure is $\frac{\lambda}{\lambda+\mu}$. After k such arrivals, a departure, with a probability $\frac{\mu}{\lambda+\mu}$ must occur for exactly k arrivals before a departure. Therefore, if the system is busy, the random variable number K of customers arriving into the system before a customer departs has the pmf

$$P[K = k] = \left(\frac{\lambda}{\lambda+\mu} \right)^k \frac{\mu}{\lambda+\mu} \tag{3.115}$$

$$= \left(\frac{\rho}{1+\rho} \right)^k \frac{1}{1+\rho} \tag{3.116}$$

$$= \frac{\rho^k}{(1+\rho)^{k+1}}, \quad k \geq 0. \tag{3.117}$$

□

THEOREM 3.5
Under the same conditions as in the above Theorem 3.4, the number of cus-

tomers in the system follows the equilibrium distribution, the time instant after the departure.

Proof

Recall that the departure is the first one observed after starting the observation at $t = 0$ and that the system was known to be in equilibrium at $t = 0$. Let M be the random variable number of customers at $t = 0$. Let N be the random variable number of customers the time instant after the first departure; that is, N does not include the departing customer. Only departures are observed. Arrivals are hidden from the observer. Let K be a random variable corresponding to the number of arrivals during an entire or remaining service time. Since service time is memoryless, the two have the same pmf. For the case of $N = 0$, the system could have had 0 customers at $t = 0$ followed by one arrival before the departure, or 1 customer at $t = 0$ and no arrival before the departure. Therefore,

$$P[N = 0] = P[K = 0 \text{ after the first arrival} \mid M = 0]P[M = 0]$$

$$+ P[K = 0 \mid M = 1]P[M = 1] \tag{3.118}$$

$$= \frac{1}{1 + \rho}(1 - \rho) + \frac{1}{1 + \rho}(1 - \rho)\rho \tag{3.119}$$

$$= 1 - \rho. \tag{3.120}$$

For $P[N = n > 0]$, we again have two subcases. If the system was empty at $t = 0$, we need a first arrival followed by n arrivals during the service time of the first arrival. If the system was not empty and had m customers at $t = 0$, we need $n + 1 - m$ arrivals in the remainder of the ongoing service time. The variable m can be of any value from 1 through $n + 1$. Therefore, for $n > 0$, we have

$$P[N = n] = P[N = n \mid M = 0]P[M = 0]$$

$$+ \sum_{m=1}^{n+1} P[N = n \mid M = m]P[M = m] \tag{3.121}$$

$$= P[K = n \text{ after the first arrival} \mid M = 0]P[M = 0]$$

$$+ \sum_{m=1}^{n+1} P[K = n + 1 - m \mid M = m]P[M = m] \tag{3.122}$$

$$= \frac{(1 - \rho)\rho^n}{(1 + \rho)^{n+1}} + \sum_{m=1}^{n+1} \frac{\rho^{n+1-m}(1 - \rho)\rho^m}{(1 + \rho)^{n+2-m}} \tag{3.123}$$

$$= \frac{(1 - \rho)\rho^n}{(1 + \rho)^{n+1}}\left(1 + \rho\frac{(1 + \rho)^{n+1} - 1}{(1 + \rho) - 1}\right) \tag{3.124}$$

$$= (1 - \rho)\rho^n. \tag{3.125}$$

That is, the pmf of the number of customers satisfies the equilibrium pmf of the number of customers in the queue, for both the cases of $N = 0$ and $N > 0$. ☐

Combining the above two theorems, we have the nice desirable result.

THEOREM 3.6

The stream of departing customers from the output of an equilibrium $M/M/1/\infty$ queue is Poisson with a rate equal to the arrival rate, λ.

Proof

If the system under consideration is at equilibrium at some time, we know from the above two theorems that

1. Time for the next departure is exponential with rate λ.

2. The system is at equilibrium, at the instant following the departure.

Following the first departure time instant, the future behavior of the system is a function only of the state at that instant which is known to be in equilibrium. Therefore, the time for the next departure is not dependent on the time for the first departure. Also, the next interdeparture time (IDT) is exponential with rate λ. Thus, the sequence of IDTs are iid exponential with rate λ. ☐

The original result of the Poisson nature of the output stream of customers from an equilibrium $M/M/1/\infty$ system is due to P. J. Burke, published in 1956. This property of $M/M/1/\infty$ queues has far reaching consequences. Over a packet communication data link, it may be initially confusing to think that packet arrivals can be Poisson, since each packet takes some time to flow into the receiver hardware. That is, an arrival does not occur at a single time instant. The packets have nonzero ON time. However, we can consider that the data packets are coming out of another $M/M/1/\infty$ system with the packet ON time being the service time of an earlier exponential server. Tracing these arguments to the origin of the packets, a computer simply creates a data packet and a *virtual arrival* by placing a pointer to the memory segment corresponding to a packet. This occurs in a negligible time (in comparison with other service times). Thereafter, all the packet movements take time intervals proportional to the data packet sizes. For hundreds and thousand of bits, the number of bits in a packet is very well approximated by a continuous random variable. At downstream points in a network, packets are coming out of a sequence of equilibrium $M/M/1/\infty$ systems. We now know that such outputs for Poisson streams. At a point, a packet is considered to have arrived just after its last bit has completed arriving. Furthermore, at some point in a network, if packets are iid probabilistically switched to two or more different queues, input streams into all the queues retain the Poisson property.

3.8   Analysis of ON-OFF Model of Packet Departures

A distinction between queues in data packet communication and some other application areas is that a data packets flows into a queue buffer over a nonzero amount of time. Contrast this with a human being walking into a queue buffer or a physical hardware being submitted to a repair facility. In all these cases, we consider that the job arrives into the queue after it has completely arrived. The fact that humans walk in with a finite speed is not of consideration here! If we assume that all the humans walk with the same speed, the time instant the customer enters the queue is the arrival time instant. In a similar way, consider cars modeled as points moving through a lane on a road. Even though cars may differ slightly in their lengths, the service time they need at an oil change facility is quite independent of their lengths. Therefore, modeling them with an arrival time instant each is an excellent approximation. However, the scenario of data bits flowing over a communication link is different. The time taken for the data packet to flow in is proportional to the number of bits in the packet. Again this is not due to a finite speed of propagation over a long distance link, but due to each bit encoded as a time function of electromagnetic quantities over a finite time-width.

In the previous section, we argued that in spite of this on-off model of packet train, we can consider that a packet arrives when its final bit has just completed arriving. Then the departure points constitute a Poisson stream and such a packet stream presents itself as Poisson arrivals into any following queue. Clearly, the on times of individual packets in such a packet train are iid exponential with the service rate of the queue from which the packet train is departing. However, what is the nature of the off-times? This is the subject of the present section. Consider a segment of time containing a few packets of the packet train; see Figure 3.7, similar to Figure 2.2 of Chapter 2. The random variable X is the on-time of a packet, corresponding to the service time in a queue whose output constitutes the packet stream. Similarly, the random variable Y is the off-time. Y starts from the completion of the departure of a packet to the beginning of the service time of the next packet. Since we now know that the system is in equilibrium at the completion of every service, successive occurrences of Y are iid. Of course, successive occurrences of X are the successive service times and are iid. Note the following. From the beginning of Y till the end of the next X is the time interval between successive time instants of completions of service of successive packets. We know this to be iid exponential with rate λ, from the previous section. The random variable starting from the beginning of X to the end of the next Y is composed of two components. The first component, X is the service time which is exponential with a rate μ. At the conclusion of service, that is, at the end of X (which is the same time instant as the beginning of Y), we now know that the system is in equilibrium. Therefore, successive Y are iid. Successive time intervals $Y + X$ are the time intervals between successive completions of service, known to form a Poisson sequence with rate λ. Successive intervals of $X + Y$ must also have the same statistical nature, simply because $Y + X = X + Y$. Therefore,

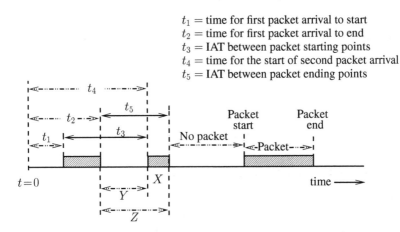

t_1 = time for first packet arrival to start
t_2 = time for first packet arrival to end
t_3 = IAT between packet starting points
t_4 = time for the start of second packet arrival
t_5 = IAT between packet ending points

FIGURE 3.7:   ON-OFF model of a packet train

we have the following result.

THEOREM 3.7
If packets start leaving the system as they begin service in an equilibrium M/M/1/∞ queue, the sequence of such points constitutes a Poisson stream with rate λ.   □

Finally, what is the distribution of the random variable Y? This is not a purely continuous random variable. Since the system is in equilibrium at the end of a departure, another packet can immediately get into service if the system is busy, which occurs with a probability ρ. Therefore, we have

$$P[Y = 0] = \rho. \tag{3.126}$$

In order for $Y > 0$, the system must be empty when at the completion of service of one packet. This occurs with a probability $(1 - \rho)$. If the system is empty, the time interval for the next service to begin is exponential with rate λ. Therefore,

$$f_Y(y, \, Y > 0) = P[Y > 0]f_Y(y|Y > 0) \tag{3.127}$$

$$= (1 - \rho)\lambda \exp(-\lambda y). \tag{3.128}$$

The cumulative distribution of Y is easily obtained as

$$P[Y \leq y] = 1 - \rho \exp(-\lambda y). \tag{3.129}$$

Therefore, Y is not exponential leading to the following cautionary statement.

THEOREM 3.8
In the ON-OFF sequence of a train of packets departing an equilibrium $M/M/1/\infty$ queue, the OFF time periods between successive packets are iid but are not exponential.   ▯

3.9   Round Robin Operating System

The following is a realistic representation of the functioning of uniprocessor systems. The operation is referred to as round robin. A user typically submits many jobs in succession and the system responses are not necessarily FIFO. The operating system (OS) has an internal timer that rings in a succession of iid exponentially distributed random intervals. If the server is serving a customer when the OS timer rings, the customer is sent back to the tail of the queue and the next customer in the waiting line starts service. Typically, the average time intervals between these rings is much less than the average service time requirement of jobs so that a job gets swapped out of service several times. Each of the continuous time segment service is called a piecemeal service. Due to the memoryless property of the total service time requirement of jobs, the remaining service time of every job is also distributed identically to the total service time requirement. Time wasted for swapping the jobs in and out of service is negligible. Therefore, the number of customers and their statistical service requirements after a feedback are identical to those before the feedback. Hence, the statistical behavior of $N(t)$ is same as in the basic $M/M/1/\infty$ system.

The overall (or total) service time is exponentially distributed with an average of $\frac{1}{\mu}$. Let the piecemeal service time be exponential with an average of $1/\alpha$. Typically, $\frac{1}{\alpha} < \frac{1}{\mu}$ although this is not necessary for the validity of the analysis. Of course, the feedback piecemeal service time is also memoryless. The probability of a job being fed back is the probability that an exponential random variable with rate α is less than another independent exponential random variable with rate μ. This is evaluated in the proof of Lemma 3.1 to be $\frac{\alpha}{\alpha+\mu}$. Figure 3.8 shows the queuing model for such a round robin system. The expected number of feedback returns a customer experiences is the expectation of the modified geometric random variable with a success probability of $\frac{\alpha}{\alpha+\mu}$. This expectation evaluates to $\frac{\alpha}{\mu}$. The expected number of passes through the queue is

$$1 + \frac{\alpha}{\mu} = \frac{\alpha + \mu}{\mu}. \tag{3.130}$$

Since each customer experiences iid number of feedback returns, the combined arrival rate into the merged waiting line is simply the product of the arrival rate and the expected number of passes a customer makes. This is given by $\frac{\lambda(\alpha+\mu)}{\mu}$. Figure 3.9 shows the rates of customers flowing at different points in the system. The rate

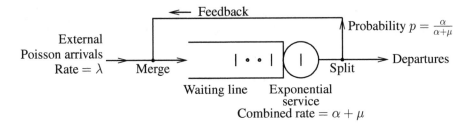

FIGURE 3.8:   The round robin queuing model

of customers departing the server is the same as the combined rate of the merged customers, $\frac{\lambda(\alpha+\mu)}{\mu}$. Note that we do not know whether or not the combined arrival stream of customers is Poisson, at this point of analysis. Figure 3.9 shows the system with rates of customers at different points.

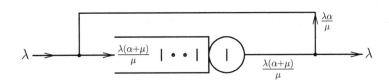

FIGURE 3.9:   Rates of customers at different points in a round robin system

The goal of this analysis is to determine the total expected waiting time of a tagged job A whose total service requirement is known to be a real variable τ. We need to find the expected number of passes. Figure 3.10 shows a typical total service time interval τ composed of segments of piecemeal service times. The successive service time segments do not occur continuously. They are laid down successively in the figure, to illustrate the relation between the number of service time segments and the total service time. Every time the job A passes through the server and is fed back, it completes an iid exponential amount of time with parameter α. Therefore,

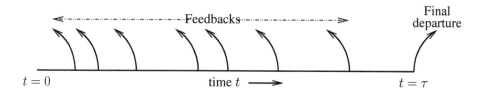

FIGURE 3.10: Individual service time segments placed successively

the number of feedback returns of A is a Poisson random variable with rate α over time τ. The number of passes job A makes through the server is one more than the number of feedback returns, which simply includes the last pass which is not fed back. Therefore, the expected number of passes job A makes through the server is $1 + \alpha\tau$. At the outset, we do not know if the expected response times of all the passes are the same. The following theorem establishes an important result required to evaluate the total expected waiting time of multiple passes.

THEOREM 3.9
Let a tagged customer A enter the round robin system at $t = 0$ when the system is known to be in equilibrium. Let the arrivals be Poisson, service times be iid exponential, and feedback times be iid exponential. When the customer A leaves the system after one pass, (either for feedback or for overall departure), the system will again be in equilibrium.

Proof
Let there be K customers in the system just before customer A enters at $t = 0$. As usual, k is the outcome of K. We know that $P[K = k] = (1 - \rho)\rho^k$. During the time period of interest here, we know that the system has at least one customer, that is the tagged customer A. During the one pass of service time of the customer under service at $t = 0$, the number of arrivals into the system is known to be modified geometric (due to Lemma 3.1 with a success probability of $q = \frac{\lambda}{\lambda+\alpha+\mu}$. Its $\mathcal{Z}$ transform is $\frac{1-q}{1-qz}$. By the time the tagged customer A leaves the server for the first time, the server would have served $k + 1$ customers, including the customer A. The $\mathcal{Z}$ transform of the number of external arrivals during this time is

$$\left(\frac{1 - q}{1 - qz}\right)^{k+1}. \tag{3.131}$$

Of the k customers served before A, each return to the tail of the queue for more service, with an iid probability of $r = \frac{\alpha}{\alpha+\mu}$ and leave the entire system with a probability of $1 - r$. The $\mathcal{Z}$ transform of each such feedback is $1 - r - rz$. The $\mathcal{Z}$ transform of the sum of these k possible feedback returns is $(1 - r + rz)^k$. Note that any feedback of the tagged customer A itself is not included. Let the total number of external arrivals plus the feedback returns be M. Therefore, M is the random variable number of customers in the system when the tagged customer A leaves the server for the first time and its $\mathcal{Z}$ transform conditioned on k customers being in the system just before A entered at $t = 0$ is

$$\mathcal{Z}_M(z|k) = (1 - r + rz)^k \left(\frac{1-q}{1-qz}\right)^{k+1}. \tag{3.132}$$

The unconditional transform is obtained by applying the theorem of total expectation.

$$\mathcal{Z}_M(z) = \sum_{k=0}^{\infty}(1 - r + rz)^k \left(\frac{1-q}{1-qz}\right)^{k+1}(1-\rho)\rho^k \tag{3.133}$$

$$= \frac{1-q}{1-qz}(1-\rho)\sum_{k=0}^{\infty}\left(\frac{(1-r+rz)(1-q)\rho}{1-qz}\right)^k \tag{3.134}$$

$$= \frac{1-q}{1-qz}(1-\rho)\frac{1}{1-\frac{(1-r+rz)(1-q)\rho}{1-qz}} \tag{3.135}$$

$$= \frac{(1-q)(1-\rho)}{1-qz-(1-r+rz)(1-q)\rho}. \tag{3.136}$$

The final expression is of the form

$$\mathcal{Z}_M(z) = \frac{u}{v - wz} \tag{3.137}$$

where u, v, and w are functions of r, q, and ρ which are, in turn, functions of λ, μ, and α. In order for the RHS of equation (3.137) to be a valid $\mathcal{Z}$ transform of a pmf, we need

$$\frac{w}{v} = 1 - \frac{u}{v} \text{ and } 0 < \frac{w}{v}1. \tag{3.138}$$

If these conditions are met, the resulting valid $\mathcal{Z}$ transform is of modified geometric pmf with a probability of success of $\frac{w}{v}$. Indeed, after some cumbersome but otherwise simple algebra, the above conditions can be verified when the system parameters are substituted in equation (3.136) and it turns out that

$$\frac{w}{v} = \frac{\lambda}{\mu}. \tag{3.139}$$

This completes the proof that soon after the tagged customer A leaves the server after its first round of service, the number of customers in the system follows the equilibrium pmf. □

The above theorem allows us to use expected response times for each round of service for the tagged customer, to evaluate the total expected response time (or the total expected waiting time). Using the theorem, the total expected waiting time of a customer with a total service time requirement of τ is given by

$$E[W] = \sum_{j=1}^{\infty} E[W_1] j P[j] \tag{3.140}$$

$$= E[W_1] E[J] \tag{3.141}$$

$$= \frac{\lambda}{(\alpha + \mu)(\mu - \lambda)} E[J] \tag{3.142}$$

where j is the number of passes for the customer A to complete service. From the earlier derivation, we know that $E[J] = 1 + \alpha\tau$. Therefore,

$$E[W] = \frac{\lambda}{(\alpha + \mu)(\mu - \lambda)}(1 + \alpha\tau). \tag{3.143}$$

Adding the total service time of τ to the total expected waiting time, we have the following result.

THEOREM 3.10
The expected response time $E[RR]$ of an M/M1/∞ round robin system with external arrival rate λ, service rate μ, and exponential feedback rate α is given by

$$E[RR] = \frac{\lambda}{(\alpha + \mu)(\mu - \lambda)} + \left(1 + \frac{\lambda\alpha}{(\alpha + \mu)(\mu - \lambda)}\right)\tau. \tag{3.144}$$

⬜

Figure 3.11 shows the expected response time as a function of the service time for the two cases. The solid line plot is for the round robin case. The external arrival rate is 1 per unit time. The service rate, 1.2 per unit time. The feedback rate α is 5 per unit time. The expected response time for the original M/M/1/∞ FIFO system is drawn with a broken line. This has a large part for the expected waiting time, followed by a slow increase due to the service time. On the other hand, the round robin constant term is small, the expected waiting time for one pass only. Thereafter, the overall expected response time increases much faster than the corresponding time in the FIFO case, due to multiple passes. A few more important properties of M/M/1∞ system are developed below.

THEOREM 3.11
The sequence of merged customer arrivals into the waiting line in an equilibrium round robin M/M/1/∞ queue is not *Poisson.*

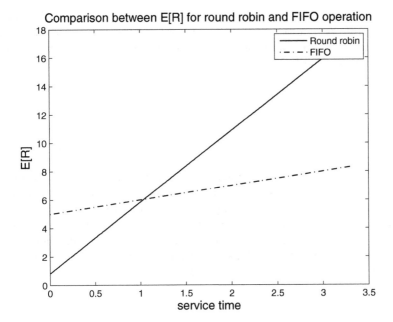

Comparison between E[R] for round robin and FIFO operation

FIGURE 3.11: Expected response time as a function of the given total service time

Proof

As in the above treatment, let the time for feedback of a customer under service be exponential with rate α. The time for the next arrival into the merged queue is a function of both the overall arrivals and the feedback time. However, feedback is possible only if there is already a customer under service. Let T be the random variable corresponding to the time for the next arrival. If N, the number of customers in the system is zero, the only arrival that can enter the system is the external arrival and in this case T is exponential with rate λ. On the other hand, if $N > 0$, the next composite arrival can be either an external arrival with rate λ or a feedback arrival with rate α. The combination is equivalent to an exponential time for arrival with rate $\lambda + \alpha$, for the case of $N > 0$. Combining the two cases, we find the pdf of the time for next arrival

$$f_T(t) = (1 - \rho)\lambda \exp(-\lambda t) + \rho(\lambda + \alpha) \exp[-(\lambda + \alpha)t], \quad t > 0, \qquad (3.145)$$

which is hyperexponential. Therefore, arrivals into the merged waiting line are not Poisson. ▯

However, the departure sequence from such a round robin system turns out to be Poisson, as shown below.

THEOREM 3.12

Consider an equilibrium round robin system with arrival rate λ and a total ser-

vice requirement which is iid exponential with rate μ. *The feedback discipline is more general, as follows. At the time instant a job enters the service area for its first or successive piecemeal service, a race ensues between the overall job completion time and a feedback time random variable* T *which is nonnegative but otherwise arbitrarily distributed. Then, the overall output sequence of customers leaving the entire system is Poisson with rate* λ.

Proof
The time for feedback here is more general and not restricted to being an exponential random variable. Nevertheless, at the time a job enters service, there is a well defined probability that it will be fed back. At any time instant, the amount of remaining service time required for all the customers in the system is exponential with rate μ, irrespective of the peculiarity of the feedback mechanism. This is due to the memorylessness of the total service time of a job. Therefore, the number of customers at any time instant is statistically identical to that in an alternative simple M/M/1/∞ system without feedback. Therefore, the IDTs corresponding to the overall departures still constitute a Poisson stream.   ☐

3.10   Examples

Example 3.1
Consider an M/M/1/∞ queuing system with an arrival rate of 3 per second and a service rate of 5 per second, operating under equilibrium.

1. A customer A enters the system when the server is free. What is the probability that another customer enters before customer A leaves the system.

2. A customer A enters the system when the number of customers in the system is 3. The exact service time requirement of customer A is known to be 0.4 second. What is the expected response time of customer A?

3. Determine the probability that the number of customers in the system does not change during a time interval of 0.1 second.

☐

Solution

1. After A enters, there is a contest between the next arrival with a rate of 3 per second and the departure of A with a rate of 5 per second.

$$P[\text{arrival occurs before} A \text{departs}] = \frac{3}{3+5} = \frac{3}{8}. \quad (3.146)$$

2.

$$E[\text{Response time of} A] \quad (3.147)$$

$$= 3E[\text{service time of each of the other s}] + A\text{'s service time}$$

$$= 3\frac{\text{sec}}{5} + 0.4 \text{ sec} = 1.0 \text{ second} \quad (3.148)$$

3. Let the S denote the event of no change in state for 0.1 second and N be the number of customers, a random variable.

$$P[S] = P[S|N=0]P[N=0] + P[S|N>0]P[N>0] \quad (3.149)$$

When $N = 0$, the only possible change in state is an arrival with a rate of 3 per second. When $N > 0$, an arrival or a departure changes the state, with a total rate of 8 per second. Under each condition, the probability of the event is the probability of an exponential random variable (with appropriate rate) being larger than 0.1 second. Or, the probability of no Poisson arrival in 0.1 second. Thus,

$$P[S] = 0.4e^{-0.3} + 0.6e^{-0.8} = 0.6. \quad (3.150)$$

☐

Example 3.2
Consider a single queue with a round robin scheme of piecemeal service. External arrivals are Poisson with a rate of 1 per second. The total service requirement of jobs are iid exponential with a rate of 2 per second. Each single service piece is a **constant time** of 0.1 second. Of course, if a job completes its service before its current piece of 0.1 second ends, it makes its final departure. At the time a job enters the service area, what is the probability that it will be fed back (as opposed to making its final departure)? ☐

Solution
Only the remaining service time is memoryless. Time for each piece of service is constant. Every time a job enters the service area, irrespective of how many pieces of service it has already received, its remaining service time is exponential with rate 2 per second.

$$P[\text{feedback}] = P[\text{service time} \geq 0.1 \text{ second}] \quad (3.151)$$

$$= \int_{t=0.1}^{\infty} 2e^{-2t} dt \tag{3.152}$$

$$= \left[-e^{2t} \right]_{0.1}^{\infty} \tag{3.153}$$

$$= e^{-0.2} = 0.82 \tag{3.154}$$

[]

Example 3.3
A processor (server) uses a round robin scheme for service, with an exponential timer of average 1 msec for each service attempt. A job is known to require exactly 3.5 msec for its total service time. What is the expected number of service attempts this particular job will need?   []

Solution
Let the time instant $t = 0$ when the job entered service for the first time. Thereafter, the average number of times it will depart strictly BEFORE completing the 3.5 msec is the average number of Poisson arrivals during a time interval $0 < T < 3.5$ msec with a rate of 1 arrival per msec. This expected number is 3.5. Thereafter, the customer will get into service one more time and complete the required full service. This is the reason strict inequality is used in defining T. And, the probability that the final timer and the final completion of full service of 3.5 msec occurs exactly at the same time is 0 and does not contribute to the expected number of rounds of service. Thus, the expected number of service attempts is 4.5.   []

3.11   Analysis of Busy Times

Let a customer enter a stable and *empty* M/M/1/∞ queue at time $t = 0$. The time interval for which the server remains continuously busy is a random variable. Denote this by random variable by B and let t be its outcome. We are interested in the probability distribution of B. Lajos Takacs (a mathematician born in Hungary in 1924) and D. G. Kendall separately studied the Laplace transforms and many properties of the busy times of the M/G/1/∞ queue. The M/G/1/∞ queue is a more general case of queues due to the service times not being restricted to be memoryless. The present section develops the pdf and the Laplace transform of the interdeparture times of an equilibrium M/M/1/∞ queue through a direct approach. Let K be the random variable number of jobs that arrive after $t = 0$ and let the server become free for the first time (after $t = 0$), after serving the initial customer arriving at $t = 0$ and exactly the K more later arrivals. Let k be the outcome of K. We will have exactly k

arrivals and k departures after $t = 0$, followed by the departure of the final customer rendering the system empty. The property of these k arrivals and k departures (after $t = 0$) is that the number of departures at any time should not exceed the number of arrivals. Let $n_{(i,j)}$ be such number of combinations of i arrivals and j departures such that $j \le i$. We have $n_{(0,0)} = 1$; $n_{(1,0)} = 1$; $n_{(1,1)} = 1$. Indeed,

$$n_{(i,0)} = 1, \quad \text{for } 0 \le i. \tag{3.155}$$

Now, if i arrivals and $j - 1 < i - 1$ departures have occurred with one of $n_{(i,j-1)}$ combinations, one more departure makes it j departures. And this can occur after one of $n_{(i,j-1)}$ ways of reaching i arrivals and $j - 1$ departures. Alternatively, after $i - 1$ arrivals and $j \le i - 1$ departures, an arrival may come in resulting in i arrivals and j departures. This can occur in one way, after one of $n_{(i-1,j)}$ ways of reaching $i - 1$ arrivals and j departures. Therefore (as long as $j < i$), we have the recursive equation

$$n_{(i,j)} = n_{(i,j-1)} + n_{(i-1,j)}, \quad \text{for } 1 \le j < i. \tag{3.156}$$

If $j = i$, after reaching i arrivals and $i - 1$ departures, we can have one more departure. Since the i-th departure must come after i arrivals, there is no other way of reaching i arrivals and i departures. Therefore,

$$n_{(i,i)} = n_{(i,i-1)}, \quad \text{for } 1 \le i. \tag{3.157}$$

The probability of a departure (as opposed to an arrival) in the above sequence of arrivals and departures is $\frac{\mu}{\lambda+\mu}$. Denote this by p. Similarly, the probability of an arrival, rather than a departure, is $\frac{\lambda}{\lambda+\mu}$. This evaluates to $1 - p$. Now, the probability of exactly k arrivals following the first arrival at $t = 0$ and the system then becoming empty for the first time after $t = 0$ is given by

$$P[k] = n_{(k,k)}[p(1 - p)]^k p. \tag{3.158}$$

The last factor p in the above equation is due to the final $(k + 1)$-th departure rendering the system empty. After $t = 0$, the time interval for the next event of an arrival or a departure satisfying the above requirement is exponential with rate $\lambda + \mu$. Successive such time intervals for all of the k arrivals, k departures, followed by the final departure (rendering the system to be empty) are all iid. The fact that some are arrivals and others are departures is expressed in the joint probability of the compound event. The Laplace transform of this total time to reach empty state, given that it occurs after k arrivals, k departures followed by the final departure is

$$\mathcal{L}_B(s|k) = \left(\frac{\lambda+\mu}{s+\lambda+\mu}\right)^{2k+1}. \tag{3.159}$$

Using the theorem of total expectation and using expressions for p and $1-p$ in terms of λ and μ, we have

$$\mathcal{L}_B(s) = \sum_{k=0}^{\infty} \left(\frac{\lambda+\mu}{s+\lambda+\mu}\right)^{2k+1} \left(\frac{\lambda}{\lambda+\mu}\right)^k \left(\frac{\mu}{\lambda+\mu}\right)^{k+1} n_{(k,k)} \qquad (3.160)$$

$$= \sum_{k=0}^{\infty} \frac{\lambda^k \mu^{k+1}}{(s+\lambda+\mu)^{2k+1}} n_{(k,k)}. \qquad (3.161)$$

3.11.1 Combinations of arrivals and departures during a busy time period

The following Lemma gives an expression for $n_{(k,k)}$.

LEMMA 3.2
Let a first customer arrive into an empty queue at time $t = 0$. The number of distinct ways in which i more arrivals and j departures can occur into the queue, keeping at least one customer in the queue from the first arrival until the last arrival or departure (whichever occurs last), is given by

$$n_{(i,j)} = \frac{(i+j)!(i-j+1)}{(i+1)!\,j!}, \qquad for\ 0 \le j < i\ and \qquad (3.162)$$

$$n_{(k,k)} = \frac{(2k)!}{k!\,(k+1)!}, \qquad for\ i = j = k \ge 1. \qquad (3.163)$$

Proof
We know that the equations (3.162) and (3.163) are true for all $i \ge 0$ and $j = 0$, as well as for $i = j = 1$. The proof technique used is induction. Assume that the equations (3.162) and (3.163) are true for all $0 \le i,\ j \le m$ and also for the combinations of $i = m + 1$ and all j satisfying $0 \le j \le l \le m - 1$, for some l. Evaluate $n_{(m+1,l+1)}$ using the known recursive equation (3.156). We have

$$n_{(m+1,l+1)} = n_{(m+1,l)} + n_{(m,l+1)}. \qquad (3.164)$$

Since $l \le m - 1$, we have $l + 1 \le m$ and by our assumption, $n_{(m,l+1)}$ is known to satisfy equation (3.162). Therefore,

$$n_{(m+1,l+1)} = \frac{(m+1+l)!\,(m+1-l+1)}{(m+2)\,l!} + \frac{(m+1+l)!\,(m-l-1+1)}{(m+1)!\,(l+1)!}$$

$$= \frac{(m+l+1)!\,(m-l+2)}{(m+2)!\,l!} + \frac{(m+l+1)!\,(m-l)}{(m+1)!\,(l+1)!} \qquad (3.165)$$

$$= \frac{(m+l+1)!}{(m+1)!\,l!} \left(\frac{m-l+2}{m+2} + \frac{m-l}{l+1} \right) \qquad (3.166)$$

$$= \frac{(m+l+1)!}{(m+2)!\,(l+1)!}(m^2 - l^2 + 3m - l + 2). \qquad (3.167)$$

The last factor $(m^2 - l^2 + 3m - l + 2)$ is also the expansion for $(m+l+2)(m-l+1)$. Substituting this, we have

$$n_{(m+1,l+1)} = \frac{(m+l+1)!\,(m-l+1)}{(m+2)!\,(l+1)!} \qquad (3.168)$$

proving that equation (3.162) is true for $i = m+1$ and $j = l+1 \le m$. From equation (3.157), we know that

$$n_{(m+1,m+1)} = n_{(m+1,m)} \qquad (3.169)$$

verifying that equation (3.162) is true for $i = m+1$ and for all $0 \le j \le m+1$. Increasing $m+1$ to $m+2$, equation (3.162) is true for all $i \ge m+2$ and $j = 0$ and this completes the proof by induction that equation (3.162) is valid for all $i > j \ge 0$. Equation (3.163) is merely an application of the known equation (3.157) in equation (3.162) completing the proof of the Lemma. $\qquad \square$

3.11.2 Density function of busy times

The Laplace transform of the busy time random variable can now be completely specified by substituting for $n_{(k,k)}$ from equation (3.163) in equation (3.161). It is

$$\mathcal{L}_B(s) = \sum_{k=0}^{\infty} \frac{\lambda^k \mu^{k+1}}{(s+\lambda+\mu)^{2k+1}} \frac{(2k)!}{k!\,(k+1)!}. \qquad (3.170)$$

The probability density function of the busy time period B is the inverse Laplace transform of the above series. The result is a weighted sum of the inverse transforms of terms of the form

$$\left(\frac{\alpha}{s+\alpha}\right)^k, \quad k \geq 1 \tag{3.171}$$

where $\alpha = \lambda + \mu$ for simpler notation. For a given k the corresponding component of the overall density of the busy time is the pdf of the sum of k iid exponential random variables, each with a rate α. Each such component is known as the Erlang density. For $k = 1$, the Erlang density reduces to the exponential density. The following states and proves an expression for the Erlang pdf.

LEMMA 3.3
The pdf of the nonnegative random variable X, the sum of k iid exponential random variables, each with the rate α is,

$$f_{X_k}(x) = \frac{\alpha^k}{(k-1)!} x^{k-1} \exp(-\alpha x), \quad x \geq 0. \tag{3.172}$$

Proof
The result is true for $k = 1$, for which X_1 is the exponential random variable itself. Proof is by induction. Let the result of equation (3.172) be true for $k = n$. Then, it follows that

$$\mathcal{L}_{X_n}(s) = \left(\frac{\alpha}{s+\alpha}\right)^n. \tag{3.173}$$

Evaluate the Laplace transform of the given expression in equation (3.172) for $f_{X_{n+1}}(x)$.

$$\mathcal{L}_{X_{n+1}}(s) = \int\limits_{x=0}^{\infty} \frac{\alpha^{n+1}}{n!} x^n \exp(-\alpha x) \exp(-sx) dx \tag{3.174}$$

$$= \frac{\alpha^{n+1}}{n!} \left(\left[\frac{x^n \exp[-(s+\alpha)x]}{-(s+\alpha)} \right]_0^{\infty} - \int\limits_{x=0}^{\infty} \frac{n x^{n-1} \exp[-(s+\alpha)x]}{-(s+\alpha)} dx \right).$$

$$\tag{3.175}$$

The first term evaluates to 0. The second term is given by

$$\mathcal{L}_{X_{n+1}}(s) = \frac{\alpha}{s+\alpha} \int_{x=0}^{\infty} \frac{\alpha^n x^{n-1} \exp[-(s+\alpha)x]}{(n-1)!} dx \qquad (3.176)$$

$$= \frac{\alpha}{s+\alpha} \mathcal{L}_{X_n}(s) \qquad (3.177)$$

$$= \left(\frac{\alpha}{s+\alpha}\right)^{n+1}. \qquad (3.178)$$

The above shows that if the given expression for $f_{X_n}(x)$ in equation (3.172) corresponds to the pdf of the sum of the n iid exponential random variables each with rate α, then the given expression for $n+1$ is the pdf of the sum of $n+1$ iid exponential random variables, each with the same rate. Since the given expression is known to be valid for $n = 1$, by induction, it follows that the given expression for $f_{X_k}(x)$ is the pdf of the sum of k iid exponential random variables, for every $k \geq 1$. □

The series expression for the pdf of the busy time is evaluated by substituting the corresponding Erlang densities for the terms in the series expression of the Laplace transform in equation (3.160) and also by using the expression for $n_{(k,k)}$.

$$f_B(t) = \sum_{k=0}^{\infty} \frac{(\lambda+\mu)^{2k+1}}{(2k)!} t^{2k} \exp[-(\lambda+\mu)t] \left(\frac{\lambda}{\lambda+\mu}\right)^k \left(\frac{\mu}{\lambda+\mu}\right)^{k+1} \frac{(2k)!}{k!\,(k+1)!}$$

$$\qquad (3.179)$$

$$= \left(\exp[-(\lambda+\mu)t]\right) \sum_{k=0}^{\infty} \frac{\lambda^k}{k!} \frac{\mu^{k+1}}{(k+1)!} t^{2k}, \quad t \geq 0. \qquad (3.180)$$

3.11.3 Laplace transform of the busy time

The infinite series expression for the Laplace transform can be simplified into a closed form. The following theorem states and proves the result.

THEOREM 3.13

The Laplace transform of the pdf of busy times in an M/M/1/∞ queue, $\mathcal{L}_B(s)$, *is given by*

$$\mathcal{L}_B(s) = \frac{s + \lambda + \mu - \sqrt{(s + \lambda + \mu)^2 - 4\lambda\mu}}{2\lambda}, \qquad if \ \lambda < \mu. \qquad (3.181)$$

Proof

The proof is based on the Maclaurin series (named after the Scottish mathematician Colin Maclaurin, 1698–1746) expansion of $y = 1 - \sqrt{1 - x}$ given by

$$y = \sum_{k=0}^{\infty} \frac{x^k}{k!} \frac{d^k y}{dx^k}\bigg|_{x=0}. \qquad (3.182)$$

For $y = 1 - \sqrt{1 - x}$, we have

$$\frac{dy}{dx} = \frac{1}{2}(1 - x)^{-\frac{1}{2}}. \qquad (3.183)$$

$$\frac{d^2 y}{dx^2} = \frac{1}{2}\frac{1}{2}(1 - x)^{-\frac{3}{2}}. \qquad (3.184)$$

$$\frac{d^3 y}{dx^3} = \frac{1}{2}\frac{1}{2}\frac{3}{2}(1 - x)^{-\frac{5}{2}}. \qquad (3.185)$$

$$\frac{d^j y}{dx^j} = \frac{1}{2^j} 1 \times 3 \times 5 \times \cdots \times (2j - 3)(1 - x)^{-\frac{2j-1}{2}}, \quad j \geq 1 \qquad (3.186)$$

$$= \frac{1}{2^j} \frac{1 \times 2 \times 3 \times 4 \times \cdots \times (2j - 3)(2j - 2)}{2 \times 4 \times \cdots \times (2j - 2)}(1 - x)^{-\frac{2j-1}{2}} \qquad (3.187)$$

$$= \frac{1}{2^j} \frac{(2j - 2)! \, (1 - x)^{-\frac{2j-1}{2}}}{2^{j-1}(j - 1)!}, j \geq 1 \qquad (3.188)$$

$$= \frac{(2j - 2)! \, (1 - x)^{-\frac{2j-1}{2}}}{2^{2j-1}(j - 1)!}, \quad j \geq 1. \qquad (3.189)$$

$$\frac{d^j y}{dx^j}\bigg|_{x=0} = \frac{(2j - 2)!}{2^{2j-1}(j - 1)!}, \quad j \geq 1 \qquad (3.190)$$

and $y(0) = 0$. Constructing the Maclaurin series, we have

$$y(x) = \sum_{j=1}^{\infty} \frac{[2(j-1)]!}{2^{2j-1}\,(j-1)!} \frac{x^j}{j!}. \tag{3.191}$$

Change the index of summation to $k = j - 1$. We have the Maclaurin series for $y = 1 - \sqrt{1-x}$ given by

$$1 - \sqrt{1-x} = \sum_{k=0}^{\infty} \frac{(2k)!}{2^{2k}\,k!} \frac{x^{k+1}}{(k+1)!}. \tag{3.192}$$

The known series expression for the Laplace transform of the busy time in equation (3.161) with the expression for $n_{(k,k)}$ substituted from equation (3.163) is

$$\mathcal{L}_B(s) = \sum_{k=0}^{\infty} \frac{\lambda^k \mu^{k+1}}{(s+\lambda+\mu)^{2k+1}} \frac{(2k)!}{k!\,(k+1)!} \tag{3.193}$$

$$= \frac{s+\lambda+\mu}{2\lambda} \sum_{k=0}^{\infty} \frac{2^{2k+2}\lambda^{k+1}\mu^{k+1}}{2^{2k+1}(s+\lambda+\mu)^{2k+2}} \frac{(2k)!}{k!\,(k+1)!} \tag{3.194}$$

$$= \frac{s+\lambda+\mu}{2\lambda} \sum_{k=0}^{\infty} \left(\frac{4\lambda\mu}{(s+\lambda+\mu)^2}\right)^{k+1} \frac{(2k)!}{2^{k+1}k!\,(k+1)!}. \tag{3.195}$$

The summation in the above equation is recognized as the above developed Maclaurin series by substituting

$$x = \frac{4\lambda\mu}{(s+\lambda+\mu)^2}. \tag{3.196}$$

Therefore, we have

$$\mathcal{L}_B(s) = \frac{s+\lambda+\mu}{2\lambda} \left(1 - \sqrt{1 - \frac{4\lambda\mu}{(s+\lambda+\mu)^2}}\right) \tag{3.197}$$

$$= \frac{s + \lambda + \mu - \sqrt{(s + \lambda + \mu)^2 - 4\lambda\mu}}{2\lambda} \tag{3.198}$$

concluding the proof.   ▯

An important conclusion from the above development is that the busy time in an $M/M/1/\infty$ queue is not exponentially distributed.

3.12   Forward Data Link Performance and Optimization

Wireless communication is less reliable than wire-line communication, in general. This application illustrates the trade-offs between high data rate and effects of errors due to noise, to maximize the throughput. A general definition of throughput of a statistically steady system is the "rate at which finished product flows out." Consider a wireless network with many stations communicating among themselves in a multi-hop fashion. Established connections between several pairs of stations are through line of sight (LOS) and over a dedicated electromagnetic frequency spectrum. That is, there is no contention for transmission opportunity among the stations. Each pair of stations that can directly communicate with each other do so over separate unidirectional sub-links. The two sub-links in opposite directions do not interact but the two computers at the extremities of the link cooperate for reliable data communication over the less reliable wireless channels.

3.12.1   Reliable communication over unreliable data links

Consider the operation of a datalink between station A and station B. Station A transmits data packets to station B. Station B examines individual data packets for possible errors through the redundancy system incorporated in the design. Lower data rates use larger time width per bit, therefore carry more energy, and result in higher probabilities of being correctly received at station B. But this may result in lower overall throughput. On the other hand, a higher data rate introduces a higher probability of the packet being erroneously received at station B. Station B signals errors to station A as follows. Data packets have a fixed serial number field to distinguish between different packets. Due to the finite size of field, serial numbers repeat in cycles. The serial numbers of data packets erroneously received at station B are inferred based on those of the correctly received packets. Note that the receiver at station B cannot detect the serial number of an erroneously received packet from that packet itself! Information about serial numbers of erroneously received packets is piggybacked over data packets intended for station A from station B. Station A is required to retransmit data packets that station B did not receive correctly. There is also the probability of station A incorrectly receiving packets containing retransmission request in which case, after a predesigned time out period, station B repeats the retransmit request. The probabilities of sequences of compounding errors decrease as the number of such erroneous events in the sequence, due to the independence of successive erroneous events. This is the basis of reliable communication over unreliable communication networks. Station B also acknowledges the correct receipt of all packets up to some serial numbers. This eliminates confusion about packets with a serial number from two different cycles. This approach to control a data link is called the cyclic window protocol.

In this section, we will consider a very simple model in which bit errors are evaluated based on a simple binary communication system introduced in Section 2.7. All erroneous packets are assumed to be detected. Pauses in transmission due to incomplete receipt of all packets in a cyclic window are ignored by implicitly assuming a large length of the cyclic window.

3.12.2   Problem formulation and solution

A transreceiver is the combination of equipment at one end of the bidirectional communication system over the two sub-links of the data link. A forward data link from transreceiver A to transreceiver B generates packets at a rate of λ packets per unit time. Packet sizes are geometric with an average packet size of $\frac{1}{q}$ bits per packet, but are very well approximated by the exponential random variable for the sake of queue analysis. The data rate s is the adjustable and it affects the packet error rate as well as the queue performance by altering the reception time for packets. The average transmission time at transmitter A is $\frac{1}{qs}$ time units per packet. The average packet service rate in the transmission queue is qs. The iid bit errors and corresponding iid packet errors are characterized by the Gaussian noise model of Section 2.7. The bit error rate (BER) for the present data link is known to be a given b_e for the given data rate. All packet errors at the receiver B are detected. Station B requests retransmissions and station A complies with the request, after some delay. Station B manages its own data rates. In our present model, the the delay between the time instant that station B detects an error and the time instant that station A retransmits is beyond our control and is not subject to optimization. Errors in requests for retransmissions are also possible. In such a case, station B repeats requests for retransmission after a *time-out* period. Retransmissions from station A to B are also subject to errors, and we consider these in the performance. Although the packet size of a transmission and its retransmission are identical, we approximate all transmissions and retransmissions as iid packet sizes and arriving at the transmitter queue of A is a Poisson stream.

Representative figures for the parameters are as follows. The BER is known to be 10^{-3} for a bit rate of 1 Mbps. The average packet size is 10^3 bits. The following problems are required to be solved.

1. Determine the maximum packet transmission rate in packets per second that the system can handle, as a function of the bit transmission rate s with s in the

range of 0.5 Mbps to 2 Mbps.

2. Use a packet transmission rate of 300 packets per second. Consider only the cumulative delay of a packet due to waiting and transmission at the queue of transmitter A, possibly multiple times due to errors. Ignore all other components of delays such as the delay in B communicating detected errors to A, etc. (assume that these are not variable as we vary s). Determine the optimal value of the data rate s that minimizes the expected total delay.

Solution

1. From Section 2.7 and Example 2.7, on page 57, we have that $\sigma_b^2 = 0.1047$ per Mbps. The combined transmission rate at transmitter A due to original and all retransmissions is

$$\frac{\lambda}{1 - e_f} \qquad (3.199)$$

where e_f is a function of the data rate s. For the queue to be stable, we need

$$\frac{\lambda}{1 - e_f} < qs \text{ or} \qquad (3.200)$$

$$\lambda < (1 - e_f)qs. \qquad (3.201)$$

Interestingly, the maximum of these allowable packet rates occurs when $s(1 - e_f)$ is a maximum, identical to the case of throughput maximization in Example 2.7 studied in Section 2.7. Figure 3.12 shows a plot of the maximum packet rate in a second of time as a function of bit rate in Mbps, for the given system parameters.

2. The expected response time in the transmitter queue for one pass is given by

$$E[R|\text{ pass }] = \frac{1}{qs - \frac{\lambda}{1 - e_f}}. \qquad (3.202)$$

The expected number of passes is $\frac{1}{1 - e_f}$. Therefore, the total expected delay in the queue at the transmitter A only is

$$E[R] = \frac{1}{(1 - e_f)qs - \lambda}. \qquad (3.203)$$

Again, the expected response time is minimized by maximizing the throughput $(1 - e_f)$. Figure 3.13 shows a plot of the total expected response time at transmitter A as a function of the transmission data rate. The minimum total expected response time is 0.003 seconds.

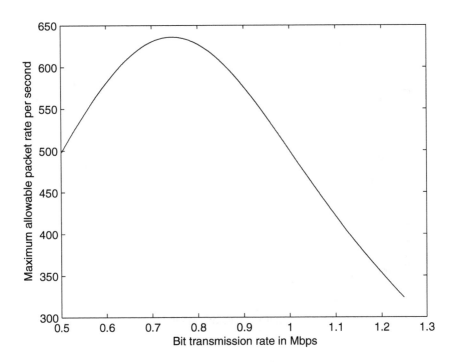

FIGURE 3.12: Maximum allowable packet transmission rate in packets per second as a function of the bit transmission rate in Mbps

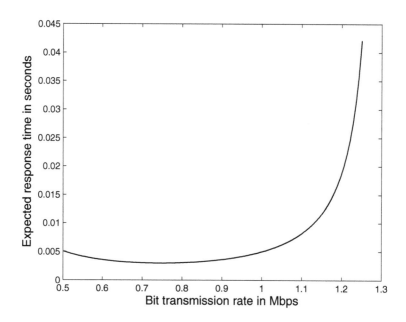

FIGURE 3.13:   Total expected response time as a function of data transmission rate

3.13 Exercises

In the following exercises, unless otherwise specified, all the queues have unlimited buffer sizes and are assumed to be in equilibrium.

1. In a queue with Poisson arrivals with a rate of 4 jobs per second, there are two jobs. Job A is the first and B is second, with a service time requirement of 0.15 and 0.2 seconds, respectively. At time zero, A begins its job service. Specify the probability mass function of the number of arrivals from time zero until job B completes service.

2. The check-in queue at the Fly By Night Airlines is M/M/1/∞ under equilibrium with an arrival rate of 10 customers per hour and a service rate of 15 customers per hour. Mr. Red Eye knows that he can spend no more than 15 minutes in the check-in queuing system so as to run and catch the flight. Determine the value of probability that he will catch the flight.

3. In a stable M/M/1/∞ system operating under equilibrium with $\lambda = 3$ per second, what is the minimum service rate to satisfy $P[\text{No one is waiting}] \geq 0.64$?

4. In a steady state M/M/1/∞ queue, the average number of customers in the system is 4.5 and the expected response time is 1 sec. Determine the arrival and service rates in the queue.

5. Determine the pmf of the number of customers waiting in an equilibrium M/M/1/∞ queue.

6. What is the probability density of time spent in state 2 of an equilibrium M/M/1/∞ system with an arrival rate of 7 jobs per msec and a service rate of 10 jobs per msec?

7. Consider a steady state M/M/1/∞ system with an arrival rate 2 per second and service rate 3 per second. Determine $P[N \leq E[N]]$ where N is the random variable corresponding to the number of customers in the system.

8. In a standard M/M/1/∞ system, the boss of the server wants the server to be busy at least 80% of the time as well as satisfy $N < 2$ at least 36% of the time. Are both possible? Justify.

9. In an M/M/1/∞ unstable queue that has already been operating for an unlimited time, $\lambda = 2/\text{sec}$ and $\mu = 1/\text{sec}$. Completely specify the nature of the departure stream.

10. In a queuing system, the expected service time is 1 sec. The system is empty (server is free) with a probability 0.3. If the system is not empty, the expected waiting time is 2 sec. Determine the expected response time of a customer. Note that this queue need not be an M/M/1/∞ system.

11. In a steady state M/M/1/∞ queue with $\lambda = 1$ and $\mu = 2$, a customer finds out that if he enters the system, he will have to wait (that is, there IS a waiting line). Under this condition, determine the probability that the length of waiting line is 2 or less.

12. A stream of Poisson arrivals with a rate of 10 per second is split with an iid probability of p and $1 - p$. The sub-stream with p is fed to a queue with an exponential service rate of 8 per jobs second. The other sub-stream is fed to another queue with an exponential server with a rate 5 per second. Determine the set of p over which the entire network is stable.

13. Repeat the above exercise with the numbers 8 and 5 respectively replaced by 20 and 3.

14. Consider our standard stable M/M/1/∞ queuing system with nonzero parameters λ and μ. We know the probability that a job does wait to begin service is nonzero; indeed it is $1 - P_0 = \rho$. If a job is known to wait for a nonzero amount of time, determine its probability density of waiting time (this is a conditional density under the condition that the waiting time is known to be nonzero).

15. Individual jobs in a stream of Poisson arrivals with a rate of 10 jobs per second are routed to one of the two queuing systems as follows. A job is routed with probability 0.4 to a queue with a service rate of 8 jobs per second. Else, it is routed to a queue with a service rate of 14 jobs per second. Both queues have exponential service times and unlimited waiting room capacities. Systematically determine the expected response times in the individual queuing systems as well as the overall expected response time of a job in the complete system.

16. A processor (server) uses a round robin scheme for service, with an exponential timer of average 1 msec for each service attempt. External arrivals are Poisson with a rate of one in 10 milliseconds. The overall service requirements for jobs is exponential with an average of 8 milliseconds. A job is known to require exactly 3.5 msec for its total service time. Determine its total expected response time.

17. In a round robin scheme, the interrupt to feedback a job being serviced occurs after a time interval that is uniformly distributed between 0.2 and 0.8 msec. from the time instant of the start of every service segment. The total service time requirement of jobs is iid exponential with an average of 4 msec. Arrivals are Poisson with a rate of 200 jobs per second. Determine the feedback probability of a job (*a*) when it enters service, (*b*) when a job has spent 0.2 msec in service, and (*c*) when a job has spent 0.5 msec in service.

18. Consider the following round robin scheme. External arrivals are Poisson with a rate of 3 job per msec and require an exponential service time with a rate of 8 per msec (that is the average service time requirement is $\frac{1}{8}$ msec). Whenever a job gets into service, the system starts an exponentially distributed timer with

a rate of 24 per msec (that is, the average time of the timer is $\frac{1}{24}$ msec). If the timer completes before the job completes its service, the job is returned (sent back, or fed back) to the tail of the queue with an unlimited buffer size.

(a) Determine the feedback probability of a job entering the service area.

(b) If the total service requirement of a particular job is known to be an exact amount of time, τ msec, determine the expected number of returns (feedbacks) from the server to the tail of the queue that this job will experience.

(c) For this particular job, determine the total expected waiting time experienced in all of its passes through the waiting line, as a function of τ. Evaluate the expected response time of this job.

19. A stream of Poisson arrivals with a rate of 10 jobs per second enters an FIFO queue with an exponential service time with rate of 18 jobs per second. A customer leaving this first queue is required to leave the entire system with a probability of 0.3 or enter a second FIFO queue of exponential service time with a rate of 10 jobs per second. Both queues have unlimited waiting room capacities. Systematically determine the expected response times in the individual queuing systems as well as the overall expected response time of a job in the complete system.

20. A computer is composed of a CPU and an I/O unit. The service time of every job submitted to the CPU is exponentially distributed with a rate of 10 jobs per second. Following the CPU service, not all jobs require an I/O operation; a job requires an I/O operation with a probability of 0.2. If an I/O operation is required the job is routed to another queue with an exponential service time of rate 2 I/O jobs per second.

(a) What is the density function of the total service time (CPU plus I/O, if any) required by a random job input to the CPU?

(b) A job input to the CPU is found to require a total time of 0.2 seconds. What is the probability that it used an I/O operation?

(c) The computer center charges each user a dollar amount equal to

$$A = 2C + 3I \qquad (3.204)$$

where C and I are CPU service time and I/O service time in seconds, respectively. Determine the expected value and the variance of the random variable A.

21. When a particular customer joins an M/M/1/∞ queue with arrival and service rates λ and μ respectively, there are exactly n customers in the system. At the time of joining the queue, this new customer wishes to leave the system within a time interval t in order to make it to a previously made appointment.

Derive a mathematical expression for the probability that the customer will not be late for the appointment.

22. A WAN router has three incoming data links A, B, and C, and three corresponding outgoing data links α, β, and γ. Each of these six links can be considered to be a unidirectional link. That is, there is no feedback. Packet arrivals at the three incoming links are independent and Poisson. All the packets are of iid (independent identically distributed) exponential number of bits with an average of 1000 bits. All the incoming packets on incoming links A, B, and C are merged and fed into the router processor which processes at a constant rate of 1 million bits per second. Every processed packet is immediately transferred to the queuing buffer at the required outgoing link. Each outgoing link transmits packets at a constant rate of 2 million bits per second. Processing at every queue is FIFO.

The entire system is a feed-forward network of four M/M/1/∞ queues. The arrival rates (in number of packets per second) and iid proportions of packets to be transferred to the different outgoing links are given in Table 3.1. Systematically evaluate the average delay experienced by a random packet arrival in the entire router system.

TABLE 3.1:   Characteristics of data packets at the router

Incoming link	Arrival rate	Outgoing to α	Outgoing to β	Outgoing to γ
A	100	0	0.4	0.6
B	200	0.7	0	0.3
C	300	0.2	0.8	0

23. A user is faced with having to decide which of the two waiting lines he should enter his job. The two waiting lines are in front of two computers S_1 and S_2. Both computers have iid exponential service times with service rates of 2 jobs/minute and 3 jobs/minute respectively. In addition to the jobs being

served by the two systems, S_1 and S_2 have 2 and 3 jobs waiting in front of them, respectively. If the user wants to decide based on the minimum expected time for him to leave after service, which station should he enter?

24. The pmf of the number of k arrivals and $k+1$ departures in a stable M/M/1/∞ queue for it to reach the empty status for the first time after a customer arrives into the empty queue is obtained from equations (3.158) and (3.163) as

$$P[k] = \frac{\lambda^k \mu^{k+1} (2k)!}{(\lambda + \mu)^{2k+1} k! \, (k+1)!}. \tag{3.205}$$

   (a) Prove that this is a valid pmf.

   (b) Evaluate its expectation.

25. Evaluate $E[B]$, the expectation of the busy time in an M/M/1/∞ queue.

Chapter 4

State Dependent Markovian Queues

4.1 Introduction

In the previous chapter, we studied the M/M/1/∞ system with constant arrival and service rates. In many applications, the arrival and service rates can change over time. If the changes are at arbitrary time instants, we cannot conduct a general analysis. However, if arrival and service rates are functions of the number of customers only, we can analyze the system. Additionally, we can also deal with several other logical combinations of situations affecting the arrival and service rates. We find many practical applications that fall within this category. The principles of continuous parameter Markov chains are essential to the analysis of such state dependent queues. In addition to state dependent queues, Markov chains have many other applications within the realm of computer networks. A Markov chain is a special case of the more general stochastic process.

4.2 Stochastic Processes

In our M/M/1/∞ queue, consider the state of the system $N(t)$ at time t. At a given time instant, the number in the system is an integer. If we continuously observe the number in the system over a long time, we get a nonnegative stepped function that increases by one at arrival time instant and decreases by one at departure time instants. Such time plots of $N(t)$ are called *sample functions*. If we observe another queue with identical parameters, we will find a different sample function. Thus, the "ensemble" of all possible $N(t)$ observations is a larger set than a sample space of just a random variable. We refer to $N(t)$ as a *random process* or *stochastic process*. Figure 4.1 shows an example sample function (only for a segment of time). The x-axis is time, and the y-axis is the number in the system.

DEFINITION 4.1 Random or Stochastic Process *A random process* $X(t)$ *is a parameterized random variable such that (a) for different values of the parameter* t, *we get different random variables and (b) an element of the*

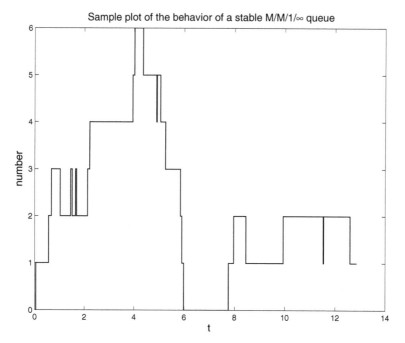

FIGURE 4.1:   Example sample function segment in an M/M/1/∞ system

sample space of the random process is a "sample function," an observation over all possible values of t. Although t is generally the time variable, the parameter of a random process can be other real-valued quantities. ☐

We will see many examples. The value taken by the random variable $X(t)$ at a given time $t = \tau$ is called the *state of the process* at τ. A random process can have a continuous or discrete state, and a continuous or discrete parameter. More complicated mixed state random processes also appear in applications. The state of a random process can also be a vector. Even simple queues, such as an M/M/1/∞ system, provide very illustrative examples of random processes. Indeed, it is preferable to use queues as application examples with the help of which to introduce the topic of stochastic processes.

Example 4.1

In M/M/1/∞ systems, $N(t)$ is a continuous parameter discrete state stochastic process. Observe the system from some arbitrary starting time instant $t = 0$. Assign serial numbers to arriving customers starting with customer number $i = 1$ for the "oldest" existing customer in the queue. If the system is empty at $t = 0$, the first observed arrival is assigned customer number $i = 1$. In this system, N_i, the number of customers in the system soon after the departure of the ith job is a discrete parameter discrete state process. R_i, the response time of the ith job, is a discrete parameter continuous state process. $R(t)$, the response time of the arrival following the continuous time variable t is a continuous parameter continuous state process. Note that the above processes can also be defined for an unstable system. ⬜

4.2.1 Markov process

In general, stochastic processes can be very abstract and very complicated. One reason for this is the possible statistical dependency of the various random variables at various values of these parameter values. However, most of the application systems we will study are well modeled by a very interesting and considerably simple class of stochastic processes. It is called the Markov process, in honor of Andrei Andreyovich Markov, the Russian mathematician (1856–1922) who originally defined and studied it. The following discussion motivates the study of such processes. Consider $N(t)$ in an M/M/1/∞ system. The number of customers at t is strongly statistically dependent on the number of customers a little amount of time before t, say at $t - \tau$. Therefore, $N(t)$ and $N(t - \tau)$ are dependent. However, if we know the number at $t - \tau$ to be $n(t - \tau)$, the number at t depends only on $n(t - \tau)$, and the number of arrivals and departures in the intervening period τ. These in turn do not depend on any event that occurred before $t - \tau$, since the times for arrivals and departures are memoryless. Therefore, given $N(t - \tau) = n(t - \tau)$, the random variable $N(t)$ does not depend on $N(t - \tau - \xi)$ for $\xi > 0$. Such processes are known as Markov processes.

DEFINITION 4.2 Markov Process *Let $t > t_k > t_{k-1} > \cdots t_{k-m}$. If*

$$P[X(t) \leq x(t) | X(t_k) = x(t_k), X(t_{k-1}) = x(t_{k-1}), \cdots, X(t_{k-m}) = x(t_{k-m})]$$

$$= P[X(t) \leq x(t) | X(t_k) = x(t_k)], \tag{4.1}$$

we say that $X(t)$ is a Markov process. Elaborating, the most recent known observation affects the future distributions. If we have many observations, other than the most recent of these observations, the earlier observations do not influence the distributions of the random variables at future times. ⬜

The restriction on $X(t)$ in the above definition is quite stringent. Condition (4.1) is required to be satisfied for all $m \geq 1$, for all $t, t_k, t_{k-1}, \ldots, t_{k-m}$, and for all $x(t)$, $x(t_k), x(t_{k-1}), \ldots, x(t_{k-m})$.

DEFINITION 4.3 Markov chain *If the set of states of a Markov process is countable, the stochastic process is called a Markov chain.* ⬜

Therefore, $N(t)$ in an M/M/1/∞ queue is a continuous parameter Markov chain.

4.3   Continuous Parameter Markov Chains

Markov processes may be of continuous or discrete parameter and of continuous or discrete state. In this chapter, continuous parameter Markov chains are studied. Discrete parameter Markov chains are studied in Chapter 6.

4.3.1   Time intervals between state transitions

Let $X(t)$ be a continuous parameter Markov chain. Given $X(t_1) = k$, what is the time, $t_1 + \tau$, at which the state changes from k to anything else? This time is a random variable. Given $X(t_1) = k$, the past events are irrelevant. So, when exactly the state reached the value k prior to t_1 is irrelevant. That is, given $X(t_1) = k$, future state changes forget the past. Since we know that *only* the exponential random variable is continuous and memoryless, time for state change must be exponential. Of course, the parameter of the exponential density may depend on the exact state k, at which the chain is, before the state transition. We have the very important result.

THEOREM 4.1
Times between successive state changes in a continuous parameter Markov chain are all mutually independent exponential random variables.   ▯

The rate of the exponential random variable corresponding to how long the chain stays in the same state before changing the state can, of course depend on the state. In addition, it can depend on the parameter value too. In many applications, these rates are not functions of the time constituting the parameter variable. Such chains are identified as homogeneous as formally defined below.

DEFINITION 4.4 Homogeneous Markov chain   *A Markov chain is said to be homogeneous if every state transition rate is invariant with time.* ▯

4.3.2   State transition diagrams

We represent a continuous parameter Markov chain as a directed graph with nodes representing states, and directed arcs, possible state transitions. If the chain is homogeneous, the transition rates are invariant with time and they are written next to each arc. Only transition arcs with nonzero rates of transitions are included in the diagram. For the M/M/1/∞ case, such a graph is shown in Figure 4.2. We associate a numerical value with each arc, or transition, as follows. Irrespective of how long the chain has been in state i, the time for it to change to $i + 1$ is exponential with rate λ. Similarly, the time for state change from $i + 1$ to i is exponential with rate μ.

If a state of a Markov chain can be reached from another state through possibly a sequence of one or more nonzero rate transitions, we say that the latter state is

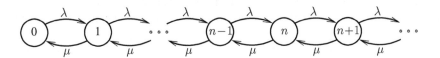

FIGURE 4.2:   The state transition diagram of an M/M/1/∞ queue

reachable from the former state. In general, a subset of states may not be reachable from another subset, even though the former subset is reachable from the latter. If a chain does not have such peculiarities, its analysis will be simple. There are many applications whose Markov chains satisfy this simplifying property. It is formally defined below.

DEFINITION 4.5 Irreducible Markov chain   *A Markov chain is said to be irreducible if every state can be reached from every other state and from itself through a finite number of transitions, each transition being of nonzero transition rate.* ⬜

Unless otherwise stated the Markov chains we will study are homogeneous and irreducible.

4.3.3   Development of balance equations

The above M/M/1/∞ queuing system is just one example of a Markov chain. In general, a Markov chain has a countable set of states that can be conveniently numbered as 0, 1, 2, ⋯ . A Markov chain may also contain a finite number of states. Over continuous time, a state transition is observed only if the system changes from a state to *any other* state. Therefore, the chain may have possible transitions from every state to *every other* state. Let the transition rate from state i to state j be α_{ij}. For convenience, define quantities $\alpha_{ii} = 0$.

A fundamental topic in the study of Markov chains is the evaluation of probabilities of different states at a given time instant. Many performance figures of application systems are functions of these state probabilities. The following derivation develops differential equations for the state probabilities as functions of time, just as in the case of M/M/1/∞ system. Let $P_i(t)$ be the probability that the system is in state i at time t, $i = 0, 1, \ldots$. For any $\tau > 0$, the statistical behavior of the chain following time t given the state at $t + \tau$ depends only on the state at t and on nothing else. Consider the state at time $t + \delta_t$, where δ_t is a positive infinitesimal time interval. Consider the probability that the chain is in a particular state i at time

$t+\delta_t$. Over the time interval $[t, t+\delta_t)$, we need to consider at most one state change, since the probability of more than one change is negligible in comparison with the probability of one change. If the chain is at state j at time t, the probability that the chain will move to state i in δ_t is the conditional probability $\alpha_{ji}\delta_t$. If the chain is in state i at time t, the probability that it will stay in state i for δ_t more time period is the probability that none of the possible changes from state i occurs. This probability is $\sum_{k=0}^{\infty} \alpha_{ik}\delta_t$. Using the theorem of total probability, we obtain the probability that the chain is in state i at time $t + \delta_t$ as

$$P_i(t + \delta_t) = P_i(t)\left(1 - \delta_t \sum_{k=0}^{\infty} \alpha_{ik}\right) + \sum_{j=0}^{\infty} P_j(t)\alpha_{ji}\delta_t. \tag{4.2}$$

Rearranging, we have

$$\frac{P_i(t + \delta_t) - P_i(t)}{\delta_t} = -P_i(t)\sum_{k=0}^{\infty} \alpha_{ik} + \sum_{j=0}^{\infty} P_j(t)\alpha_{ji}, \quad i = 0, 1, \cdots. \tag{4.3}$$

The limit of the above LHS as $\delta_t \to 0$ is the derivative $\frac{dP_i(t)}{dt}$. We have an additional equation specifying that the state probabilities must sum to one. That is,

$$\sum_{i=0}^{\infty} P_i(t) = 1. \tag{4.4}$$

As in the case of M/M/1/∞ systems, we will be especially interested in the steady state solution to the set of differential equations and in the conditions under which such steady state is possible.

DEFINITION 4.6 Equilibrium *A continuous parameter Markov chain is said to be in equilibrium at time τ if the time derivatives of all its state probabilities are zero at time τ. That is, if*

$$\frac{dP_i(t)}{dt} = 0 \text{ at } t = \tau \text{ for all } i = 0, 1, \cdots. \tag{4.5}$$

▯

Note that this definition is identical to the definition of equilibrium in the case of M/M/1/∞ queue. If equilibrium is possible for a Markov chain, the above equations (4.3) and (4.4) must be satisfied with time invariant state probabilities p_i replacing $P_i(t)$, respectively for $i = 0, 1, \cdots$. Therefore, we have the following result.

THEOREM 4.2
If the equations

$$p_i \sum_{k=0}^{\infty} \alpha_{ik} - \sum_{j=0}^{\infty} p_j\alpha_{ji} = 0, \quad i = 0, 1, \cdots \text{ and} \tag{4.6}$$

$$\sum_{i=0}^{\infty} p_i = 1 \qquad (4.7)$$

possess a unique solution for p_0, p_1, $\cdots$, then that solution is the set of equilibrium state probabilities for the Markov chain. ☐

COROLLARY 4.1
If the balance equations (4.6) and (4.7) do not sport any solution, the Markov chain can never be in equilibrium. ☐

Clearly, the set of equations (4.6) alone does not have a unique solution since any solution multiplied by a constant is also a solution.

COROLLARY 4.2
If equilibrium state probabilities exist for a chain,

1. *every state has a nonzero equilibrium probability and*

2. $\lim_{i\to\infty} p_i = 0.$

Proof
As mentioned earlier, since nothing is said about the chain, it is assumed to be irreducible and the result holds for irreducible chains. Rearrange the balance equations as

$$p_i \sum_{k=0}^{\infty} \alpha_{ik} = \sum_{j=0}^{\infty} p_j \alpha_{ji}, \quad i = 0, 1, \cdots \text{ and} \qquad (4.8)$$

$$\sum_{i=0}^{\infty} p_i = 1. \qquad (4.9)$$

The quantity p_i does not appear on the RHS of equation (4.8), since $\alpha_{ii} = 0$. As a consequence of equation (4.9), at least one of the equilibrium state probabilities is nonzero. Due to irreducibility, this state must have a transition to at least one of the other states. The equilibrium state probability of such a latter state must also be nonzero, due to the following reason. Equation (4.8) expresses every state probability as a positive weighted sum of equilibrium probabilities of all other states from which there is a transition to the state in question. Continuing this argument further, since every state is so reachable from every other state through a sequence of transitions, every equilibrium state probability must be nonzero.

To prove the second part, we know that $p_i > 0$ for all i. Define b_i to be the maximum of the infinite tail sequence of p_i, p_{i+1}, $\cdots$. Since all the probabilities are nonzero and the sum of all of them is one, we have

$$b_i = \max\{p_i, \ p_{i+1}, \cdots\} \qquad (4.10)$$

$$\leq \sum_{j=i}^{\infty} p_j. \tag{4.11}$$

$$\leq 1 - \sum_{j=0}^{i-1} p_j. \tag{4.12}$$

$$\lim_{i \to \infty} b_i \leq \lim_{i \to \infty} 1 - \sum_{j=0}^{i-1} p_j \tag{4.13}$$

$$\leq 0 \tag{4.14}$$

$$= 0, \tag{4.15}$$

since b_i is nonnegative. The limit of b_i, the maximum of the tail sequence of a nonnegative sequence of probabilities tends to zero. Therefore, the limit of the tail sequence itself must tend to zero, completing the proof.   ☐

DEFINITION 4.7 Stability   *A Markov chain is said to be stable if there exists a solution to its balance equations.*   ☐

Note that a Markov chain can be stable but not in equilibrium at some time instant. Stability is a property of the chain. Whether or not a chain is in equilibrium at a particular time instant depends on the operating condition of the chain at that time instant.

THEOREM 4.3
If a chain is in equilibrium at a time instant $t = 0$, it will continue to be in equilibrium for all $t > 0$ as well.

Proof
The differential equations governing the behavior of $P_i(t)$, $i = 0, 1, \cdots$, are

$$\frac{dP_i(t)}{dt} = \sum_{j=0}^{\infty} P_j(t)\alpha_{ji} - P_i(t) \sum_{k=0}^{\infty} \alpha_{ik}, \quad i = 0, 1, \cdots . \tag{4.16}$$

The proof is identical to the proof of Theorem 3.2 which is concerned with an identical property of M/M/1/∞ queue. The only difference is that the present arguments are made about the above differential equations (4.16) and not about the differential equations in (3.29).   ☐

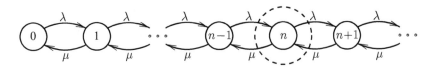

FIGURE 4.3: Global balancing around state n in an M/M/1/∞ state diagram

4.3.4 Graphical method to write balance equations

Let the time invariant equilibrium state probabilities be denoted by p_k, $k = 0, 1, \ldots$. Equations (4.6) for the equilibrium state probabilities are easily written by examining the state transition diagram of the Markov chain, as follows. The resulting equations are called the balance equations since they equate some quantities going into and out of a state. This is demonstrated with the help of Figure 4.3, the state transition diagram of an M/M/1/∞ system. The product of the equilibrium probability of a state and the rate of an outgoing arc is the unconditional rate of the arc; this is a joint rate and not a conditional rate conditioned on the chain being in the state. One equation for the equilibrium probability of a state is obtained by equating the sum of the joint rates going out of a state to that coming into the state. The resulting equation around state $n > 0$ is

$$p_n(\lambda + \mu) = p_{n-1}\lambda + p_{n+1}\mu \qquad (4.17)$$

for the M/M/1/∞ queue. Since this approach balances the sum of the unconditional rates of incoming and outgoing arcs across a boundary between one state and *all other states*, it is called global balancing around that state. We have one global balance equation around each state.

Writing a similar equation across a boundary partitioning the set of states into two sets leads to a linear combination of several of the original global balance equations. This approach leads to an equation between the equilibrium probabilities of a few states only. This is demonstrated in Figure 4.4, in which each local balance equation is between the equilibrium probabilities of only two states. The resulting equation between states n and $n + 1$ is

$$p_n\lambda = p_{n+1}\mu, \ n \geq 0. \qquad (4.18)$$

These equations are equivalent to equations obtained in Chapter 3 for the analysis of M/M/1/∞ system.

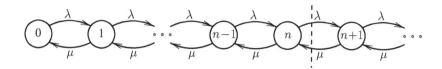

FIGURE 4.4:   Local balancing between states n and $n+1$ in an M/M/1/∞ state diagram

4.4   Markov Chains for State Dependent Queues

4.4.1   State dependent rates and equilibrium probabilities

State dependent queues are applications of general Markov chains. In many applications, the assumptions of constant arrival rate and unlimited waiting line room of the M/M/1/∞ may be unrealistic. In real-life situations, the arrival rate may be less if the number of customers in the system is large. Shrewd market vendors also know to be deliberately slow in service if the number of customers is small, to give the appearance of credibility due to implicit validation from waiting customers. Later on, we will also introduce very specific applications wherein state dependent arrival and service rates arise due to the peculiarity of the system, such as multiple servers, finite size waiting room, etc. Let

- λ_i = Arrival rate when there are i customers in the system.

- μ_i = Service rate when there are i customers in the system.

If the system's buffer capacity is finite, let m be the maximum number of customers possible in the system. If the buffer capacity is unlimited, $m \to \infty$. For finite m, if $\lambda_m \neq 0$, some arrivals see a full buffer. Note that $\mu_0 = 0$, for every case (even for the state independent M/M/1/∞ case). The state transition diagram of the Markov chain is shown in Figure 4.5. Using balance equations,

$$p_1\mu_1 = p_0\lambda_0 \tag{4.19}$$

$$\vdots$$

$$p_n = \frac{\lambda_{n-1}}{\mu_n}p_{n-1} \tag{4.20}$$

$$= \frac{\lambda_{n-1}\lambda_{n-2}}{\mu_n\mu_{n-1}}p_{n-2} \tag{4.21}$$

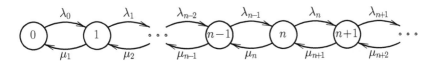

FIGURE 4.5: State transition diagram of a state dependent queue

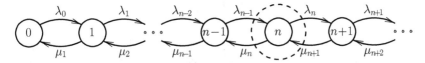

FIGURE 4.6: Global balancing around state n

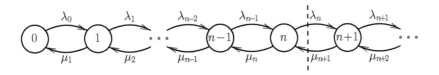

FIGURE 4.7: Local balancing across a boundary between states n and $n + 1$

$$= \frac{\lambda_{n-1}\lambda_{n-2}\cdots\lambda_0}{\mu_n\mu_{n-1}\cdots\mu_1}p_0. \tag{4.22}$$

Recall that

$$p_0, p_1, \cdots, p_n, \cdots$$

are the equilibrium probabilities of states

$$0, 1, \cdots, n, \cdots,$$

respectively. Each state probability is thus expressed as a function of p_0 and the arrival and service rates. We solve for p_0 by using

$$\sum_{n=0}^{M} p_n = 1. \tag{4.23}$$

That is,

$$p_0\left\{1 + \sum_{n=1}^{M}\prod_{i=1}^{n}\frac{\lambda_{i-1}}{\mu_i}\right\} = 1. \tag{4.24}$$

A useful result from equation (4.24) is that since all the probabilities can be expressed as a function of one unknown p_0, the balance equations have at most one solution. If equating the sum of all probabilities to one results in $p_0 = 0$, the system is unstable and the balance equations have no solution. If the resulting $p_0 > 0$, then the balance equations have a unique solution.

Example 4.2
A simple state dependent system can hold no more than two customers including any under service. The arrival and service rates are $\lambda_0 = 7$, $\lambda_1 = 2$, $\lambda_2 = 0$, $\mu_1 = 3$, and $\mu_2 = 6$. Analyze it. ⬚

Solution

$$3p_1 = 7p_0, \tag{4.25}$$

$$p_1 = \frac{7}{3}p_0, \tag{4.26}$$

$$6p_2 = 2p_1, \tag{4.27}$$

$$p_2 = \frac{2}{6}p_1 = \frac{7}{9}p_0, \tag{4.28}$$

$$p_0 + \frac{7}{3}p_0 + \frac{7}{9}p_0 = 1, \tag{4.29}$$

$$p_0 = \frac{9}{37}, \tag{4.30}$$

$$p_1 = \frac{21}{37}, \tag{4.31}$$

$$p_2 = \frac{7}{37}. \tag{4.32}$$

☐

4.4.2 General performance figures

We can define many more expectations of quantities about the state dependent case, than in the simple case of the M/M/1/∞ queue. Performance figures specific to applications examples are common in the case of state dependent queues. The following defines some general performance figures.

4.4.2.1 Throughput

The general definition of throughput of any system is the rate of production of successful output. In the state independent equilibrium M/M/1/∞ queue, throughput is λ, same as the arrival rate. If we have a finite buffer state-dependent case and if $\lambda_m \neq 0$, some arrivals experience a full buffer. They are turned away without service and let into the waiting line. The most common model is to treat them as lost and that they will not "wait outside" or affect future arrival rates. If we exclude lost jobs, throughput is also the rate at which customers "enter" the system, those that are not turned away. Therefore, the throughput is

$$\overline{Y} = E[Y] = \sum_{i=1}^{M} p_i \mu_i = \sum_{i=0}^{m-1} p_i \lambda_i. \tag{4.33}$$

4.4.2.2 Blocking probability

Blocking probability is simply the probability that an attempted arrival sees a full buffer and is turned away. Note that this is not the fraction of jobs turned away. In fact, if m is finite and $\lambda_m = 0$, there will be no lost jobs. The emphasis is on "an attempted" arrival, in defining p_b, the blocking probability. If an arrival attempts, the probability that it will be lost is the same as the probability that the buffer is full. Hence, $p_b = p_m$.

4.4.2.3 Expected fraction of lost jobs

This is defined as the ratio of the rate of lost jobs to the rate of attempted arrivals. That is,

$$\frac{\lambda_m p_m}{E[Y] + \lambda_m p_m}. \tag{4.34}$$

If the attempted arrival rate is zero whenever the buffer is full, the expected fraction of lost jobs is zero.

4.4.2.4   Expected number of customers in the system

The expected number of customers in the system is $E[N] = \sum\limits_{n=1}^{M} n p_n$.

4.4.2.5   Expected response time

The expected response time of a customer that enters a system is a function of the state of the Markov chain at the time the customer enters the system. Let the states of the system be 0, 1, 2, $\cdots$. Let R be the response time random variable. Let $E[R|i]$ denotes the conditional response time of a customer known to enter the system when the state of the system is i. Using the theorem of total expectation, we have the expected response time given by

$$E[R] = \sum_{i=0}^{\infty} E[R|i] a_i, \tag{4.35}$$

where a_i is the probability that an arrival sees state i. In the case of the simple M/M/1/∞ system, the evaluation of $E[R]$ in equation (4.35) is simple since for every condition i, the response time is the sum of $i + 1$ iid service times. In a general Markov chain, the total response time of a customer is not so easily decomposed into known components. Therefore, even though the final expectation is a simple expression of the conditional expectations, $E[R|i]$, in equation (4.35) may not be easy to evaluate. Also, note that the states of the chain have been assumed to be the natural numbers. In general, the state may not be identical to the number of customers; the state may include additional information such as from which server a customer is getting service. It is still possible to map such a set of states into the set of nonnegative integers and the number of customers in the system can be a more general function of the state, as opposed to being the state itself. This aspect is illustrated in some examples later.

In addition to the difficulty in evaluating expected response time, there is another concern about performance figures. In practical applications, we are interested in the performance figures of the one sample function of the Markov process corresponding to the operation of the physical system. The performance figures defined above are the ensemble expectations. We may anticipate that the expectations over the sample space of all possible sample functions would be the same as the required "time averages" of the one sample function that the physical system experiences. We need to examine such hypotheses through a formal analysis of long-term average behaviors and their expectations. To evaluate the expected response time performance figure defined above, we will develop and use a general and a powerful result known as the Little's theorem (also known as Little's result and Little's law). The result was published in 1961 by John D. C. Little. It is applicable to long-term time averages and this is another reason to study the long-term behavior of a sample function of a Markov chain.

4.5   Intuitive Approach for Time Averages

Let the time variable start from zero and progress without bounds. In reality, we have only one sample function for the stochastic process of the physical system represented by the Markov chain. We imagine an ensemble of an innumerable number of sample function satisfying the definition of the sample space for the chain. In many cases, the evaluation of expectations over the sample space appears simpler than the evaluation of averages of corresponding quantities about the one sample function being observed, over the infinite time interval. Therefore, we would like to develop general results of the following nature. The averages over time of the sample function of a "nice" Markov chain tends to the corresponding expectations of the ensemble of all sample functions of the Markov chain. An important point to note here is that the "average over time of the sample function" is a random variable and not a constant, since averaging is taken over the time variable and no expectation over the ensemble of the Markov chain is taken. However, intuitively, it appears reasonable that as we let time increase without bounds, the averages over an infinite amount of time, converges to the ensemble expectations of the corresponding random variables.

A mathematical examination of such hypothesis is tricky, because we would be comparing a limiting random variable to a constant. What does it mean to say that a limiting random variable tends to a constant? As discussed in Section 2.6.1, even the average of an infinite sequence of iid random variables with a finite variance is not certain to converge to the expectation of the original random variable; but there is a probability of 1 that the limiting average is the expectation. Similarly, in the same Section 2.6.1, the number of Poisson arrivals is shown to tend to infinity with probability 1, as the time of observation of the Poisson arrivals tends to infinity. Such principles and methods are used in the rigorous analysis of the statistical behavior of the sample function of a Markov chain. The following lists important results with some intuitive justification. They provide an overview and a guided tour of the formal analysis in the following sections. The analysis is generally conducted for an infinite state chain. Specializing results for a finite state chain is usually simple.

1. We already know that in an irreducible and stable chain, all the equilibrium probabilities, p_i are strictly larger than zero. Furthermore, we know that

$$\lim_{i \to \infty} p_i = 0. \qquad (4.36)$$

2. As the continuous time variable increases without bounds, the limiting number of state transitions observed in a sample function tends to infinity with probability 1. The reason for this is similar to the reason for the number of Poisson arrivals of a constant rate to tend to infinity with probability 1, as the time interval of observation tends to infinity. The only difference is that in the case of the sample function of a Markov chain, the rate of the exponential random variable of the time for every transition is dependent on the state. However, each such rate is finite, since, from every state, there must be transitions with nonzero rates for the chain to be irreducible.

3. The expected fraction of total time spent in every state (due to multiple transitions into the state), q_i, tends to the equilibrium probability p_i of the state in question, as time of observation tends to infinity. This is an important result and is not difficult to prove. As a consequence and since every equilibrium state probability is also nonzero, we have the following.

    (a) The expected amount of time spent in every state tends to infinity, as the observation time tends to infinity, with probability 1.

    (b) The number of transitions into and out of every state tends to infinity, as the time of observation tends to infinity, with probability 1.

    (c) Note that even though the expected amount of time spent in every state tends to infinity, the expected long-term fraction of time spent in state i tends to zero as the state index i tends to infinity.

4. The rate of arrival of customers is nonzero in at least in one state of the chain; else we would have no arrivals at all! Since the expected amount of time that the chain spends in each state tends to infinity with probability 1, the number of customer arrivals tends to infinity, as time of observation tends to infinity.

5. Using similar arguments, the number of departures of customers tends to infinity with probability 1, as the observation time tends to infinity.

6. We can now consider the limiting variances of many such averages. Note that between successive entries of the chain into any particular state, the behaviors of the chain are iid. Therefore, we have the following.

    (a) The amount of time spent by the chain in a state during multiple visits to the state are iid.

    (b) The rate of a customer arrival, the rate of a customer departure, whether or not an arrival occurs, whether or not a departure occurs, the response time of a customer entering during a particular state, are independent during successive visits to a state and are also correspondingly identical during successive visits to a state.

7. As a consequence, the properties of cumulative averages of infinite sequences of iid random variables are applicable. These properties are that if X_i are iid, with a finite expectation η and variance σ^2, the following are satisfied.

$$P[\lim_{n \to \infty} \frac{1}{n} \sum_{i=0}^{n} X_i = \eta] = 1 \quad \text{and} \tag{4.37}$$

$$\lim_{n \to \infty} \text{var}[\frac{1}{n} \sum_{i=0}^{n} X_i] = 0. \tag{4.38}$$

8. Some random variables are defined for every time instant of the chain. Examples of these random variables are the state of the chain itself and the number of customers in the system. Note that the number of customers need not be equal to the state. We will make the assumption that the number of customers in the system tends to infinity, as the integer variable state tends to infinity. This is just a mapping from the state to the number of customers. This will be true in every application system we will consider. Let $Y(t)$ be a random variable for every t. The long-term time average of $Y(t)$ is defined as

$$\lim_{t \to \infty} \frac{1}{t} \int_{\tau=0}^{t} Y(\tau) d\tau. \tag{4.39}$$

In the case of Markov chains, the sample function $Y(t)$ changes values (by jumping) only when the state changes. Therefore, it is piecewise constant. The above integral is equivalent to weighted averaging, with the weights being the time intervals during which the state does not change. Note that these time periods are statistically repetitive as the chain repeatedly visits the same states. The application of these properties to the various quantities of the sample function will lead to the following properties.

(a) The overall observed arrival rate in the sample function converges to its ensemble expectation with probability one. The variance of the same overall observed arrival rate tends to zero.

(b) Similar results are true for the overall departure rate, the number of customers, and the response time of a customer entering the system.

The above properties allow us to use the results based on the ensemble expectations for time averaged performance figures. There is one exception, though. The expected response time is not easy to evaluate using ensemble expectations only, since the expected response time of a customer known to enter when the chain is in a particular state is not easy to evaluate, in general. That is, $E[R|i]$ in equation (4.35) can be very difficult to evaluate in many applications. This difficulty is overcome with the help of a result based on time averages, known as the Little's result. The above

properties of the Markov chains about the convergences of long-term time averages
to the corresponding ensemble averages is required for the application of the Little's
result, developed in a subsequent Section 4.7.

4.6　Statistical Analysis of Markov Chains' Sample Functions

Consider an irreducible and stable continuous time (parameter) Markov chain with
states $0, 1, \cdots$. Let it possess a unique solution of equilibrium state probabilities p_0,
$p_1, \cdots$, for its balance equations. Let the arrival rate of customers be λ_i when the
system is in state i. Similarly, let μ_i be the rate at which a customer leaves when
the system is in state i. Since the number of customers in the system may not be
identical to the state itself, let n_i be the number of customers in the system, when
the state is i. Let $n_0 = 0$ and $n_\infty = \infty$, without loss of generality. This study is
centered around the following questions. Is there an overall arrival rate? If yes, what
is it? What is the expectation of its long-term time average? Similar questions arise
for the time average number of customers in the system and average response time
of customers who complete service. Note that quantities such as "long-term time
average" are random variables and have their corresponding expectations. To clarify
this, consider the sample space of all possible outcomes of an equilibrium queue.
The sample space consists of a continuum of iid sample functions. Each sample
function is a function of time, that is, the state as a function of time. When we
pick an outcome of the random process, we pick an entire sample function over time
$t = [0, \infty)$. If we pick one sample function and observe it at time t, we observe the
random variable corresponding to the equilibrium state of the chain. If we evaluate
the time average of the state, the number of arrivals, or the expected response time of
customers who completed service up to a time t, we still have only random variables.

We will study time averages of functions of the continuous time variable such as
the average number of customers over a time interval. The number of customers is
defined for all time instants and hence averaging over the time interval is applicable
and useful. On the other hand, the random variable response time is defined for every
customer. The average response time that is useful in applications is the average
over a number of customers. Hence we have two types of long-term averages. Since
we will be using these two lengthy expressions, the following abbreviations and
definitions are used. We generally study the system over the time (parameter) interval
$t \in [0, \infty)$. The averages will be taken over this time interval, even if the averaging
is over a number of observations as opposed to over the continuous time variable.
The definitions below make this clear.

DEFINITION 4.8　*The expectation of the long-term average of a random process, $X(t)$ that is defined for every time instant and taken over the* *continuous time (or parameter) is denoted and given by*

$$E_\infty[X(t)] = \lim_{t\to\infty} \frac{1}{t} \int_{\tau=0}^{t} X(\tau)d\tau. \tag{4.40}$$

▯

DEFINITION 4.9 *Let $n(t)$ be the number of occurrences of random variables $Y_j, j = 1, \ldots n(t)$ over the time interval $[0, t)$. Consider the expectation of the long-term average of a sequence of random variables $Y_{n(t)}$ occurring over the entire time interval $t \in [0, \infty)$. The expectation of the average of all these random variables is the "expected long-term average over number" of observations. It is denoted and given by*

$$E_\infty[Y_{n(t)}] = \lim_{t\to\infty} \frac{1}{n(t)} \sum_{j=1}^{n(t)} Y_j. \tag{4.41}$$

▯

In both the above cases, note that the limit on the RHS is taken as the time $t \to \infty$.

Let us now consider the long-term operation of a Markov chain, over a time interval $t \in [0, T)$, with $T \to \infty$. Let T_i be the total amount of time spent by the chain in state i during $t \in [0, T)$, possibly in several disjoint time periods. These T_i are random variables; however,

$$\sum_{i=0}^{\infty} T_i = T. \tag{4.42}$$

Let q_i be the expectation of the long-term fraction of time the chain spends in state i. That is,

$$q_i = \lim_{T\to\infty} E[\frac{T_i}{T}] = \lim_{T\to\infty} \frac{1}{T} E[T_i]. \tag{4.43}$$

Let $\mathcal{D}_i$ be the number of times the system departs from state i for some other state over the time interval T. Similarly, let $\mathcal{A}_i$ be the expected number of times the system enters state i from some other state. These entries into a state and departures from a state are not to be confused with customer arrivals and customer departures. The expected numbers of entries into and departures from a state over a continuous time interval can differ by at most one. Let $\Delta_i = \mathcal{A}_i - \mathcal{D}_i$. Thus, $\Delta_i \in \{-1, 0, 1\}$. We also have an even more restricted condition. Among all the states, Δ_i is zero for all except, perhaps, two. This is due to the fact that only the states at $t = 0$ and $t = T$ can have nonzero Δ values. Any time the chain reaches state i, the chain is attempting to leave the state i with a combined rate of the sum of rates of all outgoing arcs from state i in the state transition diagram. Therefore, the chain continuously stays in that state i for an expected amount of time given by $\frac{1}{\sum_{j=0}^{\infty} \alpha_{ij}}$. Successive entries to the state result in the same expected amount of time of stay since the behavior of the chain depends only on the fact that the chain is in state i

and nothing else of the past. Therefore, the expectation of the total amount of time spent in state i over a time interval T is

$$q_i T = E[\mathcal{D}_i] \frac{1}{\sum_{j=0}^{\infty} \alpha_{ij}} \quad \text{or} \tag{4.44}$$

$$E[\mathcal{D}_i] = q_i T \sum_{j=0}^{\infty} \alpha_{ij}, \quad i = 0, 1, \cdots . \tag{4.45}$$

Of the departures from state i causing the system to enter various different states, the expected number of times the system enters state j is proportional to α_{ij}. Summing up all such entries into state j we have

$$E[\mathcal{A}_j] = T \sum_{k=0}^{\infty} q_k \alpha_{kj}, \quad j = 0, 1, \cdots . \tag{4.46}$$

We know that

$$E[\mathcal{A}_i] = E[\mathcal{D}_i] + E[\Delta_i] \tag{4.47}$$

and the absolute value of Δ_i is no more than 1. Therefore,

$$\lim_{T \to \infty} \frac{1}{T} E[\mathcal{A}_i] = \lim_{T \to \infty} \frac{1}{T} E[\mathcal{D}_i] + \lim_{T \to \infty} \frac{1}{T} E[\Delta_i] \tag{4.48}$$

$$= \lim_{T \to \infty} \frac{1}{T} E[\mathcal{D}_i] \quad i = 0, 1, \cdots . \tag{4.49}$$

Using the above in equations (4.45) and (4.46), we have

$$q_i \sum_{j=0}^{\infty} \alpha_{ij} = \sum_{k=0}^{\infty} q_k \alpha_{ki}. \tag{4.50}$$

Since the expected fractions of time of occupancies of different states by the system sum to one, we also have

$$\sum_{i=0}^{\infty} q_i = 1. \tag{4.51}$$

Equations (4.50) and (4.51) for $q_0, q_1, \cdots$ are exactly the same as the balance equations for the equilibrium state probabilities p_i, $i = 0, 1, \cdots$. Therefore, we have the following result.

THEOREM 4.4
If the balance equations for the equilibrium state probabilities of a continuous parameter Markov chain possess a unique solution, the long-term expected fractions of time occupancies of different states respectively correspond to their equilibrium state probabilities. □

It is very important to note that the above Theorem 4.4 *does not* assume the condition that the system is known to be in equilibrium at any time instant. It does assume that the balance equations possess a unique solution. Therefore, we have

$$E[\lim_{t \to \infty} \frac{1}{t} T_i] = q_i = p_i, \tag{4.52}$$

the equilibrium state probability.

DEFINITION 4.10 *Let the chain be in equilibrium and observed starting from some arbitrary time instant $t = 0$. The random variable $A_i(t)$ is defined as the total number of customer arrivals that enter the system while the chain is in state i, during the time period $[0, t)$. The random variable $A(t) = \sum_{i=0}^{\infty} A_i(t)$ is the total number of all arrivals of customers up to and including time instant t. The quantity $\overline{A}(t)$ is the random variable corresponding to the observed arrival rate up to and including time t. That is,*

$$\overline{A}(t) = \frac{A(t)}{t}. \tag{4.53}$$

The number of customers in the system at a time instant is a random variable $N(t)$. The time average number of customers up to and including time instant t is another random variable defined as

$$\overline{N}(t) = \frac{1}{t} \int_{\tau=0}^{t} N(\tau) d\tau. \tag{4.54}$$

Let $D(t)$ be the integer random variable corresponding to the number of customers who have completed their response time and departed by time instant t. The average rate of departure over $[0, t)$ is

$$\overline{D}(t) = \frac{D(t)}{t}. \tag{4.55}$$

Individual customers experience a response time which is a random variable. Let $i = 1, 2, \cdots$ be the serial numbers of customers arriving in sequence, starting from the observation time instant of $t = 0$. Let $R_l(i)$ be the response time of the l-th of the subsequence of arrivals counted during the times that the state of the chain is i. Let R_i be the random variable response time of customer i. The average of response times of all the customers who have completed their response times and departed by time instant t is a random variable defined as

$$\overline{R}(t) = \frac{1}{D(t)} \sum_{j=1}^{D(t)} R_j. \tag{4.56}$$

Over a time of observation $t = [0, T)$, let T_i be the random variable corresponding to the total amount of time spent in state i. ☐

THEOREM 4.5

Let $K(t)$ be the random variable number of state transitions over a time period of operation given by t. As the real (nonrandom) variable time tends to infinity, each of the random variables, the number of state transitions of the chain, numbers of arrivals, the number of departures, and the number of state transitions of the Markov chain tend to infinity, with probability one. That is,

$$P[\lim_{t\to\infty} K(t) = \infty] = 1 \qquad (4.57)$$

$$P[\lim_{t\to\infty} A_i(t) = \infty] = 1, \quad i = 0, 1, \cdots \qquad (4.58)$$

$$P[\lim_{t\to\infty} A(t) = \infty] = 1 \qquad (4.59)$$

$$P[\lim_{t\to\infty} D(t) = \infty] = 1, \qquad (4.60)$$

Here is some elaboration about the meaning of the statement. It implies that the total number of arrivals seen as the observation time tends to infinity *can be* finite as opposed to being infinity. However that such an event of observing only a finite number of arrivals over an infinite time period occurs with zero probability. Alternatively, the number of arrivals increasing without bounds as time increases without bounds is *almost certain*, but not *certain*, as defined in Section 2.6.1.

Proof

The proof is based on the simple fact that the probability of an exponential random variable taking an outcome of infinity is zero. The sample space of an exponential random variable is $[0, \infty)$. Let the rate of the exponential random variable be α. Consider the probability

$$P[X \geq x] = \exp(-\alpha x) \qquad (4.61)$$

so that

$$P[X \to \infty] = 0. \qquad (4.62)$$

The infinite additivity extension of the axioms of probability stated in equation A.1 is useful and repeated below. If an infinite sequence of events $e_1, e_2, \ldots$ are mutually exclusive,

$$P[e_1 \cup e_2 \cup \cdots] = P[e_1] + P[e_2] + \cdots. \qquad (4.63)$$

This in turn implies that if the infinite sequence of events $e_1, e_2, \ldots$ are not mutually exclusive,

$$P[e_1 \cup e_2 \cup \cdots] \leq P[e_1] + P[e_2] + \cdots. \qquad (4.64)$$

Therefore, if each of the infinite sequence of random variables X_1, X_2, ... satisfies

$$P[X_i \to \infty] = 0, \tag{4.65}$$

then the following is true.

$$P[\text{at least one } X_i \to \infty] = 0 + 0 + \cdots \tag{4.66}$$

$$= 0. \tag{4.67}$$

Clearly, at some particular states of the Markov chain, the arrival rates of customers may be zero. The departure rate of customers is definitely zero at state zero, during which there are no customers to depart. However, the chain is irreducible and hence at every state, there is a nonzero rate of change to one or more of some other states. Therefore, the probability of the chain spending an infinite amount of time is zero for every state, based on equation (4.62). Therefore, as the amount of time of operation of the chain tends to infinity, the probability of the number of transitions tending to infinity is 1. That is

$$P\left[\lim_{t \to \infty} N(t) = \infty\right] = 1. \tag{4.68}$$

From equation (4.52), we know that the expected amount of time the chain spends in every state, $E[T_i]$ tends to infinity as time of operation tends to infinity. Therefore, the expected total amount of time the chain spends in all the states that have nonzero arrival rates also tends to infinity. Similarly, the expected total amount of time the chain spends in all the states that have nonzero departure rates tends to infinity. During all of the infinite time periods with nonzero arrival rates, the number of arrivals during each state tends to infinity with probability one, for the same reason that every exponential time period for the next arrival has zero probability of being infinity. The argument for the probability of infinite number of departures is identical, completing the proof. ⬚

Consider Poisson arrivals with a rate β over a random time period X with a pdf $f_X(x)$ whose expectation is finite and given by $E[X]$. The expected number of arrivals, $E[J]$, over the time X is given by the theorem of total expectation as

$$E[J] = \int_{x=0}^{\infty} E[J|X = x] f_X(x) dx \tag{4.69}$$

$$= \int_{x=0}^{\infty} \beta x f_X(x) dx \tag{4.70}$$

$$= \beta E[X]. \tag{4.71}$$

The arrival rates can be state dependent. The expectation of the total number of arrivals during all of the time periods of state i is $\lambda_i E[T_i]$. Therefore,

$$E[\lim_{t \to \infty} \overline{A}(t)] = E[\lim_{t \to \infty} \frac{A(t)}{t}] \tag{4.72}$$

$$= \lim_{t \to \infty} \sum_{i=0}^{\infty} \lambda_i \frac{E[T_i]}{t} \tag{4.73}$$

$$= \sum_{i=0}^{\infty} \lambda_i p_i. \tag{4.74}$$

That is, the expectation of the long-term arrival rate, which is a limit, exists and is given by the ensemble expectation of the arrival rates. Similarly, we have

$$E[\lim_{t \to \infty} \overline{D}(t)] = \sum_{i=0}^{\infty} \mu(i) p_i. \tag{4.75}$$

Consider the average response time now.

$$E\left[\lim_{t \to \infty} \frac{1}{D(t)} \sum_{j=1}^{D(t)} R_j\right] = E\left[\lim_{t \to \infty} \frac{1}{A(t)} \sum_{j=1}^{A(t)} R_j\right] \tag{4.76}$$

since $A(t)$ and $D(t)$ both tend to infinity with probability 1, as t tends to infinity. Rearrange the order of R_j in the summation by grouping the response times corresponding to arrivals occurring during different states. We have,

$$E\left[\lim_{t \to \infty} \frac{1}{D(t)} \sum_{j=1}^{D(t)} R_j\right] = E\left[\lim_{t \to \infty} \sum_{i=0}^{\infty} \frac{A_i(t)}{A(t)} \frac{1}{A_i(t)} \sum_{l=1}^{A_i(t)} R_l(i)\right]. \tag{4.77}$$

All the $R_l(i)$ have the same expectation $E[R|i]$. We know that

$$\lim_{t \to \infty} \frac{A_i(t)}{t} = \lambda_i p_i$$

with probability 1 and $\qquad$ (4.78)

$$\lim_{t \to \infty} \frac{A(t)}{t} = \sum_{i=0}^{\infty} \lambda_i p_i$$

with probability 1. $\qquad$ (4.79)

Using these, we have

$$E\left[\lim_{t \to \infty} \frac{1}{D(t)} \sum_{j=1}^{D(t)} R_j\right] = \sum_{i=0}^{\infty} \frac{\lambda_i p_i}{\sum_{j=0}^{\infty} \lambda_j p_j} E[R|i] \tag{4.80}$$

with probability one. Also, the inner average in equation (4.77) given by

$$\frac{1}{A_i(t)} \sum_{l=1}^{A_i(t)} R_l(i)$$

is an average of iid random variables with a finite expectation and a finite variance. Therefore, when this average is taken in the limit, the variance of the limiting random variable

$$\lim_{t \to \infty} \frac{1}{D(t)} \sum_{j=1}^{D(t)} R_j$$

is zero. Another byproduct of the above derivation is that a_i, the probability that an arriving customer sees state i in equation (4.35) evaluates to the intuitively satisfying

$$a_i = \frac{\lambda_i p_i}{\sum_{j=0}^{\infty} \lambda_j p_j}.$$

Finally, note that $N(t) = A(t) - D(t)$ at every time instant t. Whereas $A(t)$ and $D(t)$ are cumulative, monotonically nondecreasing, and generally increase as t increases, $N(t)$ is the number of customers and it fluctuates. The equilibrium probability and the expected fraction of time the system sees an infinite number of customers is 0, from Corollary 4.2. Therefore, we have

$$E\left[\lim_{t \to \infty} \frac{1}{t} N(t)\right] = E\left[\lim_{t \to \infty} \frac{1}{t}(A(t) - D(t))\right] \tag{4.81}$$

$$= 0. \tag{4.82}$$

Each of the above random variables are cumulative averages of independent (but not necessarily identical) random variables. From Theorem 2.2 in Chapter 2, their limiting variances are all zero. The foregoing discussion is formally stated in the following theorem.

THEOREM 4.6

Let a continuous time state dependent queue be an irreducible Markov chain with a unique solution for balance equations and let it function in equilibrium starting from time $t = 0$. Let n_i be the number of customers in the system when the state of the system is i. Let $n_0 = 0$ and $n_\infty = \infty$.

1. *The number of arrivals, the number of transitions, and the number of departures each tends to infinity, with probability one, as time tends to infinity.*

2. *The random variables corresponding to long-term averages of the arrival rate, departure rate, response time, the state $S(t)$, and the number of customers satisfy the following properties.*

   (a) *Their expectations correspond to their respective ensemble expectations. That is,*

   $$\lim_{t \to \infty} E[\overline{A}(t)] = E\left[\lim_{t \to \infty} \frac{1}{t} A(t)\right] = \sum_{i=0}^{\infty} \lambda_i p_i \qquad (4.83)$$

   $$\lim_{t \to \infty} E[\overline{D}(t)] = E[\lim_{t \to \infty} \frac{1}{t} D(t)] = \sum_{i=0}^{\infty} \mu_i p_i \qquad (4.84)$$

   $$\lim_{t \to \infty} E[\overline{S}(t)] = E[\lim_{t \to \infty} \frac{1}{t} S(t)] = \sum_{i=0}^{\infty} i p_i \qquad (4.85)$$

   $$\lim_{t \to \infty} E[\overline{N}(t)] = E[\lim_{t \to \infty} \frac{1}{t} \int_{\tau=0}^{t} N(\tau)] = \sum_{i=0}^{\infty} n_i p_i \qquad (4.86)$$

   $$\lim_{t \to \infty} E[\overline{R}(t)] = E[\lim_{t \to \infty} \frac{1}{D(t)} \sum_{j=1}^{D(t)} R_j] = \sum_{i=0}^{\infty} E[R|i] a_i \qquad (4.87)$$

   (b)

   $$\lim_{t \to \infty} E[\overline{A}(t)] = \lim_{t \to \infty} E[\overline{D}(t)] \text{ so that} \qquad (4.88)$$

   $$\sum_{i=0}^{\infty} \lambda_i p_i = \sum_{i=0}^{\infty} \mu_i p_i \qquad (4.89)$$

   (c) *The limiting variances are all zero.* ▢

In other words, the random variables of overall arrival rate, departure rate, the state, and response time corresponding to the averages over the time variables are all statistically steady. Their limits exist with probability one. Their limiting expectations respectively converge to corresponding ensemble averages. All their limiting variances converge to zero. These properties together are referred to as the ergodicity property of Markov chains. They are favorable to the applicability of a result connecting the overall time averages of arrival rate of customers, number of customers in the system, and the response time. This is known as the Little's result. A particular motivation to develop and use the Little's result is that while the equilibrium probabilities, the expected number in the system, the expected arrival rates are simple to evaluate, the expected response time is not, in general, due to the difficulty of evaluating $E[R|i]$.

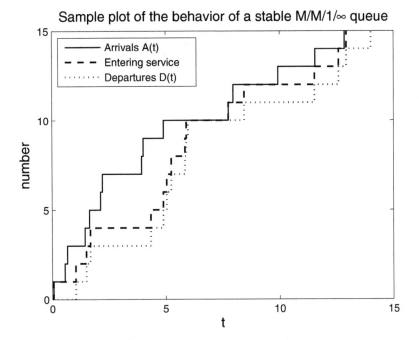

FIGURE 4.8: Use of time plots of arrivals and departures to derive Little's result

---

4.7 Little's Result

A surprisingly generalized equation connecting the long-term averages of the arrival rate, number of customers in a system, and their response time holds. The result holds for any enclosure with statistically steady input and output of integer numbers of customers. Let us first concentrate on the FIFO case. Relaxing this assumption is easy, as we will see later.

4.7.1 FIFO case

Study a typical plot of arrivals $A(t)$ and departures $D(t)$ plotted in Figure 4.8. In Figure 4.8, each horizontal bar is the response time of some job. Therefore, the total area between the two plots $A(t)$ and $D(t)$, denoted by $S(t)$ is the sum of all response times of all jobs.

$$S(t) = \text{ total area } = A(t)\overline{R}(t).$$

Therefore, the total area is also the integral of $N(t) = A(t) - D(t)$ over time up to t. So,

$$S(t) = \int_0^t N(t)dt = t\overline{N}(t) \tag{4.90}$$

where $\overline{N}(t)$ is the average number of customers in the system up to time t. We know that

$$\lim_{t \to \infty} \frac{A(t) - D(t)}{t} = 0 \tag{4.91}$$

with probability one.

$$S(t) = A(t)\overline{R}(t) = t\overline{N}(t) \quad \text{and} \tag{4.92}$$

$$\overline{N}(t) = \frac{A(t)}{t}\overline{R}(t) = \overline{\lambda}(t)\,\overline{R}(t). \tag{4.93}$$

For every sample function of an FIFO queue for which limits for $\overline{N}(t)$, $\overline{\lambda}(t)$, and $\overline{R}(t)$ exist as $t \to \infty$, we have that the average number in the system equals the average arrival rate multiplied by the average response time. In the case of state dependent queues whose behavior are governed by equilibrium Markov chains, we know that these limits exist with probability one. We know that the expectations of long-term averages are the same as the expectations of the ensemble or the sample space. Therefore, for an FIFO equilibrium state dependent queuing system, we have

$$E[N] = \lambda E[R] \tag{4.94}$$

where λ is the overall arrival rate, $E[R]$ is the expected response time of a customer, and $E[N]$ is the expected number of customers in the system. We also know that the variance of the long-term averages of the arrival rate, the number in the system, and the response time of customers are zero.

4.7.2   Non-FIFO case

Let a_i and d_i be the arrival and departing time instants respectively, of the ith job. The only difference in the sample functions of Figure 4.8 is that the order of departing customers may be different. However, the total area $\sum_i (d_i - a_i)$ is the same even if the order of departure time instants is different. All other arguments stay the same. This result is indeed powerful.

Little's result implicitly assumes that all the customers are statistically identical so that all of them have the same expected response time. In some cases, it may not be advisable to make such an assumption. An illustrative example is the following case of noninteracting systems enclosed in an imaginary box merely for the sake of applying Little's result. Consider two independent M/M/1/∞ queues being fed by two independent arrival streams of customers with arrival rates λ_1 and λ_2, respectively. Let the expected response times be $E[R_1]$ and $E[R_2]$, different for the two systems. Now, enclose the two in a box. Let the arrival streams come from a single stream with rate $\lambda_1 + \lambda_2$, probabilistically split into two substreams of rates λ_1 and λ_2. Applying Little's result to this large box will give us an overall expected response time of

$$\frac{\lambda_1 E[R_1] + \lambda_2 E[R_2]}{\lambda_1 + \lambda_2}. \tag{4.95}$$

The above is not strictly erroneous, but we can get better performance figures for the two individual queues, instead of clubbing them into a single stream and evaluating an overall expectation.

Example 4.3
Into a restaurant, customers come in at the rate of 100 per hour to attempt dining. Customers wait in a separate lounge to be seated and this takes quite some time, occasionally. As a consequence, on the average, 10% of the customers that come in leave without dining. Customers who eventually dine take an average of 40 minutes in the dining hall. The dining hall has a capacity of 20% in excess of the average number of customers dining at any time.

Determine the capacity of the dining hall, in terms of the number of customers that can be simultaneously dining. ▯

Solution
The arrival rate into the dining hall is 90% of the total arrival rate and it is 90 customers per hour. The average time spent by a customer in the dining hall is 40 minutes = $\frac{2}{3}$ hour. Applying Little's result, we get the average number of customers in the dining hall as 60. The capacity is 1.2 times the average number and it is 72. ▯

Many other performance figures of state-dependent queues, such as average number of busy servers, average service time, average waiting time, etc., depend on the peculiarity of construction of the physical systems. Some very important and illustrative examples of these are studied next.

4.8 Application Systems

4.8.1 Constant rate finite buffer M/M/1/k system

$$\lambda_i = \lambda, \quad i = 0, \cdots, k-1 \tag{4.96}$$

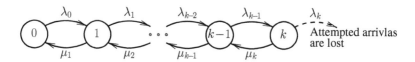

FIGURE 4.9:   The M/M/1/k state transition diagram

$$\lambda_k = \lambda, \quad \text{but arrivals at state } k \text{ are lost.} \tag{4.97}$$

$$\mu_i = \mu, \quad i = 1, \cdots, k \tag{4.98}$$

$$\mu_0 = 0, \quad \text{of course.} \tag{4.99}$$

Let $\rho = \frac{\lambda}{\mu}$.

$$\prod_{i=1}^{n} \frac{\lambda_{i-1}}{\mu_i} = \left(\frac{\lambda}{\mu}\right)^n, \quad n = 1, 2, \cdots, k, \tag{4.100}$$

$$1 + \sum_{n=1}^{k} \prod_{i=1}^{n} \frac{\lambda_{i-1}}{\mu_i} = \sum_{n=0}^{m} \left(\frac{\lambda}{\mu}\right)^n = \frac{1 - \rho^{k+1}}{1 - \rho}, \tag{4.101}$$

$$p_0 = \frac{1 - \rho}{1 - \rho^{k+1}}. \tag{4.102}$$

As expected, $\rho \geq 1$ is also possible and we still get nonzero state probabilities. From equation (4.22),

$$p_n = \rho^n \frac{1 - \rho}{1 - \rho^{k+1}}. \tag{4.103}$$

As a special case, if $\rho = 1$,

$$p_n = \frac{1}{k + 1}, \quad n = 0, \cdots, k. \tag{4.104}$$

Performance figures
Load

$$P[\text{busy}] = 1 - p_0 \tag{4.105}$$

$$= 1 - \frac{1 - \rho}{1 - \rho^{k+1}} \tag{4.106}$$

$$= \frac{\rho - \rho^{k+1}}{1 - \rho^{k+1}} \tag{4.107}$$

$$p_b = P[\text{blocking}] = \rho^k \frac{1 - \rho}{1 - \rho^{k+1}} \tag{4.108}$$

Throughput

$$E[Y] = \sum_{i=0}^{k-1} \lambda p_i = (1 - p_k)\lambda, \quad \text{from the input side} \tag{4.109}$$

$$= \sum_{i=1}^{k} \mu p_i = (1 - p_0)\mu \quad \text{at the output side} \tag{4.110}$$

$$= \frac{\rho - \rho^{k+1}}{1 - \rho^{k+1}} \mu = \frac{1 - \rho^k}{1 - \rho^{k+1}} \lambda. \tag{4.111}$$

Fraction of lost jobs

In this case, the rate of attempted arrivals is constant at λ. The expected number of lost jobs in a unit time is λp_k. Therefore, fraction of lost jobs is

$$\frac{\lambda p_k}{\lambda} = p_k, \tag{4.112}$$

$$p_k = \frac{\rho^k - \rho^{k+1}}{1 - \rho^{k+1}}. \tag{4.113}$$

Expected number in the system

$$E[N] = \overline{n} \tag{4.114}$$

$$= \sum_{n=1}^{k} n p_n \tag{4.115}$$

$$= \frac{(1 - \rho)}{1 - \rho^{k+1}} \sum_{n=1}^{k} n \rho^n \tag{4.116}$$

$$= \frac{(1 - \rho)\rho}{1 - \rho^{k+1}} \frac{d}{d\rho} \sum_{n=1}^{k} \rho^n \tag{4.117}$$

$$= \frac{(1-\rho)\rho}{1-\rho^{k+1}} \frac{d}{d\rho} \rho \sum_{k=0}^{k-1} \rho^k \qquad (4.118)$$

$$= \frac{(1-\rho)\rho}{1-\rho^{k+1}} \frac{d}{d\rho} \left[\rho \frac{1-\rho^k}{1-\rho} \right] \qquad (4.119)$$

$$= \frac{\rho[1-(k+1)\rho^k + k\rho^{k+1}]}{(1-\rho)(1-\rho^{k+1})}. \qquad (4.120)$$

The final expression is obtained by simply differentiating as required and simplifying.

Expected response time

This is obtained by applying the Little's result.

$$E[R] = \frac{E[N]}{E[Y]} \qquad (4.121)$$

$$= \frac{\rho[1-(k+1)\rho^k + \rho^{k+1}]}{(1-\rho)(1-\rho^{k+1})} \times \frac{1}{\frac{1-\rho^k}{1-\rho^{k+1}}\lambda} \qquad (4.122)$$

$$= \frac{1}{\mu - \lambda} \times \frac{1-(k+1)\rho^k + k\rho^{(k+1)}}{1-\rho^k}. \qquad (4.123)$$

4.8.2 Forward data link with a finite buffer

Let us generalize the forward data link analysis of Section 3.12 further with a finite buffer at the receiver queue. The transmitter queue at station A has unlimited buffer but the receiver queue at station B has a finite buffer and packets are dropped at the receiver queue in station B if too many packets come in during a short time. Let the receiver queue at station B have room for only k packets, including any packet under service. The overall input at the receiver queue in station B continues to be Poisson due to the Poisson nature of departures from the M/M/1/∞ transmitter queue in station A. All other aspects and representative parameters are the same as in Section 3.12. Let p_b be the probability of blocking (or dropping) at the receiver queue. This blocking probability is a function of several parameters and will remain unknown until later in the analysis. The probability of a packet entering the receiver queue and it being correct (nonerroneous) is

$$p_c = (1-p_b)(1-e_f) \qquad (4.124)$$

since blocking and packet errors are not influenced by one another. Expected number of transmissions per correct receipt of a packet is

$$\frac{1}{(1-p_b)(1-e_f)}. \qquad (4.125)$$

The combined arrival rate of packets for transmission and all retransmissions at the transmitter A is

$$\frac{\lambda}{(1-p_b)(1-e_f)}.$$ (4.126)

This is also the "attempted" arrival rate at the receiver B. Note that this emphasizes that there is no packet loss in the propagation channel. The propagation channel may only add noise. Any packet loss is due only to the finite buffer at the receiver. Once the receiver successfully receives and processes the packet, any packet error due to added noise during propagation is detected. The time for receiving a bit is the bit-width y and the average number of bits in the packet is $\frac{1}{q}$. Therefore, the service rate at the receiver queue is $\frac{q}{y}$ packets per unit time. The normalized attempted load in the receiver queue is

$$\rho = \frac{\lambda y}{q(1-p_b)(1-e_f)}.$$ (4.127)

From equation (4.108) giving the probability of blocking for a finite buffer M/M/1 queue, we have

$$p_b = \rho^k \frac{1-\rho}{1-\rho^{k+1}}.$$ (4.128)

If we substitute for ρ from equation (4.127) into equation (4.128) for p_b we obtain a nonlinear equation for the unknown p_b in terms of all other quantities about the system. The expected response time for one pass can be obtained by using the Little's result. The overall expected response time including possible multiple passes is

$$E[R] = \frac{E[R| \text{ one pass }]}{(1-p_b)(1-e_f)}.$$ (4.129)

The overall objective is to minimize the expected response time as a function of the control parameter, which is the bit-width y. The corresponding mathematical expressions are algebraically cumbersome. Clearly, this is a nonlinear optimization over one variable y. Numerical techniques using commercial software such as Matlab are fairly straightforward to implement.

4.8.3   M/M/∞ or immediate service

Imagine that we have an unlimited number of servers, each with an iid service rate μ, and a constant arrival rate of λ. Therefore, anytime a customer arrives, its service will begin instantaneously. We are interested in finding the probability mass function of the number of customers in the system. The departure rate is state dependent and is $n\mu$ where n is the state, since all the busy servers (as many as the number of customers) will be outputting a job each at a rate of μ. The arrival rate is constant, λ. The state transition diagram is shown in Figure 4.10. From the balance equations,

$$n\mu p_n = \lambda p_{n-1}, \ n \geq 1,$$ (4.130)

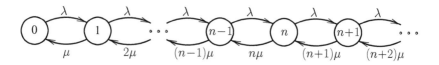

FIGURE 4.10: State diagram of an M/M/∞ queue

$$p_n = \frac{\lambda}{n\mu}p_{n-1} = \frac{\lambda^2}{n(n-1)\mu^2}p_{n-2} = \cdots = \frac{\lambda^n}{n!\mu^n}p_0 \qquad (4.131)$$

$$p_n = \frac{\rho^n}{n!}p_0. \qquad (4.132)$$

Summing all the state probabilities,

$$\sum_{n=0}^{\infty} p_n = p_0 \sum_{n=0}^{\infty} \frac{\rho^n}{n!} = p_0 e^{\rho} = 1. \qquad (4.133)$$

Hence,

$$p_0 = e^{-\rho} \qquad (4.134)$$

$$p_n = \frac{e^{-\rho}\rho^n}{n!}. \qquad (4.135)$$

That is, the number in the system is Poisson distributed with the dimensionless parameter ρ.

Performance Figures

$$E[N] = \bar{n} = \rho \qquad (4.136)$$

from the expectation of the Poisson random variable.

$$P[\text{ empty system }] = p_0 = e^{-\rho}. \qquad (4.137)$$

4.8.4   Parallel servers

By now it should be clear that in most cases, the important step is to write the correct state transition diagram. Using this, the state probabilities can be evaluated

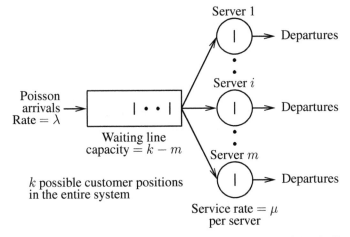

FIGURE 4.11:   Queue with parallel servers and a finite buffer

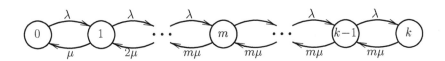

FIGURE 4.12:   State transition diagram for the parallel server case

from first principles, without using the general formulas. The second step is to formulate and evaluate interesting performance figures peculiar to the applications. Let us consider m parallel servers with a capacity k in the system including those under service. Each server's service rate is μ. Arrival rate is λ. Customers wait in a single line until a server is free. If more than one server is free when a customer gets a chance to get into service mode, the customer chooses one at random. Alternatively, under the same circumstances, the management uses a random scheduling algorithm to assign one of the free servers to the customer. The queuing system is shown in Figure 4.11. The state transition diagram is in Figure 4.12.

$$\lambda_n = \lambda, n = 0, 1, 2, \cdots k - 1, \tag{4.138}$$

$$\lambda_k = \lambda, \text{ but such customers will be lost}, \tag{4.139}$$

$$\mu_i = i\mu, i = 1, \cdots, m, \tag{4.140}$$

$$\mu_n = m\mu, m < n \le k, \tag{4.141}$$

$$p_i = \frac{\lambda}{i\mu} p_{i-1}, i = 1, \cdots, m, \tag{4.142}$$

$$p_n = \frac{\lambda}{m\mu} p_{n-1}, n = m, \cdots, k. \tag{4.143}$$

The solutions for these equations with $\sum_{j=0}^{\infty} p_j = 1$ are cumbersome and are not particularly illustrative. Let us just note that they can be easily evaluated for any given numerical values of the parameters and proceed.

Performance Figures

$$P[\text{all servers are free}] = p_0. \tag{4.144}$$

$$P[\text{all servers are busy}] = \sum_{k=m}^{k} p_k. \tag{4.145}$$

$$E[\text{number of busy servers}] = \sum_{i=1}^{m} ip_i + m \sum_{i=m+1}^{k} p_i. \tag{4.146}$$

$$E[N_w] = \sum_{i=m+1}^{k} (i - m)p_i, \tag{4.147}$$

the expected number in waiting.
Throughput

$$E[Y] = \lambda(1 - p_k). \tag{4.148}$$

Expected response time

$$E[R] = \frac{E[N]}{E[Y]}. \tag{4.149}$$

For average waiting time, $E[T_w]$, we have two ways

$$E[T_w] = E[R] - \frac{1}{\mu}. \tag{4.150}$$

Also, we can apply Little's result to an imaginary box around the waiting line and obtain

$$E[T_w] = \frac{E[N_w]}{E[Y]}. \tag{4.151}$$

Fraction of time a server is busy
If k servers are busy at a time instant, all combinations of k servers are equally probable since

1. a server is chosen at random by the customer if more than one is available to choose from and

2. service times at all the servers are iid.

Therefore,

$$P[\text{a particular server busy}|k \text{ are busy}] = \frac{k}{m}, \quad k \le m \tag{4.152}$$

$$P[\text{busy}] = P[\text{a particular server busy}] \tag{4.153}$$

$$= \sum_{j=1}^{m} \frac{j}{m} p_j + \sum_{j=m+1}^{j} p_j. \tag{4.154}$$

The mathematical expression for the blocking probability in an M/M/m/m queue is known as Erlang's B formula. The expression for the probability that an arriving customer waits in an M/M/m/m queue is known as Erlang's C formula. These expressions were originally derived by Agner Krarup Erlang, a Danish scientist (1878–1929), for (and extensively used in) traditional telephone systems. These derivations are left as exercises listed at the end of this chapter.

Example 4.4
Poisson arrivals with rate 28 per second enter a single queue for processing by one of two *iid* exponential servers, each with service rate 20 jobs per second. If a job arrives when the system is empty, it chooses one of the servers at random. The total number of jobs that the entire system can hold is only 3 (including any under service). Arrivals to a full system are lost. Evaluate the expected response time of a job that got admitted into the system. ▯

Solution
The state diagram has states 0, 1, 2, and 3 only, with constant arrival rate of 28. The rate from state 1 to 0 is 20. The rate from 2 to 1 as well as from 3 to 2 is 40. Writing balance equations,

$$28p_0 = 20p_1 \tag{4.155}$$

$$p_1 = 1.4p_0 \tag{4.156}$$

$$28p_1 = 40p_2 \tag{4.157}$$

$$p_2 = 0.7p_1 = (0.7)1.4p_0 \tag{4.158}$$

$$28p_2 = 40p_3 \qquad\qquad (4.159)$$

$$p_3 = 0.7p_2 = (0.7)^2 1.4p_0 \qquad (4.160)$$

$$p_0[1 + 1.4 + (0.7)1.4 + (0.7)^2 1.4] = 1 \qquad (4.161)$$

$$p_0 = \frac{1}{4.066} \qquad\qquad (4.162)$$

$$E[N] = \frac{1}{4.066}[1.4 + (0.98)2 + (0.686)3] \qquad (4.163)$$

$$= 1.3325. \qquad\qquad (4.164)$$

The effective arrival rate (rate of admitted jobs), η is given by

$$\eta = \lambda(1 - p_3) = 23.28 \qquad (4.165)$$

$$E[R] = \frac{E[N]}{\eta} = 0.057 \text{ seconds.} \qquad (4.166)$$

□

4.8.5   Client-server model

The system and the "customers" are defined as follows. The k client machines depend on a central server for some service. Each client machine can be in two modes: local, during which the client has no service request pending at the server. During the local mode, a client is working on other things or preparing to send a request to the server. The "local mode" time is modeled as an exponential random variable. Note that the mean local mode time can depend on the person sitting at the client machine. However, to keep the details simple, and to illustrate the concepts better, clients are all iid. The second mode in which each client can be is the "request" mode, after sending a request for the server's function. These requests are queued up in front of the server. Finally, each client can send only one request at a time and can have only one request for service pending at the server. Service time requirements for the client's requests are iid exponential with parameter μ. The physical nature of the function of the system is depicted in Figure 4.13. The buffer capacity at the server needs to be only m. There is no waiting line at any client machine.

The state transition diagram for the Markov chain is shown in Figure 4.14. For a given set of numerical values, obtaining the equilibrium probabilities and performance figures is straightforward, as in other cases. The most important performance

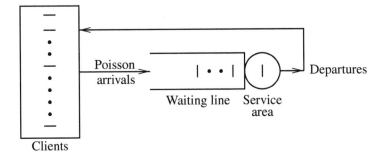

FIGURE 4.13: Queuing model for the client-server problem

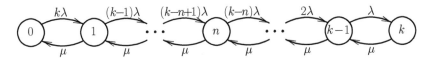

FIGURE 4.14: State transition diagram for the client-server queue

figure is the expected response time in the the server queue which can be evaluated with the help of Little's result.

Example 4.5
Balking is the phenomenon in which a customer arrival rate reduces when a longer waiting line is seen. Let us consider another simple numerical example to illustrate it. We have two identical servers and an additional waiting room for only one more customer.

Arrival rates:

- $\lambda_0 = \lambda_1$, the arrival rate when there is no waiting.

- $\lambda_2 < \lambda_1$, indicating balking.

- $\lambda_3, \lambda_4, \cdots = 0$

Let us use $\lambda_0 = \lambda_1 = 2, \lambda_2 = 1, \mu = 1$. Analyze the system. ⬜

Solution
Note that the system is always stable due to a finite buffer. That is, the "effective" $\lambda_3 = 0$ meaning that even if customers attempt to arrive when the system is full, they get lost. Writing balance equations

$$2p_0 = p_1 \Rightarrow p_1 = 2p_0, \tag{4.167}$$

$$2p_1 = 2p_2 \Rightarrow p_2 = p_1 = 2p_0, \tag{4.168}$$

$$p_2 = 2p_3 \Rightarrow p_3 = \frac{p_2}{2} = p_0, \tag{4.169}$$

$$p_0 + p_1 + p_2 + p_3 = p_0 + 2p_0 + 2p_0 + p_0 = 1. \tag{4.170}$$

Therefore,

$$p_0 = \frac{1}{6} \tag{4.171}$$

$$p_1 = \frac{2}{6} \tag{4.172}$$

$$p_2 = \frac{2}{6} \tag{4.173}$$

$$p_3 = \frac{1}{6}. \tag{4.174}$$

Performance figures:

$$\text{Throughput} = \sum_{i=0}^{N-1} \lambda_i p_i \tag{4.175}$$

$$= \frac{1}{6}(2 \cdot 1 + 2 \cdot 2 + 1 \cdot 2) \tag{4.176}$$

$$= \frac{4}{3}. \tag{4.177}$$

Throughput is also given by:

$$\sum_{i=1}^{N} \mu_i p_i = \frac{1}{6}(1 \cdot 2 + 2 \cdot 2 + 2 \cdot 1) \tag{4.178}$$

$$= \frac{4}{3} \tag{4.179}$$

$$\bar{n} = E[\text{number in system}] \tag{4.180}$$

$$= \sum_{i=1}^{N} i p_i \tag{4.181}$$

$$= \frac{1}{6}(1 \cdot 2 + 2 \cdot 2 + 3 \cdot 1) \tag{4.182}$$

$$= \frac{3}{2}$$

$$E[R] = \frac{\overline{n}}{\text{Throughput}} \qquad (4.183)$$

$$= \frac{9}{8}. \qquad (4.184)$$

□

Example 4.6

A single exponential server with a service rate of 10 jobs per second is input with the following peculiar process of jobs. Single Poisson arrivals occur with a rate of 3 jobs per second. Additionally and independently, pairs of jobs arrive with a Poisson distribution of 1 pair per second. There is room for only 4 jobs including any being served. If a pair of jobs arrives when the system already has 3 jobs, one of them (at random) enters the system and the other gets lost. Arrivals to a full buffer are lost. Develop the state transition rates of the Markov chain for the above system. Let $p_0, ..., p_4$ be the steady state probabilities of the corresponding states. Determine the following as functions of $p_0, ..., p_4$.

1. The fraction of lost jobs.

2. Among the successful jobs, the ratio of individually arriving jobs to jobs arriving in pairs.

□

Solution

The transition rates $r_{i,j}$ from state i to state j are as follows. All the numerical values for rates are in number of jobs per second.

$$r_{i,i+1} = 3, \quad \text{for} \quad i = 0, 1, 2. \qquad (4.185)$$

$$r_{i,i+2} = 1, \quad \text{for} \quad i = 0, 1, 2. \qquad (4.186)$$

$$r_{i,i-1} = 10, \quad \text{for } i = 1, 2, 3, 4. \qquad (4.187)$$

$$r_{3,4} = 3 + 1 = 4. \qquad (4.188)$$

All other rates are zero. The rate $r_{3,4}$ has two components. The component of 3 is due to single arrivals when the state is 3. The component of 1 is due to a pair arriving when the state is 3 and one of the pair being lost due to buffer full condition. When the state is 3, jobs are lost with a rate of 1 due to pairs of jobs arriving with a rate

1 and one of the pair being lost. When the state is 4, individual job arrivals are lost at a rate of 3. Both jobs of pairs of arrivals at the rate of 1 pair are also lost making the loss rate 5 when the state is 4. Therefore, the total rate of lost jobs is $p_3 + 5p_4$. Rate of attempted arrivals is always three plus one pair, that is a total of five jobs per second. Therefore, fraction of lost jobs is

$$\frac{p_3 + 5p_4}{5}. \tag{4.189}$$

Rate of successful jobs among the individual arrivals is $3 - 3p_4$. Rate of successful jobs among pairs of arrivals is $2 - p_3 - 2p_4$. The required ratio is

$$\frac{3 - 3p_4}{2 - p_3 - 2p_4}. \tag{4.190}$$

☐

Example 4.7 Sluggish operating system

A computer system has a Poisson job arrival stream with rate λ. Payload jobs have iid exponential service time with rate μ and arrive into an unlimited size buffer. Whenever there are no payload jobs, the operating system executes internal jobs. There are two equivalent ways to model this. In the first, the system continuously executes such internal jobs. Whenever a payload job arrives, the system completes its housekeeping operations before attending to the payload job. This takes an exponential amount of time with rate α. Upon completion of a payload job, if the buffer has any other payload job, the system attends to it and does not take up internal jobs. Alternatively, the internal jobs are modeled as requiring iid exponential times with rate α and the system executes them one after another until a payload job arrives. Once such a payload job arrives, the remaining time to complete its current internal job is exponential with rate α. Both modes are equivalent from the point of view of the payload jobs.

1. Draw the state transition diagram of the Markov chain.

2. Verify that the following pmf satisfies the balance equations. Let $P[n, s]$ be the equilibrium probability of n external customers in the system with the external customer at the head of the queue being serviced. Similarly, let $P[n, b]$ be the equilibrium probability of n external customers in the system with the server executing the internal system job; b stands for *blocked*. Show that the pmf is of the form

$$P[n, s] = \frac{(1 - \rho)(1 - v)\rho}{\rho - v}\left(\rho^n - v^n\right) \tag{4.191}$$

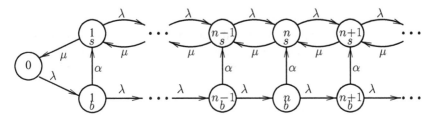

FIGURE 4.15: State transition diagram for the sluggish operating system queue

$$P[n, b] = (1 - \rho)(1 - v)v^n \tag{4.192}$$

where $n \geq 1$ is the number of external customers in the system, $\rho = \frac{\lambda}{\mu}$, and $v = \frac{\lambda}{\lambda + \alpha}$. Note that $P[0] = P[0, b]$ and $P[0, s] = 0$.

3. Solve the balance equations and obtain the above equilibrium pmf. Use $\mathcal{Z}$ transform.

4. What is the value of α for which the system collapses to the standard M/M/1/∞ queue? Verify that the results for this case corresponds to those of the M/M/1/∞ queue.

5. Show that the expected number of payload jobs in the system is

$$E[N] = \frac{\rho + v - 2\rho v}{(1 - \rho)(1 - v)}. \tag{4.193}$$

6. Specialize the result for the case when $\alpha = \mu$.

□

Solution

1. Consider the time just before and after an arrival into an empty buffer. Just before the arrival, the system is executing internal job. After an arrival the system takes an exponential amount of time with rate α to start servicing the external customer. During this time, potentially, any number of additional external customers can arrive. Therefore, it is necessary to distinguish between whether or not an external customer is being serviced for every number of customers in the system. Of course, when the system is empty of external customers, there is only one combination. The state diagram is shown in Figure 4.15. For every number of customers $n > 0$, there are two states; n with s indicating that a customer is being serviced and b indicating that the customer at the head of the queue is blocked since the system has still not recovered from internal job

it was executing before all the external customers in the system arrived. From any state (n, b), there is an arc with rate α to state (n, s) corresponding to the completion of the system job and starting servicing the external customer at the head of the queue. The rest of the state transitions are straightforward.

2. From the equations for the given pmf, $P[0] = (1 - \rho)(1 - v)$ and $P[1, s] = (1 - \rho)(1 - v)\rho$. Balancing around state 0 in Figure 4.15, we have

$$P[0]\lambda = P[1, s]\mu \tag{4.194}$$

as the balance equation. Substituting the given values of $P[0]$ and $P[1, s]$ above, the balance equation is verified to hold. Around any state $(n, b), n \geq 0$, the balance equation is

$$P[n, b](\lambda + \alpha) = P[n - 1, b]\lambda, \quad n = 1, 2, \ldots \tag{4.195}$$

The given pmf expression $P[n, b] = (1 - v)v^n$ with $v = \frac{\lambda}{\lambda + \alpha}$ satisfies this balance equation. Now, balance across a line between states corresponding to n and $n + 1$. The resulting balance equation is

$$(P[n, s] + P[n, b])\lambda = P[n + 1, s]\mu, \quad n = 1, 2, \ldots \quad \text{or} \tag{4.196}$$

$$P[n, s] + P[n, b] = \rho P[n + 1, s], \quad n = 1, 2, \ldots \tag{4.197}$$

From the given pmf for $P[n, s]$ and $P[n, b]$ respectively in equations (4.191) and (4.192), we have

$$P[n, s] + P[n, b] = (1 - \rho)(1 - v)\left(\frac{\rho^{n+1} - \rho v^n}{\rho - v} + v^n\right) \tag{4.198}$$

$$= (1 - \rho)(1 - v)\left(\frac{\rho^{n+1} - v^{n+1}}{\rho - v}\right). \tag{4.199}$$

The final expression is the same as for $P[n + 1, s]$ as seen from equation (4.191).

3. The rate $\alpha = \infty$ lets the system collapse to the standard M/M/1/∞ queue.

4.

$$E[N] = \sum_{n=0}^{\infty} n\left(P[n, s] + P[n, b]\right) \tag{4.200}$$

$$= \sum_{n=0}^{\infty} nP[n + 1, s] \quad \text{from earlier}$$

$$= \sum_{n=1}^{\infty} n\frac{(1 - \rho)(1 - v)}{\rho - v}(\rho^{n+1} - v^{n+1})$$

$$= \frac{\rho(1-v)}{\rho-v} \sum_{n=1}^{\infty}(1-\rho)\rho^n \sum_{n=1}^{\infty}(1-v)v^n \qquad (4.201)$$

$$= \frac{\rho(1-v)}{\rho-v}\frac{\rho}{1-\rho} - \frac{v(1-\rho)}{\rho-v}\frac{v}{1-v} \qquad (4.202)$$

$$= \frac{\rho+v-2\rho v}{1-\rho)(1-v)}. \qquad (4.203)$$

5. For $\alpha = \mu$, we have

$$v = \frac{\lambda}{\lambda+\mu}, \qquad (4.204)$$

$$1-v = \frac{\mu}{\lambda+\mu}, \quad \text{and} \qquad (4.205)$$

$$1-\rho = \frac{\mu-\lambda}{\mu}. \qquad (4.206)$$

Using these in $E[N]$, we obtain

$$E[N] = \frac{\mu}{\mu-\lambda} - \frac{\mu-\lambda}{\mu} \qquad (4.207)$$

$$= \frac{\rho}{1-\rho}(2-\rho) \qquad (4.208)$$

$$= \frac{\rho}{1-\rho} + \rho. \qquad (4.209)$$

The final expression points out that the expected number in the system is more than the corresponding quantity in the simple M/M/1/∞ system. This is anticipated since the service of some packets are delayed due to sluggishness of the server when an arrival occurs into an empty buffer. Indeed, whenever the system is called upon to start serving a payload customer which arrives when there are no other payload customers, the system delays starting service by an average time of $\frac{1}{\mu}$ during which an average of $\frac{\lambda}{\mu}$ additional payload customers arrive. This is the additional part of $E[N]$ over and above that in a conventional M/M/1/∞ system.

4.9   Medium Access in Local Area Networks

4.9.1   Heavily loaded channel with a contention based transmission protocol

Consider the following very simple model of continuous time Medium Access. Many computers communicate data packets over a single cable channel. At any time, at most one computer can be successfully transmitting a packet onto the cable. Therefore, the following carrier sense, collision detection (CSMA/CD) scheme is used. The totality of all channel access attempts, including reattempts, by all the computers together, is a Poisson process with a constant rate of α attempts per unit time, all the time. This rate is not decreased, even if one transmitter is successfully transmitting. At any instant of time, the channel is in one of the following states.

- Free state F: In this state, the channel is not being used by any attempted access. Any arrival of an attempt to access when the channel is in this state will change the state. The combined rate of attempted access to take the channel away from this free state is α.

- Contention followed by collision state C: This is a short but random time period. A transmitter (say transmitter A) senses the channel, finds it free, and starts transmitting. Another transmitter, B, may start transmitting a short time after A started transmission, before the electromagnetic signal from A reaches B. If no other transmitter starts transmitting within a short random period (exponential with an average of $\frac{1}{\gamma}$ time units) after A starts, there will be no more collisions for this transmission from A. This is because, after the short random time is complete, the electromagnetic signal from station A would be available all over the channel for others to sense and note that the channel is busy. After A starts, the short exponential timer with rate γ competes with any other transmission that can start with a rate α. Therefore, the probability of the original transmission being successful is $\frac{\gamma}{\alpha+\gamma}$. The probability that it will collide with another transmission is $\frac{\alpha}{\alpha+\gamma}$. Therefore, the rate of changing to the contention and collision state from state F is $\frac{\alpha^2}{\alpha+\gamma}$. The rate of changing from state F to a successful transmission state is $\frac{\alpha\gamma}{\alpha+\gamma}$. The start of the original transmission from transmitter A that is destined to meet with a collision renders the system to be in contention followed by collision state C. The residence time of state C is exponential with a rate γ.

- Recovery state R: Following a collision, both transmitters detect collision, abort transmission, and recover. The time period between the instant a collision is detected and the instant the channel becomes free again is modeled as an exponential random variable with rate δ.

- Successfully transmitting state T: After the first transmitter starts transmitting and if no other transmitter starts during the short contention period, the original transmission will continue successfully; after the contention time, every other transmitter is able to sense and detect an ongoing transmission. As argued above, the rate of attempted transmission when the channel is free is α. Once a transmission starts, other possible transmissions are attempted with the rate of α until the contention period ends. Therefore, the proportion of original attempts escaping collision is $\frac{\gamma}{\alpha+\gamma}$. The proportion of original attempts leading to collision is $\frac{\alpha}{\alpha+\gamma}$. The rate of change from the free state to the successful transmission state is $\frac{\alpha\gamma}{\alpha+\gamma}$. Once in this successful transmission state, the remaining time of transmission is memoryless with rate μ.

4.9.1.1 Consequences of modeling approximations

In reality the small time period of contention and recovery may not be accurately exponential. There is a small probability of the transmission beginning and ending before the contention period ends. However, the successful throughput contributed to this is very small. Also, the contention followed by collision state is fictitious. This state is defined to occur right when the first transmitter starts and given that it will lead to a collision, as if the system knows ahead of time that a collision is guaranteed to occur! But we do account for the probability of this event occurring. In any case, the model is for performance evaluation only. There is no suggestion to change the details of operation to suit the model. The inaccuracies in the model will be reflected in the accuracy of the results. Fortunately, the inaccuracy of the model does not lead to inconsistencies which might otherwise render the entire analysis useless.

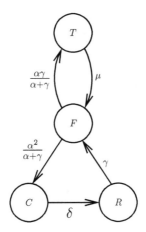

FIGURE 4.16: State transition diagram for the saturated MAC system

4.9.1.2   Analysis steps

1. Draw a complete state diagram of the Markov chain for the system. The state transition diagram is given in Figure 4.16.

2. Let P_F, P_C, P_T, and P_R be the equilibrium probabilities of corresponding states. Solve for and obtain expressions for them as functions of α, μ, γ, and δ.

3. Determine the throughput, that is, the rate of successful packet transmission.

4. Plot the throughput as a function of α when all other parameters are constants.

5. Determine expressions for other important performance figures such as the expected number of channel sensing per successful transmission, and the expected number of collisions per successful transmission.

The state diagram is very simple. Balancing around states F, C, R, and T, respectively, we obtain

$$\mu P_T = \frac{\alpha\gamma}{\alpha + \gamma} P_F \text{ or} \tag{4.210}$$

$$P_T = \frac{\alpha\gamma}{\mu(\alpha + \gamma)} P_F, \tag{4.211}$$

$$\gamma P_C = \frac{\alpha^2}{\alpha + \gamma} P_F \text{ or} \tag{4.212}$$

$$P_C = \frac{\alpha^2}{\gamma(\alpha + \gamma)} P_F, \text{ and} \tag{4.213}$$

$$\delta P_R = \gamma P_C \text{ or}$$

$$P_R = \frac{\gamma}{\delta} P_C = \frac{\alpha^2}{\delta(\alpha + \gamma)} P_F. \tag{4.214}$$

Summing all the probabilities, we have

$$P_F \left(1 + \frac{\alpha\gamma}{\mu(\alpha + \gamma)} + \frac{\alpha^2}{\gamma(\alpha + \gamma)} + \frac{\alpha^2}{\delta(\alpha + \gamma)} \right) = 1. \tag{4.215}$$

When the state of the chain is T, a packet is being successfully output at a rate of μ. Therefore, the conditional throughput is μ when the state is T and zero during other states. That is, the throughput in packets per unit time, denoted by $E[Y]$ is given by

$$E[Y] = \mu P_T = \frac{\alpha\gamma}{\alpha + \gamma} P_F \tag{4.216}$$

$$= \frac{1}{\frac{1}{\gamma} + \frac{1}{\alpha} + \frac{1}{\mu} + \frac{\alpha}{\gamma^2} + \frac{\alpha}{\gamma\delta}}. \tag{4.217}$$

The throughput is maximized by differentiating $E[Y]$ wrt α, equating it to zero, and evaluating α. Equivalently, we can minimize

$$\frac{1}{\alpha} + \alpha \left(\frac{1}{\gamma^2 + \frac{1}{\gamma\delta}} \right) \tag{4.218}$$

wrt α. The result is easily evaluated as

$$\alpha = \gamma \sqrt{\frac{\delta}{\gamma + \delta}} \tag{4.219}$$

maximizes the throughput. The maximum throughput is obtained by substituting $\gamma \sqrt{\frac{\delta}{\gamma+\delta}}$ for α in $E[Y]$. We obtain

$$\max E[Y] = \frac{1}{\frac{1}{\gamma} + \frac{2}{\gamma}\sqrt{\frac{\gamma+\delta}{\delta}} + \frac{1}{\mu}}. \tag{4.220}$$

Over Ethernet, the maximum time over which a newly started transmission can result in a collision is about 50 microseconds. Therefore, maximum time for all the transmitters to detect a collision is 100 microseconds Similarly, after a collision, a noise burst is sent by the first station that senses a collision to warn all others. This also lasts for about 50 microseconds. Using these as nominal values in our model and also an average transmission time of 1 millisecond for a packet, we have the following rates in millisecond^{-1} units.

$$\gamma = 20, \tag{4.221}$$

$$\delta = 20, \text{ and} \tag{4.222}$$

$$\mu = 1. \tag{4.223}$$

The optimal $\alpha = \frac{20}{\sqrt{2}} 14.1421$ per millisecond. The maximum possible throughput is $\frac{1}{1.05+0.1\sqrt{2}} = 0.8393$ packet per millisecond. This is a small reduction from the maximum of 1 packet per millisecond, since the average transmission of a packet takes 1 millisecond. Figure 4.17 shows a plot of the variation of the throughput as a function of α.

4.9.2 A simple contention-free LAN protocol

A LAN has m transmitters connected to it. Packets arrive into the ith buffer as a Poisson stream at a rate λ_i. All packets in all the buffers are iid and each requires an

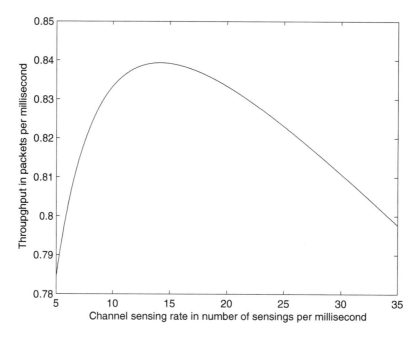

FIGURE 4.17:   Throughput as a function of sensing rate α

exponentially distributed transmission time with rate μ. At the end of a transmission, the packet includes the identification of the transmitting node that gets the right to transmit. The identity of the transmitter for this purpose is selected randomly with a probability q_i for transmitter i. All the transmitters use the same random number generating algorithms and successively selected transmitters are iid. It is possible that the next transmitter picked by a transmitting station is itself, in which case, it transmits the next packet. When it is transmitter i's turn to transmit, if it does not have any payload packet to transmit, it transmits a dummy packet whose transmission time is iid as other packets. This dummy packet includes the identification of the next transmitter.

The above description is idealized. But it has the advantage of a very well defined service time distribution that is independent of the states of the different queues. What is the time interval between successive attempts for transmission at a station i? When transmitter i gets a chance, it spends an exponential time with rate μ. Thereafter, the number of transmissions at different stations before i is scheduled again   is modified geometric with a probability of success $1 - q_i$. Including its first transmission, the number of transmissions K_i between successive chances for transmitter i has the pmf

$$P[K_i = k] = (1 - q_i)^{k-1}q_i, k = 1, \ldots. \tag{4.224}$$

Each of the K_i transmissions takes an iid exponential time with rate μ. The Laplace transform of the total time between successive chances for transmission at transmitter i is

$$\mathcal{L}_{T_i}(s) = \sum_{k=1}^{\infty} \frac{(1-q_i)^{k-1} q_i \mu^k}{(\mu+s)^k}. \tag{4.225}$$

Evaluating the geometric sum in the equation above, we obtain the result that T_i is exponential with rate $q_i \mu$. This result is analogous to the response time in an M/M/1/∞ queue evaluating to an exponential distribution. We now have the following result. Let each transmitter transmit a payload packet with rate μ when it gets a chance to transmit. If it does not have a payload packet when it gets a chance to transmit, let it transmit a dummy packet with rate μ. Then the equivalent service rate of transmitter i is $\mu_i i = q_i \mu_i$.

However, a transmitter queue in such a network is not a perfect M/M/1/∞ queue for the following reason. When the empty queue of a transmitter receives a new arrival, its service does not begin immediately, but only after a memoryless time with the rate μq_i. But as long as the buffer has packets to transmit, successive packets are transmitted contiguously, with a memoryless time of the same rate between their starting time instants. The operation of the queue of such a transmitter is identical to that of the sluggish operating system in which the average delay due to sluggishness is the same as the average service time of payload customer. Using the result from equation (4.209), we have

$$E[N_i] = \frac{\lambda_i}{\mu q_i - \lambda_i} + \frac{\lambda_i}{\mu q_i}, \quad i = 1, 2, \ldots, m \tag{4.226}$$

where λ_i is the rate of packet arrivals into the buffer of the ith transmitter, q_i is the probability with which a transmitter will be scheduled for transmission, and μ is the common rate of transmission completion whenever any transmitter is transmitting. Denote $\frac{\lambda_i}{\mu q_i}$ by ρ_i. The expected response time of a random payload packet entering the LAN at a randomly chosen transmitter is minimized by minimizing the expectation of the sum of the number of payload packets in all the transmitters. This is a consequence of the Little's result and the fact that the overall throughput $\sum_{i=1}^{m} \lambda_i$ is a constant. We have

$$E[N] = \sum_{i=1}^{m} \rho_i \left(\frac{1}{q_i - \rho_i} + \frac{1}{q_i} \right). \tag{4.227}$$

The design of the LAN requires the determination of the probability values, q_i, which will minimize $E[N]$.

Optimization

The m probabilities $q_1, \ldots, q_m$ are required to sum to 1. Use

$$q_m = 1 - \sum_{j=1}^{m-1} q_j. \tag{4.228}$$

We have

$$E[N] = \sum_{i=1}^{m-1} \rho_i \left(\frac{1}{q_i - \rho_i} + \frac{1}{\rho_i} \right) + \rho_m \left(\frac{1}{1 - \sum\limits_{j=1}^{m-1} q_j - \rho_m} + \frac{1}{1 - \sum\limits_{j=1}^{m-1} q_j} \right).$$

$$\tag{4.229}$$

In order to obtain the optimal probabilities $\{q_i\}$, take the partial derivatives of $E[N]$ wrt q_i, $i = 1, 2, \ldots, m-1$ and equate each to zero. We have

$$\frac{\partial E[N]}{\partial q_i} = \rho_i \left(\frac{-1}{(q_i - \rho_i)^2} + \frac{-1}{q_i^2} \right)$$

$$+ \rho_m \left(\frac{1}{(1 - \sum\limits_{j=1}^{m-1} q_j - \rho_m)^2} + \frac{1}{(1 - \sum\limits_{j=1}^{m-1} q_j)2} \right),$$

$$i = 1, 2, \ldots, m-1 \tag{4.230}$$

$$= 0. \tag{4.231}$$

The condition for vanishing partial derivatives simplifies to

$$\rho_i \left(\frac{1}{(q_i - \rho_i)^2} + \frac{1}{q_i^2} \right) = \rho_m \left(\frac{1}{(q_m - \rho_m)^2} + \frac{1}{q_m^2} \right), \qquad i = 1, 2 \ldots, m-1$$

$$\tag{4.232}$$

which implies that the LHS evaluates to the same quantity for every i. Denote this by a constant c. We have

$$\rho_i \left(\frac{1}{(q_i - \rho_i)^2} + \frac{1}{q_i^2} \right) = c, \qquad i = 1, 2 \ldots, m. \tag{4.233}$$

This leads to the interesting optimization problem of finding a c whose inverse functions will give us $q_1, \ldots, q_m$ that will add to one. As q_i decreases from 1 to ρ_i, the quantity c shoots up without bounds. The domain of feasible solutions is given by

$$\rho_i < q_i < 1 \quad i = 1, \ldots, m \quad \text{and} \tag{4.234}$$

$$\sum_{i=1}^{m} q_i = 1. \tag{4.235}$$

Define m functions

$$c_i(q_i) = \rho_i \left(\frac{1}{(q_i - \rho_i)^2} + \frac{1}{q_i^2} \right), \quad i = 1, 2 \ldots, m. \tag{4.236}$$

The function $c_i(q_i)$ is a strictly monotonically decreasing function of q_i in the open interval domain of $\rho_i < q_i \leq 1$. Define the function

$$q_i = g_i(c) \tag{4.237}$$

as the inverse function of $c_i(q_i)$. That is, for every given c, the quantity q_i is given by the unique value of q_i for which c_i in the equation (4.236) takes the given value of c. Clearly, $g_i(c) = q_i$ is also strictly monotonically decreasing in the open interval range of $\rho_i < q_i \leq 1$. Following is a brute-force method to evaluate the optimal solution for the transmission probabilities q_i. Evaluate and store an array for each $c_i(q_i)$ as a function of q_i over a range from $q_i = 1$ through a value close to $q_i = \rho_i$, with a fine grain size of increments in q_i. Invert the arrays so that each q_i is a function of c_i. Sweep the range of c. For each c, evaluate the corresponding values of q_i, with linear interpolation, if necessary. Find the value of c corresponding to the values of q_i summing to a value closest to one. One of the exercises at the end of this chapter suggests the study of a mathematical optimization approach.

Implementation details
There are two ways to generate the identity of the next station to transmit. In the first method, all the stations generate pseudorandom numbers with an identical algorithm and an identical seed. In this case, every transmitter knows the identity of the next station scheduled for transmission. If a transmitter gets a chance to transmit when it is empty, it still needs to transmits a dummy or a control packet so that the sequence of transmitting stations is not disturbed. In the second method, every transmitter that

gets a chance to transmit, includes in its transmitted packet, the randomly selected identification of the station for the next transmission. This is a token passing scheme, except that the sequence is not only random, but possibly with skewed probabilities.

Instead of transmitting dummy packets as suggested above, a transmitter with an empty buffer may be designed to transmit useful control packets. These can be used to exchange messages about currently estimated load at the transmitter transmitting the control packet. Other transmitters can use such parameter values to update their probability evaluations. This adaptive method to update the parameters whenever necessary is very powerful.

Another very useful feature can be incorporated to sign in transmitters that want to connect to the LAN. When a transmitter scheduled for transmission does not have any payload packet to transmit, it can transmit a short "beacon" signal which is understood to be an invitation for an alien transmitter to ask for permission to join the LAN, within a prespecified time period. This facility is contention based, since more than one alien stations can contend to join. Conventions for handling contentions would have to be designed.

A useful closed form approximation to the above solution (which is by search or mathematical programming) can be determined as follows. The composite service time is determined by accounting for sluggishness caused by dummy or control packets of size iid to payload packets. Now, let the dummy packet simply pass the token to the next transmitter in a short packet that takes a negligible time to transmit. This reduces the delay caused by sluggishness. Following through, in the analysis of the individual queues with the composite service time, neglect the entire effect of the already reduced sluggishness. Each queue then becomes an M/M/1/∞ system with arrival rate λ_i and a composite service time with a rate μq_i. This model lends itself to simple analysis.

Optimization of the M/M/1/∞ approximation
The resulting objective function for minimization is

$$E[N] = \sum_{i=1}^{m} E[N_i] \tag{4.238}$$

$$= \sum_{i=1}^{m} \frac{\rho_i}{q_i - \rho_i} \tag{4.239}$$

$$= \left(\sum_{i=1}^{m-1} \frac{\rho_i}{q_i - \rho_i} \right) + \frac{\rho_m}{(1 - \sum_{j=1}^{m-1} q_j) - \rho_m}. \tag{4.240}$$

Evaluate the partial derivatives of $E[N]$ wrt q_i and equate each partial derivative to 0.

$$\frac{\partial E[N]}{\partial q_i} = \frac{-\rho_i}{(q_i - \rho_i)^2} + \frac{\rho_m}{(1 - \sum\limits_{j=1}^{m-1} q_j - \rho_m)^2} \tag{4.241}$$

$$= \frac{-\rho_i}{(q_i - \rho_i)^2} + \frac{\rho_m}{(q_m - \rho_m)2}, \quad i = 1, \ldots, m \tag{4.242}$$

$$= 0, \quad i = 1, \ldots, m \tag{4.243}$$

This implies that

$$\frac{\rho_1}{(q_1 - \rho_1)^2} = \frac{\rho_2}{(q_2 - \rho_2)^2} = \cdots = \frac{\rho_m}{(q_m - \rho_m)^2} = \frac{1}{b^2} \tag{4.244}$$

where b is an unknown constant. Equivalently,

$$\frac{q_i - \rho_i}{\sqrt{\rho_i}} = b, \quad i = 1, \ldots, m. \tag{4.245}$$

Summing all the probabilities and equating the sum to 1, we have

$$\sum_{i=1}^{m} q_i = b \sum_{i=1}^{m} \sqrt{\rho_i} + \sum_{i=1}^{m} \rho_i = 1. \tag{4.246}$$

Therefore,

$$b = \frac{1 - \sum\limits_{i=1}^{m} \rho_i}{\sum\limits_{i=1}^{m} \sqrt{\rho_i}} \quad \text{and} \tag{4.247}$$

$$q_i = \frac{1 - \sum\limits_{j=1}^{m} \rho_j}{\sum\limits_{j=1}^{m} \sqrt{\rho_j}} \sqrt{\rho_i} + \rho_i. \tag{4.248}$$

4.10   Exercises

1. Determine the expectation of the time spent during a continuously busy time period in an M/M/1/∞ queue. Do not use results on its pdf or on its Laplace transform derived in Chapter 3.

2. Consider a general Markov chain and two of the balance equations written by enclosing each of states i and j, respectively inside a boundary. Add the two equations and simplify by canceling identical terms on the two sides of the resulting equation. Could the resulting equation have been obtained by writing a single equation after observing the state transition diagram of the chain? Generalize the result. Also, show that if the chain has finite number of states, the number of linearly independent balance equations can be at most the number of states minus one.

3. In a real-time computing system, the processor attends to only one request at a time, and additional requests are not allowed to wait in a line. That is, if a request A comes in when the processor is busy, A gets lost (and will not return later). Requests are attempted as a Poisson process with a rate of 1 per millisecond. Service requirements of requests are iid exponential with an average of 2 milliseconds of time. Determine the probability that the processor is busy, under equilibrium.

4. (a) Formulate the Little's result for the service area of a single queue.

   (b) Formulate the Little's result for the "waiting customers" in a single queue.

5. A computer network has a dual processor server for computation intensive jobs. Jobs appear from clients in a Poisson stream with a constant rate of 1 job per millisecond and wait in a common FIFO waiting line with unlimited buffer capacity. If both the processors are available for serving a job at the head of the line, one of the two processors is scheduled to serve, with equal probabilities. Service times in each processor is iid exponential with a rate of 1 job per millisecond.

   (a) Draw the Markov chain for the above system.

   (b) Evaluate the numerical value of p_0, the probability of zero customers in the system under equilibrium.

   (c) Evaluate the fraction of time each processor is busy, as a function of p_0.

6. A special purpose computer laboratory has two identical computers. Students arrive in a Poisson stream; each student uses a computer for an exponential amount of time and leaves. There is a common waiting line. If any computer is free for use, the students' arrival rate is 10 per hour. If both computers

are occupied, the arrival rate is 5 per hour. If there is anyone waiting, no more students arrive. The average time a student uses a computer is 15 minutes if no one is waiting, and it is 5 minutes if anyone is waiting. Develop the complete Markov chain for the queuing system including all transition parameters.

7. Consider an $M/M/1/7$ system (finite buffer) with $\lambda = 5$ per second and $\mu = 5$ per second. Determine the average response time, throughput, and the variance of the number of customers in the system. Also determine the probability that an arriving customer finds the system full.

8. A queuing system with Poisson arrivals of rate $\lambda = 1$ has a capacity of 3 customers in the system. That is, if there are three customers in the system including any being serviced, the arrival rate into the system is 0. The service is exponential. If there is only one customer in the system, the service rate is 2. If there are two or more customers in the system, the server works harder and the service rate goes up to 3. Draw the complete rate transition diagram; fill in the values of the parameters. Calculate the probability that the system is empty.

9. In a state dependent M/M/1 queuing system with unlimited buffer, the arrivals are Poisson with the rate being inversely proportional to "one plus the number of customers in the system." That is

$$\lambda(i) = \frac{\lambda_0}{i+1}, i = 0, 1, ..., . \tag{4.249}$$

The service time is exponential with a state independent (constant) μ. Answer the following.

 (a) Is there a maximum value for λ_0 to ensure stability?

 (b) Assuming that the parameters imply stability, what is p_0, the probability that the system is empty?

 (c) Under stability, what is the expected response time (time spent in the entire system) of an incoming job?

10. Consider the following state dependent M/M/1 system with unlimited buffer. Customers balk. That is, the arrival rate reduces as the number of customers in the system increases, and is given by $\lambda(0) = \lambda$ and

$$\lambda(n) = \frac{\lambda(n-1)}{\alpha}, n = 1, ..., \tag{4.250}$$

with $\alpha > 0$. The service rate is a constant μ. What is the condition for the stability of the system?

11. In an office, there are three incoming telephone lines and only two operators who only receive calls (but never make a call). Call durations are iid exponential with an average of one minute per call. If both operators are busy with

calls and a third call comes in, the caller waits for an operator to finish earlier call and pick up. If there are 3 callers (with one waiting as the phone rings), and a fourth caller rings, he hears a busy tone and "gets lost." Call arrivals are Poisson with a rate of 1 call in 2 minutes.

Find the probability that both operators are busy and the third line is ringing. Assume that a free operator picks up a ringing phone immediately.

12. Consider two independent parallel exponential servers with rates 3 and 1, respectively. Arrivals are Poisson with rate 2. If both servers are free, an arriving customer prefers the server with higher service rate. The capacity of the entire system is only 3 customers. Are the arrival and service rates dependent only on the number of customers in the system? Write the complete rate transition diagram for the system. Fill in the values of all rates of state transitions. Evaluate important performance figures including the expected fractions of times that the servers are busy.

13. We have an unlimited buffer in a single server FIFO queue with Poisson arrivals of rate 1 job per minute. The strange boss of the server insists that the server should take breaks (and not serve) for all time periods when there are exactly 2 customers in the system. Other than this peculiarity, the service time is exponential with a constant rate of 2 jobs per minute. Is the system stable? If yes, find the equilibrium probability mass function of the number of customers in the system.

14. Consider a single queuing system with a capacity of two customers. Interarrival times are exponential with an average of 0.2 hour. However, each arrival brings in one customer with a probability of 0.7 or two customers together (holding hands) with a probability of 0.3. Arrivals to a buffers-full system are lost. Indeed, if two simultaneous arrivals come in and find room only for one customer, both arrivals get lost. Two simultaneous arrivals join the waiting line in a random order. Server takes one customer at a time and the service time is exponential with a rate of 10 customers per hour. Write the state transition diagram including the rates of each arc. Determine the probability that the system is empty. Evaluate the probability that

   (a) a single customer is lost.

   (b) an arriving couple is lost.

15. Consider a PC lab with only three computers. Customers for use form a Poisson arrival stream with a rate of 6 arrivals per hour. When a customer arrives, he/she chooses a computer at random (if one or more computers are available) and uses it for an exponentially distributed time with an average of 20 minutes. If an arriving customer finds no free computer, he/she gets lost. Determine the fraction of time a computer is free without any customer using it.

16. A bank office has two tellers A and B and a single waiting line with a capacity for two customers (totally, there can be only four customers in the entire system). Arrivals to a full buffer are lost. Arrivals are Poisson with a rate of 12 per hour. Servers are iid exponential, each with a rate of 10 per hour. At the time of entering service, a customer always chooses server A instead of server B if both are free (available). Otherwise, the customer is required to go to the free server. Draw the complete Markov chain for the system, including all arcs with their nonzero transition rates.

17. Poisson arrivals with a rate of 28 per second enter a single queue for processing by one of two iid exponential servers, each with a service rate of 20 jobs per second. If a job arrives when the system is empty, it chooses one of the servers at random. The total number of jobs that the entire system can hold is only 3 (including any under service). Arrivals to a full system are lost. Evaluate the expected response time of a job that got admitted into the system.

18. In a continuous time Markov chain, α_{ij} is the rate with which the state of the system changes from state i to state j, after the system has entered the state i. Recall that $\alpha_{ii} = 0$. Once the system enters state i, what is the probability that the state to which the system will change is j (whenever the state change occurs)?

19. In our usual speech sounds, there are three distinct states, V for voiced as in vowels, U for unvoiced as in fricatives such as in the syllables "f" and "s," and S for silence that occurs between words and for short times before plosive sounds such as during the pressure build up to say syllables like "p" and "t." A good model for the sequence of such states is a continuous time Markov chain with the average transition times from one state to another given in milliseconds in the following matrix. The rows are for V, U, and S in order from top to bottom, and the columns, similarly in order from left to right.

$$\begin{bmatrix} 0 & 50 & 70 \\ 60 & 0 & 15 \\ 40 & 30 & 0 \end{bmatrix}. \qquad (4.251)$$

Note that the state of this Markov chain is not a random variable (since a random variable is required to take numerical values for outcomes). It is a Markov chain of three non-numerical states. This model is useful to determine the effective bit rate necessary to code speech for transmission, etc. Answer the following.

    (a) Draw the Markov chain with correct values and dimensions on the arcs.

    (b) Let the equilibrium state probabilities be p_v, p_u, and p_s. Write the three global balance equations for the same.

    (c) Write any set of a minimum number of equations that uniquely determine the equilibrium state probabilities.

(d) Express the same set of equations in the above part in a matrix form.

(e) Find the inverse of the coefficient matrix.

(f) With the help of the inverse, find the equilibrium state probabilities.

(g) Over a long time interval T, what is the expected number of times the state moves into V? Note that the answer to this is not $p_v T$. Give similar results for U and S.

(h) With the help of a computer program, simulate an equilibrium sequence of 30 states. Plot a straight line with segments marked by notches. The distance between successive notches should correspond to the time intervals of the states. Write the state names above each interval. You can use a computer program to generate this plot.

20. Consider a two iid processor, continuous time, Markovian, single queuing system with room for up to 3 jobs including any under service. Attempted arrival rate is λ. Service rate of each processor is μ. If both the processors are free, the next job arrival is routed to whichever processor has been free for the longer time. These times are measured from the most recent time instants when the processors became free, respectively. Develop the complete Markov chain of the system, including all transition rates.

21. Consider a two processor, continuous time, Markovian, single queuing system with room for up to 3 jobs including any under service. Attempted arrival rate is 5 per second. Service rate of processor A is 3 per second and of processor B is 1 per second. Therefore, when both processors are free, the next job arrival is routed to processor A for service. Draw the state transition diagram. Let p_2, p_3 be the probabilities of finding 2, 3 jobs, respectively. Let p_A be the probability of finding exactly one job in the system, being served by processor A. Similarly, p_B is the probability of finding exactly one job in the system, being served by processor B. Of course, $p_0 = 1 - (p_A + p_B + p_2 + p_3)$.

Determine the throughput flowing through each (separately) of the processors, as functions of p_A, p_B, p_2, and p_3

22. Into a single queue with unlimited buffer size, customers always arrive in pairs but line up one after another in the waiting line for service. One of an arriving pair joins the line ahead of the other, by a random choice. The single server takes up one customer at a time from the head of the queue and serves. Each customer leaves immediately upon completion of his/her service (that is, without waiting for the completion of the partner's service). Arrivals of pairs are Poisson with a rate of 1 pair per hour. Service times of individual customers are independent and identically distributed exponential random variables with a mean of 0.25 hour for each customer (and not for a pair). Determine the expected response time of an individual customer.

23. In an office shared by two people A and B, at any time, both are quiet or only one is talking (both do not talk at the same time). When it is quiet, A will

start talking after an exponentially distributed time with an average time of 2 minutes. Likewise, when it is quiet, B will start talking after an exponentially distributed time with an average of 3 minutes. The lengths of times that each person talks (during their respective talk bursts) are also independent exponential with average times of 20 seconds and 50 seconds, respectively. Draw the complete Markov chain for the different states in the office. Over a long time, what is the expected fraction of the time that each person is talking?

24. A single server, single queue has a capacity of only 2 customers. Customers arrive ONLY as couples and both members of a couple try to join the queue one after another, in a random order. Arrivals to full buffer are lost. When a couple arrives, if there is room for only one customer, one member of the couple enters and the other leaves (is lost). Customers are served one at a time. Poisson arrivals of couples is at the rate of 1 couple per time unit. Service time is exponential with a rate of 1 customer (not couple) per unit time.

   (a) Draw the Markov chain for the above system.

   (b) Evaluate the numerical values of the equilibrium probabilities of all the states.

   (c) What is the probability that one member of an arriving couple will have to leave without service?

25. A wireless transmitter cannot detect a collision of its own transmission because it cannot simultaneously receive a different transmission while it is transmitting. Any attempted simultaneous reception will be saturated with its own transmission. Since collisions cannot be detected, a collided transmission cannot be aborted. In the approach generally used for reliable communication, the receiver transmits a short acknowledgment immediately after successfully receiving a packet. If the transmitter does not receive such an acknowledgment, it knows that its transmission failed due to collision. The time for an acknowledgment is counted as part of the packet transmission, as another simple but very good approximation. Approaches to reduce the incidence of collisions are known as collision avoidance approaches.

The following is a simple model (approximation of real life operation) for a wireless LAN operating with a CSMA/CA (carrier sense multiple access with collision avoidance) protocol. There are 10 wireless transreceivers (nodes) which are all within the reception ranges of one another (hence the term LAN). The packet sizes are all iid exponential with an average time of $\frac{1}{\mu} = 1$ millisecond (ms). We assume that a packet attempted for transmission multiple times has statistically iid transmission times, even though the successive times must be the very same (ignoring minor differences due to acknowledgments). In this exercise, every transmitter senses the channel with a statistical regularity, whenever it is not transmitting. The average time between such sensing by a single transmitter is $\frac{1}{\alpha}$, a parameter for optimization. A transmitter sends a dummy (or control) packet when it gets a chance to transmit but does not have the payload packet. This eliminates the dependency of the model on buffer lengths. The average time at the end of which a newly started transmission will be successfully sensed is $\frac{1}{\delta}$, a physical parameter of the system. All time periods are modeled as exponentially distributed.

We are now ready to describe the Markov chain governing the operation of the above wireless LAN. When the wireless medium (channel) is in the free state (F), the rate at which the state will change to a newly beginning transmission (S) is 10α. During the state S, 9 other transmitters are racing to start what they "think" will be a new transmission, but what might turn out to be a collision, with a combined rate of 9α. However, the physical time period of possible contention may end before any of these 9 transmitters actually start and cause a collision. This contention time period ends after an exponential time period with an average of δ time units. If the contention time period ends before one of the other 9 transmitters start and cause a collision, the state of the chain will change to T, a successfully transmitting state. If one of the 9 transmitters causes a collision, two simultaneous transmissions will continue in a state C_2 with a rate of 2μ. At the end of this period of two simultaneous transmissions, one of the two will continue in a state C_1 and complete with a rate of μ, when the channel will finally become free again. On the other hand, if the system had moved to the successfully transmitting state T, the transmission will continue and complete with a rate μ, when the channel will again become free.

(a) Draw the complete state transition diagram of the resulting Markov chain. Include the rate parameters for each transition arc.

(b) Solve for the equilibrium state probabilities.

(c) Express the throughput (rate of successfully transmitted packets) as a function of α and δ.

(d) An optimum α is one that maximizes the throughput. Determine the optimum α as a function of δ. Evaluate the optimum α for a representative numerical value of δ.

26. Develop the equilibrium pmf of the Markov chain in the sluggish operating system from first principles; use $\mathcal{Z}$ transform.

27. In the analysis of a simple contention-free protocol in Section 4.9.2, the individual queues are mathematically identical to the sluggish operating system. A simple brute-force optimization was suggested. Analyze the following optimization algorithm and examine if it is guaranteed to converge to the optimal probabilities. First, it is required to determine the value of q_i for a given c. Replace the function $c_i(q_i)$ by $f(q)$ for convenience. For a given c, we need q satisfying

$$c = f(q). \tag{4.252}$$

Manipulate the above as

$$f(q) - c + q = q. \qquad (4.253)$$

Analytically examine whether or not the following fixed-point algorithm

$$q(0) = 1 \qquad (4.254)$$

$$q(n+1) = f[q(n)] - c - q(n), \quad n = 0, 1, 2, \ldots \qquad (4.255)$$

will converge to the required q. Next, we need a procedure to start from some particular $c(0)$ and evaluate the optimal probabilities. Define $y(c)$ as the sum of all corresponding probabilities a function of $\{q_i\}$. That is

$$y(c) = \sum_{i=1}^{m} g_i(c). \qquad (4.256)$$

We want $y(c)$ to converge to 1 and we need the corresponding value of c. Analytically examine the following algorithm for convergence to the optimal probabilities. The starting point, $c(0)$ below, is selected to be the minimum of the values of c_i obtained by using $q_i = 1$, for the different i.

$$c(0) = \min\{c : q_i = 1, i = 1, \ldots, m\} \qquad (4.257)$$

$$c(n+1) = y[c(n)] - 1 + c(n). \quad n = 0, 1, \ldots \qquad (4.258)$$

28. Derive Erlang's B formula.

29. Derive Erlang's C formula.

Chapter 5

The M/G/1 Queue

5.1 Introduction

The state independent M/M/1/∞ and the many cases of state dependent M/M/1 queues are very easily represented as continuous time Markov chains. If the inter-arrival times or the service times are not memoryless, the number of customers in the queue is not a continuous time Markov chain. In these cases, the distribution of time for the next arrival or departure depends not only on the number in the system at that time, but also on how long ago the previous arrival or departure took place. The M/G/1 system, the present topic, allows for a general service time distribution, instead of the more restrictive exponential service time. Arrivals are restricted to be Poisson, with rate λ, as usual. Let the mean and variance of the service time distribution be $\frac{1}{\mu}$ and σ_s^2, respectively. The M/G/1 system has many practical applications. The following examples are cited here as a motivational introduction. The service time may be a constant, or uniformly distributed. It may be a combination of two or more exponentially distributed times as follows. If service is conducted in two successive stages of exponential times, Y_1 and Y_2, the composite service time distribution is called hypoexponential. However, this is an applicable case of M/G/1 system only if no more than one customer is allowed to be present in the combined service area of the two service stations at any time. Likewise, if service is rendered by one of a few possible exponential servers with different service rates, the composite service time is not exponential, but hyperexponential. If the service is exponential with rate μ_1 with probability P_1 and exponential with rate μ_2 with probability P_2, the overall hyperexponential service time Y has the density function

$$f_Y(y) = \begin{cases} P_1\mu_1 e^{-\mu_1 y} + P_2\mu_2 e^{-\mu_2 y}, & y \geq 0 \\ \\ 0, & y < 0. \end{cases} \tag{5.1}$$

Again, no more than one customer may be in the service area for this model to be valid.

Following is the plan of study in this chapter. In order to analyze the M/G/1/∞ queue, we consider the number of customers at a sequence of points in time that allow us to construct a discrete parameter Markov process. The sequence of points are the time instants of customer departures. The state of the system can be expressed using recurrence equations connecting the current state with the previous state and the number of arrivals over a service time. The state transition diagram possesses nonzero probability transitions from a state to itself and to every larger state. The expectation of the long-term time average of different states are shown to be the same as the corresponding equilibrium state probabilities at departure time instants. The expected number in the system is evaluated by taking the second moment of the recurrence equations, simplifying individual terms, and manipulating the equations. A few simple performance figures are easily evaluated. Straightforward application examples are constructed with the help of popular pdfs for service times. The case of a stable system but with infinite variance of the service time is briefly dealt with.

The finite buffer M/G/1/k system is also studied in this chapter. The corresponding finite state transition diagram is easily obtained by modifying the one for the M/G/1/∞ system. A simple algorithm to evaluate the equilibrium state probabilities for the finite buffer case is available. However, the state probabilities at arbitrary time instants are not the same as those at the departure time instants for the two largest states. The required expectations of time averages are evaluated for use in the Little's result for expected response time. The buffer size is not always explicitly included in referring to an M/G/1 queue. Whether the buffer size is finite or not is unambiguous from the context.

5.2 Imbedded Processes

The stochastic process $N(t)$, the number of customers in an M/G/1/∞ system, with the continuous time parameter, is not Markov simply because the distribution of time for the next departure is not exponential. However, the time for the next arrival is always exponential. If we observe the state of the system only at departure time instants, the only uncertainty about future observations is the number of arrivals which depend on the arrival rate and "whole" service times as opposed to "fractions" of service times. This overcomes the problem of keeping track of the fraction of completed service time. Therefore, we define a new stochastic process N_i as the number in the system "soon after" the departure of the i-th job from the system. The qualifier "soon after" is used to indicate that the departing job is not included in the count; thus N_i is the number in the system exactly at the time instant of the i-th departure, not including the departing job. The discrete parameter random process N_i is called an imbedded stochastic process, observed only at certain times. Now-a-days, imbedded processes are also being called embedded processes. Since this Markov process is also a discrete state Markov process, we call it a discrete parameter Markov chain. The subject of discrete parameter Markov chains is studied in detail in Chapter 6. However, the required properties of the imbedded discrete parameter Markov chain corresponding to M/G/1 queues are fairly simple and are proved in this chapter. This helps to reinforce some concepts during the generalization in Chapter

6. When do we start counting the number in the M/G/1/∞ system? We can consider the system that has been operating for any amount of time. However, the serial numbers of the jobs can be relative. We can start counting with any departure as the first departure.

5.3 Equilibrium and Long Term Operation of M/G/1/∞ Queue

5.3.1 Recurrence equations for state sequence

Let N_i, the number of customers soon after the i-th job departs, be zero. In this particular case, the next departure occurs after the arrival of the next, $(i + 1)$-th, job and soon after whenever it completes its service. Soon after the $(i + 1)$-th job departs, the number "left" in the system is the number of arrivals during the service time of the $(i + 1)$-th job, in this case of $N_i = 0$. Let A_{i+1} be the random variable corresponding to the number of arrivals during the service time of the $(i + 1)$-th job. The randomness of this quantity arises from two features: the randomness of the Poisson arrivals in any given time interval and the randomness of the amount of time itself, the service time of the $(i + 1)$-th job.

The state $N_{i+1} = A_{i+1}$, if $N_i = 0$. If $N_i \neq 0$, after the i-th job leaves, we have N_i left. To this, the number of arrivals, A_{i+1}, is added during the service time of $(i + 1)$-th job. When the $(i + 1)$-th job leaves, the number is reduced by one. Therefore, $N_{i+1} = N_i - 1 + A_{i+1}$ if $N_i \neq 0$. The distinction between the two cases of $N_i = 0$ and $N_i \neq 0$ is the following. If $N_i = 0$, the $(i + 1)$-th arrival is not counted as part of N_{i+1} since the $(i + 1)$-th arrival does not come in during the service time of any job. The combined recursion equation is

$$N_{i+1} = \begin{cases} N_i - 1 + A_{i+1}, & N_i > 0 \\ A_{i+1}, & N_i = 0. \end{cases} \tag{5.2}$$

Given the random variable N_i, the random variable N_{i+1} depends only on N_i and not on N_{i-1}, N_{i-2}, etc. The probability distribution of the random variable A_{i+1} depends only on the arrival rate and the pdf of the iid service time distribution. Thus, A_{i+1} is independent of i. Therefore, the discrete parameter stochastic process N_i is a Markov process. Let

$$a_{(j)} = P[j \text{ arrivals during the complete service time of any job}],$$
$$\text{for } j = 0, 1, 2, \cdots. \tag{5.3}$$

These probabilities are invariant to the serial number of the customer during whose service times, the j arrivals occur. Figure 5.1 shows the state transition diagram of the imbedded Markov chain for the M/G/1/∞ queue. This is a discrete parameter Markov chain. There are some important differences between the state transition diagrams of continuous and discrete parameter Markov chains. The values associated with the transition arcs in the case of a discrete parameter Markov chain are conditional probabilities called the state transition probabilities. We have the restriction that the sum of transition probabilities of all the arcs originating from any state evaluate to one. Also, in the case of a discrete parameter Markov chain, two successive states observed in a sequence of observations can be the same. Therefore, we can have a transition from a state back to itself, with nonzero probability, in a discrete parameter Markov chain. Recall the following in the case of continuous parameter Markov chains. The values associated with transition arcs are nonnegative rates but otherwise arbitrary (there is no sum requirement). There can be no nonzero rate transition arc from a state back to itself.

Using the above recurrence equations (5.3) in our present discrete parameter Markov chain, we have

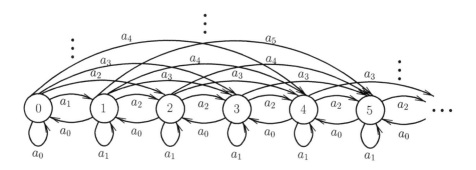

FIGURE 5.1: The state transition diagram of the imbedded Markov chain for the M/G/1/∞ queue

$$P[N_{i+1} = n | N_i = 0] = a_{(n)}, \quad n = 0, 1, 2, \cdots \tag{5.4}$$

$$P[N_{i+1} = n | N_i = k > 0] = a_{(n-k+1)}, \quad n = k-1, k, k+1, \cdots . \tag{5.5}$$

Using the theorem of total probabilities, we have

$$P[N_{i+1} = n] = a_{(n)} P[N_i = 0] + \sum_{k=1}^{n+1} a_{(n-k+1)} P[N_i = k], \text{ for } n = 0, 1, \cdots .$$

$$\tag{5.6}$$

We are interested in the expectation of N_i.

DEFINITION 5.1   *An M/G/1/∞ queue is in equilibrium at the obser-*

vation point $i + 1$, if a valid sequence of probabilities exists for $\{P[N_i = n],$ $n = 0, 1, 2, \cdots\}$ and if

$$P[N_{i+1} = n] = P[N_i = n], \quad \text{for all } n = 0, 1, \cdots. \tag{5.7}$$

□

5.3.2 Analysis of equilibrium operation

Is it enough if the system is in equilibrium at some particular i? The following theorem answers favorably.

THEOREM 5.1
Let an $M/G/1/\infty$ queue be in equilibrium at some $i + 1$. Then the system is guaranteed to be in equilibrium at every $j > i + 1$.

Proof
From equation (5.6), we have

$$P[N_{i+1} = n] = a_{(n)} P[N_i = 0] + \sum_{k=1}^{n+1} a_{(n-k+1)} P[N_i = k], \quad \text{for } n = 0, 1, \cdots. \tag{5.8}$$

Since the system is in equilibrium at $i + 1$, we have

$$P[N_{i+1} = n] = P[N_i = n], \quad \text{for all } n = 0, 1, \cdots. \tag{5.9}$$

Substituting $P[N_{i+1} = n]$ in place of $P[N_i = n]$ for all corresponding n on the RHS of equation (5.8), we obtain

$$P[N_{i+1} = n] = a_{(n)} P[N_{i+1} = 0] + \sum_{k=1}^{n+1} a_{(n-k+1)} P[N_{i+1} = k], \quad \text{for } n = 0, 1, \cdots. \tag{5.10}$$

But, we know that the RHS of equation (5.10), evaluates to $P[N_{i+2} = n]$ by changing i to $i + 1$ in equation (5.6). Therefore, substituting $P[N_{i+2} = n]$ for the RHS in equation (5.10), we find that

$$P[N_{i+1} = n] = P[N_{i+2} = n], \quad \text{for all } n = 0, 1, \cdots \tag{5.11}$$

implying that the system is in equilibrium at $i + 2$. That is, if the system is in equilibrium at some index $i + 1$, it will be in equilibrium at $i + 2$. By induction, we find that the system is in equilibrium at $i + 2, i + 3, i + 4, \cdots$. □

DEFINITION 5.2   *If there exists a valid solution of a sequence of prob-abilities $\{P[N = n], \ n = 0, \ 1, \ 2, \ \dots\}$ for the following equations,*

$$P[N = n] = a_{(n)}P[N = 0] + \sum_{k=1}^{n+1} a_{(n-k+1)}P[N = k]$$

for $n = 0, 1, \cdots$ and   (5.12)

$$\sum_{n=0}^{\infty} P[N = n] = 1,$$ (5.13)

we say that the system is stable.   The above equations (5.12) and (5.13) are known as the balance equations.   □

Redefine the equilibrium probabilities with simpler symbols since the parameter value is irrelevant. That is, let $P[N = n] = P_n$ for all n. Then, the above equation (5.12) takes the form

$$P_n = a_{(n)}P_0 + \sum_{k=1}^{n+1} a_{(n-k+1)}P_k, \text{ for } n = 0, 1, \cdots .$$ (5.14)

$$= a_{(n)}P_0 + \sum_{k=1}^{n-1} a_{(n-k+1)}P_k + a_{(1)}P_n + a_{(0)}P_{n+1}$$ (5.15)

where $\sum_{k=1}^{0}(\cdot)$ is defined to be zero as a convention. Express P_{n+1} as a function of $P_0, \dots, P_n$. We obtain

$$P_1 = \frac{1}{a_{(0)}}(1 - a_{(0)})P_0 \quad \text{and}$$ (5.16)

$$P_{n+1} = \frac{1}{a_{(0)}}\left((1 - a_{(1)})P_n - a_{(n)}P_0 - \sum_{k=1}^{n-1} a_{(n-k+1)}P_k\right),$$

for all $n = 1, 2, \cdots .$ (5.17)

In equation (5.14), $a_{(n)}$, the probability of n arrivals during a complete service time is strictly positive for every $n \geq 0$. This follows from the probabilities of all numbers of Poisson arrivals being nonzero during a complete service time. The only exception is if the service time is zero, which is a trivial degenerate case. Therefore, from equation (5.14), every P_n, $n \geq 1$ must be nonzero, if $P_0 > 0$. Equations (5.16) uniquely determine P_1 as a multiple of P_0. Equation (5.17) uniquely determines every P_n, $n > 1$ as a linear combination of $P_0, \cdots, P_{n-1}$. These in turn imply that if $P_0 = 0$, every other P_n, $n \geq 1$ must also be zero in the equations for equilibrium state probabilities. That is, the equilibrium condition is not possible with $P_0 = 0$. Furthermore, the above also implies that every equilibrium state probability P_n, $n > 0$ is a multiple of P_0. Hence, in order for all the probabilities to sum to 1, if equilibrium is possible, P_0 is uniquely determined by the equation (5.14). Therefore, we have the following result.

THEOREM 5.2
If a sequence of equilibrium state probabilities exist for the imbedded Markov chain of an $M/G/1/\infty$ queue, the following are true.

1. *All the equilibrium state probabilities are strictly positive. That is, $P_n > 0$, for all $n = 0, 1, \cdots$.*

2. *If the value of P_0 is known, the sequence of other equilibrium state probabilities P_n, $n = 1, 2, \cdots$ is easily obtained. Each P_i is a linear combination of $P_0, \cdots, P_{i-1}$ as in equations (5.16) and (5.17).*

3. *As a consequence of item 2 above, $\sum\limits_{n=0}^{\infty} P_n$ can be expressed as a multiple of P_0. The value of P_0 is uniquely determined by equating the sum $\sum\limits_{n=0}^{\infty} P_n$ to 1. If the evaluated P_0 is zero because the sum evaluates to infinity, the system cannot be in equilibrium.*

$\Box$

Therefore, the balance equations (5.12) and (5.13) determine if the system is stable, and if it is stable, possess a unique solution for the equilibrium state probabilities.

5.3.3 Statistical behavior of the discrete parameter sample function

We can modify the balance equation to be in a more concise generic form as follows. In equations (5.4) and (5.5), let

$$P[N_{i+1}|N_i = 0] = a_{(n)} \tag{5.18}$$

be denoted by p_{0n}. Similarly, let

$$P[N_{i+1}|N_i = k > 0] = a_{(n-k+1)}, \quad n \geq k - 1 \tag{5.19}$$

$$= 0, \quad n < k - 1 \tag{5.20}$$

be denoted by p_{kn}. We then have the balance equation (5.14) equivalently represented by

$$P_j = \sum_{k=0}^{\infty} P_i p_{ij}. \tag{5.21}$$

If we observe one sample function of an M/G/1/∞ queue at departure time instants for a long time, what is the statistical behavior of the relative occurrences of different states? In Chapter 4, the following is shown about a continuous parameter Markov chain for which equilibrium is possible: The long-term expected fractions of times of occupancies of different states are the same as the equilibrium state probabilities. Does a similar result hold for the discrete parameter imbedded Markov chain of a stable M/G/1/∞ queue? The following favorably answers the question. The system need not be in equilibrium at the beginning of the observation, but the equations for equilibrium probabilities must have a unique valid probability sequence as a solution. That is, the system must be stable. The solution need not be known. Let such a system be observed from serial number or the customer parameter observation epoch 1 onwards, up to and including epoch n.

The expected time between successive departures is never more than the sum of the expected interarrival time and the expected service time. The interarrival time has a finite variance (for a nonzero and finite arrival rate). We assume that the service time random variable also has a finite variance and that the expected number of service completions over a time period $t \to \infty$, also tends to infinity, with probability 1. Therefore, in the following arguments, n, the number of state observations at departure points is let to tend to infinity. We now know that this event occurs with probability one, as $t \to \infty$.

Let N_i be the random variable number of observations of state i during the run of n contiguous observations; as usual, n_i is the outcome of N_i. Note the following.

$$\sum_{i=0}^{\infty} n_i = n, \quad \text{so that} \tag{5.22}$$

$$\sum_{i=0}^{\infty} N_i = n \quad \text{and} \tag{5.23}$$

$$\sum_{i=0}^{\infty} E[N_i] = n. \tag{5.24}$$

The above simply points out that the sum of the numbers of observations of different states is the same as the total number of observations. The same is true about their expectations, by simply taking expectations on both sides of the equations. In an infinite run of the system, after the chain visits state i for the first time, due to the Markov property, the behavior of the chain is statistically identical between successive visits to a state i. Therefore, after the first visit, the number of observations between successive visits to a state are iid. That is, in an infinitely large number of observations, the number of different observations between successive occurrences of state i are iid. Therefore, as $n \to \infty$, the limiting random variable

$$\lim_{n \to \infty} \frac{N_i}{n} \tag{5.25}$$

has a limiting expectation and its variance is zero. Denote the expected value of the limit by

$$r_i = E\left[\lim_{n\to\infty} \frac{N_i}{n}\right].$$ (5.26)

The quantity r_i is called the *expectation* of the long-term average number of times that the chain is found to be in state i. Note the expression "expectation of the average." Here the average is taken over all the observations and the expectation is taken over the probability space of all the sequences of possible observations. The objective is to show that the sequence $\{r_j, \ j = 0, 1, \cdots\}$ is the same as the sequence of equilibrium state probabilities $\{P_j, \ j = 0, 1, \cdots\}$. In order to accomplish this, we consider the behavior of the numbers of times the M/G/1/∞ queue sees a change in state to and from state i.

Let $E[L_i]$ be the expected number of entries into state i the chain makes from *other states*. That is, if the chain remains in state i during the next observation after entering it during one observation, the second occupation of state i by the chain is not considered to be an entry into state i *from other states*. Similarly, let $E[M_i]$ be the expected number of exits the chain makes from state i to *some other states* during the run. The number of times the chain enters (from some other states) and exit (to some other states) can differ by at most one during a run. This is identical to a person leaving an office room and entering it from other office rooms in a building during a time period. Since the person is required to be inside a room in order to leave it and must be outside the room in order to enter it, the numbers of times of leaving and entering can differ by at most one. The two quantities are equal if the person is found to be in the same state (inside or outside the particular office room) at the beginning and end of the observation period. Let

$$\Delta_i = E[L_i] - E[M_i], \ \ i = 0, 1, \cdots \ \ \ \text{and}$$ (5.27)

$$\Delta_i \in \{-1, 0\, 1\}.$$ (5.28)

The limits $\lim_{n\to\infty} \frac{E[L_i]}{n}$ and $\lim_{n\to\infty} \frac{E[M_i]}{n}$ exist due to arguments similar to those used for the limit $\lim_{n\to\infty} \frac{E[N_i]}{n}$. Therefore,

$$\lim_{n\to\infty} \frac{\Delta t_i}{n} = 0 \ \ \ \text{and}$$ (5.29)

$$\lim_{n\to\infty} \frac{E[L_i]}{n} = \lim_{n\to\infty} \frac{E[M_i]}{n}, \ \ \ i = 0, \ldots.$$ (5.30)

After every observation that showed state j, the chain will move to a state k with a probability p_{jk}. Events following successive visits to state j are iid. Therefore, the expected number of times the chain leaves state j for some other state is

$$E[N_j] \sum_{\forall k \neq j} p_{jk} = E[N_j](1 - p_{kk}). \tag{5.31}$$

This is the same as $E[M_j]$, the definition of the expected number of times the chain makes a state transition from state j to *some other* state. Therefore,

$$E[M_i] = E[N_j] \sum_{\forall k \neq j} p_{jk} = E[N_j](1 - p_{kk}). \tag{5.32}$$

The expected number of times the chain enters state j from some other state because of leaving some other state during the course of n observations is

$$\sum_{\forall i \neq j} E[N_i] P_{ij} \tag{5.33}$$

which is the same as $E[L_j]$, the definition of the expected number of times the chain makes a state transition from *some other* state i to state j. Therefore,

$$E[L_j] = \sum_{\forall i \neq j} E[N_i] p_{ij}. \tag{5.34}$$

If we divide both sides of the two equations (5.31) and (5.33) by n and take limits as $n \to \infty$, we can equate the RHS of the resulting equations. We have

$$\lim_{n \to \infty} \frac{E[N_j]}{n}(1 - p_{jj}) = \lim_{n \to \infty} \sum_{\forall i \neq j} \frac{E[N_i]}{n} p_{ij} \quad \text{or} \tag{5.35}$$

$$r_j(1 - p_{jj}) = \sum_{\forall i \neq j} r_j p_{ij}, \quad j = 0, 1, \cdots \tag{5.36}$$

$$r_j = \sum_{i=0}^{\infty} r_j p_{ij}, \quad j = 0, 1, \cdots . \tag{5.37}$$

Equation (5.37) for $j = 0, 1, \cdots$ is identical to the balance equation (5.21) for the equilibrium state probabilities. Therefore, $r_j = P_j$, the equilibrium state probability for $j = 0, 1, \cdots$. This important result is stated as a theorem below.

THEOREM 5.3
Let the variance of service times of a stable $M/G/1/\infty$ be finite. Let the system operate for an unlimited amount of time $t \in [0, \infty)$. Consider the number of state transitions in the imbedded Markov chain of the system. Then, the long-term expectation of the number of observations of a state j, expressed as a fraction of the total number of observations is the same as the equilibrium probability of the state j. This is true for all states. □

5.3.4 Statistical behavior of the continuous time stochastic process

The analysis in the above Section 5.3.3 dealt with the numbers of observations of different states at the observation time instants of customer departures. In order to apply Little's result, we need the expectation of the time average of customers in the system, taken over the continuous time variable. This section studies the behavior of the number in the queue over the continuous time variable. This continuous parameter stochastic chain is *not* Markov. Over $t \in [0, \infty)$, let n_a be the total number of arrivals observed starting from time zero, up to and including time instant t. Similarly, let n_d be the number of departures in the same time interval. Over $[0, t)$, compare $n_d(j)$, the number of times state j is observed at (soon after) departure time instant to $n_a(j)$, the number of times state j is observed just before an arrival occurs. That is, $n_d(j)$ is the number of times the state changes from $j + 1$ to j over the continuous time interval. Similarly, $n_a(j)$ is the number of times the state changes from j to $j + 1$ over the continuous time interval. Over *any* time interval, these two numbers can differ by at most one. Recall that over any nonzero time period, the probability of two *simultaneous* Poisson arrivals is zero. If $P[\text{service time} = 0] > 0$, two simultaneous departures can occur. We order the departures as occurring one after another, in the order in which they arrived. Therefore, a state change from $j + 2$ to j is considered as two state changes, $j + 2$ to $j + 1$ soon after which another change occurs from state $j + 1$ to j. Let

$$\delta_j = n_a(j) - n_d(j). \tag{5.38}$$

As time t tends to infinity, we know from the analysis of the imbedded Markov chain that n_a, n_d, $n_d(j)$ tend to infinity with probability one. The difference $n_a - n_d$ is the number of customers left in the queue at the final time instant t. Let

$$n(t) = n_a - n_d. \tag{5.39}$$

From the imbedded process analysis above, we know that the expectation of the long-term average number of observing state j is the equilibrium probability p_j of state j at the departure process. We also know that

$$\lim_{j \to \infty} p_j = 0, \tag{5.40}$$

since $\sum_{j=0}^{\infty} = 1$. Therefore, the number of customers in the system, $n(t) = n_a - n_d$ is finite with probability one, even as time t tends to infinity. Recall that $n_a(j)$ and $n_d(j)$ can differ by at most one. Therefore, we have

$$E\left[\lim_{n \to \infty} \frac{n_a(j)}{n_a}\right] = E\left[\lim_{n \to \infty} \frac{n_d(j) - \delta(j)}{n_d + n(t)}\right] \tag{5.41}$$

$$= E\left[\lim_{n\to\infty} \frac{n_d(j)}{n_d}\right] \qquad (5.42)$$

$$= p_j, \qquad (5.43)$$

the equilibrium probability of state j in the imbedded process. The limit

$$E\left[\lim_{n\to\infty} \frac{n_a(j)}{n_a}\right] \qquad (5.44)$$

is often called the state probability at arrival time instants. of state j analogous to the departure time instant probability of state j obtained from the imbedded process. The next section develops the result that these arrival time instant probabilities are also the expected long-term time averages of state occupancies. These time averages are useful in the application of the Little's result to evaluate the expected response time.

5.3.5   Poisson arrivals see time averages

We still do not have the expected time averages of different state occupancies over the limiting continuous time period! We would like to evaluate these expectations as functions of state probabilities at departure time instants, which have also been shown to be the expected long-term proportions of the number of arrivals that see the different states. It turns out that the expected long-term time average of the number of customers in the system evaluate to these expected long-term proportions of the arrivals seeing the different states. This property is known as "Poisson Arrivals See Time Averages" or PASTA. A general statement including sufficient conditions and a simple proof are given below.

Conditions for PASTA

Consider a continuous time stochastic (not necessarily Markov) chain $N(t)$ with states 0, 1, 2, $\cdots$. The ensemble of the stochastic process consists of innumerable sample functions each of which is a plot of the state $n(t)$, as a function of the continuous time variable over $t \in [0, \infty)$. We would like to separately examine the time plot of the chain being in each state. Therefore, define $U_i(t)$ as the binary random process that takes a value 1 whenever the chain is in state i and takes a value 0 whenever the chain is not in state i. As usual, $u_i(t)$ is a sample function of the two state random process $U_i(t)$.

It is not necessary for the chain to be in equilibrium in any sense, but the following are assumed to be satisfied about long-term time averages.

1. The expected long-term time average of each state exists as a limit, for each state i. That is

$$E\left[\lim_{t\to\infty} \frac{1}{t}\int_{x=0}^{t} U_i(x)dx\right] = q_i \qquad (5.45)$$

exists. Note that the averaging is over the time variable and the expectation is over the sample space of the random process $U_i(t)$. Of course, the sequence $\{q_0, q_1, q_2, \cdots\}$ is a pmf.

2. The random variable corresponding to the limiting long-term time average of each state, i, converges to the corresponding expectation with probability one. That is, the random variable

$$\lim_{t \to \infty} \frac{1}{t} \int_{x=0}^{t} U_i(x)dx = q_i \qquad (5.46)$$

with probability one.

3. The variance of the random variable corresponding to the limiting long-term time average of each state, i, evaluates to zero. That is,

$$\text{var}\left[\lim_{t \to \infty} \frac{1}{t} \int_{x=0}^{t} U_i(x)dx\right] = 0. \qquad (5.47)$$

Other than the above conditions, the stochastic chain $N(t)$ is general. Consider a sequence of Poisson time instants with any finite and nonzero rate λ. In particular, the time instants of when $U_i(t)$ change from 0 to 1 as well as from 1 to 0 can depend on the sequence of the Poisson time instants. Let $M_i(t)$ be the random variable number of Poisson points that see state i of the stochastic chain $N(t)$, over the time interval $t \in [0, t)$. We also have

$$M(t) = \sum_{i=0}^{\infty} M_i(t) \qquad (5.48)$$

as the total number of Poisson points over the same time interval $t \in [0, t)$.

The above notation and conditions are detailed, but simple; they make it easy to prove the PASTA theorem.

THEOREM 5.4
Under the above conditions for PASTA, the following is true.

1. *The limiting expectation*

$$E\left[\lim_{t \to \infty} \frac{M_i(t)}{t}\right] \qquad (5.49)$$

exists and evaluates to λq_i, for every state i.

2. *The limiting random variable*

$$\lim_{t \to \infty} \frac{M_i(t)}{t} \qquad (5.50)$$

converges to λq_i with probability one, for every state i.

3. *The limiting variance*

$$var\left[\lim_{t\to\infty}\frac{M_i(t)}{t}\right]=0 \qquad (5.51)$$

for every state i.

Proof

Consider the function $u_i(t)$. This function fluctuates between 0 and 1. Consider the cumulative number of Poisson events (arrivals) over all the time segments during which $u_i(t)=1$. Due to the memorylessness of the times between successive arrivals, the expected number of arrivals in each segment corresponding to $u_i(t)=1$ depends only on the time interval for which $u_i(t)=1$. This is true even if the time instants of $u_i(t)$ changing to 1 or 0 are dependent on the Poisson arrivals. The number of arrivals in the multiple mutually exclusive segments during which $u_i(t)=1$ are mutually independent. Therefore, the number of Poisson events (arrivals) during all of the cumulative time intervals corresponding to $u_i(t)=1$ is simply the number of Poisson events over the entire sum of all time intervals for which $U_i(t)=1$. The expectation of this number is proportional to the cumulative amount of time intervals for which $U_i(t)=1$. Therefore, we have

$$\lim_{t\to\infty}\frac{E[M_i(t)]}{t}=\lambda E\left[\lim_{t\to\infty}\frac{1}{t}\int_{x=0}^{t}U_i(x)dx\right] \qquad (5.52)$$

$$=\lambda q_i. \qquad (5.53)$$

That is, the long-term time average of the expected number of Poisson arrivals during state i of the stochastic chain $N(t)$ is the same as the product of the rate of the Poisson events and the expected long-term time average of occupancy of state i of $N(t)$, even if $N(t)$ is not a Markov chain. Over an unbounded amount of time, the time averages of random numbers of Poisson events converge to their respective expectations with probability one. Their variances vanish to zero. Therefore, the three statements of the theorem are valid. ∎

A minor manipulation of the above result gives us

$$\lim_{t\to\infty}\frac{E[M_i(t)]}{E[M(t)]}=\frac{q_i}{\sum\limits_{j=0}^{\infty}q_j} \qquad (5.54)$$

$$=q_i. \qquad (5.55)$$

In the case of the M/G/1/∞ queue, recall that $M_i(t)$ are the number of Poisson arrivals "seeing" state i which we proved to be the same as the number of departures seeing state i over the long-term time averages, in equations (5.41) through (5.43). The above Theorem 5.4 shows that this number of Poisson arrivals seeing state i is the same as the time average of the occupancy of state i by $N(t)$, in the sense of the expected long-term time average. Therefore, we finally have the following needed result.

THEOREM 5.5

The equilibrium state probabilities of the imbedded Markov chain for a stable M/G/1/∞ queue are the same as the expectation of the long-term time averages of corresponding state occupancies by its continuous time stochastic chain. ☐

In the next section, the expectation of the imbedded Markov chain is developed without any intermediate evaluation of the state probabilities.

5.4 Derivation of the Pollaczek-Khinchin Mean Value Formula

The objective here is to derive the expected number of customers in a stable M/G/1/∞ system under equilibrium. From the development in Section 5.3.1, the recurrence relations of an M/G/1/∞ system are

$$N_{i+1} = \begin{cases} A_{i+1}, & \text{if } N_i = 0 \\ N_i - 1 + A_{i+1}, & \text{if } N_i > 0 \end{cases}. \tag{5.56}$$

Define

$$u(N_i) = \begin{cases} 0, & \text{if } N_i \leq 0 \\ 1, & \text{if } N_i > 0 \end{cases}. \tag{5.57}$$

The distinction between the random variable $u(N_i)$ and its outcome $u(n_i)$ is implicit. We have

$$N_{i+1} = N_i - u(N_i) + A_{i+1}. \tag{5.58}$$

Square both sides and take expectations. We have

$$E[(N_{i+1})^2] = E[N_i^2] + E[u^2(N_i)] + E[A_{i+1}^2] - 2E[N_i u(N_i)]$$

$$-2E[u(N_i)A_{i+1}] + 2E[N_iA_{i+1}]. \tag{5.59}$$

The individual terms on the right-hand side of equation (5.59) are evaluated as follows.

$$E[N_{i+1}^2] = E[N_i^2] \quad \text{under equilibrium,} \tag{5.60}$$

$$E[u^2(N_i)] = E[u(N_i)], \tag{5.61}$$

since $u^2(N_i) = u(N_i)$. We have

$$E[u(N_i)] = \sum_{N_i=0}^{\infty} P[N_i]u(N_i) \tag{5.62}$$

$$= 1 - P[N_i = 0] \tag{5.63}$$

$$= P[\text{server is busy}]. \tag{5.64}$$

$$E[\text{Number in service area}] = 0 \cdot P[N_i = 0] + 1 \cdot P[N_i > 0] \tag{5.65}$$

$$= 1 \cdot P[\text{server is busy}]. \tag{5.66}$$

We know from Section 5.3.5 that the equilibrium state probabilities correspond to their respective expected long-term time averages. Therefore, Little's result is applicable with $P[N_i]$ as time average state occupancies. Applying Little's result to the service area, we obtain

$$E[\text{Number in service area}] = \lambda E[\text{service time}] \tag{5.67}$$

$$= \frac{\lambda}{\mu} \tag{5.68}$$

$$= \rho. \tag{5.69}$$

Therefore, we have the result

$$P[\text{busy}] = \rho, \tag{5.70}$$

the normalized load, for M/G/1/∞ queue also. Continuing with further simplification of various terms, we have

$$E[N_i u(N_i)] = E[N_i], \tag{5.71}$$

since $N_i u(N_i) = N_i$. Next,

$$E[u(N_i)A_{i+1}] = E[u(N_i)]E[A_{i+1}], \tag{5.72}$$

since N_i and A_{i+1} are independent. Therefore,

$$E[u(N_i)A_{i+1}] = \rho E[A_{i+1}]. \tag{5.73}$$

In order to obtain $E[A_{i+1}]$, recall equation (5.58) from which we get the expectation of N_i as

$$E[N_{i+1}] = E[N_i] - E[u(N_i)] + E[A_{i+1}]. \tag{5.74}$$

Under equilibrium, $E[N_{i+1}] = E[N_i]$ and therefore, the above equation simplifies to

$$0 = -E[u(N_i)] + E[A_{i+1}] \quad \text{or} \tag{5.75}$$

$$E[A_{i+1}] = E[u(N_i)] = \rho. \tag{5.76}$$

Using this in equation (5.73), we have

$$E[u(N_i)A_{i+1}] = E[u(N_i)]E[A_{i+1}] \tag{5.77}$$

$$= \rho \cdot \rho \tag{5.78}$$

$$= \rho^2. \tag{5.79}$$

Realize that A is a random variable representing the number of arrivals during a service time. Also, define T to be the random variable representing the service time of the system. Therefore,

$$E[A(A-1)] = \int_{t=0}^{\infty} E[A(A-1)|T=t] f_T(t) dt \tag{5.80}$$

$$= \int_{t=0}^{\infty} \sum_{k=0}^{\infty} k(k-1) \frac{e^{-\lambda t}(\lambda t)^k}{k!} f_T(t) dt \tag{5.81}$$

$$= \int_{t=0}^{\infty} f_T(t)(\lambda t)^2 \sum_{k=2}^{\infty} \frac{e^{-\lambda t}(\lambda t)^{k-2}}{(k-2)!} dt \tag{5.82}$$

$$= \int_{t=0}^{\infty} f_T(t)(\lambda t)^2 dt \tag{5.83}$$

$$= \lambda^2 \int_{t=0}^{\infty} f_T(t) t^2 dt \tag{5.84}$$

$$= \lambda^2 E[T^2]. \tag{5.85}$$

Now,

$$E[T^2] = \text{Var}(T) + \frac{1}{\mu^2} \tag{5.86}$$

$$= \sigma_s^2 + \frac{1}{\mu^2}. \tag{5.87}$$

Therefore, we have

$$E[A(A-1)] = \lambda^2 \left(\sigma_s^2 + \frac{1}{\mu^2} \right) \quad \text{or} \tag{5.88}$$

$$E[A^2] - E[A] = \lambda^2 \sigma_s^2 + \rho^2 \tag{5.89}$$

$$E[A^2] = \lambda^2 \sigma_s^2 + \rho^2 + \rho. \tag{5.90}$$

We need to substitute appropriate values for the different terms in equation (5.59) and reproduced below.

$$E[(N_{i+1})^2] = E[N_i^2] + E[u^2(N_i)] + E[A_{i+1}^2] - 2E[N_i u(N_i)]$$

$$-2E[u(N_i)A_{i+1}] \quad + 2E[N_i A_{i+1}]. \tag{5.91}$$

Under equilibrium, $E[(N_{i+1})^2] = E[N_i^2]$. Also, denote the equilibrium $E[N_i]$ by $E[N]$. Using this and substituting for other terms, we have

$$0 = \rho + E[A_{i+1}^2] - 2E[N_i] - 2\rho^2 + 2E[N_i]\rho \quad \text{or} \tag{5.92}$$

$$2E[N_i](1 - \rho) = \rho - 2\rho^2 + E[A_{i+1}^2] \tag{5.93}$$

$$= \rho - 2\rho^2 + \lambda^2 \sigma_s^2 + \rho^2 + \rho \text{ or} \tag{5.94}$$

$$E[N] = \frac{\lambda^2 \sigma_s^2 + 2\rho - \rho^2}{2(1 - \rho)}. \tag{5.95}$$

The mean number in the system depends only on the arrival rate, the service rate, and σ_s^2, the variance of the service time. It does not depend on other characteristics of the service time distribution. Therefore, two different service time distributions but with correspondingly equal means and variances will yield the same mean number in the system (for the same λ and μ, of course). The expression for $E[N]$ in the equation (5.95) is known as the Pollaczek-Khinchin mean value formula. Felix Pollaczek (1892–1981) was an Austrian-French scientist. Aleksandr Yakovlevich Khinchin (1894–1959) was a Russian mathematician. They developed the expression for the expected buffer occupancy in the early nineteen thirties through the use of Laplace and $\mathcal{Z}$ transforms. Their expression for the transform of the pmf of the number in the system is known as the Pollaczek-Khinchin transform formula. The present approach to directly derive the expression for the mean number in the systems is due to D. G. Kendall, 1951. The mean value formula gives the mean number in the system at departure time instants. As shown in Section 5.3.4, the equilibrium state probabilities at departure time instants are also the expected fractions of time the system is in the corresponding states. Therefore, the Pollaczek-Khinchin mean value formula is also the expected number of customers of the continuous time stochastic process of the M/G/1/∞ queue.

5.4.1   Performance figures

The most important figures are $P_0 = 1 - \rho$, load = $P[\text{busy}] = \rho$, and the mean response time $E[R] = \frac{E[N]}{\lambda}$ from Little's result, in addition to the mean number in the system. The mean number in the waiting line is obtained by applying Little's result to the waiting line only. The expected waiting time is the difference between the expected response time and the expected service time. Hence,

$$E[N_W] = \lambda\left(E[R] - \frac{1}{\mu}\right) \tag{5.96}$$

$$= \lambda E[R] - \rho \tag{5.97}$$

is the mean number in the waiting line. To examine the mean number and mean response times, we can vary λ from 0 to μ for any specified variance. Note that for any $\mu > 0$, the variance of service time can be as low as 0, as is the case for a constant service time, or as high as desired (∞, as is the case of a Pareto distributed service time).

5.5   Application Examples

Interesting examples are obtained not only for specific service time distributions but also for practical combinations of these. In each case, the task of performance evaluation is straightforward once we have the variance of service time.

5.5.1   M/D/1/∞: Constant service time

The variance $\sigma_s^2 = 0$ and the mean number in the system reduces to

$$E[N] = \frac{\rho(2 - \rho)}{2(1 - \rho)}. \tag{5.98}$$

5.5.2   M/U/1/∞: Uniformly distributed service time

If the service time is uniformly distributed over a continuous time segment (a, b),

$$\mu = \frac{2}{a+b} \quad \text{and} \tag{5.99}$$

$$\sigma_s^2 = \frac{(b-a)^2}{12} \tag{5.100}$$

from standard evaluation. These can be substituted in the Pollaczek-Khinchin mean value formula.

5.5.3 Hypoexponential service time

Let the service be in two independent exponential stages with rates μ_1 and μ_2. Let there be at most one job allowed in the service area enclosing both the service stages. Then the service time is the sum of two independent, exponential random variables. From standard probability theory, the variance of a sum of independent random variables is the sum of their individual variances. Of course, the expectation of sum of random variables is the sum of their individual expectations - even if they are not independent. Therefore, for a sum of two independent exponential random variables with rates μ_1 and μ_2,

$$E[Y] = \frac{1}{\mu_1} + \frac{1}{\mu_2} \tag{5.101}$$

$$\sigma_Y^2 = \frac{1}{\mu_1^2} + \frac{1}{\mu_2^2}. \tag{5.102}$$

These are used to evaluate the performance figures.

5.5.4 Hyperexponential service time

In some cases, whenever a job enters service mode, one of two different exponential processors may be allocated for service. Again, at most one customer can be in service area, for M/G/1 system results to be valid. Let the probability of allocating a server with rate μ_1 be P_1 and, similarly, μ_2 and P_2. Since there are only two servers, $P_1 + P_2 = 1$. From the theorem of total expectation,

$$E[Y^i] = P_1 E[Y^i|\text{server 1}] + P_2 E[Y^i|\text{server 2}] \tag{5.103}$$

$$E[Y] = \frac{P_1}{\mu_1} + \frac{P_2}{\mu_2} \tag{5.104}$$

$$E[Y^2] = \frac{2P_1}{\mu_1^2} + \frac{2P_2}{\mu_2^2} \tag{5.105}$$

$$\sigma_Y^2 = \frac{2P_1}{\mu_1^2} + \frac{2P_2}{\mu_2^2} - \left(\frac{P_1}{\mu_1} + \frac{P_2}{\mu_2}\right)^2. \tag{5.106}$$

These are used in the Pollaczek-Khinchin mean value formula for performance figure calculations.

5.6   Special Cases

5.6.1   Pareto service times with infinite variance

Performance figures of the M/G/1/∞ queue in which service times are Pareto but with finite variance follows the development so far. If the expectation of service times is finite but its variance is infinite, the continuous time periods between successive departures have finite mean and infinite variance. However, the probability that a service time extends without bounds, to infinity, is zero. Therefore, the probability that the number of transitions of the corresponding imbedded discrete parameter Markov chain tends to infinity as the time period of operation tends to infinity is one. Therefore, as long as the expected service time is less than the expected interarrival time, all the properties of the Markov chain, including the Pollaczek-Khinchin mean value formula are valid. Substituting ∞ for the variance of service time distribution in the Pollaczek-Khinchin mean value formula, the expected number in the system is found to be ∞. This is an illustrative case of a stable Markov chain with unbounded expected state.

5.6.2   Finite buffer M/G/1 system

Consider a finite buffer queue with at most k positions for customers, including any under service. Arrivals are Poisson with rate λ. Arrivals to a full buffer are lost. Service times are iid. The expectation of service times is finite (and positive) but otherwise unrestricted; this also implies that the probability of a service time extending without bounds is zero. The variance of service times can be infinity. The discrete parameter imbedded Markov chain operates with an unbounded number of transitions with probability one, as the continuous time of operation extends without bounds, to infinity.

The state diagram of the imbedded Markov chain is shown in Figure 5.2. Observations are soon after a departure. Therefore, the possible state of k is never observed in the imbedded chain, but is observed in the continuous time stochastic process $N(t)$. The balance equations across a boundary drawn between states n and $n+1$ expresses p_{n+1}, the equilibrium probability of state $n + 1$ as a function of those of states 0, 1, $\cdots$, n. Therefore, every one of the finite number of state probabilities can be expressed as a function of p_0, and p_0 can then be evaluated through normalization. Thus, the evaluation of equilibrium state probabilities of the imbedded Markov chain

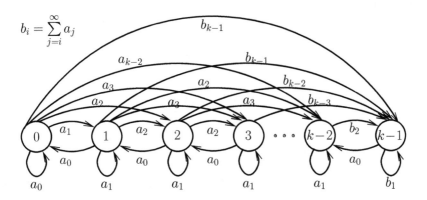

FIGURE 5.2: The state transition diagram of an M/G/1/k queue

is simple.

The arguments about the numbers of times the chain sees a change from state i to $i-1$ and from $i-1$ to i can differ by at most one over any time interval is definitely valid for all $i \leq k-1$. The PASTA property that the ratio of expected times spent in two states is the same as the ratio of expected numbers of arrivals in those respective states is also valid. Therefore, q_i, the long-term expected fractions of time spent in state i by the continuous time stochastic process is the same as the equilibrium state probabilities of the discrete parameter Markov chain, for $j = 0, \ldots, k-1$. That is

$$q_i = p_i, \quad i = 0, \ldots, k-1. \tag{5.107}$$

During the continuous time periods that the stochastic process is in state $k-1$, if an arrival occurs, the state changes to k. Further arrivals are lost until a departure takes place. Therefore, the long term expected fractions of times spent in states $k-1$ and k add up to p_k. The component q_k of p_k is easily evaluated by equating the two different evaluations of the throughput carried out by observing the arriving and departing customers. At the departure point, throughput is the service rate multiplied by the probability that the system is busy. That is,

$$E[Y] = (1 - p_0)\mu. \tag{5.108}$$

At the arrival point, customers are lost whenever the state of the continuous time stochastic process is k. During all other time periods, the arrival rate is λ. Therefore, the throughput is also given by

$$E[Y] = (1 - q_k)\lambda. \tag{5.109}$$

Comparing equations (5.108) and (5.109), we have

$$(1 - q_k)\lambda = (1 - p_0)\mu \quad \text{or} \tag{5.110}$$

$$q_k = \frac{p_0 + \rho - 1}{\rho} \quad \text{and} \tag{5.111}$$

$$q_{k-1} = p_{k-1} - q_k \tag{5.112}$$

$$= p_{k-1} - \frac{p_0 + \rho - 1}{\rho}. \tag{5.113}$$

From this, it is simple to show that

$$E[N(t)] = E[N] + q_k \tag{5.114}$$

where $E[N]$ is the equilibrium expectation of the finite state imbedded Markov chain for the finite buffer system.

5.7   Exercises

1. In a computer system, jobs arrive in a Poisson stream with a rate of 20 per second. A job can be serviced by one of three computers in the service area. Each of these computers takes a constant amount of time to service a job. There can be at most one job in the service area. A job is serviced by the first processor for 0.05 second with a probability of 0.2, or by the second processor for 0.03 second with a probability of 0.3, or by the third processor for 0.02 second with a probability of 0.5. Determine the service rate and the variance of service time. Is the queuing system stable?

2. Consider the following queuing system. The arrival stream is Poisson distributed with a rate of 4 jobs per second. The service times are exponentially

distributed with rates 3 and 5 jobs per second. An arriving job is routed to the first processor (with rate 3) with a probability p, and to the other processor with a probability $(1 - p)$. At any time, at most one processor is allowed to be busy. Determine the expected response time of a random job as a function of p.

3. A computer is composed of a CPU and an I/O unit. The service time of every job submitted to the CPU is exponentially distributed with a rate of 10 jobs per second. Following the CPU service, not all jobs require an I/O operation; a job requires an I/O operation with a probability of 0.2. If an I/O operation is required, its service time is exponentially distributed with a rate of 2 I/O jobs per second.

   (a) What is the density function of the total time (CPU plus I/O, if any) required by a random job input to the CPU?

   (b) A job input to the CPU is found to require a total time of 0.2 second. What is the probability that it used an I/O operation?

   (c) The computer center charges each user a dollar amount equal to

   $$A = 2C + 3I \qquad (5.115)$$

   where C and I are CPU time and I/O time in seconds, respectively. Determine the expected value and the variance of the random variable A.

   (d) A job arrives at the CPU and finds two jobs in the waiting line for the CPU and one being serviced by the CPU. What is the expected time for the arriving job to enter the CPU and begin being serviced?

4. In an M/G/1/∞ queuing system, the processor service time is a constant (deterministic) equal to 1 second for each job. The Poisson arrival rate is 0.5 job per second. Determine the steady state probability of finding three or more jobs in the system (including the one being serviced).

5. A computer server has its own internal jobs in addition to those submitted by external clients into a single queue. It devotes only 65% of its time to the client jobs. This implies that for every millisecond of time spent on client jobs, the server is busy for a total of $\frac{100}{65}$ millisecond. The jobs submitted by clients have exponential time requirement with an average of 3 milliseconds. However, 20% of the jobs are erroneous and the server spends exactly 0.2 millisecond on each of these defective jobs. Arrivals from all the clients put together are Poisson with a rate of one job in 8 milliseconds. Evaluate the expected number of client jobs in the system and their average response time.

6. A computer system is made of a CPU followed by an I/O device. Each is an exponential server with service rates of 20 per second and 10 per second respectively. There are two ways of organizing the system. In the first, there

is only one queue in front of the CPU. After a job is serviced by the CPU and the I/O device, the CPU starts on the next job.

In the second organization, there is a queue in front of the CPU and a queue in front of the I/O device. So, as soon as the CPU completes servicing a job, it is sent to the queue in front of the I/O and the CPU begins servicing the next job (if there is one) in its queue. Determine the improvement in the overall average response time of the second organization over the first form of organization. The Poisson arrival rate of jobs to the system is 4 per second.

7. Consider a finite buffer data link queue which can hold at most 2 packets including any being transmitted. Packets arrive in a Poisson process with a rate of 1000 packets per second. Successive packet transmission times are independent and identical, but not exponentially distributed. A packet's transmission time is exactly 300 microseconds with a probability of 0.4 and exactly 700 microseconds with a probability of 0.6. Answer the following.

   (a) During the complete service time a random packet, determine each of the probabilities of (*a*) no arrival, (*b*) one arrival, (*c*) two arrivals, and (*d*) more than two arrivals.

   (b) Develop the discrete parameter Markov chain of the system. The state of the system is defined as the number of packets in the system at the time of a packet departure (the number does not include the departing packet).

   (c) Let x_i be the steady state probability of finding i packets in the system. Write a set of equations in a matrix form the solution of which will give us all the x_i.

8. A computer is made of a CPU whose service time is exponentially distributed with an average of 1 sec followed by an I/O whose service time is uniformly distributed between 0 and 2 seconds. Jobs queue up in front of CPU only and until a job completes its I/O, the CPU does not take in the next job. The CPU and I/O service times are statistically independent of each other. Arrivals are Poisson with a rate of one job in 4 secs. Determine the average response time of a job (i.e., the sum of waiting, CPU, and I/O times).

9. In an M/G/1/∞ queuing system, the arrival rate is 10 per second. The service time is uniformly distributed between 0.03 and 0.06 second. Find the average response time and the average waiting time a job will experience.

10. Consider a queuing system which has only one waiting line at the entry point. Arrivals at this entry point are Poisson with rate of 1 job per second. The first stage of processing of a job is done by a processor S_1 which consumes a uniformly distributed amount of time between 0 and 0.2 second. After this first stage, the job is sent to one of two processors S_2 or S_3 with probabilities 0.4 and 0.6 respectively, for final processing. The service times in S_2 and S_3 are both independent and exponential with service rates 3 per second and 5

per second, respectively. Again note that there is only one waiting line at the entry point and until a job completes service in (S_1 AND (S_2 OR S_3)), all other jobs wait in the waiting line. Determine the average response time in the queuing system.

11. In a computer system, jobs that complete CPU service leave in a Poisson stream with rate 10 jobs per second and queue up for I/O. The I/O service times are *iid* and each service time is 0 with probability 0.5 and a constant 0.05 second, with probability 0.5 (that is, all the jobs queue up, but half of them find that they do not require I/O, when they get to I/O service point). Service times for the jobs are mutually independent of one another.

   (a) Determine the expected response time of the I/O queuing system.

   (b) What is the expected response time of a corresponding M/M/1 system with the same arrival and service rates? If this equals the expected response time of the above original I/O system, is the output process of the original I/O system Poisson?

12. In a simple computer system, only one job can be under service. "Service" consists of CPU time followed by I/O time. There is unlimited waiting room. Job arrivals are Poisson with a rate of 1 per second. CPU times are iid exponential with rate 2 jobs per second. I/O times are iid uniform from 0 to some T. What is the value of T for each of the following possible cases.

   (a) An incoming job finds the system busy with probability 0.75.

   (b) Overall expected response time is 3 seconds.

13. In an M/D/1 system under equilibrium, determine the cumulative distribution function of the interdeparture time between successive jobs leaving the system. Sketch the function.

14. In a steady state M/G/1 system, service time is uniformly distributed between 0 and b seconds. The arrival rate is 0.4 jobs per second. The expected time for the next departure, under the condition that the server is free is known to be 3 seconds. Determine the expected number of customers in the waiting line (not including the customer in service).

15. In a steady state queuing system, the service time is composed of a uniformly distributed preprocessing time between 0 and 1 millisecond followed by an independent exponentially distributed CPU time with an average of 3 milliseconds. The preprocessor is never functioning when the CPU is busy. Arrival rate is 100 jobs per second. Systematically determine the expected number of customers in the waiting line (not including any under service).

16. In a steady state M/G/1 system, service time is uniformly distributed between 0 and b second. The arrival rate is 0.4 job per second. The expected time for the next departure, under the condition that the server is free is known to be

3 seconds. Systematically determine the expected number of customers in the waiting line (not including the customer in service).

17. In a computer server, the CPU followed by I/O together constitute a single service area. Poisson job arrivals are at the rate of one job per second. If a job runs without any error, its CPU time is exactly 100 milliseconds. and its I/O time is exactly 300 milliseconds. If the job is erroneous, its CPU time is 50 milliseconds. and its I/O time is 100 milliseconds. The system is found to be empty 70% of the time. Let Y be the service time random variable. Determine the variance of Y.

18. Consider a stable M/G/1/∞ queuing system with an arrival rate of λ. The service time is uniformly distributed between a and b. Determine P_1, the steady state probability of finding one customer in the system, as a function of λ, a, and b.

19. Consider a sluggish M/G/1/∞ queue with a hyperexponential service time composed of a mixture of m exponential times with rates α_i and corresponding mixing probabilities h_i. The Poisson arrival rate of payload packets is λ. Whenever the queue becomes free of payload packets, the server gets busy with its internal jobs whose service times are iid as the payload packets.

   (a) Determine the probability that a payload packet arrives when the server is executing its internal job.

   (b) Between the time instant that the server becomes free of payload jobs and the time instant that a new payload job arrives, the server completely executes a random number K internal jobs. A payload packet arrives during its execution of the $(K + 1)$th internal job. Develop the pmf of this random variable K.

   (c) Determine the probability distribution of the time remaining for completion of an internal job, after a payload job arrives. This time amount quantifies the sluggishness of the server.

   (d) Develop an expression for the equilibrium expected number of payload packets in the system, which is different from the Pollaczek-Khinchin mean value formula, due to the sluggish server.

20. Analyze the following extension of the simple contention-free LAN protocol studied in Section 4.9.2. Let the payload packet sizes in different transmitters be different, with rates μ_i instead of a common μ. If a transmitter does not have any payload packets in its buffer at the time it gets a chance to transmit, it transmits a token packet, of size iid to its payload packets. The payload packet arrival rate at transmitter i is λ_i. The algorithm to give the right for transmission to a transmitter selects one through a random experiment with probabilities, $q_1, \ldots, q_m$. A useful feature of this LAN organization is that even within one transmitter, there may be multiple heterogeneous queues. For example in

voice over IP (VOIP) communication packet arrival rates and packet sizes for voice packets are usually different from the corresponding parameters for data packets.

(a) Evaluate the exact mean and variance of the time interval that transmitter i experiences between its successive chances for transmitting.

(b) Optimize the set of probabilities $\{q_i\}$ that minimize the expected number in the entire LAN. Recall that each transmitter operates in a sluggish mode due to the transmission of dummy or control packets, whenever there are no payload packets.

Chapter 6

Discrete Time Queues

6.1 Introduction

The interarrival times and service times of many queues in real computer networks are modeled as continuous (as opposed to discrete) random variables. Section 3.1 describes some justification and data networks applications for such a model. Many other computer systems, small scale computer networks, and some wireless networks are organized with complete synchronization. In such wireless networks, nodes synchronize their activities with the clock of one node. Channel requests, grants, data transmissions, and receptions all proceed in predetermined fixed time intervals. Data frames are necessarily of fixed sizes. Analysis and performance evaluation of such systems are crucial, especially since these systems have limited resources. A proper understanding and modeling of timing and synchronization is required to correctly analyze such discrete time queues. Identification of when a data packet cannot enter due to a full buffer is important. Making assumptions with regard to synchronization issues also influences when exactly the last customer has left the system and the buffer is empty. Analysis and performance evaluation of discrete time queues is based on discrete parameter Markov chain models. The structure and operation of simple discrete parameter Markov chains are easy to visualize. Development of their statistical properties, however, require a careful study of the possible variations in the nature of interconnections (state transitions) and probabilities of transitions. Nevertheless, the final results are simple to comprehend.

6.2 Timing and Synchronization

In discrete time systems, progression of activities is controlled by a clock. The clock divides time into a succession of equal intervals or slots (see Figure 6.1). These activities persist for a nonzero, finite amount of continuous time within a slot, and are simple enough that they will be completed in a small amount of time. An example of such an activity is the transmission of a packet in a wireless communication system. The end points of a slot are called slot edges. At the beginning of a slot, data and physical components are ready to execute an activity. By the end of a slot, the activity is complete. Even if some activity is complete before the end of the slot, the next activity cannot start until the beginning of the successive slot. Thus, the discrete time model is not an approximation to continuous time operation, but arises due to the strictly digital nature of the operation. In the analysis of discrete time queuing systems, the details of the activities that take place within a slot and of the service received by the customers are unimportant. Only the numbers of customers in various positions within the system at different times are relevant. The positions of different customers should never change within the body (the open interval) of a slot in order to ensure that no activity is interrupted.

Arrival and departure events are the most common causes of changes that take place in a queuing system. Even movement of a customer within a queue is a departure from one buffer position and an arrival into another position. We make a distinction between an arrival and an arrival event (compare departure and departure event). An arrival event is the occurrence of one or more simultaneous arrivals. There is at most one arrival event per slot. Arrival and departure events (including movement of customers from one position to another) do not persist over a continuous time period, but instead are changes in the system that take place instantaneously at slot edges. Throughout this chapter, unless otherwise stated, it is assumed that an arrival occurs during an infinitesimal time period soon after the slot edge and a departure, during an infinitesimal time period just before a slot edge. Figure 6.1 illustrates this terminology. This type of system is referred to as an early arrival system (EAS). This model is consistent with the movement of data in digital systems, for example, in shift registers. Any activity between successive slot edges belongs to that slot.

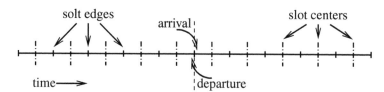

FIGURE 6.1:   Slot arrival and departure instances

Hence, the slot edge is a natural choice of epoch to make observations. However, the numbers of customers in various positions do not change during the continuous time period starting from soon after a slot edge and ending just before the next slot edge. Therefore, counting the numbers at slot centers leads to another choice of the epoch. In a practical scenario, the slot center represents the point in the slot where arrivals are guaranteed to have fully entered the system. Compare this to the slot edge, which represents the point in a slot at which a departure is guaranteed to have completely left the system and no arrivals have begun entering the system. The number of customers varies depending on whether the count is made at the slot edge or at the slot center.

As an illustration of the difference between counting at slot edges versus counting at slot centers, let a system be empty at the beginning of slot 0, as in Figure 6.2 (the numbers on the time axis indicate the slot to the right of the numbers, in this figure). Let there be four successive packet arrivals in slots 1 through 4, and three successive departures in slots 2 through 4. The system has 1, 2, 2, 2, 1 packets at the centers of slots 1 through 5, respectively. At the beginning edges of slots 1 through 5 there are 0, 1, 1, 1, 1 packets in the system, respectively. At the ending edges of slots 1 through 5 there are 1, 1, 1, 1, 1 packets. The sequences of numbers of packets at the beginning edges of slots and ending edges of slots are the same except for one discrepancy: the ending edge of a slot is the beginning edge of the next slot. From

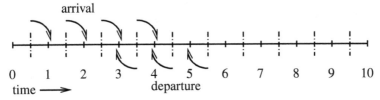

FIGURE 6.2:   A plot of 4 arrivals and 3 departures

the previous example, it is evident that the number in the system at any given slot depends on whether the count is made at slot edges or at slot centers. The following section develops methods to evaluate the probabilities for possible changes in the number of packets between successive observations in discrete time queues.

6.3   State Transitions and Their Probabilities

In simple discrete time queues, the state of the system at any time is the number of customers. An example of a customer is one of the packets in a store and forward queue obtaining or waiting for service. The possible set of state transitions is unambiguously determined by the epoch at which the state is evaluated. An empty state corresponds to zero customers, and the full state corresponds to the maximum number of customers possible in the system. Particular attention should be paid to the impossible transitions from empty and full states. The properties dictating these transitions are simple. Obviously, a customer cannot leave from an empty buffer and a customer cannot enter a full buffer. If the state is evaluated at the slot center, then between the present epoch and the next, any possible departure occurs before any possible arrival. On the other hand, if the state is evaluated at slot edges, then any possible departure occurs after any possible arrival, between the present epoch and the next. Therefore, if the observations are at slot edges, then, between successive observations, the following hold. First, a customer can enter into an empty buffer and depart from the system after the slot of service. Second, a customer cannot enter a full buffer. In contrast, if observations are at slot centers, then, between successive observations, the following hold. First, a customer can enter into an empty buffer but cannot leave. Second, a customer can depart from a full buffer and another customer can enter.

The sets of events triggering possible transitions for a system which can have at most one arrival and at most one departure between the present and the next epoch are listed in Table 6.1*. Elements in a row correspond to possible transitions. The second and third rows correspond to the cases of two different epochs. The symbol n_b denotes the size of the buffer. The event A denotes an arrival, and $\overline{A}$ denotes no arrival. Likewise, D and $\overline{D}$ denote a departure and no departure, respectively. The symbol · denotes logical AND, and + denotes logical OR. The variable i in the table has the range $0 < i < n_b$. The probability of each transition is evaluated from the

TABLE 6.1:   Events triggering various state transitions

Transition	$0 \to 0$	$0 \to 1$	$i \to i+1$	$i \to i$	$i \to i-1$	$n_b \to n_b - 1$	$n_b \to n_b$
Center	$\overline{A}$	A	$\overline{D} \cdot A$	$\overline{D} \cdot \overline{A} + D \cdot A$	$D \cdot \overline{A}$	$D \cdot \overline{A}$	$\overline{D} + D \cdot A$
Edge	$\overline{A} + A \cdot D$	$A \cdot \overline{D}$	$A \cdot \overline{D}$	$\overline{A} \cdot \overline{D} + A \cdot D$	$\overline{A} \cdot D$	D	$\overline{D}$

probability of the compound event required for the execution of the transition. These transition probabilities are functions of the arrival and service completion probabilities.

We use $p = [p_{ij}]$ to denote the one step transition probabilities from state i to state j, if observations are made at slot centers. If observations are made at slot edges, we use $q = [q_{ij}]$ for transition probabilities from state i to state j.

Example 6.1

In a slotted LAN (local area network), a transmitter functions as a discrete time queue. In this example, the buffer has two positions (for two packets)

---

*Tables 6.1, 6.2, 6.3, and 6.4 are reproduced (with copyright permission) from the article G. R. Dattatreya and L. N. Singh, "Relationships among different models for discrete-time queues," *WSEAS Transactions on Systems*, volume 4, issue 8, August 2005, pp. 1183–1190.

only, including for any packet under service. Arrivals enter the system and join the queue. Service consists of transmitting a packet at the head of the queue over the outgoing physical medium. Due to contentions for transmission, transmission is not always successful during an attempt. The probability of one arrival in a slot is a and the probability of no arrival is $1 - a$. If a packet is present in the service mode in the queuing system, the probability of its service completion during the present slot is s. Probabilities of arrivals and service completions in successive slots are independent among themselves and independent of one another. An attempted arrival to a full buffer gets lost. In other words, such an arrival is not admitted into the system and this event does not affect future arrival probabilities. These arrival and service processes are also known as memoryless, since their past history does not affect the probabilities of their future occurrences.

For $a = 0.3$ and $s = 0.6$, the resulting transition probability matrix for counting at slot centers is given by:

$$p = \begin{bmatrix} 0.70 & 0.30 & 0.00 \\ 0.42 & 0.46 & 0.12 \\ 0.00 & 0.42 & 0.58 \end{bmatrix}. \tag{6.1}$$

The state transition diagram for the above LAN when the system is observed at slot centers is given in Figure 6.3. The transition probability matrix for counting at slot edges is:

$$q = \begin{bmatrix} 0.88 & 0.12 & 0.00 \\ 0.42 & 0.46 & 0.12 \\ 0.00 & 0.60 & 0.40 \end{bmatrix}. \tag{6.2}$$

The state transition diagram for the above LAN when the system is observed at slot edges is given in Figure 6.4.

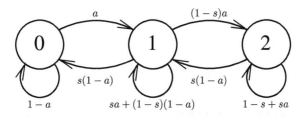

FIGURE 6.3: State diagram for Example 6.1. Observations are at slot centers

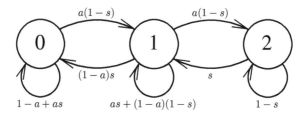

FIGURE 6.4:   State diagram for Example 6.1. Observations are at slot edges

Example 6.2
A slight modification to the above Example 6.1 is to allow at most two packets to arrive during one time slot. Let the probability of one arrival in a slot be 0.3 and the probability of two arrivals, 0.1. In addition, the capacity of the system is increased to hold a maximum of three packets. All other aspects are the same as in Example 6.1. If two arrivals attempt to arrive in a slot and there is room for only one of them in the buffer, one of the two at random will be admitted and the other one will be dropped.

The arrival and departure events for different state transitions in this example are a little more involved than those in Table 6.1. The approach for computing the transition probabilities is similar, however. Let the events in which one and two arrivals occur be A_1 and A_2, respectively. Tables 6.2 through 6.4 give the transition probabilities for the possible transitions. The resulting transition probability matrix for counting at slot centers is given by:

$$p = \begin{bmatrix} 0.60 & 0.30 & 0.10 & 0.00 \\ 0.36 & 0.42 & 0.18 & 0.04 \\ 0.00 & 0.36 & 0.42 & 0.22 \\ 0.00 & 0.00 & 0.36 & 0.64 \end{bmatrix}. \tag{6.3}$$

The state transition diagram for the above LAN when the system is observed at slot centers is given in Figure 6.5. The state transition probability matrix for counting at slot edges is:

$$q = \begin{bmatrix} 0.78 & 0.18 & 0.04 & 0.00 \\ 0.36 & 0.42 & 0.18 & 0.04 \\ 0.00 & 0.36 & 0.48 & 0.16 \\ 0.00 & 0.00 & 0.60 & 0.40 \end{bmatrix}. \tag{6.4}$$

The state transition diagram for the above LAN when the system is observed at slot edges is given in Figure 6.6.   ☐

Performance analysis of such discrete time queues require the foundations of analysis of discrete parameter Markov chains, just as we needed to understand the analysis of continuous parameter Markov chains to evaluate performances of continuous

TABLE 6.2: Events triggering state transitions from state 0 given 2
possible arrivals per slot

Transition	$0 \to 0$	$0 \to 1$	$0 \to 2$
Center	$\overline{A}_1 \overline{A}_2$	A_1	A_2
Edge	$\overline{A}_1 \cdot \overline{A}_2 + A_1 \cdot D$	$A_1 \cdot \overline{D} + A_2 \cdot D$	$A_2 \cdot \overline{D}$

TABLE 6.3: Events triggering state transitions from state i given 2
possible arrivals per slot

Transition	$i \to i-1$	$i \to i$	$i \to i+1$	$i \to i+2$
Center	$D \cdot \overline{A}_1 \cdot \overline{A}_2$	$\overline{D} \cdot \overline{A}_1 \cdot \overline{A}_2 + D \cdot A_1$	$\overline{D} \cdot A_1 + D \cdot A_2$	$\overline{D} \cdot A_2$
Edge	$\overline{A}_1 \cdot \overline{A}_2 \cdot D$	$\overline{A}_1 \cdot \overline{A}_2 \cdot \overline{D} + A_1 \cdot D$	$A_1 \cdot \overline{D} + A_2 \cdot D$	$A_2 \cdot \overline{D}$

TABLE 6.4: Events triggering state transitions from state n_b and
$n_b - 1$ given 2 possible arrivals per slot

Transition	$n_b - 1 \to n_b$	$n_b \to n_b - 1$	$n_b \to n_b$
Center	$\overline{D} \cdot (A_1 + A_2) + D \cdot A_2$	$D \cdot \overline{A}_1 \cdot \overline{A}_2$	$\overline{D} + D \cdot (A_1 + A_2)$
Edge	$(A_1 + A_2) \cdot \overline{D}$	D	$\overline{D}$

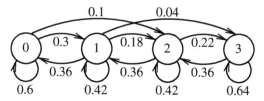

FIGURE 6.5:   State diagram for Example 6.2. Observations are at slot centers

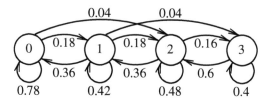

FIGURE 6.6:   State diagram for Example 6.2. Observations are at slot edges

time queues. The following sections develop the required foundations of discrete parameter Markov chains. A cursory glance at the entire development may give the impression that it is long-winded. Important properties are developed one small step at a time that allows us to concentrate on only a small number of aspects. These results are successively integrated for the final result that helps us to examine simple conditions on the Markov chain for the existence of equilibrium and for the evaluation of equilibrium state probabilities.

6.4   Discrete Parameter Markov Chains

In many applications of discrete time queues, the probabilities of arrivals and departures in the future depend only on the present situation or condition in the system and that the present condition that can be specified from a countable set. In many cases, the present condition can be as simple as the number of customers in the system at the time of observation. In other cases, the present condition specification may need to include, for example, which servers are busy. We call the description of the present condition as the present or current "state." In such systems, the future behavior of the system is not influenced by the past, except that it depends on the present state. That is, the current state is sufficient to describe the future statistical behavior of the states, as time slots progress. How the current state was reached is irrelevant for occurrences of future states, if the current state is known. The appropriate mathematical model to represent the behavior of such systems is that of a Markov chain.

In Section 4.2, a stochastic process is defined as a parameterized random variable. In the present study of discrete time queues, the parameter is the sequence of integers representing the progression of time slots. The random variable is the state of the system, represented by integers. The state may be a vector of discrete random variables. We therefore have a discrete parameter, discrete state stochastic process, also called a discrete parameter stochastic chain. Consider the following further restrictions on the nature of such stochastic chains. If the states at some of the parameter values (slots) are known, the conditional distribution of states at a larger parameter value depends only on the largest value of the parameter value for which the state is known. If this restriction is true for the entire stochastic chain, we call the chain a Markov chain, with a discrete parameter, in this case. We have already seen the specific discrete parameter Markov chain in Chapter 5. We have also seen them in Examples 6.1 and 6.2. The following is a formal definition, to begin a systematic study of the topic.

DEFINITION 6.1   *Let $X(i)$ be a discrete state stochastic process, that is, a parameterized discrete random variable, with the parameter i taking integer values. The discrete sample space can be, for example, all nonnegative integers. Let $i > i_k > i_{k-1} > i_{k-2} \cdots$. If*

$$P[X(i) \le x(i)|X(i_k) = x(i_k), X(i_{k-1}) = x(i_{k-1}), \cdots] \qquad (6.5)$$
$$= P[X(i) \le x(i)|X(i_k) = x(i_k)]$$

is true for all possible $x(i)$ and for all possible $i > i_k > i_{k-1} > i_{k-2} \cdots$, we say that $X(i)$ is a discrete parameter Markov chain. ▯

A simple example of a Markov chain is a store, process, and forward queue in a discrete time data packet communication system. Let us say that soon after every slot, a packet attempts to arrive with a probability a. If there is at least one packet in the system, the packet at the head of the queue (the oldest arrival among the packets present) successfully completes processing and departs the system with a probability s. The arrival and successful probabilities depend on the current number of packets in the system, but do not depend on other aspects of past behavior. Successful departures are forwarded on one of the outgoing communication links. In this case, the current state is adequately described by the number of packets in the system (including any at the transmission head) at the current time instant. The future behavior, that is, the probabilities of finding various numbers of packets at future time instants, depend only on the number of packets at the current observation. These future probabilities do not depend on, for example, whether or not the current state was reached as a consequence of an arrival or departure. In the present example, if we imagine that there is no limit on the number of packets the communication system buffer can hold waiting for service, the analysis gets simplified. Therefore, we allow a Markov chain to have a countably infinite number of states, in general. Particular examples can have limited finite buffers, of course. Examples 6.1 and 6.2 are illustrative cases of finite buffer systems.

The number of packets in a discrete time queue changes from one observation to the next; it is also possible for the number to remain the same between two such successive observations. The change is caused by possible arrivals and successful completions (departures). If the number of packets forms the state of the Markov chain representing the stochastic behavior of the queue, the probability of the number of packets at the $(i + 1)$th observation depends only on the exact number of packets at the ith observation and the probabilities of arrivals and of successful completions. For the state of the Markov chain to be the number of packets in the system only, the probabilities of arrivals and successful completions following the ith observation should be independent of how the state at the ith observation was reached. These arrival and departure probabilities, following the ith observation, can depend on the exact state found at the ith observation. For example, if the system has a finite buffer in which to hold a limited number of already arrived packets waiting for service, any attempted packet arrival would be dropped, if there is no departure between the ith and the $(i+1)$th observations. Such dropped packets are also called lost and they do not surreptitiously wait outside the buffer to make more attempts for arriving later. In other words, lost packets do not influence the probabilities of arrivals following their loss. This is certainly the scenario in data communication systems. The probabilities of successful completions also can depend on the current state. As an example, if the system has multiple packet servers (processors and transmitters), the probabilities of departure depend on whether or not more than one server is busy trying to complete packet service. The probability corresponding to a change in state from k at the ith observation to a state l at the $(i + 1)$th observation is known as a transition probability. In general, in discrete parameter Markov chains, the state k can be a discrete vector. The transition probability is a function of the current state and the next state. It (the transition probability) can also be a function of the parameter i, the index of progression of slots. The dependency or otherwise on the parameter i give us two classes of Markov chains developed below. The symbol $p_{kl}(i)$ is convenient to represent the transition probability from the state k at the ith observation to the state l at the next, $(i + 1)$th observation. Such transition probabilities are also called one step transition probabilities to emphasize that k and l represent states before and after one transition starting at the observation index i and not multiple transitions.

6.4.1   Homogeneous Markov chains

The dependency of the transition probabilities on the parameter corresponding to the index of progression of slots is clearly the more general of the two cases. The following definition distinguishes between the two cases.

DEFINITION 6.2   *If the transition probabilities of a Markov chain are completely invariant to the parameter values, the Markov chain is said to be* *homogeneous. If the chain is not homogeneous, it is said to be inhomogeneous.* ▯

A simple way to bring about the inhomogeneous generality is to let the probabilities of packet arrivals and packet processing speeds to be functions of time. Since time is divided into discrete slots, this translates to the transition probabilities being dependent on the slot-index parameter. A more illustrative real-life example follows.

Example 6.3
A popular car dealer's service shop has the following policy. Cars needing service should be dropped before 7:00 AM on weekdays; any car dropped before 7:00 AM including even those dropped on the previous evening are logged in as incoming at 7:00 AM. At 5:00 PM every weekday, service completions are logged. Repaired cars can be picked up only after 5:00 PM. Of course, any car picked up on the day or days after service completion are not in the register of internal service shop. The service shop is closed during weekends. Car owners plan to have serviced cars for the weekends. Also, cars breaking down during weekends would be brought in first thing Monday morning. Therefore, it is common for more cars to be logged in for repair on Monday and Friday mornings, than on Wednesdays, for example. As a consequence, the shop allocates more repair personnel during early and late weekdays than during the midweek.

The above example illustrates two features. One, that we can construct a discrete time queuing system with a progression of slots, each slot lasting from 7:00 AM through 5:00 PM the same day, and only for weekdays. The nights and weekends are squeezed out from our progression of slots. Also note that the arrivals and departures occur at slot edges in these progression of slots with any departure occurring before any arrival. The second feature of this example is the time varying nature of arrival and service completion probabilities of numbers of cars. These time varying arrival and departure probabilities in turn render the Markov chain transition probabilities to be functions of the slot index. That is, $p_{kl}(i)$ explicitly depends on i. ▯

The above is an example of inhomogeneous Markov chains. In contrast, in simple packet communication system, the arrival and service completion probabilities are not functions of the slot index parameter. They are functions of the current state, though. Therefore, they are homogeneous Markov chains. In the study of homogeneous Markov chains, i is dropped from the symbol $p_{kl}(i)$. The symbol p_{kl} completely represents the one step transition probability from the state k to the state l, starting at any observation slot index. Inhomogeneous Markov chains are difficult to specify, since transition probabilities are required to be specified for all parameter values, i, possibly different for each i. They are also difficult to analyze for the reason that even average quantities are time (slot index) varying. The concepts and definitions of homogeneity apply to both finite state and countably infinite state

Markov chains. Unless otherwise stated, any Markov chain considered in this chapter is assumed to be homogeneous.

6.4.2   Chapman-Kolmogorov equations

In a homogeneous Markov chain, if the current state is known, the transition probabilities specify the probabilities of observing different possible states after a transition. However, if the current state is uncertain and if only the probabilities with which the current state takes the possible values are given, how can the probabilities of the next state be evaluated? Let the states of the Markov chain be $0, 1, \cdots, n_b$ where n_b can be finite or infinite. Let p_{ij} be the transition probability from state i to state j, the elements of the transition probability matrix p. The definition of a matrix is extended to include infinite rows and columns. We should be careful to not conduct invalid or ambiguous operations on such infinite size matrices. Inverse is an example operation that is invalid for infinite size matrices. These transition probabilities are also called one-step transition probabilities. Let $P(t) = P_0(t), \cdots, P_{n_b}(t)$ be the probabilities of observing different states at slot number t. The probability that the state is j at slot index $t + 1$ is given by the theorem of total probabilities

$$P_j(t+1) = \sum_{i=0}^{n_b} P_i(t)p_{ij}. \qquad (6.6)$$

In matrix notation, we have

$$P(t+1) = P(t)p. \qquad (6.7)$$

The above equations in any form are known as the Chapman-Kolmogorov equations, in honor of the British scientist Sydney Chapman (1888–1970) and the Russian mathematician Andrey Nikolaevich Kolmogorov (1903–1987). Applying these again, we obtain

$$P(t+2) = P(t+1)p = P(t)p^2. \qquad (6.8)$$

Extending this, the so called n-step transition probabilities evaluate to the elements of p^n. That is if the current state is i, the probability of state j after n slots is given by the ij-th element of the matrix p^n.

6.4.3   Irreducible Markov chains

In many practical Markov chains, especially in those with a finite set of states, each state is repeatedly visited. The number of slots between successive visits to a state is a random variable, in general. However, even in some practical Markov chains, there may be some undesirable states that may be visited a few times before the chain settles into repeatedly visiting (with random number of slots between successive visits) every state in a proper subset of the original set of states. In some other improperly designed practical systems, the chain may settle into an undesirable proper subset of states, after switching in. Proper definitions and a study of some simple properties help the understanding of these issues and better design techniques.

DEFINITION 6.3 *In a (homogeneous, by default) Markov chain, starting from any state, at a particular slot, if every other state as well as itself can be reached, each in a finite number of transitions, and each with nonzero probability, we say that the Markov chain is irreducible. If a Markov chain is not irreducible, it is called reducible.* ⬜

As in the case of homogeneous and inhomogeneous Markov chains, it is illustrative to consider a specific example of the more complex system, a homogeneous but reducible Markov chain, in this case.

Example 6.4

A computer CPU (central processing unit) and its DMA (direct memory access) hardware access, mutually exclusively, the RAM (random access memory unit) through a common bus. The hardware that controls which of the subsystems will access the RAM during a clock period (slot) has two flip-flops C for CPU and D for DMA. During a slot, if a flip-flop shows a Boolean value 1, it allows its corresponding device to access the RAM. In practice, the device that will access the RAM during a slot is actually decided in the previous slot and the hardware enters this information into the flip-flops during the previous slot itself, so that the flip-flops can memorize it for the current slot. The control hardware and the two flip-flops C and D together form a four-state synchronous sequential machine. Obviously, for the successful operation of the entire system, only three states, $CD \in \{00,\ 01,\ 10\}$, are valid. If the probabilities of attempted accesses by the CPU and the DMA are constant over time (that is over a sequence of slots), and the control hardware has an unchanging way of arbitration if both devices attempt to access the RAM, we obtain a desirable Markov chain with three states with $CD \in \{00,\ 01,\ 10\}$. The state diagram for this chain is shown in Figure 6.7

However, when the system is started with a fresh power-up (also called switching-in), each of the the flip-flops C and D may find itself in the state 1, for several successive slots. Clearly, a proper design of the control hardware must ensure that if $CD = 11$ during any slot, the states of the flip-flops are driven to one of the desirable states, 00 for example, in the next slot. The corresponding Markov chain for the sequence of states of the flip-flops will then have four states $CD \in \{00,\ 01,\ 10\ 11\}$. A transition from the state 11 to state 00 occurs with a probability 1. There will be no transitions from any of the states 00, 01, and 10, to the state 11. This four state Markov chain is a reducible Markov chain, since starting from any state, including from state 11, the state 11 cannot be reached at all. After any possible switching-in transients, the Markov chain settles into the irreducible subchain with states

00, 01, and 10.

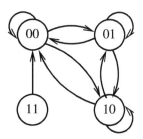

FIGURE 6.7:   State diagram for the properly designed DMA hardware

It is worth noting that if the control hardware is improperly designed, we can have a transition from state 11 back to itself with probability 1, in the final product. In such a case, if the state at the switching-in time turns out to be the undesirable state 11, the hardware will never get out of it! Figure 6.8 shows the state diagram of such a chain. Not only is it reducible, but it is also composed of two completely disjoint chains.   ∏

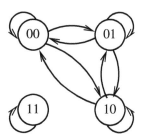

FIGURE 6.8:   State diagram for an improperly designed DMA hardware

If a Markov chain is made of multiple irreducible chains, the study of the entire chain is usually split up into studies of its individual irreducible subchains. Therefore, unless otherwise specified, Markov chains in our study are irreducible.

6.5 Classification of States

6.5.1 Aperiodic states

DEFINITION 6.4 *In a homogeneous and irreducible discrete parameter Markov chain, starting from a particular state, say A, it may be possible to return to itself (state A), for the first time, only after $i_1, \cdots, i_n$ slots, each with a nonzero probability. If this set of integers $\{i_1, \cdots, i_n\}$ has its highest common factor $m > 1$, we say that state A is a periodic state with period m. If the highest common factor is one, we say that the state is aperiodic. Aperiodic states may also be called periodic with period 1.* □

The behavior of the sequence of states visited has a peculiar property, if the Markov chain has one or more periodic states. It is illustrated with the help of the following example.

Example 6.5

Consider a simple computer system's hardware executing a machine language program. A machine instruction is fetched during the first clock period (slot) and executed during the succeeding slots. After the completion of execution of one instruction, the next instruction to be executed is fetched and the process continues. Register mode instructions take exactly one slot for execution, after the fetch slot. In the memory access addressing mode, the hardware requires three successive slots for execution, beyond the fetch. The three slots are used for evaluating the effective address, executing the operation and a memory read or memory write operation. Only one memory operation is allowed, either read or store, but not both. Therefore, the three operations in the three slots mentioned above are not always in the same succession. In any case, these result in a total of two slots for fetch and execute of a register mode instructions and four slots for a memory mode instruction. Let us assume that in the long run of the computer, the sequence of instructions encountered for execution is an independent and identically distributed sequence of the two types. Let the probability of a memory mode instruction be 0.3. The Markov chain for the sequence of states experienced by the control hardware has four states, 0, 1, 2, 3. During the state 0, the instruction is fetched. If the instruction is register mode, the states change from 0 to 1, and then back to 0. For a memory mode instruction, the states change from 0, 1, 2, 3, and back to 0, in this sequence. The state transition diagram for the Markov chain is in figure 6.9.

We see that the number of slots required for the chain to return to state 0 for the first time (starting from state 0, of course) can be 2 or 4, even numbers,

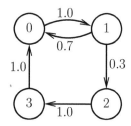

FIGURE 6.9:   State diagram for the periodic chain of Example 6.5

with a common factor of 2. Due to this property, we say that the state 0 is periodic. It is important to note that an exact sequence of states visited can be, for example, 4, 6, 8, 12, 16, $\cdots$. These numbers do have a common factor. To determine periodicity of a state, we collect all possible numbers of slots after which the chain can return for the first time to the state in question with nonzero probabilities, and examine them for a common factor larger than 1. ▯

It is illustrative to point out the following. In a chain, a state B may return to itself for the first time only after certain numbers of slots $i_1, \cdots, i_n$ with nonzero probabilities. However, if the collection of these numbers do not have a common integer factor $m > 1$, then state B is not periodic. The following modification to the above example illustrates this.

Example 6.6

In the previous Example 6.5, let the memory mode instruction check for the presence of an interrupt and require an additional slot to ready the hardware for interrupt service, if it finds an interrupt upon checking. Let the probability that the hardware finds an interrupt, when checked for, be a constant 0.1. The resulting Markov chain now has five states as shown in Figure 6.10. Therefore, starting from state 0, the chain can return to state 0, for the first time, after 2, 4, or 5 slots. State 0 in this new Markov chain is aperiodic.   ▯

What are the consequences of a periodic state? By and large, we are interested in the behavior of a Markov chain in the long run, that is, after the chain has been in operation for a large number of slots. We subjectively anticipate that the Markov property renders the influence caused by the exact state at some starting slot to drop down as the slots progress. If the chain is homogeneous, irreducible, and aperiodic, after a large number of slots, the probability of being in any particular state is nonzero, irrespective of the starting state. This property does not hold for chains with periodic states. In Example 6.5, if the starting state at slot 0 is 0, then the probability that the chain is in state 0 is 0 for each slot numbered $2j + 1$, representing odd numbers, however large.

Does the above peculiarity hold for the previous Example 6.5, even though the

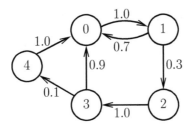

FIGURE 6.10:   State diagram for the aperiodic chain of Example 6.6

chain can return to state 0 for the first time only after 2, 4, or 5 slots? The answer is no and the justification follows. Assume that the chain with five states in the previous Example 6.5 is at state 0 during slot 0. The chain can return to state 0, possibly after many such returns, at slot numbers $2, 4, 5, 6 = 2+4, 7 = 2+5, 8 = 4+4, 9 = 4+5$, etc. That is, after any number of slots beyond three!

In other words, if the number of slots required for the first return to state A in two different ways are positive integers i_1 and i_2 with no common factor larger than 1, there exists a positive integer i such that for all integers $j > i$, the chain can return to state A. The value of i is given by $j = k_1 i_1 + k_2 i_2$, for some positive integers k_1 and k_2. That is, for every slot beyond a large enough number of slots, the chain can return to an aperiodic state with nonzero probability. How does the periodicity or otherwise of a state affect other states in a chain? The following theorem answers the question.

THEOREM 6.1
If one state of an irreducible chain is periodic with a period n, all other states are also periodic and with the same period n.

Proof
Note that a period of 1 corresponds to aperiodicity. Let state k be known to be periodic with period n. Consider a different state l. Let l be periodic with a period $m \neq n$. Therefore, it must be possible to transition from l to k with n_A transitions, return to k as many as n times each taking $i \times n$ transitions, and transition back to l in n_B transitions. The total number of transitions for this way of returning to l is $n_A + in + n_B$ transitions. Since l is periodic with a period m, the above number of transitions must also be $j \times m$ for some j. That is, for all i, the following integer equality must hold.

$$n_A + ni + n_B = j \times m, \quad i = 1, \cdots . \tag{6.9}$$

This is possible only if m is an integer factor of n. If we now consider the chain transitioning from k to l, returning to l many times and transitioning back to state l, similar to the above conclusion, we find that n is an integer factor of m. Combining the two results, $m = n$, concluding the proof. □

6.5.2   Transient and recurrent states

We now study the long term repetitiveness or otherwise of states.

DEFINITION 6.5   *In a chain, starting from the state k, if the probability of eventually returning to it is less than one, state k is said to be a transient state.*   ☐

DEFINITION 6.6   *In a chain, starting from the state k, if the probability of eventually returning to it is exactly one, state k is said to be a recurrent state.*   ☐

Clearly, a state can be either transient or recurrent, but not both. In a reducible Markov chain, the chain may leave a subset of states and never return to any of them. Reducible Markov chains are studied by first splitting the chain into multiple irreducible chains. Of course, each irreducible split chain contains all the states that can be visited from one another and from themselves. Therefore, the following discussion assumes a single irreducible chain.

LEMMA 6.1
An irreducible finite Markov chain has no transient states.

Proof
Let the number of states in the finite state irreducible chain be m. Due to the irreducibility, the probability of visiting state k from any state in m transitions is nonzero, since there exists a sequence of transitions m long or shorter from any state to state k. Therefore the probability of not visiting state k in m slots is strictly less than 1. Let $b < 1$ be the upper bound on the probability of not visiting state k in m slots. The upper bound is taken over all possible starting states in the sequence of m transitions. The exact value of b and its evaluation are irrelevant here. Now, consider a sequence of transitions, starting from state k. The sequence is made of n successive runs each run composed of m transitions. Therefore, at the end of $n \times m$ transitions, the chain would have completed n such rounds. As n increases, the probability of not visiting state k is bounded from above by a product of b with itself, n times. That is

$$P[\text{no revisits to state } k \text{ in } n \text{ rounds of } m \text{ transitions in each round}] \leq b^n. \quad (6.10)$$

Clearly, as n tends to infinity, the limit of the RHS of the above equation (6.10) is zero. That is, the probability that the chain never returns to a state is 0. This is true of all the states in the chain. Hence a finite irreducible chain has no transient states. ☐
    The following gives an additional description of why and how a state in only an infinite chain can be transient. Let a state k of an infinite state irreducible chain be transient. Let $t_k < 1$ be the probability that the chain will ever visit state k at least

once starting from itself. Since successive attempts to return are iid, after visiting k every time, the pmf of M, the number of additional visits to k, after being in k is modified geometric with a success probability of t_k. That is,

$$P[M = m] = t_k^m (1 - t_k). \tag{6.11}$$

That is, after some number of trials the chain never returns to state k. The meaning of this needs to be clearly understood. If we imagine a sample function of the entire infinite sequence of state transitions, after some number of returns to state k, the chain never returns. If we imagine the entire infinite sequences of an innumerable number of iid but different realizations of sample functions of the same ensemble Markov chain, the number of returns is distributed modified geometrically. However, there is no limit on the exact number of returns to state k; only that the probability of the exact number of returns decreases exponentially, as the exact number under consideration increases. The expectation of this distribution is

$$E[M] = \frac{t_k}{1 - t_k}. \tag{6.12}$$

Now, imagine examining the entire infinite sequence of transitions of one realization. If we examine the sample function one transition at a time, we never know whether or not the chain has already made its final visit to state k. But suppose we examine all the remaining infinite sequence of transitions and find that the chain has already made its final visit to state k. As the slots progress beyond the final visit, the states visited by the chain must tend to a set of states such that the product of transition probabilities from any state in this set to state k decreases and tends to zero, in order to make the probability of return to state k tend to zero. Due to irreducibility, there is always a sequence of transitions from every state to state k. Therefore, the only way by which the product of the transition probabilities of the sequence of transitions can tend to zero is if the number of transitions in the sequence tends to infinity.

DEFINITION 6.7 *The symbol $\lceil s_{(k,n)} \rceil$ denotes the largest of the serial numbers of states visited by an irreducible chain starting from state k and running n transitions for n slots.* ▯

If state k is transient and if we know that the chain will not return to state k after it has been in k,

$$\lim_{n \to \infty} \lceil s_{(k,n)} \rceil \text{ denoted by } \lceil s_{(k,\infty)} \rceil = \infty. \tag{6.13}$$

But, as emphasized earlier, we do not know for certainty that the chain will not return to k. We only know that the pmf of the number of visits is modified geometric. That is, the number of visits in an endless run of transitions can be infinity, but that such an event occurs with zero probability. The difference between an impossible event and an event that occurs with zero probability is that, for example, in an infinite run of iid trials, an event with zero probability can occur a finite number of times. However, even in an infinite run of iid trials, an impossible event never occurs. We now have the conclusion:

LEMMA 6.2
If k is a transient state in an irreducible chain,

$$P[\lceil s_{(k,\infty)}\rceil = \infty] = 1. \tag{6.14}$$

That is, the probability of the state of the chain running away to infinity is one. □

We can now prove the following important theorem easily.

THEOREM 6.2
In an irreducible chain, if one state is transient, all others states are also required to be transient.

Proof

Let state k be transient. Consider the probability that the state of the chain runs away, starting from another state j, that is, $P[\lceil s_{(j,\infty)}\rceil = \infty]$. Now consider two mutually exclusive conditions once the chain starts making state transitions for an infinite number of slots, after visiting state j. The first condition, called condition A, is that the chain makes at least one visit to the state k. The second condition, called condition B, is that the chain makes no visits whatsoever, to state k. Since the chain is irreducible, $P[A] > 0$ and clearly, $P[B] = 1 - P[A] < 1$. Using the theorem of total probability, we have

$$P\left[\lceil s_{(j,\infty)}\rceil = \infty\right] =$$

$$P\left[\lceil s_{(j,\infty)}\rceil = \infty|A\right]P[A] + P\left[\lceil s_{(j,\infty)}\rceil = \infty|B\right](1 - P[A]). \tag{6.15}$$

Due to the Markov property, if the chain visits state k, its behavior after that is independent of the earlier state j and depends only on state k. Therefore, we can replace the first occurrence of j on the RHS of the above equation (6.15) by k. That is,

$$P\left[\lceil s_{(j,\infty)}\rceil = \infty\right] = P\left[\lceil s_{(k,\infty)}\rceil = \infty\right]P[A] + P\left[\lceil s_{(j,\infty)}\rceil = \infty|B\right](1 - P[A]) \tag{6.16}$$

$$= t_k P[A] + P\left[\lceil s_{(j,\infty)}\rceil = \infty|B\right](1 - P[A]) \tag{6.17}$$

$$\leq t_k P[A] + 1 - P[A] \tag{6.18}$$

$$< 1. \tag{6.19}$$

The inequality (6.18) follows by substituting an upper bound of 1 for the probability $P\left[\lceil s_{(j,\infty)}\rceil = \infty | B\right]$. The inequality (6.19) follows because $t_k < 1$ due to state k being known to be transient. ◻

Although obvious, the converse is stated below due to its importance.

COROLLARY 6.1
If one state of an irreducible chain is recurrent, all other states of the chain are also recurrent. ◻

These lead to the following definitions.

DEFINITION 6.8
A chain with all transient states is called a transient chain. A chain with all recurrent states is called a recurrent chain. ◻

It turns out that there is a further distinction within the class of recurrent states. This is based on the finiteness or otherwise of the expected number of slots between successive visits to a state. Let R_{ij} be the random number of slots the chain takes to make a first visit to state j, after it has visited state i. Let $E[R_{ij}] = \bar{r}_{ij}$.

DEFINITION 6.9
A state i is called positive recurrent or recurrent non-null if $\bar{r}_{ii}$ is finite. A state j is called recurrent null or null recurrent if $\bar{r}_{jj} = \infty$. ◻

LEMMA 6.3
If one state of an irreducible chain is null recurrent, all other states of the chain are also null recurrent.

Proof
Let state k of an irreducible chain be null recurrent. Therefore,

$$\bar{r}_{kk} = \infty. \tag{6.20}$$

Now consider the behavior of the chain after visiting another state j. Between successive visits to state j, the chain may pass through state k at least twice (event A) or pass through it at most once (event B). Events A and B are mutually exclusive. Clearly, due to irreducibility, $P[A] > 0$. Also, in the first condition of passing through k at least twice, as the chain visits intermediate states, its follow-up behavior depends only on successively visited states. Using the theorem of total expectation, we have

$$\bar{r}_{jj} = E[R_{jj}|A]P[A] + E[R_{jj}|B]P[B] \qquad (6.21)$$

$$\geq (E[R_{jk}] + E[R_{kk}] + E[R_{kj}]) P[A] \qquad (6.22)$$

$$\geq (\bar{r}_{jk} + \bar{r}_{kk} + \bar{r}_{k}j)P[A] \qquad (6.23)$$

$$\geq \infty \qquad (6.24)$$

$$= \infty. \qquad (6.25)$$

The following converse obviously holds.

COROLLARY 6.2

If one state in an irreducible chain is positive recurrent, all other states are also positive recurrent.

The above results are concisely stated in the following very important theorem. Recall that a chain with a periodicity of one is also called an aperiodic chain.

THEOREM 6.3

All the states of an irreducible discrete parameter Markov chain are of the same type. They all have the same period. Furthermore, exactly one of the following three statements is true:

1. all the states are transient, or

2. all the states are null recurrent, or

3. all the states are positive recurrent.

The terms stability and positive recurrence are used interchangeably in Markov chains. In computer networks, data rates are very high and systems operate for a very large number of slots before the system parameters change. Therefore, many such practical applications are very well served by positive recurrent Markov chain models. The next section develops properties of the equilibrium operation of chains.

6.6 Analysis of Equilibrium Markov Chains

In Section 5.3.1, a preliminary equilibrium analysis of a special class of discrete parameter Markov chains is studied. The analysis there is made simple due to the structure of the state transition diagram for which we could easily show the existence of a unique solution for equilibrium state probabilities. This section develops similar results for a general class of discrete parameter Markov chains. The development in the present section reinforces some concepts introduced in Section 5.3.1. But it is not a repetition; new concepts and results are required and are developed. We start with Chapman-Kolmogorov equations (6.6) and (6.7) developed in Section 6.4.2 and reproduced below, with a slight modification in the notation.

$$P_j(i+1) = \sum_{i=0}^{\infty} P_i(i)p_{ij}. \tag{6.26}$$

$P_j(t+1)$, $j = 0, 1, \cdots$ are the state probabilities at the slot $i+1$. The one step transition probabilities of the homogeneous Markov chain are p_{ij}. The buffer size n_b corresponding to the largest numbered state is replaced by the more general ∞. In matrix notation, we have

$$\boldsymbol{P}(i+1) = \boldsymbol{P}(i)\boldsymbol{p}. \tag{6.27}$$

Expressions for the elements of the product of two matrices are obvious extensions with limits as the number of states tends to infinity. However, we should be careful to avoid invalid or ambiguous operations on infinite size matrices.

DEFINITION 6.10 *A discrete parameter Markov chain is said to be in equilibrium at slot $i+1$ if all the state probabilities at slot $i+1$ are correspondingly equal to those at slot i.* ▯

THEOREM 6.4
If a chain is in equilibrium at slot $i+1$, it will be in equilibrium for all the slots $j > i+1$ also.

Proof
Since $\boldsymbol{P}(i+1)$ is known to be the same as $\boldsymbol{P}(i)$, use $\boldsymbol{P}(i+1)$ in place of $\boldsymbol{P}(i)$ on the RHS of equation (6.27) to yield

$$\boldsymbol{P}(i+1) = \boldsymbol{P}(i+1)\boldsymbol{p}. \tag{6.28}$$

But, the RHS of (6.28) evaluates to $\boldsymbol{P}(i+2)$, as per Chapman-Kolmogorov equations. Hence we find $\boldsymbol{P}(i+2) = \boldsymbol{P}(i+1)$ or that the chain is in equilibrium at slot $i+2$. By induction, the chain is found to be in equilibrium at any slot $j > i+1$. ▯

6.6.1   Balance equations

The above property of equilibrium initiates interest in exploring conditions under which a chain can be in equilibrium. An obvious necessary condition for the existence of equilibrium state probabilities is that the Chapman-Kolmogorov equations (6.27) possess a solution when $P(i + 1)$ and $P(i)$ are both replaced by candidate equilibrium state probability vector P. If the system is in equilibrium, the slot index parameter for P is irrelevant and hence dropped. A necessary condition is that the sum of all such candidate equilibrium state probabilities evaluate to one. That is

$$\sum_{j=0}^{\infty} P_j = 1. \tag{6.29}$$

DEFINITION 6.11   *For an irreducible chain with a transition probability matrix* p,

$$\sum_{i=0}^{\infty} P_i p_{ij} = P_j \tag{6.30}$$

$$\sum_{j=0}^{\infty} P_j = 1 \tag{6.31}$$

are known as balance equations for the equilibrium state probabilities $P = [P_0 \ P_1 \cdots]$.   ⬚

DEFINITION 6.12   *If the balance equations for an irreducible chain have no valid solution, the chain is said to be unstable. A chain is said to be stable if it is not unstable.*   ⬚

Henceforth we will refer to any valid solution to the set of balance equations (6.30) and (6.31) as equilibrium state probabilities, even though we have not yet shown that the balance equations of a stable Markov chain produce a unique set of state probabilities corresponding to the equilibrium state probabilities. The required result is shown in Theorem 6.9.

THEOREM 6.5
The state probabilities obtained by solving the balance equations (6.30) and (6.31) for stable and irreducible Markov chain are all strictly positive. That is, $P_i > 0$, *for all* $i = 0, 1, \cdots$.

Proof
At least one of the probabilities, say P_i, must satisfy $P_i > 0$ in order for the sum of all the probabilities to be 1. The balance equations are modified below to express P_j

on the LHS to be a function of all other state probabilities on the RHS.

$$P_j(1 - p_{jj}) = \sum_{\forall i \neq j} P_i p_{ij} \tag{6.32}$$

Note that for an irreducible chain, $p_{jj} < 1$. Since the chain is irreducible, there must be a nonempty set of states S_i such that for each state $j \in S_i$, $p_{ij} > 0$. From equation (6.32), the equilibrium probabilities of all the states in S_i must be larger than zero. Considering such successive state transitions from states in S_i to other states, and in turn all states reachable through a finite number of transitions from the original state i, we find that the state probabilities of all such states reachable from i must have nonzero equilibrium state probabilities. Due to irreducibility, all the states in the chain are so reachable from i. Hence, every state m of an irreducible and stable chain must satisfy $P_m > 0$. ⬚

The balance equations can be graphically visualized with the help of the state transition diagram of a chain. Construct a boundary around state j in the state transition diagram. The RHS of equation (6.30) is the sum of the products of the equilibrium state probability P_j and the probabilities of all transition arcs going out of state j into all other states including to itself. This is so due to the sum of the transition probabilities of all the arcs originating from the state j. The LHS of the same equation (6.30) is the sum of similar products of the equilibrium state probabilities and corresponding transition probabilities of all transition arcs coming from all states into state j, including from itself. This is the reason for calling them the balance equations. The equation is often referred to as balancing between state j and all other states, or balancing across the boundary around state j. We obtain one such equation for every state. If we add two such equations, we get an equation corresponding to balancing across a boundary enclosing the two particular states. This is very similar to the balance equations and their graphical equivalents for the case of continuous parameter Markov chains studied in Section 4.3.4.

If we have a finite chain with $n_b + 1$ states in the chain, it is now easy to see that the last of the equations in (6.30) can be obtained by summing all other equations in the same set. Equivalently, any equation in the set can be obtained by adding all other equations in the set of equations (6.30). That is, for a finite chain, the set of equations (6.30) contains at least one redundant equation. Any redundant equation is a linear combination (in this case a simple sum) of all other equations. Therefore if we eliminate one redundant equation from the set of $n_b + 1$ equations (6.30) and use the other n_b equations in the set with the remaining equation (6.31), we have as many linear equations, $n_b + 1$, as the number of states in the chain. A set of k linear equations in k unknowns has at least one solution. Therefore, for a finite chain, the balance equations will have at least one solution. Therefore, we have the following simple result.

THEOREM 6.6
Every irreducible finite state chain is stable. ⬚

The study of a chain with infinite number of states is more involved. The following apply to both finite and infinite state chains, unless otherwise stated.

DEFINITION 6.13   *In a discrete parameter Markov chain, the long term time average of the expectation of the number of visits to state j starting from state i is denoted by v_{ij} and is defined as*

$$v_{ij}$$

$$= \lim_{n \to \infty} \frac{1}{n} E[number\ of\ visits\ to\ j\ in\ slots\ 1, 2, \cdots, n | state\ at\ slot\ 0 = i].$$
(6.33)

$\Box$

If a state j is transient, the expected number of repeated visits made to state j after the first visit to state j is the expectation of a modified geometric distribution, as in equation (6.12). Thus, starting from any state, the expected number of repeated visits made to a transient state during an infinite slot run ($n \to \infty$) of the chain is finite and we have the following result.

LEMMA 6.4
In an irreducible chain, the long term time average of the expected number of visits to a transient state, starting from any state is zero. $\Box$

LEMMA 6.5
If state j of an irreducible Markov chain is recurrent null, the expectation of the long term time average of the number of visits to state j starting from any state i is zero.

Proof
Construct a sequence of random variables $K_0, K_1, K_2, \cdots$. Here, K_0 is the number of slots for the chain to visit j for the first time, after being in state i at slot *zero*. The random variable K_l represents the number of slots for the jth visit of the chain to state j, starting from state j at some slot. Clearly, $K_1, K_2, \cdots$ are iid. For a null-recurrent state j, $E[K_l] = \infty$, for all $l = 1, 2, \cdots$. Let the random variable number of number of visits made to state j up to and including n slots be denoted by M. Due to the iid nature of K_l, we have

$$E[K_l]E[M] \leq n$$
(6.34)

$$E[M] \leq \frac{n}{E[K_l]}.$$
(6.35)

Therefore,

$$v_{ij} = \lim_{n \to \infty} \frac{1}{n} E[M] \tag{6.36}$$

$$\leq \lim_{n \to \infty} \frac{1}{n} \frac{n}{E[K_l]} \tag{6.37}$$

$$\leq \frac{1}{E[K_l]} \tag{6.38}$$

$$= 0. \tag{6.39}$$

□

LEMMA 6.6

If states i and j of an irreducible Markov chain are positive recurrent, the long term time average of the expected number of visits to state j starting from state i satisfies all of the following.

1. *It is nonzero.*

2. *It is independent of the starting state i.*

3. *It is given by the reciprocal of the expected number of slots between successive visits to the state in question, state j. That is, it is given by $\frac{1}{\bar{\tau}_{jj}}$.*

Proof

$K_0, K_1, \cdots$, and M are as defined in the proof of the above Lemma 6.5. In this case, due to the positive recurrence of of states i and j, the expectations $E[K_l]$ are all finite and $K_1, K_2, \cdots$, are iid. Over n slots, $E[K_0]$ slots are spent for the first visit. Of the remaining $n - E[K_0]$ slots, for an expected number $E[M]$ visits, the total number of slots is $E[K_0] + E[M]E[K_l]$. This number of slots is limited by n. The difference, if any is less than $E[M]$. Let the difference be a fraction a times $E[K_l]$. Therefore,

$$n = E[K_0] + (E[M] + a)E[K_l]. \tag{6.40}$$

Using this in the definition of v_{ij}, we have

$$v_{ij} = \lim_{n \to \infty} \frac{1}{n} \times \frac{n - E[K_0] - aE[K_1]}{E[K_1]} \tag{6.41}$$

$$= \frac{1}{E[K_1]} \tag{6.42}$$

$$= \frac{1}{\bar{\tau}_{jj}}. \tag{6.43}$$

The final expression results due to the original definition and notation of $\bar{r}_{jj}$ for the expected number of slots between successive visits of the chain to state j.   ▯

Combining the three Lemmas 6.4, 6.5 above, and 6.6, we have the following important result.

THEOREM 6.7

For an irreducible chain, v_{ij}, the long term time average of the expected number of visits made to a state j, starting from any state i exists and is independent of i.   ▯

We can now concentrate on computing this limit for a chain given its one-step transition probabilities.

THEOREM 6.8

In any irreducible Markov chain,

$$\lim_{n \to \infty} \frac{1}{n} \sum_{k=1}^{n} (\boldsymbol{p}^n)_{ij} = \frac{1}{\bar{r}_{jj}} = v_{jj}. \qquad (6.44)$$

That is, the above limit exists and evaluates to the long term time average of the expected number of visits to state j, independent of the starting state i. Note that this theorem statement is not restricted to aperiodic chains.

Proof

The quantity $(\boldsymbol{p}^n)_{ij}$ is the ij-th element of the matrix $\boldsymbol{p}^n$. This ij-th element therefore corresponds to the n-step transition probability that the chain is in state j at slot n, starting from state i at slot 0. In other words, starting from slot 0, the chain is in state j during slot n with a probability $(\boldsymbol{p}^n)_{ij}$. The expectation of the number of visits the chain makes to state j over slots 1 through n, again, starting from state i at slot 0 is obtained by summing the probabilities with which a visit is made at each slot, given by

$$\sum_{k=1}^{n} (\boldsymbol{p}^n)_{ij}. \qquad (6.45)$$

From Theorem 6.7, the long term average of the quantity in expression (6.45) exists and is independent of the starting state i. Furthermore, such a long term average is zero for transient and null recurrent chains and is given by v_{jj} for positive recurrent chains. Therefore, we have

$$\lim_{n \to \infty} \frac{1}{n} \sum_{k=1}^{n} (\boldsymbol{p}^n)_{ij} = \frac{1}{\bar{r}_{jj}} = v_{jj}. \qquad (6.46)$$

The quantity v_{jj} is zero for transient and recurrent null chains.   ▯

The following theorem is important because it helps constructively helps us to evaluate the equilibrium state probabilities.

THEOREM 6.9

Let $0, \cdots, n_b$ *be the states of an irreducible Markov chain. The number of states,* $n_b + 1$ *can be finite or infinite. If* $q_i, i = 1, \cdots, n_b$ *is a sequence of numbers satisfying*

$$\sum_{i=1}^{n_b} q_i = 1 \text{ and} \tag{6.47}$$

$$q_j = \sum_{k=1}^{n_b} q_k p_{jk}, \; j = 1, \cdots, n_b, \tag{6.48}$$

also written as

$$\boldsymbol{q} = \boldsymbol{q}\boldsymbol{p}, \tag{6.49}$$

then $q_j = v_{jj}$, $j = 1, \cdots, n_b$, *are the equilibrium probabilities of the states and the Markov chain turns out to be positive recurrent. That is, the balance equations of a positive recurrent Markov chain possess a unique solution and it corresponds to the equilibrium state probabilities.*

Proof

Starting from the balance equations (6.49) that are known to be true for equilibrium state probabilities, we know that

$$\boldsymbol{q} = \boldsymbol{q}\boldsymbol{p}^k, \quad k = 1 \cdots . \tag{6.50}$$

Summing and taking the average of all these equations for $k = 1 \cdots$, we have

$$\boldsymbol{q} = \lim_{n \to \infty} \frac{1}{n} \sum_{k=1}^{\infty} \boldsymbol{q}\boldsymbol{p}^k. \tag{6.51}$$

Expressing the above equation for each component q_j, we have

$$q_j = \lim_{n \to \infty} \frac{1}{n} \sum_{k=1}^{\infty} \sum_{i=0}^{\infty} q_i (\boldsymbol{p}^k)_{ij} \tag{6.52}$$

$$= \sum_{i=0}^{\infty} q_i \lim_{n \to \infty} \frac{1}{n} \sum_{k=1}^{\infty} (\boldsymbol{p}^k)_{ij}. \tag{6.53}$$

We know that

$$\lim_{n \to \infty} \frac{1}{n} \sum_{k=1}^{\infty} q_i (\boldsymbol{p}^k)_{ij} = v_{jj} \tag{6.54}$$

and that it is independent of the starting state i, for each of the three types of chains. Therefore,

$$q_j = \sum_{i=0}^{\infty} q_i v_{jj} \tag{6.55}$$

$$= v_{jj} \sum_{i=0}^{\infty} q_i \tag{6.56}$$

$$= v_{jj}. \tag{6.57}$$

The conclusion is that if a valid probability vector q exists for the solution to the balance equations, it is unique.   □

The above result has many direct implications listed below.

1. The only possible solution q to the balance equations satisfy $q_i \geq 0$ for every $i = 0, 1, \cdots$.

2. The only possible reason the balance equations the balance equations of a chain have no solution at all is that $q = 0$ is the only solution for $q = qp$. From the above, the solution for q_i is nonnegative for every $i = 0, 1, \cdots$. Any solution for $q = qp$ other than $q = 0$ can be normalized so that the probabilities sum to one and will become a valid solution for both parts of the balance equation.

3. If any valid solution can be obtained for the balance equations, the chain is stable and solution corresponds to strictly positive equilibrium state probabilities.

4. If it can be shown that no solution exists for a set of balance equations, the chain is either transient or null recurrent.

Example 6.7

Let $\pi_c = [\pi_c(1), \ldots, \pi_c(n_b)]^T$ be the vector of equilibrium probabilities at the slot center. Similarly, $\pi_e = [\pi_e(1), \ldots, \pi_e(n_b)]^T$ represents the vector of equilibrium probabilities at slot edges. Solution for the balance equations results in the following equilibrium state probabilities. For the system in Example 6.1,

$$\pi_c = [0.521277 \quad 0.37234 \quad 0.106383]^T, \tag{6.58}$$

$$\pi_e = [0.744681 \quad 0.212766 \quad 0.0425532]^T. \tag{6.59}$$

For Example 6.2,

$$\pi_c = [0.264826 \quad 0.294251 \quad 0.253383 \quad 0.18754]^T, \tag{6.60}$$

$$\pi_e = [0.441377 \quad 0.26973 \quad 0.213877 \quad 0.0750159]^T. \qquad (6.61)$$

☐

6.6.2 Time averages

Consider a positive recurrent chain that is in equilibrium. Let the equilibrium state probabilities be P_j, $j = 0, 1, \cdots$. Consider the sample space, the set of all possible outcomes of the random process. The sample space is also called the ensemble of the random experiment. Each outcome is a sample function and is an infinite sequence of exact observations of states. If we pick a random sample function from the ensemble (the sample space) of all possible infinite sequences at slot 0 and consider its state, the probability of observing state j is P_j, the equilibrium state probabilities. If we observe many different sample functions at slot 0, their state probabilities are iid. The expected value of the state is the expectation of the random process or of the ensemble. Due to equilibrium, the expectation at any slot is independent of the slot index. Let X denote the equilibrium state of the chain observed at any single slot. The sample space of X is the set of states $0, 1, \cdots$. Its expectation is given by

$$E[X] = \sum_{j=0}^{\infty} j P_j. \qquad (6.62)$$

Now, consider observing one sample function from the ensemble, for slots $0, 1, \cdots$, indefinitely. What is the long term average of the expectation of states over this infinite sequence of states? We know that the long term time average of the expected number of visits made to state j is $v_{jj} = P_j$, the equilibrium probability of state j and that it is independent of the starting state i. Let $X(k)$ be the random variable state at slot k. We know that $X(0) = i$ is observed. Denote the the long term time average of the expectation of the state by $\overline{E[X]}$. The bar over the entire expectation indicates that the expectation is taken over the time average.

$$\overline{E[X]} = \lim_{n \to \infty} \frac{1}{n} \sum_{k=1}^{n} E[X(k)|X(0) = i]$$

$$= \lim_{n \to \infty} \frac{1}{n} \sum_{k=1}^{n} \sum_{j=0}^{\infty} j P[X(k) = j|X(0) = i] \qquad (6.63)$$

$$= \sum_{j=0}^{\infty} j \lim_{n \to \infty} \frac{1}{n} \sum_{k=1}^{n} P[X(k) = j|X(0) = i]. \qquad (6.64)$$

We know that the inside limit in the above equation (6.64) is the long term time average of the expected number of visits to state j. It is given by $v_{jj} = P_j$ and that it is independent of the starting state i. Using this in equation (6.64), we have

$$\overline{E[X]} = \sum_{j=0}^{\infty} j P_j \tag{6.65}$$

$$= E[X]. \tag{6.66}$$

Note also that in equation (6.63), since the limit exists, the expectation can be taken after time averaging over the infinite sequence of slots. Hence, we have

$$E[X] = \overline{E[X]} = E[\overline{X}]. \tag{6.67}$$

What is the variance of the long term time average of states? The behavior of the chain is repetitive between successive visits to a state, say to state i, the starting state. Therefore, as the number of slots tends to infinity, the numbers of visits to every state between successive states is an iid sequence. As the number of slots tend to infinity, if the number of visits to state i tends to infinity, the variance of the state tends to zero. If the number of visits to state i does not tend to infinity, the variance of the state for the finite average over the number of visits to state i is finite. However, we know that the probability of the number of visits to state i tending to infinity is 1. And the number of visits to state i not tending to infinity occurs with zero probability. Therefore, the overall variance is the same as under the condition that the number of visits to state i tends to infinity. Therefore, the variance of the long term time average of the state sequence is zero. The two properties about the expectation and the variance of the long term time average of states is stated in the following theorem.

THEOREM 6.10
The following results hold for a positive recurrent chain.

1. *The expectation of the long term time average of the states is the expected state.*

2. *The variance of the long term time average of the states is zero.*   ⬚

6.6.3   Long term behavior of aperiodic chains

The previous subsection considered only long term time averages. This subsection studies the evolution of Markov chains starting from some state at slot 0. We consider only the special case of positive recurrent aperiodic chains. These have the most interesting behavior of evolving towards equilibrium starting from any state, as slots progress. Therefore, for the remainder of this subsection, the qualifications of positive recurrence and aperiodicity are assumed without explicit mention.

DEFINITION 6.14 $f_{ij}^{(n)}$ *is the probability that the chain visits state j for the first time at slot n, since visiting state i at slot 0.*   ⬚

We can use $f_{ij}^{(n)}$ to determine the probability that the chain is in state j at slot n, starting from state i at slot 0, irrespective of other possible visits to state j during slots $1, \cdots, n-1$. We know that $(\boldsymbol{p}^n)_{ij}$ is the probability of the chain being in state j at slot n, starting from state i at slot 0. For simpler notation, denote $(\boldsymbol{p}^n)_{ij}$ by $p_{ij}^{(n)}$. The chain can be in state j for the first time during slot k and then again in state j at slot n, $k = 1, 2, .. \, n-1$. The probability of visiting state j for the first time during slot k and then being in state j again at slot n is given by $f_{ij}^k p_{jj}^{(n-k)}$. These constitute mutually exclusive events over $k = 1, 2, \cdots, n$. Therefore,

$$p_{ij}^{(n)} = \sum_{k=1}^{n} f_{ij}^{(k)} p_{jj}^{(n-k)}. \tag{6.68}$$

Take the $\mathcal{Z}$ transform of the sequence on both sides with respect to the slot number n. This is not the $\mathcal{Z}$ transform of a probability mass function, but of the sequence of probabilities over the progression of slots. Since the probabilities are bounded from above by 1, the transform exists for all fractional real parts of the complex variable z. Denote the $\mathcal{Z}$ transform of the sequence $\{p_{ij}^{(n)}, \, n = 0, 1 \cdots\}$ by $P_{ij}(z)$ and of the sequence $\{f_{ij}^{(n)}, \, n = 0, 1 \cdots\}$ by $F_{ij}(z)$. We have

$$P_{ij}(z) = \sum_{n=0}^{\infty} p_{ij}^{(n)} z^n \tag{6.69}$$

$$= p_{ij}^{(0)} + \sum_{n=1}^{\infty} \sum_{k=1}^{n} f_{ij}^{(k)} p_{jj}^{(n-k)} z^n. \tag{6.70}$$

The range of sum in the two dimensional plane can be seen to be identical to an inner sum with n varying from k to ∞ and an outer sum with n varying from k to ∞. Therefore,

$$P_{ij}(z) = p_{ij}^{(0)} + \sum_{k=1}^{\infty} f_{ij}^{(k)} z^k \sum_{n=k}^{\infty} p_{jj}^{(n-k)} z^{n-k} \tag{6.71}$$

$$= p_{ij}^{(0)} + \sum_{k=1}^{\infty} f_{ij}^{(k)} z^k \sum_{l=0}^{\infty} p_{jj}^{(l)} z^l \tag{6.72}$$

$$= p_{ij}^{(0)} + F_{ij}(z) P_{jj}(z). \tag{6.73}$$

The quantity p_{ij} is the probability of reaching state j in zero transitions (slots) starting from state i. Therefore, $p_{ii}^{(0)} = 1$ for all i and $p_{ij}^{(0)} = 0$ for all $i \neq j$. Therefore, we have

$$P_{ii}(z) = 1 + F_{ii}(z) P_{ii}(z) \tag{6.74}$$

$$= \frac{1}{1 - F_{ii}(z)}. \tag{6.75}$$

In order to evaluate $\lim_{n\to\infty} p_{jj}^{(n)}$, construct a new sequence defined by

$$w_0 = p_{jj}^{(0)} \tag{6.76}$$

$$w_n = p_{jj}^{(n)} - p_{jj}^{(n-1)}, \quad n > 0. \tag{6.77}$$

We have

$$p_{jj}^{(n)} = \sum_{k=0}^{n} w_k \tag{6.78}$$

so that

$$\lim_{n\to\infty} p_{jj}^{(n)} = \sum_{k=0}^{\infty} w(n). \tag{6.79}$$

The $\mathcal{Z}$ transform of $\{w_n\}$ is given by

$$W(z) = P_{jj}(z) - zP_{jj}(z) = P_{jj}(z)(1 - z) \tag{6.80}$$

from elementary properties of the $\mathcal{Z}$ transform in Section A.11. Using this in equation between the $\mathcal{Z}$ transforms $P_{ii}(z)$ and $F_{ii}(z)$ in equation (6.75), we have

$$W(z) = P_{ii}(z)(1 - z) = \frac{1 - z}{1 - F_{ii}(z)}. \tag{6.81}$$

We know that

$$\lim_{z\to1} W(z) = \sum_{k=0}^{\infty} w(n). \tag{6.82}$$

Evaluating this limit, we have

$$\lim_{z\to1} W(z) = \lim_{z\to1} \frac{1 - z}{1 - F_{ii}(z)} \tag{6.83}$$

$$= \lim_{z\to1} \frac{1}{\frac{dF_{jj}(z)}{dz}}. \tag{6.84}$$

The quantity $f_{ii}^{(n)}$ is the probability that the first return to state i takes n slots. Hence, the expectation of the pmf $f_{ii}^{(n)}$ is the expected number of slots between successive returns of the chain to state i which we know to be the reciprocal of the equilibrium state probability P_i of the state i, from equations (6.43) and (6.57). The expectation can also be obtained with the help of the $\mathcal{Z}$ transform of $\{f_{jj}^{(n)}\}$ as follows.

$$\frac{dF_{ii}(z)}{dz} = \sum_{n=1}^{\infty} f_{ii}^{(n)} n z^{n-1}. \tag{6.85}$$

If we evaluate the above derivative at $z = 1$, we get the needed expectation. Obtaining the expectation and equating it the reciprocal of the equilibrium probability of state i, we have

$$\left. \frac{dF_{ii}(z)}{dz} \right|_{z=1} = \frac{1}{P_i}.$$

Combining equations (6.87), (6.84), and (6.86), we have

$$\lim_{n \to \infty} p_{jj}^{(n)} = \lim_{z \to 1} W(z) \tag{6.86}$$

$$= \lim_{z \to 1} \frac{1}{\frac{dF_{jj}(z)}{dz}} = P_i, \tag{6.87}$$

the equilibrium state probability of state i. Now,

$$\lim_{n \to \infty} p_{ij}^{(n)} = \lim_{n \to \infty} f_{ij}^{(k)} p_{jj}^{(n-k)} \tag{6.88}$$

from equation (6.68). The probability of being in state j in the limit, after a run of an unlimited number of transitions (one transition per slot), given that the state at slot i was i is given from equation (6.68) by

$$\lim_{n \to \infty} p_{ij}^{(n)} = \lim_{n \to \infty} \sum_{k=1}^{n} f_{ij}^{(k)} p_{jj}^{(n-k)}. \tag{6.89}$$

In the limit, for every k in the sum, $p_{ij}^{(n-k)}$ tends to P_j, the equilibrium state probability of j, from equation (6.87). So,

$$\lim_{n \to \infty} p_{ij}^{(n)} = \lim_{n \to \infty} P_j \sum_{k=1}^{n} f_{ij}^{(k)}. \tag{6.90}$$

The sum in the above equation is the sum of the probabilities of first time visits to state j being at various slots $1, 2, \cdots$, after being in state i at slot 0. For our positive recurrent aperiodic chain, this sum is 1, since the chain is guaranteed to visit state j. Therefore, we have

$$\lim_{n \to \infty} p_{ij}^{(n)} = \lim_{n \to \infty} P_j. \tag{6.91}$$

The above development shows that a positive recurrent aperiodic chain will evolve towards equilibrium as the number of slots progress, irrespective of the state at any earlier slot. The result is formally stated in the following theorem known as the ergodic theorem for Markov chains.

THEOREM 6.11
Let a positive recurrent aperiodic Markov chain be at an arbitrary state to begin with and operate for an unbounded number of transitions. In the limit, as the number of transitions tends to infinity, the the probability distribution of states tends to its equilibrium distribution. □

6.6.4 Continuous parameter Markov chains

In Chapter 4, the continuous parameter irreducible chain was defined. Balance equations for the equilibrium state probabilities were developed as the steady state solution to the differential equations. We also proved that if the balance equations have a unique solution, the long term time average of the state occupancies satisfy the same balance equations. We did not show the uniqueness of equilibrium state probabilities, if such a set exists, for a general case. Neither did we address the question of whether or not a Markov chain evolves towards equilibrium, if operated for a long time (as the parameter value tends to infinity). Both these aspects are best examined with the help of the results on discrete parameter Markov chains which are developed above in this chapter. Continuous parameter Markov chains have no distinction of periodicity. Corresponding to every irreducible continuous parameter chain, there is an irreducible, aperiodic discrete parameter Markov chain with identical balance equations. The approach to show this is simply to normalize state transition rates to correspond to probability values. To accommodate for any necessary difference as opposed to a factor, we can introduce transitions from a state back to itself in the discrete parameter chain being constructed. Since transition arcs from a state to itself occurs identically on both sides of the balance equations, such newly introduced transitions do not change the balance equations.

Consider an irreducible continuous parameter Markov chain with states $0, 1, \cdots$. Let the transition rate from a state i to state j be α_{ij}. Of course $\alpha_{ii} = 0$ for all i. Let

$$\beta_i = \sum_{j=0}^{\infty} \alpha_{ij} \tag{6.92}$$

be the total rate with which the chain is leaving state i for some other state, given that the chain is in state i. Let

$$\gamma = \delta + \max\{\beta_0, \ \beta_1, \cdots\} \tag{6.93}$$

where δ is a rate of transition. The value of δ is strictly positive but otherwise arbitrary, in principle. In practice, visualizing a small rate (in comparison with other rates) helps. Now, define transition probabilities by normalizing all the rates with respect to γ. That is, define

$$p_{ij} = \frac{\alpha_{ij}}{\gamma}, \ \forall j \neq i, \quad \text{and } i = 0, 1, \cdots \tag{6.94}$$

$$p_{ii} = 1 - \frac{\beta_i}{\gamma}, \quad i = 0, 1, \cdots . \tag{6.95}$$

The above transition probabilities ensure that for every transition in the original continuous parameter chain, there is a corresponding transition with nonzero transition probability. Furthermore, the introduction of δ above ensures that there is a transition from every state to itself. Therefore the chain is aperiodic. The balance equations for the original continuous parameter Markov chains are equivalent to those for the newly constructed discrete parameter Markov chain. That is, both the chains have correspondingly identical equilibrium state probabilities. Furthermore, due to the aperiodicity of the discrete parameter chain, the corresponding continuous parameter chain evolves to equilibrium as the number of transitions tends to infinity. We know from the earlier result of Theorem 4.5 that as time of operation tends to infinity, the number of transitions of an irreducible continuous parameter chain tends to infinity with probability one. Hence we have the following result.

THEOREM 6.12

If an irreducible continuous parameter chain is stable, there is a unique set of strictly positive equilibrium state probabilities associated with it. If the chain is stable and allowed to run for a long time (that is, as the parameter value increases without bounds), the state probabilities evolve and converge to their equilibrium probabilities. □

This also proves that the original stable M/M/1/∞ queue reaches equilibrium, if it is operated for an unbounded amount of time.

6.7   Performance Evaluation of Discrete Time Queues

6.7.1   Throughput

Throughput[†] is the rate of the number of successful service completions, per slot. In general, different throughput occur conditioned on different states due to state dependent arrivals or services, or both. Even in the simple Example 6.1, throughput appears to be zero when the buffer is full, if evaluated at the input. The throughput appears to be zero under the empty system condition, if evaluated at the output. Throughput is commonly evaluated by first evaluating conditional throughput, i.e., the throughput of the system given that the system is in a particular state. The weighted average of the state dependent throughput gives the overall throughput.

In general, a queuing system may receive simultaneous multiple arrivals soon after a slot edge as in Example 6.2. In other applications, simultaneous multiple departures may be allowed just before a slot edge if the system has multiple servers. Let a_{ij} be the probability of j arrivals being admitted when the state of the system is i at the arrival instant. Since the number of arrivals that can be admitted into the buffer cannot exceed the number of vacant positions in the buffer,

$$a_{ij} = 0, \quad i + j > n_b. \tag{6.96}$$

[†]Some parts in this section are rewritten (with copyright permission) from material appearing in the article G. R. Dattatreya and L. N. Singh, "Relationships among different models for discrete-time queues," *WSEAS Transactions on Systems*, volume 4, issue 8, August 2005, pp. 1183–1190.

Also,

$$\sum_{j=0}^{n_b-i} a_{ij} = 1, \quad i = 0, ..., n_b - 1 \quad \text{and} \quad (6.97)$$

$$a_{n_b 0} = 1. \quad (6.98)$$

Similarly, let s_{ij} be the probability of j departures given that the state of the system is i at the time of departure (i.e., at the slot center).

$$s_{ij} = 0, \ j > i, \quad (6.99)$$

since there cannot be more departures than there are customers in the system. Of course,

$$\sum_{j=0}^{i} s_{ij} = 1. \quad (6.100)$$

In practice, the probabilities of arrivals that are actually admitted into the system are state dependent, and the same is true for departure probabilities. Furthermore, the state transition diagram of such a Markov will have arcs (or arrows) between non-adjacent states. Consequently, calculation of both a_{ij} and s_{ij} requires some care and thought. The throughput, nonetheless, can be easily expressed in general form as

$$E[Y] = \sum_{i=0}^{n_b-1} \pi_e(i) \left[\sum_{j=1}^{n_b-i} j \, a_{ij} \right] \quad (6.101)$$

if evaluated by considering customers admitted into the system. If evaluated by considering all the departures, the same throughput is evaluated as

$$E[Y] = \sum_{i=1}^{n_b} \pi_c(i) \left[\sum_{j=1}^{i} j \, s_{ij} \right]. \quad (6.102)$$

The throughput of the system in Example 6.1 evaluates to 0.2872 packet per slot. For Example 6.2, it evaluates to 0.4411 packet per slot.

6.7.2   Buffer occupancy

The buffer occupancy is the time average of the number of customers in the system and is a very important performance criterion. Buffer occupancy is denoted by $E[N]$ and is evaluated as the weighted average of the buffer occupancies at different states. The weights are the equilibrium probabilities of different states in the system. Again, we have two different Markov chains giving us two different sets of steady state probabilities requiring some resolution. The expected numbers of customers at the slot center and at the slot edges are clearly two distinct quantities representing the physical averages of the number of customers observed at the two different epochs. Hence,

$$E[N_c] = \sum_{i=1}^{n_b} i\, \pi_c(i) \text{ and} \tag{6.103}$$

$$E[N_e] = \sum_{i=1}^{n_b} i\, \pi_e(i). \tag{6.104}$$

For Example 6.2, $E[N_c] = 1.3636$ and $E[N_e] = 0.9225$. These results lead us to the following questions. Which is the more useful quantity? Which (if either) represents the true time average of buffer occupancy? Finally, which should be used in the Little's result to evaluate the average response time? In reality, the overall time average of the number of customers is

$$\frac{1}{\tau} \int_{t=0}^{\tau} E[N(t)] dt \tag{6.105}$$

where $E[N(t)]$ is the expected number of customers at the real variable time t and $(0, \tau]$ is the time period of one slot. However, in our ideal discrete time queue, arrivals occur within an infinitesimal amount of time after the slot edge and departures occur during an infinitesimal time before a slot edge. Thus, $E[N_c]$ is the expected number of customers for the entire slot time not including the slot edge points. The $E[N_e]$ is the expected number of customers for only an infinitesimal time period during a slot and hence, its contribution vanishes in the above integral. A byproduct of this discussion is that the difference $E[N_c] - E[N_e]$ is the average number of customers that leave the system just before a slot edge. Of course, the same difference also represents the average number of customers that arrive soon after a slot edge. Hence,

$$E[N_c] - E[N_e] = E[Y]. \tag{6.106}$$

For Example 6.2, $E[N_c] = 1.3636$, $E[N_e] = 0.9225$ and the difference 0.4411 equals $E[Y]$ in number of packets per slot.

6.7.3 Response time

The average response time is the expected number of slots spent by a customer in the system, and is denoted by $E[R]$. This is easily evaluated by using the Little's result,

$$E[R] = \frac{E[N]}{E[Y]}, \tag{6.107}$$

provided we have the correct values for $E[N]$ and $E[Y]$. Little's result establishes a relationship among "time averages" of the number in the system, number of arrivals per slot, and the average response time of customers. As stated in the previous section, $E[N_c]$ is the true time average of the number of customers in the system and hence, should be used in the Little's result. Therefore,

$$E[R] = \frac{E[N_c]}{E[Y]} = \frac{E[N_e]}{E[Y]} + 1. \tag{6.108}$$

6.7.4   Relationship between π_c and π_e

The treatment in the previous section identifies the role and the physical interpretations of the various quantities in the two different Markov chains (one depicting number of customers at slot centers, and the other at slot edges). Since both Markov chains represent the same system, it is possible to work with just one Markov chain, as long as correct interpretations are used and accounted for. In view of this observation, explicit relationships between both Markov chains are now developed. For simplicity, it is assumed that at most one arrival with probability a, and at most one service completion with probability s are allowed. The results, however, may be easily extended to allow for bulk arrivals and departures. Note that the number of customers at a slot center is governed by the number at the preceding slot edge and any intervening arrival. Similarly, the number of customers at a slot edge is governed by the number at the preceding slot center and any intervening departure. Hence,

$$\pi_c(0) = \pi_e(0)(1 - a), \tag{6.109}$$

$$\pi_c(i) = \pi_e(i - 1)a + \pi_e(i)(1 - a), \tag{6.110}$$

$$\pi_c(n_b) = \pi_e(n_b) + \pi_e(n_b - 1)a, \quad \text{and} \tag{6.111}$$

$$\pi_e(0) = \pi_c(0) + \pi_c(1)s, \tag{6.112}$$

$$\pi_e(i) = \pi_c(i)(1 - s) + \pi_c(i + 1)s, \tag{6.113}$$

$$\pi_e(n_b) = \pi_c(n_b)(1 - s), \tag{6.114}$$

where $0 < i < n_b$ in equations (6.110) and (6.113).

6.8 Applications

Example 6.8

A discrete time packet transmitter has a capacity of 3 packets including any under service. If a packet is under service, the transmitter attempts to transmit it with a probability of 0.6. If attempted, the probability of collision requiring reattempt is 0.3. At most one packet can arrive at the queue, with a probability of 0.8, in any slot. Express each $\pi_e(i)$ as a function of one or more $\pi_c(j)$ and other required parameters.

Solution

If there is at least one packet in the system, the probability of a service completion, s, is the product of the probability of attempt, 0.6, and the probability of success if attempted, $(1 - 0.3)$. This evaluates to 0.42. If the system has at least one packet, the probability of no service completion, $(1 - s)$ is 0.58.

$$\pi_e(0) = \pi_c(0) + 0.42\pi_c(1), \tag{6.115}$$

$$\pi_e(i) = 0.58\pi_c(i) + 0.42\pi_c(i+1), \quad i = 0, 1, 2 \tag{6.116}$$

$$\pi_e(3) = 0.58\pi_c(3). \tag{6.117}$$

▯

Example 6.9

Evaluate the important performance figures of the system in Example 6.2.

Solution

Familiarization with the details of the original statement of Example 6.2 and the calculations so far in successive examples on this system are helpful at this juncture. We know from equations (6.60) and (6.61) that the equilibrium state probabilities for the the states 0, 1, 2, and 3 of the system are

$$\pi_c = [0.264826 \quad 0.294251 \quad 0.253383 \quad 0.18754]^T, \tag{6.118}$$

$$\pi_e = [0.441377 \quad 0.26973 \quad 0.213877 \quad 0.0750159]^T \tag{6.119}$$

at the slot centers and slot edges, respectively. Evaluation of the probability that an attempted arrival will be dropped is illustrative. The conditional probability that a random attempted arrival will be dropped is evaluated as follows. If the state is 3, any attempted arrival will definitely be dropped. If the state is 2 and the attempted arrival is part of a pair of simultaneous arrivals, one it will be dropped with a probability of 0.5. A random attempted arrival is a singleton with a probability of

$$P[\text{singleton} \mid \text{at least one attempt}]$$

$$= \frac{P[\text{singleton and at least one attempt}]}{P[\text{at least one attempt}]} \tag{6.120}$$

$$= \frac{P[\text{singleton}]}{P[\text{at least one attempt}]} \tag{6.121}$$

$$= \frac{0.3}{0.1 + 0.3} \tag{6.122}$$

$$= 0.75. \tag{6.123}$$

Similarly, the probability that an attempted arrival is one of a pair evaluates to

$$P[\text{one of a pair} \mid \text{at least one attempt}] = 0.25 \tag{6.124}$$

$$P[\text{drop} \mid \text{attempt}] = \pi_2(3) + \pi_e(2) \times 0.25 \times 0.5 \tag{6.125}$$

$$= 0.0750159 + 0.213877 \times 0.25 \times 0.5 \tag{6.126}$$

$$= 0.101750525. \tag{6.127}$$

The expected number of attempted arrivals in a slot is $(0.3 + 0.1 \times 2) = 0.5$. The (actual) throughput is easier to evaluate by examining the output since only one departure is possible and occurs with a probability $s = 0.6$ whenever the system is not empty at the slot center. Therefore,

$$E[Y] = (1 - 0.264826) \times 0.6 \tag{6.128}$$

$$= 0.4411044. \tag{6.129}$$

The expected loss of packets per slot is not necessarily the same as the probability of drop! It should be evaluated as an expectation:

$$E[\text{packet loss per slot}] = P[\text{lose 1}] + 2P[\text{lose 2}] \tag{6.130}$$

$$= 0.3\pi_e(3) + 0.1\pi_e(2) + 2 \times 0.1\pi_e(3) \tag{6.131}$$

$$= 0.5\pi_e(3) + 0.1\pi_e(2) \tag{6.132}$$

$$= 0.5 \times 0.0750159 + 0.1 \times 0.213877 \tag{6.133}$$

$$= 0.03750795 + 0.0213877 \tag{6.134}$$

$$= 0.05889565. \tag{6.135}$$

As a check, adding the expected loss of packets per slot and the throughput gives

$$E[\text{packet loss per slot}] + E[Y]$$

$$= 0.05889565 + 0.4411044 \tag{6.136}$$

$$= 0.50000005 \tag{6.137}$$

which is the expected number of attempted arrivals per slot, correct to seven decimal places. The above illustrates the importance of representing the intermediate probabilities accurate to a sufficient number of decimal places. A difference between inaccurate representations of two small probabilities can be disastrous to the accuracy and consistency of the overall results. The expected number of packets at slot centers represents that time average occupancy.

$$E[N_c] = \sum_{n=0}^{3} n\pi_c(n) \quad \text{which evaluates to} \tag{6.138}$$

$$= 1.363637. \tag{6.139}$$

Using Little's result, the expected response time evaluates to

$$E[R] = \frac{1.363637}{0.4411044} \tag{6.140}$$

$$= 3.09 \quad \text{slots.} \tag{6.141}$$

The expected response time is represented above with only two decimal places. The evaluation of state probabilities at slot centers using those at slot edges is illustrative in this example, due to the possibility of two arrivals in a slot. We have

$$\pi_c(0) = \pi_e(0)P[\text{no arrival}] \tag{6.142}$$

$$= 0.441377 \times 0.6 \tag{6.143}$$

$$= 0.2648262 \tag{6.144}$$

$$\pi_c(1) = \pi_e(0)P[1 \text{ arrival}] + \pi_e(1)P[0 \text{ arrival}] \tag{6.145}$$

$$= 0.441377 \times 0.3 + 0.26973 \times 0.6 \tag{6.146}$$

$$= 0.294251 \tag{6.147}$$

$$\pi_c(2) = \pi_e(0)P[2 \text{ arrivals}] + \pi_e(1)P[1 \text{ arrival}]$$

$$+ \pi_e(2)P[0 \text{ arrivals}] \tag{6.148}$$

$$= 0.441377 \times 0.1 + 0.26973 \times 0.3$$

$$+ 0.213877 \times 0.6 \tag{6.149}$$

$$= 0.2533829 \tag{6.150}$$

$$\pi_c(3) = \pi_e(1)P[2 \text{ arrivals}]$$

$$+\pi_e(2)P[\text{attempt one or two}] + \pi_e(3) \qquad (6.151)$$

$$= 0.26973 \times 0.1 + 0.213877 \times 0.4 + 0.0750159 \qquad (6.152)$$

$$= 0.1875397. \qquad (6.153)$$

The resulting state probabilities at slot centers are consistent with those originally obtained and given in equation (6.118), correct to several decimal places. □

6.8.1 The general Geom/Geom/m/k queue

In this system, there is one waiting line and m servers. The maximum number of customers the system can hold, including any under service, is called the buffer capacity and it is k. Arrivals to a full buffer are lost. During a slot, at most one arrival occurs, and with probability p. Service completion probability during a slot is s. We observe the number in the system at slot edges.

6.8.1.1 Transition probabilities

The first task in analyzing the system is the determination of transition probabilities. This system illustrates that the changeover to discrete time can introduce many possible combinations of situations. In the following, the variable l is the reduction in the number in the system during the time between successive observations. Thus, l is the number of departures minus the number of arrivals. Therefore, l can range from -1 to m. If there is an arrival, the number of departures is $l + 1$. If there is no arrival, the number of departures is l. Let $a_{n,n-l}$, $n, n - l \in \{0, \cdots, n\}$, be the one-step transition probability from the state n to the state $n - l$. The various cases and their corresponding transition probabilities are listed below.

case i) $n < m, 0 \le l \le n.$

$$a_{n,n-l} = p \binom{n+1}{l+1} s^{l+1}(1-s)^{n-l} + (1-p) \binom{n}{l} s^l(1-s)^{n-l} \tag{6.154}$$

case ii) $m \le n < k, 0 \le l < m.$

$$a_{n,n-l} = p \binom{m}{l+1} s^{l+1}(1-s)^{m-l-1} + (1-p) \binom{m}{l} s^l(1-s)^{m-l} \tag{6.155}$$

case iii) $m \le n < k, l = m.$

$$a_{n,n-l} = (1-p)s^m \qquad (6.156)$$

case iv) $n = k, 0 \le l \le m.$

$$a_{n,n-l} = \binom{m}{l} s^l (1-s)^{m-l} \qquad (6.157)$$

case v) $n < m, l = -1.$

$$a_{n,n+1} = p(1-s)^{n+1} \qquad (6.158)$$

case vi) $m \le n < k, l = -1.$

$$a_{n,n+1} = p(1-s)^m \qquad (6.159)$$

All other $a_{ij} = 0$. That is, if a combination of a_{ij} is not covered by any of the above cases, such a transition from state i to state j is impossible, and $a_{ij} = 0$.

6.8.1.2 Equilibrium state probabilities

The Markov chain for this system has a convenient property. There is only one arc from state $n - 1$ to state n. The several arcs from state k to others are all multiplied by P_k, the steady state probability of state k. Thus

$$P_{k-1}a_{k-1,k} = P_k(1 - a_{kk}) \qquad (6.160)$$

$$P_{k-1} = \frac{P_k}{a_{k-1,k}}. \qquad (6.161)$$

Similarly, the balance equation across a boundary between states $n - 1$ and n is

$$P_{n-1}a_{n-1,n} = \sum_{i=n}^{k} P_i \sum_{j=0}^{n-1} a_{ij}. \qquad (6.162)$$

The above equations can be used recursively to evaluate all the probabilities from $P_{k-1}, \cdots, P_0$ as multiples of P_k. Summing $\sum_{i=0}^{k} P_i = 1$ yields actual steady state probabilities. Evaluation of performance figures is a straightforward application of the corresponding techniques developed earlier. Equations(6.161) and (6.162) above can use $P_k = 1$. After all probabilities are calculated they can all be multiplied by a factor to ensure $\sum_{i=0}^{k} P_i = 1$.

The following example is a variation of the the above general Geom/Geom/m/k queue. In Example 6.10, the two servers are not identical.

Example 6.10

In a discrete time queuing system with room for 3 customers (including any under service), the arrival process is geometric with probability of an arrival being 0.3 in any slot. There are two servers, A and B. Both servers have independent geometric service times. However, the probability of service completion in a slot is 0.5 for server A and 0.4 for server B. Therefore, if both servers are free, the customer about the get service prefers server 1. Develop the complete state transition diagram of the system with all transition probabilities. The number of customers in the state diagram should be counted at the center of the slot. Analyze the system.

Solution
This is an illustrative example with many possible state transitions. Since there is a preference of one server over the other, we need to keep track of which server the packet is at, if there is only one packet in the system. State 1_a denotes the condition that the system has only one packet and that it is with server A. Similarly, the state 1_b denotes the condition that the system has only one packet and that it is with server B. Clearly, there is no transition from state 0 to state 1_b because a packet arriving into an empty system always chooses server A. The combination of Boolean conditions for various state transitions are complicated. But a systematic enumeration of various mutually exclusive conditions will help in correct evaluation of the state transition probabilities. The final state transition diagram is drawn in Figure 6.11. The equilibrium state probabilities can be obtained by solving

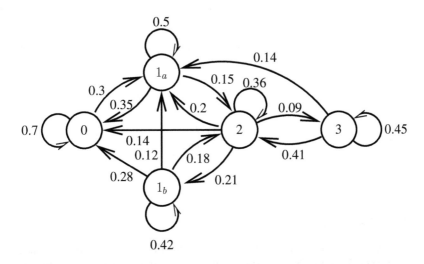

FIGURE 6.11: State diagram for the Markov chain in Example 6.10

the simultaneous equations. Let them be p_0, p_{1a}, p_{1b}, p_2, and p_3. All the performance figures can be obtained from the state transition diagram and the equilibrium state probabilities.

The probability that the system is empty at a slot edge is given by

$$q_0 = p_0 + 0.35p_{1a} + 0.28p_{1b} + 0.14p_2. \tag{6.163}$$

The coefficients of the probabilities on the RHS of the above equation (6.163) are obtained directly from the state transition diagram. The probability that the system is full at a slot edge is useful to evaluate the throughput. This is given by

$$q_3 = 0.45p_3. \tag{6.164}$$

Now, the throughput is easily evaluated as

$$E[Y] = 0.3(1 - q_3) \tag{6.165}$$

where the 0.3 is due to the probability of an arrival in a slot; an arrival occurs with probability 0.3, as long as the system is not full at slot edges. We can also evaluate the throughput of each server, separately.

$$E[Y_a] = 0.5(1 - p_0 - p_{1b}) \quad \text{and} \tag{6.166}$$

$$E[Y_b] = 0.4(1 - p_0 - p_{1a}). \tag{6.167}$$

Finally the probability that a packet is serviced by server A is given by

$$\frac{E[Y_a]}{E[Y_a] + E[Y_b]}. \tag{6.168}$$

⬜

6.8.2   Slotted crossbar

A very simple example that clearly illustrates the advantages of considering the two different Markov chains and selecting the one that is better suited for the problem at hand is the "Output Queuing in a Space-Division Packet Switch," or crossbar switch.[‡] The slotted system has N input lines and N output lines. Packets appear at the inputs of each line with an independent and identical probability p. Each packet is required to be forwarded to one of the output lines. For each packet, all the destination lines are equally likely. The output queued system functions as follows. At the beginning of a slot, the hardware for the output line under consideration (which is referred to as line A) quickly scans all the input lines, picks the packets meant for the output line A, and drops all those packets into a queuing buffer (also called buffer A here). The server of this queue forwards exactly one packet, if one or more are available in the buffer. The forwarded packet departs from the buffer at the end of the slot. Therefore, every packet spends at least one slot in the crossbar. One of the quantities under study is the number of packets left over at the end of the slot, for a large N. These are the packets that spend longer than the minimum one slot of life time in the crossbar. The number of arrivals during a slot into the buffer A is very well approximated as a Poisson random variable with a mean number of p. All such arrivals can be considered to be dropped instantaneously into the buffer right at the beginning of the slot, since the packets spend all of the slot in the system, and one packet leaves the system at the end of the slot, irrespective of the exact time instant during the slot that the packet is dropped into the buffer. Let the probability of k of these arrivals be a_k.

A discrete parameter Markov chain for the number of packets left at the end of the slot can be constructed. Then the state is the "packets in the waiting line." The transition probabilities in their Markov chain are

$$q_{ij} = a_{j-i+1}, \text{ if } i > 0 \text{ and } j \geq -1 \tag{6.169}$$

$$q_{00} = a_0 + a_1 \tag{6.170}$$

$$q_{0j} = a_{j+1}, \text{ if } j > 0. \tag{6.171}$$

The Markov chain at the slot center can also be formulated easily. The following are the transition probabilities,

$$p_{ij} = a_{j-i+1}, \text{ if } i > 0 \text{ and } j \geq -1 \tag{6.172}$$

$$p_{0j} = a_j, \quad j \geq 0. \tag{6.173}$$

The transition probabilities in equations (6.172) and (6.173) correspond exactly to those in the standard M/G/1/∞ queuing system All the necessary quantities such as the equilibrium probabilities of the number of packets in the system, their expected number, the expected response time (including the exact one slot service time), etc.

[‡]Some parts in this and the next subsection are rewritten (with copyright permission) from material appearing in the article G. R. Dattatreya and L. N. Singh, "Relationships among different models for discrete-time queues," *WSEAS Transactions on Systems*, volume 4, issue 8, August 2005, pp. 1183–1190.

are readily obtained by using p as the arrival rate, and a constant of 1 slot for service time with zero variance, in the widely available results for the standard M/G/1/∞ queuing system. The expected number of customers in an M/G/1/∞ queue with a constant service time of one unit and an arrival rate of p per unit time is given by the Pollaczek-Khinchin mean value formula in equation (5.95).

$$E[N_{mg1}] = p + \frac{p^2}{2(1-p)}. \tag{6.174}$$

The above expected number corresponds to the expected number in the discrete time system in the body of the slot, since the M/G/1 Markov chain is identical to the Markov chain at the slot center. At the slot edges, the expected number momentarily dips by the throughput p and hence

$$E[N_e] = \frac{p^2}{2(1-p)}. \tag{6.175}$$

Using the results in equations (6.112) and (6.113), we obtain

$$\pi_e(0) = \pi_c(0) + \pi_c(1) \tag{6.176}$$

$$\pi_e(i) = \pi_c(i+1), \text{ for } i > 0, \tag{6.177}$$

where $\pi_c(i)$ corresponds to equilibrium probabilities of the M/G/1 system and $\pi_e(i)$ corresponds to equilibrium probabilities of the number in the waiting line of the crossbar system.

6.8.3   Late arrival systems

In our discrete time system studied so far in this chapter, a packet is required to be in service for at least one slot. This is typical of every synchronous, electronic hardware. A peculiar alternative is called a late arrival system (LAS). In LAS, any arrival occurs just before the slot edge and any departure occurs soon after the slot edge. This can easily be accommodated in our Markov chain at the slot center by simply disallowing an arrival when the buffer is full. All other aspects of the Markov chain and performance evaluations remain the same as in our development. LAS systems can allow for instantaneous service completion, and such systems are referred to as LAS-IA (immediate access). LAS systems which enforce that an arriving packet must wait for a minimum of one slot, even if the service facility is free, are referred to as LAS-DA (delayed access). The distinction between LAS-IA and LAS-DA systems manifests itself in the definition of the service time probabilities.

6.9 Conclusion

This chapter introduced the proper use of timing and synchronization to help with the formulation of Markov chains for slotted systems. In such systems, the state can be observed at two distinct epochs during a slot. This possibility leads to two distinct Markov chains that represent the same physical system. These Markov chains, one observed at slot centers and the other at slot edges, are interrelated. Indeed, the steady state probabilities of one of these chains can be determined with the help of those of the other chain. This is a useful feature, since expectations from both chains can be used to evaluate the common performance figures.

The mathematical properties of homogeneous and irreducible discrete parameter Markov chains are developed. These properties provide us with the following important constructive results. Unstable systems possess no solution for the corresponding balance equations. Stable systems have a unique solution for their balance equations. A stable aperiodic Markov chain evolves to its equilibrium operation as the number of slots of operation increases without bounds. These results also used to develop the following properties of irreducible and stable continuous parameter Markov chains. There is no distinction of periodicity or otherwise for continuous parameter Markov chains. Their balance equations possess a unique solution. They evolve towards equilibrium operation as the time of their operation increases without bounds.

The performance figures of discrete time queuing systems, including throughput, buffer occupancy and expected response time are developed using the equilibrium probabilities from the appropriate Markov chains. The methods developed are applied to illustrative examples. The approach used here is quite simple to follow and easily extended to more complex scenarios. The end result is a systematic, coherent method for performance analysis of slotted systems.

6.10 Exercises

1. If we split a long speech signal into slots in which each slot is "talk" or "silent," we get the following model. If a slot is talk, the next slot continues to be talk with a probability of 0.7. If a slot is silent, the next slot continues to be silent with a probability 0.4. What is the average fraction of time used for talk?

2. An M/M/1/1 system is a two state continuous time Markov chain with a free state F lasting for an exponentially distributed time with rate λ and a busy state B, with rate μ. Construct a discrete parameter Markov chain as follows. We observe the system state at discrete time instants separated by iid exponential time intervals with rate α. Prove that the resulting transition probabilities are as follows. Probability of transition from F to B is $\frac{\lambda}{\lambda+\mu+\alpha}$ and the probability

of transition from B to F is $\frac{\mu}{\lambda+\mu+\alpha}$.

3. Now, consider the same continuous time system as in the above problem. That is, an M/M/1/1 system is a two state continuous time Markov chain with a free state F lasting for an exponentially distributed time with rate λ and a busy state B, with rate μ. Construct a different discrete parameter Markov chain as follows. We observe the state at time instants separated by a constant amount of time τ. Try to formulate the resulting discrete parameter Markov chain. You may stop at reasonably developed mathematical expressions for the state transition probabilities.

4. A discrete time packet transmitter functions over time slots of equal time interval T. The system has buffer for only two packets, including any being transmitted. At most one customer can arrive during a slot. However, the probabilities of arrival are state dependent. The arrival probability is 0.5 if the state is 0 at the time of arrival. It is 0.3 if the state is 1 at the time of arrival. Service completion is iid with a probability of completion of 0.4 in any slot.

    (a) Draw the complete Markov chain of the number of packets in the system, observed at the slot center.

    (b) Evaluate the equilibrium probabilities of the different states.

5. Show that, in general, two arbitrary states of a Markov chain cannot be merged into one. That is, in the contemplated merged chain, the transition probabilities from the merged state may depend on the state from which the chain entered the merged state, rendering the state sequence "non-Markov."

6. Starting from an arbitrary Markov chain with transition probabilities p_{ij}, split a particular state k into two states k_1 and k_2 so that the resulting chain is Markov and equivalent to the original chain. Are the transition probabilities into and out of each of the states k_1 and k_2 uniquely determined from p_{ij}? If not develop the relations that the transition probabilities in the new chain satisfy.

7. From the solution to the above problem, develop the conditions that the transition probabilities p_{ij} of a Markov chain should satisfy such that a particular pair of states i and j can be merged into one state resulting in an equivalent Markov chain to the original.

8. Consider a discrete time packet buffer with a total buffer space for N packets including any under service. Arrivals are Bernoulli with a probability a for an arrival. Service completion is Bernoulli with a probability of completion of s. Let P_0 be the steady state probability of finding 0 customers at the slot center. Determine P_b, the probability that an attempted arrival will be lost, as a function of P_0, N, a, and s.

9. A discrete time packet transmitter has a buffer for only 3 packets including any under transmission. Multiple packets can simultaneously attempt to arrive soon after a slot edge. The buffer will allow arrivals up to its capacity only and the others will get lost. Number of attempted arrivals in a slot is Poisson distributed with a mean number of 0.7 in a slot. At most one packet completes service during a slot, with an iid probability 0.8 in a slot. Answer the following.

   (a) Let P_0, P_1, P_2, and P_3 be the equilibrium state probabilities at slot centers. Find the throughput as a function of P_0, P_1, P_2, and P_3.

   (b) What is the probability that all the attempted arrivals will be dropped at the time of one or more attempted arrivals? Again, answer this in terms of the algebraic quantities P_0, P_1, and P_2.

10. Consider a Geom/Geom/1/3 (one server with buffer size of two including any being serviced) queuing system with arrival probability = 0.6 and service completion probability = 0.4. Completely draw the Markov chain of the system. Calculate the equilibrium state probabilities at slot centers, the average number of jobs in the system, and the average throughput.

11. Consider a discrete time packet transmission system. The station has a buffer with a capacity of three packets including any under service. There can be at most one arrival to a buffer with a probability of 0.4. If a packet arrives in a slot, or if there is already a packet in the transmitter of the station transmission is attempted with a probability 0.7, during a slot. If a transmission is attempted, it fails (due to collisions) with a probability 0.1 requiring reattempt. Draw the Markov chain for the state of the transmitter, at slot centers.

12. Consider an equilibrium discrete time packet transmitter system with a capacity to hold 3 packets including any packet/s under transmission. Arrivals are iid with at most one arrival occurring with a probability of 0.6. The transmitter can transmit up to two packets simultaneously. During any slot, the transmitter attempts to transmit one packet with a probability of 0.5 and two packets with a probability of 0.2. If there are i packets in the system and the transmitter attempts to transmit $j > i$ packets, then i packets will be transmitted.

   (a) Draw the complete Markov chain at slot centers, including transition probability values.

   (b) Let $P_0, \cdots, P_3$ be the equilibrium probabilities of the four states at slot centers. Determine the throughput of the transmitter as a function of these $P_0, \cdots, P_3$, by observing the successful departures for various conditions.

   (c) Determine $Q_0, \cdots, Q_3$, the equilibrium state probabilities at slot edges, as functions of $P_0, \cdots, P_3$.

13. Two independent Bernoulli arrival streams are merged. Their slot edges are synchronized. Note that two arrivals can appear simultaneously. When such an event occurs, one of the two at random is considered to be the first of the two arrivals. Under such a condition, the interarrival times has a sample space of all nonnegative integers. Determine the pmf of such IAT.

14. A heavily loaded closed queuing system consists of a CPU with a queue and an I/O with another queue. The degree of multiprogramming is two. This means the number of jobs in the system is always two. That is, whenever one of the two jobs depart from inside, an external job from the ever heavily loaded external queue enters the system to ensure that two jobs are present in the system all the time. The jobs can be distributed any way in the two queuing stations. The service times of the CPU and the I/O are independent of each other and both memoryless discrete time random variables. If a job is being serviced by the CPU during a time instant, it has a probability 0.5 of completing service at the end of the discrete time instant. Similarly, if a job is being serviced by the I/O during a time instant, it has a probability 0.2 of completing service by the end of the discrete time instant. This completely determines a discrete parameter Markov chain for the number of jobs in the CPU queuing system (any being serviced plus any waiting). Obviously, the states of the Markov chain are 0, 1, or 2 only. Determine the steady state probabilities of these states.

15. In a computer system, a bus (a resource) is used by three devices, CPU, I/O_1, and I/O_2. Only one device can use the bus at a time, of course. Time is measured in discrete units called clock periods. During a free clock period, the devices attempt to access the bus mutually exclusively with probabilities of 0.6, 0.2, and 0.1, respectively, for the CPU, I/O_1, and I/O_2. Once a device grabs the bus, it can continue to have it for as long as it needs. During any clock period a device has the bus, it opts to have it for one more clock period (irrespective of how long it has had it) with the following probabilities 0.1, 0.4, and 0.6 respectively for CPU, I/O_1, and I/O_2. Determine the utilization of the bus by each of the three devices.

16. Consider a homogeneous discrete parameter Markov chain with states 0, 1, 2, and 3 and the following transition probability matrix.

$$\begin{pmatrix} 0.1 & 0.2 & 0.4 & 0.3 \\ 0.0 & 0.3 & 0.0 & 0.7 \\ 0.3 & 0.4 & 0.2 & 0.1 \\ 0.0 & 0.5 & 0.0 & 0.5 \end{pmatrix} \qquad (6.178)$$

Determine if the chain is irreducible. Determine if the state 0 is transient.

17. In a digital system, a hardware piece is invoked by an arriving data, in discrete clock periods. Every clock period, a job may come in with a probability 0.5.

Jobs are independent. No more than one job can appear in a clock period. If an arriving job finds the hardware busy, it can wait in a queue buffer of waiting room size 1 job only (so, no more than 2 jobs can be in the system at any time). If an arriving job finds the waiting room buffer full, it is "lost" and will not return later. The service time is one clock period with a probability 0.8 and two clock periods with probability 0.2. Draw a clear and complete state transition diagram; identify the events (arrival and/or departure) on every transition arc. Fill in numerical values of probabilities for all arcs.

18. In a discrete time queuing system with room for 3 packets (including any under service), the arrival process is as follow. The probability of one arrival is 0.3 in any slot. The probability of two arrivals in a slot is 0.1. No more than two arrivals can occur in a slot. Arrivals to a full system get lost. If two arrivals come in and there is room only for one packet, one of the arrivals enters the system and the other gets lost. The service rate is iid Bernoulli with a probability of service completion of 0.6 during any slot. Develop the complete transition probability diagram including the probabilities of all arcs.

19. Consider a slotted packet switched crossbar with three lines. A line does not communicate with itself. The probability of a packet arrival is iid Bernoulli 0.3 on any line. Possible destinations are equally likely. Packets come in soon after the beginning of a slot and leave just before the end. Number of packets is counted at the slot edges. The output queues have a buffer of size 3 (including the packet being served). Draw the complete Markov chain of one of the queuing systems. Determine and write the probability values on the arcs of the transition diagram.

20. There is a sequence of two discrete time Geom/Geom/1 queuing systems with the number of customers counted at the center of the slot. Both the queues have room for only one customer each (that is no waiting room). Arrivals to the first queue are lost if the first queue is full. The output of the first queue feeds to a second queue. If the output from the first queue finds the second queue full, it leaves the system at that point. The probability of an attempted arrival to the first queue is p. The probability of service completion in a slot is s in each station. Develop a clear state transition diagram for the Markov chain representing the system. Clearly write down ALL the transition probabilities.

21. Consider a discrete time switching element. It has two input lines (top and bottom) and two output lines. Each input port has room for only one packet. A packet at an input port has either destination with equal probabilities. The iid probability of an input at the top is p and at the bottom is q. Outputs are not blocked and they move out freely. If only one input port has a packet, it gets transmitted without any clash. If both the input ports have packets, both of them get transmitted only if they have different output ports as destinations. If both have the same required destination, one of the input packets is chosen at random for transmission and the other one stays in the buffer. Properly define

the state of the system (state is checked at the edge of a slot). Develop a clear state transition diagram for the Markov chain including the expressions for ALL the state transition probabilities.

22. A parallel computation system has 3 processors, 2 memory modules and functions in a slotted mode in which a processor can access at most one memory module for a number of successive slots. Similarly, a memory module can serve at most one processor at a time. During every slot, a free processor attempts to access a memory module (either module will do) with a probability 0.4. If a processor has a memory module in its control, it releases it at the end of the slot with a probability 0.7. Draw the Markov chain of the number of busy memory modules, at the slot center.

23. Consider a discrete time packet buffer with a total space for two packets. Packets arrive to a buffer according to a Bernoulli process, with p being the probability of a packet arriving in a time slot. Packets are transmitted from the buffer only if the buffer contains two packets. If there are two packets in the buffer, then, with probability s_2, both packets will be transmitted, and with probability s_1 only one packet will be transmitted ($s_1 + s_2 = 1$).

   (a) Draw the state diagram, clearly labeling the transition probabilities.
   (b) Write the set of equations to solve for the steady state probabilities P_0, P_1, ...
   (c) Find the throughput of the system, as functions of assumed steady state probabilities P_0, P_1, $\cdots$.

24. Analyze an equilibrium Geom/Geom/1/∞ queue with an arrival probability of a and a service completion probability of s. Specifically, prove the following. The departure process is iid Bernoulli, the same as the arrival process. Use the following approach.

   (a)

   $$P_0 = \frac{s-a}{s} \tag{6.179}$$

   $$P_n = \frac{s-a}{s(1-s)}\left(\frac{(1-s)a}{(1-a)s}\right)^n, \text{ for } n > 0. \tag{6.180}$$

   (b)

   $$Q_n = (1-\rho)\rho^n, \text{ for } n \geq 0 \text{ where} \tag{6.181}$$

   $$\rho = \frac{a(1-s)}{s(1-a)}. \tag{6.182}$$

   (c) The probability of a departure from the queue is a.
   (d) Following a departure, the state distribution in the next slot is the equilibrium.

(e) Following a slot in which there is no departure, the state distribution is the equilibrium distribution.

(f) Hence, the departure process from the queue is the same as the arrival process.

25. The purpose of a wireless sensor network is to transfer as many data packets as possible to a central base station. Consider an intermediate store and forward node of such a network, operating in a slotted (discrete time) mode.

   The node can be in receive (packet arrival) or transmit (service) mode, but not both, during a slot. The buffer can hold at most two packets including any under service. If the node is in receive mode, one packet arrives with a probability of 0.7. At most one arrival is possible in a slot. When the node is in transmit mode, it successfully transmits a packet, if there is at least one packet in the buffer. The node operates in receive or transmit mode, with probabilities. These probabilities are independent in successive slots. But they can be dependent on the state of the system during a slot. The designer's job is to assign probabilities for optimal operation (maximum throughput). Let q_0, q_1, and q_2 be the operating probabilities that the system is in receive mode when there are 0, 1, or 2 packets in the system, respectively. Clearly, $(1 - q_0)$, $(1 - q_1)$, and $(1 - q_2)$ are the corresponding operating probabilities that the system is in transmit mode. Obviously, the activity for the following slot is decided based on the state at the slot edge. Your ultimate task is to find the optimal values for q_0, q_1, and q_2. Do this by systematically answering the following.

   (a) Draw the complete state transition diagram. Assume that the system state is observed at slot edges. Include all the state transition probabilities. If you can find out optimal values for some of q_0, q_1, and q_2, you can use them here, after stating them.

   (b) Determine the equilibrium state probabilities. These can be functions of variable or optimal values of q_0, q_1, and q_2.

   (c) Determine the optimal values for q_0, q_1, and q_2, that maximize the throughput of the node.

26. A slotted wireless communication node cannot receive and transmit simultaneously to prevent interference between the two activities. If the node is in a field of other wireless nodes, both its reception and transmission links may be disabled during some slots, to allow other nodes in the field to function. If the reception link is open, at most one arrival can come in with iid probabilities. If the transmission link is open and if the buffer has at least one packet, the packet at the head of the buffer will be definitely transmitted. There are no collisions due to static TDMA scheduling. During any clock period, in addition to any external arrival, at most one packet may be internally generated at the node and placed in the queue for eventual transmission.

Consider such a wireless node with unlimited buffer space. Let

$$r = P[\text{reception link is open}] \tag{6.183}$$
$$a = P[\text{exactly one arrival} \mid \text{reception link is open}] \tag{6.184}$$
$$g = P[\text{exactly one packet is generated in the node}] \tag{6.185}$$
$$t = P[\text{transmission link is open}]. \tag{6.186}$$

Characterize the packet arrival process (not including the generated packets). That is, are the successive external packet arrivals iid in successive slots? Draw the Markov chain at slot edges. Determine the equilibrium state probabilities and condition for stability. Determine the throughput. What is the packet transmission process? Are successive packet transmissions iid in successive slots?

27. Study the following slotted LAN. There are m transmitting stations connected to the LAN. Each has a buffer of unlimited size. The buffer of station i receives at most one payload packet arrival in each slot. During successive slots, packets arriving at the ith buffer for transmission are iid as a Bernoulli random variable, with a probability a_i. All the stations are equipped with an identical random number generation algorithm with an identical starting seed. Therefore, they successively generate identical random numbers. During a slot, station i is picked for transmission with a probability q_i. Successive generation of the identity of the station for transmission are iid. All the stations know which transmitter's turn it is for transmission, during every slot. Therefore, there is no collision. When a station is scheduled for transmission, and it has no packets to transmit, it stays silent for the duration of the slot, or transmits a control packet. Both are equivalent for the performance analysis. Determine the set of probability values $\{q_1, \ldots, q_m\}$ that minimizes the overall expected response time of payload packets through the LAN.

In practice, the optimal probabilities can be rounded off to rational numbers so as to make each probability, multiplied by a particular reasonable integer value K, return integers. The nodes can then be scheduled for transmission in a periodic fashion with K as the period of the cycle. The resulting schedule will not be optimal for two reasons. First, of course, is due to the approximation of the probabilities. The second is the deterministic (as opposed to iid probabilistic) nature of the suggested scheduling. However, this deterministic and cyclic scheduling has the advantage of the ability to turn on and off the transmission circuit as and when necessary to reduce battery usage.

Chapter 7

Continuous Time Queuing Networks

7.1 Introduction

Single queues are useful models in many applications wherein one or more servers attend to customers in a single waiting line. They are also useful building blocks in more comprehensive systems of queues; a single queue may be a component in a large network.

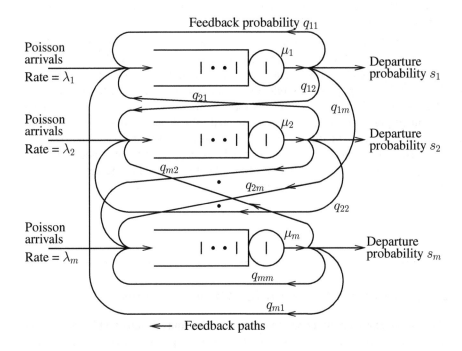

FIGURE 7.1: Open queuing network

In this chapter, we will study networks of queues with exponential servers and Poisson external arrivals. The queues are interconnected as follows. A stream of customers leaving a queue is split into substreams and fed back to the entry points of possibly all the queues. Splitting is probabilistic and splits of successive customers are mutually independent. In practice, some scheduler realizes and implements the transfer of jobs from service completing queues to tails of queues. There are two classes of such networks. In the first class, there is at least one entry point and at least one exit point in the entire network as follows. Customers from outside the network arrive as independent Poisson streams at the entry points of the queues. They depart from the network at exit points. If the system is in equilibrium, the overall rate of entry must equal the overall departure rate. Such networks which field external traffic of customers are called open queuing networks. Figure 7.1 shows the general structure of such a system. In a practical application network, it is typical for a job originating at one point to process a little and either ship the rest to another server or trigger an additional job. Generally, the completion of a job in such a network requires attention at several points in the network and the job cycles through a random number of stations, with possible repetitions. Memoryless models and probabilistic switching are good approximations for such applications. Development of such a model for a practical application and specifying its parameters can be a comprehensive case study, and it is usually very application dependent. We will only develop the analysis, after an application system has been modeled as a network and its parameters have been specified.

In the second class of queuing networks, there are no arrivals to or departures from outside the network. A constant number of customers circulate within the different queues. These are called closed queuing networks. A closed queuing network may be thought of as an appropriate model of a computer network that admits a constant number of jobs when there are always jobs waiting outside the system to fill up these limited positions, as and when completed jobs depart. Alternatively, we can imagine the network to be running a fixed set of processes like the operating system's procedures. All external jobs are viewed only as data for these procedures to run. This way, we have a constant number of jobs floating around in the network. Both open and closed networks find applications in performance modeling of computer and data networks.

7.2   Model and Notation for Open Networks

There are m exponential servers (with rates μ_i) in front of each of which customers form a waiting line. Each waiting line with its corresponding server is also called a station or a node of the network. The queue at each station, i, receives a Poisson stream of customers from outside the network, with a rate λ_i. These are appropriately called external arrivals. Customers leaving a station i are routed to the tails of various stations with probability q_{ij} for the station j and with probability s_i towards the overall departure or destination point. The stream of external arrivals to station i and and the streams of customers fed back from various stations are merged at the tail of the queue of station i. The sum of the probabilities of routing a customer completing service at station i through various branches must evaluate to 1. That is,

$$s_i + \sum_{j=1}^{m} q_{ij} = 1, \quad i = 1, \ldots, m. \tag{7.1}$$

Figure 7.2 shows the connections, splitting probabilities, and rates of customers moving through various arcs around a single queue within the open network.

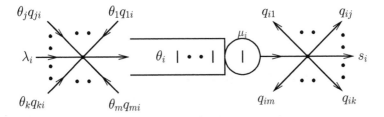

FIGURE 7.2: Input streams and distributing the output stream for one queue

We assume that the network is connected. That is, an external customer entering any station can eventually pass through all the stations, with nonzero probabilities. If the network is not connected, it can be split into two or more nonoverlapping networks that do not interfere with one another. In such a case, each of the connected networks can be studied separately, as we do here. The state of the system is defined as a vector of nonnegative integers corresponding to the ordered set of numbers of customers in each station. The vector state $n = (n_1, \ldots, n_i, \ldots, n_m)$, where n_i is the number of customers in station i. We use the lower case n_i to represent the random variable as well as its outcome. The exact usage will be clear from the context. We define a unit vector corresponding to each station as follows.

$$v_i = (0, \ldots, 0, 1, 0, \ldots, 0) \tag{7.2}$$

with a 1 in the i-th position and zeros in all other positions represents the state with a single customer in the i-th station and no other customer anywhere else. Clearly,

$$n = \sum_{i=1}^{m} n_i v_i \tag{7.3}$$

where the multiplication of a vector by a scalar results in a vector with each component of the vector being the product of the original component and the scalar multiplier.

Why is the the stochastic process $n(t)$ Markovian? The next change from a state $n(t)$ to another occurs whenever there is an arrival into or a service completion from any station. A service completion from a station being routed back to the waiting line of the same station does not change the number of customers in any station. How an arrival or a departure is routed is independent of the past. Therefore, the composite random variable time for any state change is memoryless. Also, the probability distributions of possible changes depends only on the present state. Hence, $n(t)$ is a continuous parameter Markov chain. If the network is stable, we know from the properties of Markov chains (Theorem 6.12) that the equilibrium state probabilities are the unique solution of the balance equations. Let $p(n)$ be the equilibrium probability of the network being in state n.

7.3   Global Balance Equations

Consider the equilibrium operation of the network. Let the current state be n. Following are the possible cases of events that can cause a state transition from a state n to some other state, and their rates of occurrences.

1. An external arrival into the queue of station i changes the network state. The rate of such a state change is λ_i.

2. A customer completing service from station i and leaving the entire network causes a change in the network state. The rate of service completion at station i is μ_i, provided that the station has at least one customer in its queue. Therefore, it is helpful to introduce a step function of an integer argument,

$$u(k) = 0, \quad \text{if } k \le 0 \text{ and} \tag{7.4}$$

$$= 1, \quad \text{if } k \ge 1. \tag{7.5}$$

A service-completing customer departs the entire network (as opposed to being fed back to one or another station) with a probability s_i. Therefore the rate of occurrence of such a state transition is $\mu_i u(n_i) s_i$. The factor $u(n_i)$ accounts for the possibility of such a transition only if $n_i > 0$.

3. A customer completing service at a station i joining the queue of a different station j, due to feedback, also causes a change in the network state. In order

to ensure that the rate of a customer being fed back to the same queue is not used in the state transition rate, the following Kronecker delta function, δ_{ij}, is used. Leopold Kronecker was a German mathematician.

$$\delta_{ij} = 1, \text{ if } i = j \text{ and}$$
$$= 0, \text{ if } i \neq j. \tag{7.6}$$

The rate such a transition is $\mu_i u(n_i) q_{ij}(1 - \delta_{ij})$. As in the above case, the factor $u(n_i)$ ensures that the rate is nonzero only if $n_i > 0$. The last factor $(1 - \delta_{ij})$ evaluates to zero if $i = j$.

Summing the above rates, the overall conditional rate of change of state from state n, given that the network is in state n, is therefore given by the expression

$$\sum_{i=1}^{m} \lambda_i + \sum_{i=1}^{m} \mu_i u(n_i) s_i + \sum_{i=1}^{m} \sum_{j=1}^{m} \mu_i u(n_i) q_{ij}(1 - \delta_{ij})$$

$$= \sum_{i=1}^{m} \lambda_i + \sum_{i=1}^{m} \mu_i u(n_i) \left(s_i + \sum_{j=1}^{m} q_{ij} - q_{ii} \right) \tag{7.7}$$

$$= \sum_{i=1}^{m} [\lambda_i + \mu_i u(n_i)(1 - q_{ii})]. \tag{7.8}$$

At any instant of time during an equilibrium operation of the network, the unconditional rate of the state changing from state n is given by the above expression multiplied by the equilibrium probability of the network being in that state, $p(n)$. This unconditional rate is denoted by $\alpha(n)$ and evaluates to

$$\alpha(n) = p(n) \sum_{i=1}^{m} [\lambda_i + \mu_i u(n_i)(1 - q_{ii})]. \tag{7.9}$$

At any instant of time, the network state may change from some other state to state n, as follows.

1. An external arrival into station i when the network state is $(n - v_i)$ is one such, provided $n_i > 0$. This occurs with a rate $\lambda_i u(n_i)$.

2. An overall departure from station i when the network state is $(n + v_i)$ changes the state to n. This occurs with a rate $\mu_i s_i$.

3. When the network state is $(n + v_i - v_j)$, a departure from station i routed to station j changes the state to state n, provided $i \neq j$ and $n_i > 0$. From earlier arguments, we know that this occurs with a rate $\mu_i q_{ij} u(n_j)(1 - \delta_{ij})$.

For each of these rates to be effective, the state of the network should be in the correspondingly required state under equilibrium. The unconditional rate of change of the network state from any other state into state n is denoted by $\beta(n)$ and evaluates to

$$\beta(n) = \sum_{i=1}^{m} p(n - v_i)\lambda_i u(n_i) + \sum_{i=1}^{m} p(n + v_i)\mu_i s_i$$

$$+ \sum_{i=1}^{m} \sum_{j=1}^{m} p(n + v_i - v_j)\mu_i q_{ij} u(n_j)(1 - \delta_{ij}) \tag{7.10}$$

$$= \sum_{i=1}^{m} p(n - v_i)\lambda_i u(n_i) + \sum_{i=1}^{m} p(n + v_j)\mu_i s_i$$

$$+ \sum_{i=1}^{m} \sum_{j=1}^{m} p(n + v_i - v_j)\mu_i q_{ij} u(n_j) - \sum_{i=1}^{m} p(n)\mu_i q_{ii} u(n_i).$$

$$\tag{7.11}$$

The global balance equations are obtained by equating the rates of transitioning into and out of every possible state n. This results in one equation for every state, as follows.

$$\alpha(n) = \beta(n).$$

Substituting for $\alpha(n)$ from equation (7.9) and for $\beta(n)$ from equation (7.11), the global balance equations for the Markov chain of the open queuing network are

$$p(n) \sum_{i=1}^{m} [\lambda_i + \mu_i u(n_i)(1 - q_{ii})]$$

$$= \sum_{i=1}^{m} p(n - v_i)\lambda_i u(n_i) + \sum_{i=1}^{m} p(n + v_j)\mu_i s_i$$

$$+ \sum_{i=1}^{m} \sum_{j=1}^{m} p(n + v_i - v_j)\mu_i q_{ij} u(n_j) - \sum_{i=1}^{m} p(n)\mu_i q_{ii} u(n_i).$$

$$\tag{7.12}$$

If the network is stable, the above equations possess a unique probability mass function $p(n)$ for the vector state variable n. That is, the above equations will be valid for all n, if and only if $p(n)$ is the correct equilibrium state probabilities for all n. However, the equations do not appear to be easy to solve for $p(n)$. Fortunately, the solution is quite simple and was obtained by J. R. Jackson in the year 1957 by guessing it and verifying that the guessed solution satisfies every one of the global balance equations. The guessed solution is known as the product form solution. The following is a development of the product form candidate solution and the verification of its validity. The rate of customers flowing through each station's queue is determined first through the development of traffic equations. These rates are functions of the arrival rates and the feedback proportions only, provided the network is stable. Their determination also makes it easy to specify conditions for stability of the entire network.

7.4 Traffic Equations

At the tail of the queue of every station, several streams of customers merge. Let θ_i be the combined rate of customers flowing through each station i. The rate θ_i is composed of the rate of external arrivals, λ_i and the rates of fed back customer streams. The traffic output rate from station j is θ_j. The component of this rate being fed back to station i is $\theta_j q_{ji}$. Summing all the components of customer rates entering station i, we have the m equations

$$\theta_i = \lambda_i + \sum_{j=1}^{m} q_{ji}\theta_j, \ i = 1, \ldots, m. \tag{7.13}$$

The above m equations are known as the traffic equations.

THEOREM 7.1
The traffic equations (7.13) possess a unique solution for $\{\theta_i, \ i = 1, \cdots, m\}$.

Proof
The idea behind the proof is to construct a fictitious discrete parameter Markov chain in which the stations of the network are states and data movement links in the network are state transition arcs of the Markov chain. Also, a new state, state 0, is introduced corresponding to a point from where all the external arrivals originate and to which all the network departures come in. Since the network is connected, the resulting Markov chain is irreducible. Introduce the following auxiliary quantities.

$$\theta_0 = \sum_{k=1}^{m} \lambda_k, \tag{7.14}$$

$$w_{0j} = \frac{\lambda_j}{\sum_{k=1}^{m} \lambda_k} = \frac{\lambda_j}{\theta_0}, \ j = 1, \cdots, m, \tag{7.15}$$

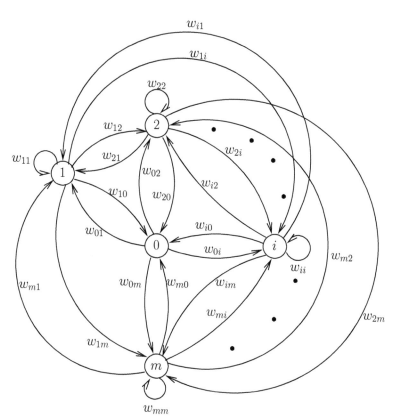

FIGURE 7.3:   Markov chain representing traffic equations

$$w_{i0} = s_i, \quad \text{and} \tag{7.16}$$

$$w_{00} = 0. \tag{7.17}$$

Of course, $w_{ij} = q_{ij}$, when $i \geq 1$ and $j \geq 1$ are true. We know that the sum of fractions of throughput routed for overall departure from the network must equal the sum of all external arrival rates. That is,

$$\sum_{j=1}^{m} \theta_j s_j = \sum_{j=1}^{m} \lambda_j = \theta_0. \tag{7.18}$$

We are now ready to manipulate the traffic equations to a form corresponding to the balance equations of a finite state irreducible Markov chain. Using $w_{0i}\theta_0$ from equation (7.15) for λ_i in the traffic equation (7.13), we obtain the following alternative form for the traffic equation.

$$\theta_i = w_{0i}\theta_0 + \sum_{j=1}^{m} q_{ji}\theta_j \text{ and} \tag{7.19}$$

$$\theta_0 = \sum_{j=0}^{m} w_{j0}\theta_j. \tag{7.20}$$

In order to express the above traffic equations in a compact form, define auxiliary variables

$$w_{ij} = q_{ij}, \quad j = 1, \cdots, m \text{ and } i = 1, \cdots, m. \tag{7.21}$$

This leads to

$$\theta_i = \sum_{j=0}^{m} w_{ji}\theta_j, \quad i = 0, \cdots, m. \tag{7.22}$$

Let $a = \sum_{j=1}^{m} \theta_j$ and define

$$x_i = \frac{\theta_i}{a} \tag{7.23}$$

so that the traffic equations now take the form

$$x_i = \sum_{j=0}^{m} w_{ji}x_j \text{ and} \tag{7.24}$$

$$\sum_{j=0}^{m} x_j = 1. \tag{7.25}$$

Equations (7.24) and (7.25) together have an identical form as the balance equations of a Markov chain. The square matrix $\{w_{ij}\}$ has the form of the transition probability matrix of an irreducible Markov chain. Therefore equations (7.24) and (7.25) possess a unique solution for x_0, through x_m. The θ_i values are easily obtained from x_0, through x_m as follows.

$$\theta_0 = x_0 a = \lambda. \tag{7.26}$$

Therefore, the required normalized factor

$$a = \frac{\lambda}{x_0}, \tag{7.27}$$

with the help of which all other θ_i are obtained as

$$\theta_i = x_i a. \tag{7.28}$$

This completes the proof. $\Box$

In order for the entire network to be stable, every station is required to be stable. That is $\frac{\theta_i}{\mu_i} < 1, i = 1, \ldots m$ is the required condition for the stability of the entire network. Therefore, given a network with all the arrival and service rates and all the splitting probabilities, the traffic equations can be solved and the stability of each station can be examined. The entire network is stable if all the stations are stable. Denote the normalized load in station i by

$$\rho_i = \frac{\theta_i}{\mu_i}, \text{ for } i = 1, \cdots, m. \tag{7.29}$$

7.5   The Product Form Solution

The vector states of the network at two slightly different time instants are definitely dependent on each other, since the state at the later of the two time instants is strongly influenced by the state at the earlier time instant. However, if we freeze the time at some particular instant during equilibrium operation of the network, could the random variable number of customers in the different stations appear to be statistically independent? In other words, can the state probability distributions of the numbers of customers in the different stations at one time instant during equilibrium operation be independent? We do not know from the analysis so far. Nevertheless, we can consider such a simple candidate solution for the equilibrium state probabilities of the entire network state. If we are able to verify the validity of such a candidate solution, we will then know that we have "caught" the correct solution. This is true since such a Markov chain has at most one solution for equilibrium state probabilities. If there is no solution, the system is unstable and cannot be in equilibrium. Such a candidate solution is known as a product form solution, since the independence hypothesis allows us to multiply marginal solutions to obtain the candidate solution for the vector state. The candidate solution for the marginal equilibrium probabilities of a station is "guessed" to be the same as for a round robin M/M/1/∞ system. Such a candidate marginal solution for the equilibrium state probability of finding n_i customers in station i is

$$P(n_i) = (1 - \rho_i)\rho_i^{n_i}, \quad \text{for all } n_i \geq 0 \text{ and for } i = 1, \cdots, m. \quad (7.30)$$

Note that the upper case P is used to distinguish this candidate solution from the unknown correct solution. Adding or subtracting 1 from n_i, the following hold, respectively.

$$P(n_i + 1) = \rho_i P(n_i), \quad \text{for all } n_i \geq 0, \text{ for } i = 1, \text{ and} \quad (7.31)$$

$$P(n_i - 1) = \frac{1}{\rho_i} P(n_i), \quad \text{for all } n_i \geq 1, \text{ for } i = 1, \ldots, m. \quad (7.32)$$

The candidate product form solution for the vector state $\boldsymbol{n}$ is

$$P(\boldsymbol{n}) = \prod_{i=1}^{m} P(n_i) \quad (7.33)$$

$$= \prod_{i=1}^{m} [(1 - \rho_i)\rho_i^{n_i}]. \quad (7.34)$$

Therefore, we have

$$P(\boldsymbol{n} - \boldsymbol{v}_i) = \frac{1}{\rho_i} P(\boldsymbol{n}), \text{ for } n_i > 0 \quad (7.35)$$

$$= \frac{1}{\rho_i} \prod_{k=1}^{m} [(1 - \rho_k)\rho_k^{n_k}], \text{ for } n_i > 0. \quad (7.36)$$

$$P(\boldsymbol{n} + \boldsymbol{v}_i) = \rho_i P(\boldsymbol{n}), \text{ and} \quad (7.37)$$

$$= \rho_i \prod_{k=1}^{m} [(1 - \rho_k)\rho_k^{n_k}]. \quad (7.38)$$

$$P(\boldsymbol{n} + \boldsymbol{v}_i - \boldsymbol{v}_j) = \frac{\rho_i}{\rho_j} P(\boldsymbol{n}), \text{ for } n_j > 0 \quad (7.39)$$

$$= \frac{\rho_i}{\rho_j} \prod_{k=1}^{m} [(1 - \rho_k)\rho_k^{n_k}], \text{ for } n_j > 0. \quad (7.40)$$

7.6   Validity of Product Form Solution

THEOREM 7.2
The product form probability mass function is the correct solution for the equilibrium vector state probabilities of a stable open queuing network.

Proof
We use product form expressions for each of $P(n - v_i)$, $P(n + v_i)$, and $P(n + v_i - v_j)$ from equations (7.38) through (7.40) in equation (7.11) to evaluate the "product form rate" of changing to state n. To distinguish this from the unknown correct transition rate, we use $B(n)$ in place of $\beta(n)$.

$$B(n) = \sum_{i=1}^{m} \frac{1}{\rho_i} \left(\prod_{k=1}^{m} [(1 - \rho_k)\rho_k^{n_k}] \right) \lambda_i u(n_i) + \sum_{i=1}^{m} \rho_i \left(\prod_{k=1}^{m} [(1 - \rho_k)\rho_k^{n_k}] \right) \mu_i s_i$$
$$+ \sum_{i=1}^{m} \sum_{j=1}^{m} \frac{\rho_i}{\rho_j} \left(\prod_{k=1}^{m} [(1 - \rho_k)\rho_k^{n_k}] \right) \mu_i q_{ij} u(n_j)$$
$$- \sum_{i=1}^{m} \left(\prod_{k=1}^{m} [(1 - \rho_k)\rho_k^{n_k}] \right) \mu_i q_{ii} u(n_i). \tag{7.41}$$

Take the common factor $\prod_{k=1}^{m}[(1 - \rho_k)\rho_k^{n_k}]$ out. Use $\rho_i = \frac{\theta_i}{\mu_i}$ for every i. We have

$$B(n) = \left(\prod_{k=1}^{m} [(1 - \rho_k)\rho_k^{n_k}] \right) \left(\sum_{i=1}^{m} \frac{\mu_i}{\theta_i} \lambda_i u(n_i) + \sum_{i=1}^{m} \theta_i s_i \right.$$
$$\left. + \sum_{i=1}^{m} \sum_{j=1}^{m} \frac{\theta_i}{\theta_j} \mu_j q_{ij} u(n_j) - \sum_{i=1}^{m} \mu_i q_{ii} u(n_i) \right). \tag{7.42}$$

The second sum on the RHS in the above equation (7.42) is the sum of the rates of departures from all the stations that are leaving the entire network. Under equilibrium, this sum is the same as the sum of all the external arrival rates. That is

$$\sum_{i=1}^{m} \theta_i s_i = \sum_{j=1}^{m} \lambda_j. \tag{7.43}$$

We can interchange the two summation signs in the double summation in equation (7.42). With these manipulations, we have

$$B(\boldsymbol{n}) = \left(\prod_{k=1}^{m}[(1-\rho_k)\rho_k^{n_k}]\right)\left(\sum_{i=1}^{m}\frac{\mu_i}{\theta_i}\lambda_i u(n_i) + \sum_{i=1}^{m}\lambda_i\right.$$

$$\left. + \sum_{j=1}^{m}\frac{\mu_j}{\theta_j}u(n_j)\sum_{i=1}^{m}\theta_i q_{ij} - \sum_{i=1}^{m}\mu_i q_{ii}u(n_i)\right). \tag{7.44}$$

The inner summation $\sum_{i=1}^{m}\theta_i q_{ij}$ in above expression evaluates to $\theta_j - \lambda_j$ through the application of the traffic equations (7.13), after reversing the roles of i and j in the traffic equations. Continue with the simplification of the expression for $B(\boldsymbol{n})$; note that the indices of summations are dummy variables. We have

$$B(\boldsymbol{n}) = \left(\prod_{k=1}^{m}[(1-\rho_k)\rho_k^{n_k}]\right)\left(\sum_{i=1}^{m}\frac{\mu_i}{\theta_i}\lambda_i u(n_i) + \sum_{j=1}^{m}\lambda_j\right.$$

$$\left. + \sum_{j=1}^{m}\frac{\mu_j}{\theta_j}u(n_j)(\theta_j - \lambda_j) - \sum_{i=1}^{m}\mu_i q_{ii}u(n_i)\right) \tag{7.45}$$

$$= \left(\prod_{k=1}^{m}[(1-\rho_k)\rho_k^{n_k}]\right)\left(\sum_{j=1}^{m}\lambda_j + \sum_{j=1}^{m}\mu_j u(n_j) - \sum_{i=1}^{m}\mu_i q_{ii}u(n_i)\right) \tag{7.46}$$

$$= \left(\prod_{k=1}^{m}[(1-\rho_k)\rho_k^{n_k}]\right)\sum_{j=1}^{m}[\lambda_j + \mu_j u(n_j)(1-q_{jj})]. \tag{7.47}$$

Now, the same candidate product form expression from equation (7.34) is substituted in equation (7.9) to evaluate the the rate at which the chain is changing its state from $\boldsymbol{n}$ to some other state. This rate is denoted by $A(\boldsymbol{n})$ instead of $\alpha(\boldsymbol{n})$, to distinguish the product form rate from the correct rate.

$$A(\boldsymbol{n}) = \left(\prod_{i=1}^{m}[(1-\rho_i)\rho_i^{n_i}]\right)\sum_{i=1}^{m}[\lambda_i + \mu_i u(n_i)(1-q_{ii})]. \tag{7.48}$$

We see that $A(\boldsymbol{n}) = B(\boldsymbol{n})$ for every possible vector state $\boldsymbol{n}$. This shows that if we use the candidate product form solution in place of unknown equilibrium state probabilities in the global balance equations, we find that the rate of transitioning into a state is the same as the rate of transitioning out of the state, respectively for every state. Since the global balance equations are known to support a unique solution for equilibrium state probabilities, this completes the proof that the product form state probabilities are indeed the correct equilibrium state probabilities. ▯

Example 7.1

The number of stations $m = 3$. The service rates are given in a vector form

$$\mu = [\mu_1, \mu_2, \mu_3]^T = [20, 25, 15]^T \text{ per millisecond each.} \qquad (7.49)$$

The external arrival rates are similarly given by

$$\lambda = [\lambda_1, \lambda_2, \lambda_3]^T = [0.8, 1.2, 2.0]^T \text{ per millisecond each.} \qquad (7.50)$$

The feedback probabilities are given in the following matrix form

$$q = \begin{bmatrix} 0.1 & 0.6 & 0.2 \\ 0.3 & 0.4 & 0.2 \\ 0.5 & 0.1 & 0.3 \end{bmatrix}. \qquad (7.51)$$

1. Solve the traffic equations.

2. Examine the network for stability.

3. Find the probability that all the servers are free.

4. Find the total expected number of customers in the entire network.

5. Find the one pass response time in each station.

6. Find the expected response time, in the entire network, of arrivals from each of the three external arrival streams.

7. Find the expected response time of a random arrival into the entire network.

□

Solution

The traffic equations take the form

$$\lambda_i = \theta_i - \sum_{j=1}^{m} q_{ji}\theta_j \text{ or} \qquad (7.52)$$

$$\lambda = \left(I - q^T \right)\theta \text{ or} \qquad (7.53)$$

$$\theta = \left(I - q^T \right)^{-1} \lambda \qquad (7.54)$$

$$\theta = \begin{bmatrix} 0.9 & -0.3 & 0.5 \\ -0.6 & 0.6 & -0.1 \\ -0.2 & -0.2 & 0.7 \end{bmatrix}^{-1} \lambda \qquad (7.55)$$

$$\theta = \begin{bmatrix} 3.7037 & 2.8704 & 3.0556 \\ 4.0741 & 4.9074 & 3.6111 \\ 2.2222 & 2.2222 & 3.3333 \end{bmatrix} \begin{bmatrix} 0.8 \\ 1.2 \\ 2.0 \end{bmatrix} \quad (7.56)$$

$$= \begin{bmatrix} 12.5185 \\ 16.3704 \\ 11.1111 \end{bmatrix}. \quad (7.57)$$

The loads on the servers are obtained below.

$$\rho_i = \frac{\theta_i}{\mu_i} \quad (7.58)$$

$$\rho_1 = \frac{\theta_1}{\mu_1} \quad (7.59)$$

$$= \frac{12.5185}{20} \quad (7.60)$$

$$= 0.6259. \quad (7.61)$$

Similarly,

$$\rho_2 = \frac{16.3704}{25} \quad (7.62)$$

$$= 0.6548 \quad \text{and} \quad (7.63)$$

$$\rho_3 = \frac{11.1111}{15} \quad (7.64)$$

$$= 0.7407. \quad (7.65)$$

From the marginal distribution of the numbers of customers in each queue, we have

$$E[n_i] = \frac{\rho_i}{1 - \rho_i}. \quad (7.66)$$

Evaluating these expectations, we have

$$E[n_1] = 1.6733, \quad (7.67)$$

$$E[n_2] = 1.8970, \quad \text{and} \quad (7.68)$$

$$E[n_3] = 2.8571. \quad (7.69)$$

The expected number of customers in the entire network is the sum of the above which evaluates to 6.4274. The network is connected in the sense that a customer entering any station can eventually pass through all the stations, with nonzero probability. Assume the following. All external traffic arrival streams originate from a single Poisson stream of iid jobs. This original stream is probabilistically split into three input streams with rates λ_1, λ_2, and λ_3.

Therefore, in order to evaluate the expected response time of a customer entering the network, we can use the Little's result with the combined arrival rate and the combined number in the network. The combined arrival rate into the network is $0.8 + 1.2 + 2.0 = 4.0$ per millisecond. The expected response time of a customer entering the network is

$$E[R] = \frac{6.4274}{4.0} = 1.6069 \text{ per millisecond.} \tag{7.70}$$

The above assumes that all the customers are iid, even those that initially enter different stations when they arrive from outside the network. An item in the exercises illustrates the evaluation of expected response time of the different classes of customers that initially enter the network at different points.

7.7 Development of Product Form Solution for Closed Networks

Continuous time Markovian Open Queuing Networks and their product form solution are fairly simple to understand. They lay useful groundwork for the present study of closed queuing networks. As mentioned earlier, in a closed queuing network, there are no external arrivals. A constant number of customers trapped in the network. They pass around the queues, as servers complete their services. The general structure of the network, the nature of customers completing service at a station, and the feedback mechanism are the same as in open networks. The mutually independent exponential service times and probabilistic switching ensure that the system is Markovian. Such networks were originally studied by W. J. Gordon and G. F. Newell in 1967.

In the following study of closed queuing networks, we use the upper case M for the total number of stations in the entire network, since a variable m number of stations will be used in iterative algorithms to evaluate performance figures. The symbol N is used to represent the constant number of customers trapped in the entire network. Since there are no external arrivals, $\lambda_i = 0, \quad i = 1, \ldots, M$. Similarly, $s_i = 0, \quad i = 1, \ldots, M$. Therefore,

$$\sum_{j=1}^{M} q_{ij} = 1, \quad i = 1, \ldots, M. \tag{7.71}$$

If there is a path from one subnetwork of the network to another but not the other way round, all the customers from the first subnetwork will eventually leave the first subnetwork and settle in the second network. Then the first subnetwork becomes degenerate with no customers. Eliminate such subnetworks after each of them is empty. The remaining network may be partitioned into subnetworks such that customers in each subnetwork will stay there indefinitely but customers can move through all the stations within the subnetwork. We select one such subnetwork for study. The selected network has M stations and N customers are in the network. Each of the N customers can move through all the stations with nonzero probability.

In the original global balance equations of open networks, if we substitute $\lambda_i = 0$ and $s_i = 0$, we obtain corresponding global balance equations for closed networks. The rate of change of state from state n in this case is obtained by modifying equation (7.9). The resulting rate is denoted by $\alpha_c(n)$. The subscript c denotes that the rate is for a closed network.

$$\alpha_c(n) = p(n) \sum_{i=1}^{M} \mu_i u(n_i)(1 - q_{ii}). \tag{7.72}$$

The rate of state change from some other state into state n is similarly obtained by modifying equation (7.11). The resulting rate, denoted by $\beta_c(n)$ is

$$\beta_c(n) = \sum_{i=1}^{M} \sum_{j=1}^{M} p(n + v_i - v_j)\mu_i q_{ij} u(n_j) - \sum_{i=1}^{M} p(n)\mu_i q_{ii} u(n_i). \tag{7.73}$$

The global balance equation for state n is obtained by equating $\alpha_c(n)$ and $\beta_c(n)$, which results in

$$p(n) \sum_{i=1}^{M} \mu_i u(n_i)(1 - q_{ii}) = \sum_{i=1}^{M} \sum_{j=1}^{M} p(n + v_i - v_j)\mu_i q_{ij} u(n_j)$$

$$- \sum_{i=1}^{M} p(n)\mu_i q_{ii} u(n_i). \tag{7.74}$$

This equation is valid for every pair of valid states $(n + v_j - v_i)$ and n that can participate in a state transition. The traffic equations are

$$\theta_i = \sum_{j=1}^{M} q_{ji}\theta_j, \quad i = 1, \ldots, M \tag{7.75}$$

where θ_i is the rate at which customers flow through station i. There is no constant term at all in any of the M linear equations. So, if $\theta = [\theta_1, \ldots, \theta_M]$ is a solution to the traffic equations, then $a\boldsymbol{\theta} = [a\theta_1, \ldots a\theta_M]$ is also a solution for any positive constant a.

Notice that the traffic equations (7.75) have a form identical to the balance equations of an M state discrete parameter Markov chain. The matrix $\boldsymbol{q}$ has the form of a transition probability matrix of an irreducible chain. In the case of the discrete parameter Markov chain, an additional equation with the all θ_i summing to 1 gives us a unique solution. Alternatively, setting any particular θ_i to a known constant is one such equation results in a unique solution for $\boldsymbol{\theta}$.

Following is the strategy used to develop and verify the validity of the product form solution. Assume that a valid $\boldsymbol{\theta}$ satisfying equation (7.75) and note that the constants in the state probabilities adjust to the $\boldsymbol{\theta}$ used. Note that $\theta_i > \mu_i$ does not imply that any station is unstable. The actual throughput in all the stations are proportional to their respective θ_i values. The physical dimension of θ_i is customers per unit time; the proportionality constant is dimensionless. The system is stable due to a constant number of customers in the network. Borrowing ideas from open networks, a candidate product form solution is

$$P(\boldsymbol{n}) = \frac{\prod_{i=1}^M \left[\frac{\theta_i}{\mu_i}\right]^{n_i}}{G(N, M)}, \qquad n_i = 1, \ldots, M \tag{7.76}$$

where $\sum_{i=1}^M n_i = N$. The constant $G(N, M)$ is used to normalize to ensure that the sum of all state probabilities is 1. The quantity $S(N, M)$ is defined as the set of all possible states. The number of possible states is the same as the number of combinations of distributing N identical objects into M bins. A simple way to derive this number is to imagine having $N + M - 1$ items in which $M - 1$ are boundaries and N are objects to be separated by the boundaries. This task is the same as picking N items to be the objects from a line-up of $N + M - 1$ items. Thus, the number of states in $S(N, M)$ is

$$\binom{N + M - 1}{N} = \binom{N + M - 1}{M - 1}. \tag{7.77}$$

This number can be large even for modest M and N. Therefore, evaluating $G(N, M)$ can pose a computational challenge. Let us show that $P(\boldsymbol{n})$ is invariant to the choice of the arbitrary proportionality constant in θ_i. We have

$$G(N, M) = \sum_{\boldsymbol{n} \in S(N,M)} \prod_{j=1}^M \left(\frac{\theta_j}{\mu_j}\right)^{n_j}. \tag{7.78}$$

Therefore,

$$P(\boldsymbol{n}) = \frac{\prod_{i=1}^M \left(\frac{\theta_i}{\mu_i}\right)^{n_i}}{\sum_{\boldsymbol{n} \in S(N,M)} \prod_{j=1}^M \left(\frac{\theta_j}{\mu_j}\right)^{n_j}}. \tag{7.79}$$

Multiply the numerator and the denominator by a^N, where a is an arbitrary constant.

$$P(\boldsymbol{n}) = \frac{a^N \prod_{i=1}^{M}\left(\frac{\theta_i}{\mu_i}\right)^{n_i}}{a^N \sum_{\boldsymbol{n}\in S(N,M)} \prod_{j=1}^{M}\left(\frac{\theta_j}{\mu_j}\right)^{n_j}}. \tag{7.80}$$

For every set of n_k, $k = 1, \ldots, M$, we have $\sum_{k=1}^{M} n_k = N$. Hence,

$$P(\boldsymbol{n}) = \frac{\prod_{i=1}^{M}\left(a\frac{\theta_i}{\mu_i}\right)^{n_i}}{\sum_{\boldsymbol{n}\in S(N,M)} \prod_{j=1}^{M}\left(\frac{a\theta_j}{\mu_j}\right)^{n_j}} \tag{7.81}$$

which implies that replacing θ_i, by $a\theta_i$, $i = 1, \ldots, M$, does not change the state probabilities. Now, let us verify that the product form candidate is the valid solution to the global balance equations. As in the case of open networks, an expression for the equilibrium probability of state in $\beta_c(\boldsymbol{n})$ is first obtained for the product form candidate solution. From the definition of the product form candidate solution in equation (7.76), we have

$$P(\boldsymbol{n} + \boldsymbol{v}_i - \boldsymbol{v}_j) = \frac{\theta_i}{\mu_i}\frac{\mu_j}{\theta_j}P(\boldsymbol{n})u(n_j). \tag{7.82}$$

Using this in the expression for $\beta_c(\boldsymbol{n})$, we obtain $B_c(\boldsymbol{n})$, the rate of change of state from any other state to state $\boldsymbol{n}$, for the product form candidate solution.

$$B_c(\boldsymbol{n}) = \sum_{i=1}^{M}\sum_{j=1}^{M} \frac{\theta_i}{\mu_i}\frac{\mu_j}{\theta_j}P(\boldsymbol{n})\mu_i q_{ij} u(n_j) - \sum_{i=1}^{m} P(\boldsymbol{n})\mu_i q_{ii} u(n_i). \tag{7.83}$$

Cancel μ_i in the double summation; interchange the order of the two summations in the double summation; change the dummy variable of i in the last summation to j. We have

$$B_c(\boldsymbol{n}) = P(\boldsymbol{n})\sum_{j=1}^{M} \frac{\mu_j}{\theta_j}u(n_j)\sum_{i=1}^{M} q_{ij}\theta_i - P(\boldsymbol{n})\sum_{j=1}^{M} \mu_j q_{jj} u(n_j). \tag{7.84}$$

The inner sum evaluates to θ_j from traffic equations (7.75). Therefore,

$$B_c(\boldsymbol{n}) = P(\boldsymbol{n}) \sum_{j=1}^{M} \mu_j (1 - q_{jj}) u(n_j). \qquad (7.85)$$

The rate of change of state from state $\boldsymbol{n}$ to any other state for the product form candidate solution is obtained by simply substituting the product form state pmf, $P(\boldsymbol{n})$ in $\alpha_c(\boldsymbol{n})$ to obtain $A_c(\boldsymbol{n})$. This takes the form

$$A_c(\boldsymbol{n}) = P(\boldsymbol{n}) \sum_{j=1}^{M} \mu_j (1 - q_{jj}) u(n_j).$$

Comparing equations (7.85) and (7.86), we find that for every state of the closed network, the rate of change of state from and to the state are equal, if we use the product form candidate solution. Since we know that the global balance equations have a unique solution for the state pmf, the product form candidate must be the valid equilibrium pmf.

The problem of obtaining the above valid product form solution reduces to computing the normalizing value $G(N, M)$. We will study two computationally efficient techniques to evaluate the product form solution. The first one develops $G(N, M)$ recursively, by generating a matrix of $g(n, m)$, $n = 0, \dots, N$, $m = 0, \dots, M$. The lowercase $g(n, m)$ is just to show that it is a variable that takes the final value of $G(N, M)$ when $n = N$ and $m = M$. The procedure is called convolution algorithm since the form of expression appears like a convolution sum. It was developed by Jeffrey P. Buzen in 1973. It turns out that all performance figures can be constructed from the matrix $g(n, m)$, $n = 0, \dots, N$; $m = 1, \dots, M$ in a computationally efficient way.

The second computationally efficient approach to obtain the product form performance figures is the mean value analysis (MVA) which is a development of performance expressions from convolution algorithms. The final form of the MVA avoids the execution of the convolution algorithm.

7.8 Convolution Algorithm

When $N = 0$, there is no customer in any station and that is the only state

$$p(\boldsymbol{n}) = 1 \qquad (7.86)$$

$$= \frac{\prod_{i=1}^{m} \left(\frac{\theta_i}{\mu_i} \right)^0}{g(0, m)} \qquad (7.87)$$

$$= \frac{1}{g(0,m)}. \tag{7.88}$$

Hence, $g(0,m) = 1$ for any $m \geq 1$. For $n > 0$, if there is only one station, $m = 1$. Then all the n customers are in it and

$$P(\boldsymbol{n}) = 1 = \frac{\rho_1^n}{g(n,1)}. \tag{7.89}$$

Therefore,

$$g(n,1) = \rho_1^n, \text{ for } n = 0,1,\ldots,N, \tag{7.90}$$

$$g(0,m) = 1, \text{ for } m = 1,2,\ldots,M \tag{7.91}$$

form the basis for iteration. Now,

$$g(n,m) = \sum_{\boldsymbol{n} \in S(n,m)} \prod_{i=1}^{m} \rho_i^{n_i}. \tag{7.92}$$

Decompose the sum into two portions. The first is the set of all states in which $n_m = 0$. The second is the set of all states with $n_m > 0$. We have

$$g(n,m) = \sum_{\substack{\boldsymbol{n} \in S(n,m) \\ n_m=0}} \prod_{i=1}^{m-1} \rho_i^{n_i} + \sum_{\substack{\boldsymbol{n} \in S(n,m) \\ n_m>0}} \left[\prod_{i=1}^{m} \rho_i^{n_i} \right]. \tag{7.93}$$

The first sum is $g(n, m-1)$ by simply comparing its mathematical form to that of $g(n, m-1)$. In the second sum, since $n_m > 0$, every term has a factor ρ_m which can be taken out. Then the rest of the n_i can be distributed over m stations in every possible way. Thus,

$$g(n,m) = g(n,m-1) + \rho_m \sum_{\boldsymbol{n} \in S(n-1,m)} \left[\prod_{i=1}^{m} \rho_i^{n_i} \right] \tag{7.94}$$

where n_i in the second sum satisfy $\sum_{i=1}^{M} n_i = n-1$. This second sum is no different from $g(n-1, m)$. So

$$g(n, m) = g(n, m-1) + \rho_m g(n-1, m) \tag{7.95}$$

is the procedure to evaluate all necessary values of $g(n, m)$, $n = 0, \ldots, N$; $m = 1, \ldots, M$. The computational complexity is MN. The results can be entered into a tabular form called the convolution matrix. To simplify the calculations even more, we can choose $\theta_1 = \mu_1$, so that $\rho_1 = 1$.

7.9　Performance Figures from the $g(n, m)$ Matrix

Evaluation of $p(n_i \geq n)$ turns out to be crucial to the evaluation of many performance figures. The key idea in evaluating $p(n_i \geq n)$ is to recognize that the possible states are those with n in station i and $N - n$ customers distributed over all stations including station i. In the argument of summation, ρ_i^n is a common factor that can be taken out. Therefore,

$$p(n_i \geq n) = \sum_{\substack{n \in S(N,M) \\ n_i \geq n}} \prod_{j=1}^{M} \frac{(\rho_j)^{n_j}}{G(N, M)} \tag{7.96}$$

$$= \frac{\rho_i^n}{G(N, M)} \sum_{n \in S(N-n,M)} \prod_{j=1}^{M} \rho_j^{n_j},$$

$$\text{with } n_j \geq 0 \text{ and } \sum_{j=1}^{M} n_j = N - n \tag{7.97}$$

$$= \rho_i^n \frac{G(N-n, M)}{G(N, M)}. \tag{7.98}$$

7.9.1　Marginal state probabilities

We can use the above to obtain the marginal state probabilities as

$$p(n_i = n) = p(n_i \geq n) - p(n_i \geq n+1) \tag{7.99}$$

$$= \rho_i^n \frac{G(N-n, M) - \rho_i G(N-n-1, M)}{G(N, M)}. \tag{7.100}$$

7.9.2   Average number in a station

This quantity is also known as the average buffer occupancy. Let $E[n_i(N)]$ be the expected number in station i.

$$E[n_i(N)] = \sum_{n=1}^{N} np(n_i = n) \tag{7.101}$$

$$
\begin{aligned}
= \quad & p(n_i = 1) + \qquad \cdots \qquad + p(n_i = N) \\
& \quad + p(n_i = 2) + \ldots + p(n_i = N) \\
& \qquad\qquad \ddots \\
& \qquad\qquad\qquad\qquad\quad + p(n_i = N).
\end{aligned}
$$

$$\tag{7.102}$$

The above decomposition clearly shows that $p(n_i \geq n)$ should be included once for each $n = 1, \ldots, n$, in a sum. The expression can be changed to

$$E[n_i(N)] = \sum_{n=1}^{N} p(n_i \geq n) \tag{7.103}$$

$$= \sum_{n=1}^{N} \rho_i^n \frac{G(N - n, M)}{G(N, M)}. \tag{7.104}$$

7.9.3   Throughput in a station

Let $E[Y_i(N)]$ be the throughput in the ith station

$$E[Y_i(N)] = \sum_{n=1}^{N} \mu_i p(n_i = n) \tag{7.105}$$

$$= \mu_i p(n_i \geq 1) \tag{7.106}$$

$$= \theta_i \frac{G(N - 1, M)}{G(N, M)}. \tag{7.107}$$

An important observation here is that we finally found the actual throughput in a station i, starting from the relative throughput θ_i. Furthermore, observe that the missing proportionality factor between θ_i and $E[Y_i(N)]$ is independent of i, scaling all relative θ's by the same factor, as required.

7.9.4   Utilization in a station

This is simply

$$U_i(N) = p(n_i > 0) \tag{7.108}$$

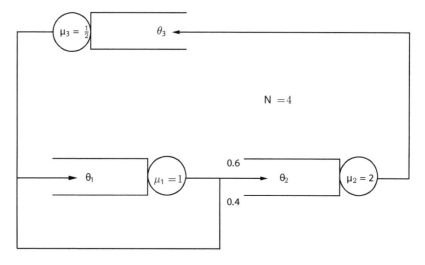

FIGURE 7.4:   The network for Example 7.2

$$= p(n_i \geq 1) \tag{7.109}$$

$$= \rho_i \frac{G(N-1,M)}{G(N,M)}. \tag{7.110}$$

7.9.5   Expected response time in a station

$$E[R_i] = \sum_{n=1}^{N} \rho_i^n \frac{G(N-n,M)}{\theta_i G(N-1,M)} \tag{7.111}$$

from Little's result.

Example 7.2
 Obtain the convolution matrix for the closed queuing network given in Figure 7.4. The service rates given in the network figure are in customers per millisecond. Calculate all performance figures.   ⬜

Solution

$$\theta_1 = 1 \text{ (by choice)}, \tag{7.112}$$

$$\theta_2 = 0.6, \tag{7.113}$$

$$\theta_3 = \theta_2 = 0.6, \tag{7.114}$$

$$\rho_1 = 1, \tag{7.115}$$

$$\rho_2 = \frac{0.6}{2} = 0.3, \text{ and} \tag{7.116}$$

$$\rho_3 = \frac{0.6}{0.5} = 1.2. \tag{7.117}$$

The convolution matrix is developed in Table 7.1. The product form solution for the

TABLE 7.1: Convolution matrix for Example 7.2

n	$m = 1$ $\rho_1 = 1$	$m = 2$ $\rho_2 = 0.3$	$m = 3$ $\rho_3 = 1.2$
0	1	1	1
1	1	$1 + 0.3 \cdot 1 = 1.3$	$1.3 + 1.2 \cdot 1 = 2.5$
2	1	$1 + 0.3 \cdot 1.3 = 1.39$	$1.39 + 1.2 \cdot 2.5 = 4.39$
3	1	$1 + 0.3 \cdot 1.39 = 1.417$	$1.417 + 1.2 \cdot 4.39 = 6.685$
4	1	$1 + 0.3 \cdot 1.417 = 1.4251$	$1.4251 + 1.2 \cdot 6.685 = 9.4472$

network is

$$p(n_1, n_2, n_3) = \frac{\rho_1^{n_1} \rho_2^{n_2} \rho_3^{n_3}}{g(N, M)} \tag{7.118}$$

$$= \frac{0.3^{n_2} 1.2^{n_3}}{9.4472}, \quad 0 \le n_2 + n_3 \le 4. \tag{7.119}$$

The total number of states we have is

$$\binom{N+M-1}{M-1} = \binom{6}{2} \tag{7.120}$$

$$= \frac{6!}{2!4!} \tag{7.121}$$

$$= 15. \tag{7.122}$$

$$U_i(N) = \rho_i \frac{G(3,3)}{G(4,3)} \tag{7.123}$$

$$U_1(4) = \frac{6.685}{9.4472} \tag{7.124}$$

$$= 0.7071 \tag{7.125}$$

$$U_2(4) = 0.2121 \tag{7.126}$$

$$U_3(4) = 1.2 \cdot 0.7071 \tag{7.127}$$

$$= 0.8485. \tag{7.128}$$

$$E[Y_1(4)] = \theta_1 \frac{G(3,3)}{G(4,3)} = 0.7071 \tag{7.129}$$

$$E[Y_2(4)] = \theta_2 \cdot 0.7071 = 0.4243 \tag{7.130}$$

$$E[Y_3(4)] = \theta_3 \cdot 0.7071 = 0.4243 \tag{7.131}$$

$$E[n_1(4)] = \frac{G(3,3) + G(2,3) + G(1,3) + G(0,3)}{9.4472} \tag{7.132}$$

$$= \frac{6.685 + 4.39 + 2.5 + 1}{9.4472} \tag{7.133}$$

$$= 1.5428. \tag{7.134}$$

$$E[n_2(4)] = \sum_{n=1}^{4} 0.3^n \frac{G(4-n,3)}{G(4,3)} \tag{7.135}$$

$$= 0.3 \cdot 0.7071 + 0.3^2 \frac{4.39}{9.4472} + 0.3^3 \frac{2.5}{9.4472} + 0.3^4 \frac{1}{9.4472}$$

$$= 0.2619. \tag{7.136}$$

$$E[n_3(4)] = \frac{1.2 \cdot 6.685 + 1.2^2 \cdot 4.39 + 1.2^3 \cdot 2.5 + 1.2^4 \cdot 1}{9.4472} \tag{7.137}$$

$$= 2.1946. \tag{7.138}$$

$$\sum_{k=1}^{4} E[n_k(4)] = 1.5428 + 0.2619 + 2.1946 = 3.9993. \tag{7.139}$$

$$E[R_1] = \frac{E[n_1(4)]}{E[Y_1(4)]} = \frac{1.5428}{0.7071} = 2.1819 \text{ milliseconds} \tag{7.140}$$

$$E[R_2] = \frac{E[n_2(4)]}{E[Y_2(4)]} = \frac{0.2619}{0.4243} = 0.6173 \text{ millisecond} \tag{7.141}$$

$$E[R_3] = \frac{E[n_3(4)]}{E[Y_3(4)]} = \frac{2.1946}{0.4243} = 5.1723 \text{ milliseconds.} \tag{7.142}$$

7.10   Mean Value Analysis

The performance figures can be evaluated in a different way starting from intermediate results obtained through the use of the convolution algorithm. The key principle is another decomposition, called the arrival theorem, which allows us to avoid generating the convolution matrix altogether. We will first state and prove this theorem. Application of this theorem first to a network of cyclic queues and then to individual stations in the cyclic network develops the mean value analysis for cyclic networks. In a cyclic network, the output of one queue is completely fed to the input of another, until the last queue outputs into the input of the first queue. This situation is simpler due to two reasons. The throughput is the same value in every queue. We can identify a fictitious quantity, average response time as the round trip time from any point back to itself after going through all the queues, once each. We will then extend the mean value analysis (MVA) to noncyclic closed queues. The following arrival theorem is valid for the general case of the network, that is, including noncyclic networks. Mean value analysis was developed by Stephen S. Lavenberg and Martin Reiser in 1980.

7.10.1   Arrival theorem

THEOREM 7.3 Arrival theorem
In a closed queuing network,

$$E[R_i(N)] = \frac{1}{\mu_i}\left(1 + E[n_i(N-1)]\right). \tag{7.143}$$

This relates the average response time in station i with N customers in the network to the average number in the station i, if the entire network had only $N-1$ customers.

Proof

$$E[n_i(N)] = \sum_{n=1}^{N} \rho_i^n \frac{G(N-n, M)}{G(N, M)} \tag{7.144}$$

from performance figures based on convolution algorithm. Separate the $n = 1$ and other terms

$$n_i(N) = \rho_i \frac{G(N-1, M)}{G(N, M)} + \frac{1}{G(N, M)} \sum_{n=2}^{N} \rho_i^n G(N-n, M). \tag{7.145}$$

Change the variable of summation in the second part to $j = n - 1$. Then

$$E[n_i(N)] = \rho_i \frac{G(N-1, M)}{G(N, M)} + \frac{\rho_i}{G(N, M)} \sum_{j=1}^{N-1} \rho_i^j G(N-j-1, M) \tag{7.146}$$

$$= U_i(N) + \rho_i \frac{G(N-1, M)}{G(N, M)} \sum_{j=1}^{N-1} \rho_i^j \frac{G(N-j-1, M)}{G(N-1, M)} \tag{7.147}$$

$$= U_i(N)\left[1 + E[n_i(N-1)]\right]. \tag{7.148}$$

From Little's result,

$$E[R_i(N)] = \frac{E[n_i(N)]}{E[Y_i(N)]} \tag{7.149}$$

$$= \frac{E[n_i(N)]}{\mu_i U_i(N)} \tag{7.150}$$

$$E[R_i(N)] = \frac{1}{\mu_i}\left[1 + E[n_i(N-1)]\right] \tag{7.151}$$

proving the arrival theorem.   ⬚

7.10.2 Cyclic network

The average response time in the entire network, from a point back to itself is the sum of average response times in each station, in a cyclic network. Let $E[Y(N)]$ be the common throughput. If we know the value of $E[n_i(N-1)]$, we can get

$$E[R_i(N)] = \frac{1}{\mu_i}\left[1 + E[n_i(N-1)]\right] \qquad (7.152)$$

from the arrival theorem. From $E[R_i(N)], i = 1, \ldots, M$, we can get the average response time of a customer from a point back to itself in the cyclic network, as

$$\sum_{i=1}^{M} E[R_i(N)]. \qquad (7.153)$$

Now, apply Little's result to the entire network, to obtain

$$E[Y(N)] = \frac{N}{\sum_{i=1}^{M} E[R_i(N)]}. \qquad (7.154)$$

Finally, we can get

$$E[n_i(N)] = E[Y(N)]E[R_i(N)] \qquad (7.155)$$

by applying Little's result to the individual stations. Thus, starting from $E[n_i(N-1)]$, we have been able to get all of $E[R_i(N)]$, $E[Y_i(N)]$, and $E[n_i(N)]$, $i = 1, \ldots, M$. For $N = 1$, $E[n_i(N-1)] = E[n_i(0)] = 0$, $i = 1, \ldots, M$. We use n as the variable to write a clearer algorithm below. N is the final number of customers in the entire network for which performance figures are required.

7.10.2.1 MVA for cyclic queues

Step 1: Set $E[n_i(0)] = 0, i = 1, \ldots, M$.

Loop steps 2 through 4 for $n = 1, 2, \ldots, N$.

Step 2:

$$E[R_i(n)] = \frac{1}{\mu_i}\left[1 + E[n_i(n-1)]\right], \ i = 1, \ldots, M \qquad (7.156)$$

Step 3:

$$E[Y(n)] = \frac{n}{\sum_{i=1}^{M} E[R_i(n)]} \qquad (7.157)$$

Step 4:

$$E[n_i(n)] = E[Y(n)]E[R_i(n)], \ i = 1, \ldots, M \qquad (7.158)$$

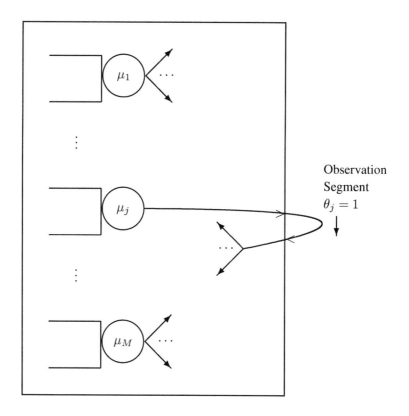

FIGURE 7.5:   Observation of traffic in a reference queue

7.10.3   Noncyclic closed networks

The main difference between a cyclic and a more general network is the following. In a cyclic network, throughput in all the stations is the same. Also, in a cyclic network, we can identify a point to which every customer returns after cycling through every station exactly once between successive returns to the point.

In the case of a noncyclic network, we can still identify a single point, at the output of a station j whose $\theta_j = 1$ and consider its movement. Enclose the entire queuing system system in a box. Pull the traffic lane that comes from station j out of the box and feed it back. See Figure 7.5. We thus have a short segment for observation of traffic, outside the box. The throughput in this observation segment is $\theta_j = 1$.

Now, successive appearances of the same customer (any single identified customer) outside the box can be considered as a sojourn through the network and an average response time is associated with this traversal of a customer through the network. How do we identify the average response times in individual stations during one sojourn through the entire network? Note that between successive appearances of the marked or the identified customer in the observation lane outside the network, the customer has passed through station j exactly once. And that the throughput $\theta_j = 1$. Therefore, during this period of one sojourn through the network, for the one pass through station j, the marked customer would pass through station i as many times as $\frac{\theta_i}{\theta_j} = \theta_i$ times, on the average. This is due to θ_i's being relative throughput made of the same set of iid customers cycling through the closed network. The expected value of the total time spent in station i during these averages of θ_i passes is $\theta_i R_i(n)$. Therefore, the expected time between successive appearances of a customer at the observation segment is

$$E[R(n)] = \sum_{i=1}^{M} \theta_i E[R_i(n)]. \tag{7.159}$$

The actual throughput in the network, at the observation point is now determined by applying the Little's result to the box at the observation segment.

$$E[Y(n)] = \frac{n}{E[R(n)]} \tag{7.160}$$

$$= \frac{n}{\sum_{i=1}^{M} \theta_i R_i(n)}. \tag{7.161}$$

We know that $E[Y(n)]$ is also the exact throughput through station j, so $E[Y_j(n)] = E[Y(n)]$. This gives us the factor by which each relative throughput θ_i should be multiplied to obtain $E[Y_i(n)]$.

$$E[Y_i(n)] = \theta_i \frac{E[Y_j(n)]}{\theta_j} \tag{7.162}$$

$$= \theta_i E[Y_j(n)] \tag{7.163}$$

$$= \theta_i E[Y(n)]. \tag{7.164}$$

Now, we apply the Little's result to individual stations and determine their respective expected number of customers.

$$E[n_i(n)] = E[Y_i(n)] E[R_i(n)] \tag{7.165}$$

$$= E[Y(n)] \theta_i E[R_i(n)]. \tag{7.166}$$

We use n as a variable that increases from 1 to N in the following algorithm.

7.10.3.1   MVA for noncyclic networks

Step 1: Solve traffic equation with $\theta_j = 1$ for any particularly selected j. $n_i(0) = 0$, $i = 1, \ldots, M$.

Loop steps 2 through 4 for $n = 1, \ldots, N$.

Step 2:

$$E[R_i(n)] = \frac{1}{\mu_i}\left[1 + E[n_i(n-1)]\right] \tag{7.167}$$

Step 3:

$$E[Y_j(n)] = E[Y(n)] \tag{7.168}$$

$$= \frac{n}{\sum_{k=1}^{M} \theta_k E[R_k(n)]} \tag{7.169}$$

Step 4:

$$E[n_i(n)] = E[Y(n)]\theta_i E[R_i(n)] \tag{7.170}$$

This concludes the MVA statement.

Example 7.3
Solve Example 7.2 with the help of mean value analysis.   ▯

Solution
From Example 7.2, we have $N = 4$, $\theta_1 = 1$, $\theta_2 = 0.6$, $\mu_1 = 1$, $\theta_3 = 0.6$, $\mu_2 = 2.0$, $\mu_3 = 0.5$. Execution of Steps 2 through 4 of the MVA for $n = 1, 2, 3$, and 4:

$n = 1$:

Step 2:

$$E[R_1(1)] = \frac{1}{1}(1+0) = 1 \tag{7.171}$$

$$E[R_2(1)] = \frac{1}{2.0}(1+0) = 0.5 \tag{7.172}$$

$$E[R_3(1)] = \frac{1}{0.5}(1+0) = 2 \tag{7.173}$$

Step 3:

$$E[Y_1(1)] = \frac{1}{1\cdot 1 + 0.6\cdot 0.5 + 0.6\cdot 2} = 0.4 \tag{7.174}$$

Step 4:

$$E[n_1(1)] = 0.4 \cdot 1 \cdot 1 = 0.4 \tag{7.175}$$

$$E[n_2(1)] = 0.4 \cdot 0.6 \cdot 0.5 = 0.12 \tag{7.176}$$

$$E[n_3(1)] = 0.4 \cdot 0.6 \cdot 2 = 0.48 \tag{7.177}$$

$$\text{Verification:} \quad \sum_i E[n_i(1)] = 1 \tag{7.178}$$

$n = 2:$

Step 2:

$$E[R_1(2)] = \frac{1}{1}(1 + 0.4) = 1.4 \tag{7.179}$$

$$E[R_2(2)] = \frac{1}{2}(1 + 0.12) = 0.56 \tag{7.180}$$

$$E[R_3(2)] = \frac{1}{0.5}(1 + 0.48) = 2.96 \tag{7.181}$$

Step 3:

$$E[Y_1(2)] = \frac{2}{1 \cdot 1.4 + 0.6 \cdot 0.56 + 0.6 \cdot 2.96} = 0.5695 \tag{7.182}$$

Step 4:

$$E[n_1(2)] = 0.5695 \cdot 1 \cdot 1.4 = 0.7973 \tag{7.183}$$

$$E[n_2(2)] = 0.5695 \cdot 0.6 \cdot 0.56 = 0.1914 \tag{7.184}$$

$$E[n_3(2)] = 0.5695 \cdot 0.6 \cdot 2.96 = 1.0114 \tag{7.185}$$

$$\text{Verification:} \quad \sum_{i=1}^{3} E[n_i(2)] = 2.0001 \tag{7.186}$$

$n = 3:$

Step 2:

$$E[R_1(3)] = \frac{1}{1}(1 + 0.7973) = 1.7973 \tag{7.187}$$

$$E[R_2(3)] = \frac{1}{2}(1 + 0.1914) = 0.5965 \qquad (7.188)$$

$$E[R_3(3)] = \frac{1}{0.5}(1 + 1.0114) = 4.0228 \qquad (7.189)$$

Step 3:

$$E[Y_1(3)] = \frac{3}{1 \cdot 1.7973 + 0.6 \cdot 0.5965 + 0.6 \cdot 4.0228} \qquad (7.190)$$

$$= 0.6567 \qquad (7.191)$$

Step 4:

$$E[n_1(3)] = 0.6567 \cdot 1 \cdot 1.7973 = 1.1803 \qquad (7.192)$$

$$E[n_2(3)] = 0.6567 \cdot 0.6 \cdot 0.5965 = 0.2347 \qquad (7.193)$$

$$E[n_3(3)] = 0.6567 \cdot 0.6 \cdot 4.0228 = 1.5851 \qquad (7.194)$$

$$\text{Verification:} \quad \sum_{i=1}^{3} E[n_i(3)] = 3.0000 \qquad (7.195)$$

$n = 4:$

Step 2:

$$E[R_1(4)] = \frac{1}{1}(1 + 1.1803) = 2.1803 \text{ milliseconds} \qquad (7.196)$$

$$E[R_2(4)] = \frac{1}{2}(1 + 0.2347) = 0.6174 \text{ millisecond} \qquad (7.197)$$

$$E[R_3(4)] = \frac{1}{0.5}(1 + 1.5851) = 5.1702 \text{ milliseconds} \qquad (7.198)$$

Step 3:

$$E[Y_1(4)] = \frac{4}{1 \cdot 2.1803 + 0.6 \cdot 0.6174 + 0.6 \cdot 5.1702} \qquad (7.199)$$

$$= 0.7076 \qquad (7.200)$$

Step 4:

$$E[n_1(4)] = 0.7076 \cdot 1 \cdot 2.1803 = 1.5428 \qquad (7.201)$$

$$E[n_2(4)] = 0.7076 \cdot 0.6 \cdot 0.6174 = 0.2621 \qquad (7.202)$$

$$E[n_3(4)] = 0.7076 \cdot 0.6 \cdot 5.1702 = 2.1950 \qquad (7.203)$$

$$\text{Verification:} \quad \sum_{i=1}^{3} E[n_i(4)] = 3.9999 \qquad (7.204)$$

The above results, obtained by using the MVA agree with those by using the convolution algorithm approach, except for round off errors in lower significant decimals. □

7.11   Conclusion

Markovian queuing networks are useful performance models for networked systems of computers. The individual computers function in round robin mode. In open networks, an overall externally arriving job may require service in more than one computer. As an example, compilation and preliminary processing may be done in one computer, intensive computation in another, database accesses in a third and input-output in the fourth. A job may move around these computers until completely processed. The equilibrium solution turns out to be a simple product form of individual solutions.

Closed networks do not have external arrivals but have a constant number of customers moving around form one queue to another. The development of product form solution is quite simple. The constant factor in the product form solution of equilibrium state probabilities and/or the final performance figures are evaluated with efficient computational algorithms. The convolution algorithm evaluates the constant in an iterative fashion. The intermediate results obtained during iterations are useful in evaluating the performance figures. The mean value analysis algorithm directly evaluates the performance figures.

7.12   Exercises

1. This exercise is a continuation of Example 7.1. Answer the following.

(a) At some time instant, the state of the system is known to be $(0, 0, 0)$. Determine the rate of change of state, from this state.

(b) The system is in equilibrium but there is no information about the state at time $t = 0$. Under this condition, determine the rate of change of state from state 0 to any other state.

(c) The system is in equilibrium. What is the rate of change of state leading a to a transition to state $(0, 0, 0)$?

(d) Answer the above questions for the state $(2, 0, 1)$.

(e) If we imagine all the customers to be iid and originate from a single external point source where they are split into different streams to be fed to different stations, they have the same overall expected response time. However, we can alternatively imagine that the streams entering the different stations from outside are of different classes. Let customers externally arriving directly to station i be called class i customers. It seems that the different classes of customers experience different expected overall expected response times, because of the differences between their activity in the first queues they enter. This is in spite of all the customers in a station experiencing iid service times, irrespective of their classes. Evaluate the conditional expected response time of a customer, given that the customer belongs to class i. Hint: Evaluate the expected numbers of passes a customer from class i makes through each station. To do this, formulate traffic equations for only class i customers.

2. Consider a continuous time Markovian open queuing network with our usual notation. Assume that the traffic equations have been solved and that θ_i, $i = 1, \cdots, M$ are known. Answer the following questions. Your answers should be reasonably simplified functions of λ, T, $\{\theta_i\}$, and $\{\mu_i\}$.

(a) Over a large (deterministic) time interval T, what is the expected number of distinct jobs passing through the entire network?

(b) In the same time interval, what is the expected total number of every repetition of every job passing through station i?

(c) What is the total number of all such passes of all the jobs in all the stations, in the time T?

(d) Note that all the jobs are statistically identical. What is the expected number of passes a particular job goes through station i?

(e) Determine the expected amount of time a job spends in station i.

(f) From the previous answer, determine the expected amount of time a job spends in the entire network.

3. In an open queuing network with two processors, $\mu_1 = 1$ and $\mu_2 = 2$. The quantity $\lambda = \frac{\lambda_0}{2}$ where λ_0 corresponds to an arrival rate below which the

network will be stable. $\lambda_{s1} = 0.6$. The feedback probabilities are r_{ij}, and the corresponding matrix is given below.

$$\begin{bmatrix} 0.3 & 0.4 \\ 0.5 & 0.3 \end{bmatrix} \tag{7.205}$$

Find the steady state probability that the two stations will have equal number of customers in them.

4. Consider a closed queuing network with two queues. Each queue has a single server. The service time of a customer in Queue 1 is exponentially distributed with an average time of 1 second. The service time of a customer in Queue 2 is exponentially distributed with an average service time of 6 seconds. Customers departing from Queue 2 are directly fed back into Queue 1. Customers departing from Queue 1 return to Queue 1 with probability $\frac{1}{2}$ and are fed into Queue 2 with probability $\frac{1}{2}$. There are a total of 2 customers in the system.

   (a) Draw the queuing diagram for the system.

   (b) Find the steady state probability that there is one customer in each of the queues.

   (c) Find the fraction of time that a customer spends in each of the queues.

   (d) Find the throughput of each queue.

5. A network made of a CPU and an I/O has exactly four total processes (jobs) all the time. The CPU takes an average of 2 msec to complete a process. 60% of the processes coming out of the CPU are routed back to the CPU itself. The I/O unit takes an average of 10 msec to complete a process. 30% of the processes coming out of the I/O are routed back to itself. The entire system is a continuous time closed Markovian network. Determine the exact throughput and the expected numbers of processes in each queue. Use any systematic method.

6. Consider the results of the mean value analysis (MVA) with our standard notation for a closed queuing network, developed with $\theta_1 = 1$ and other θ values satisfying the traffic equations. How do we obtain the $G(N, M)$ for the network from the MVA results?

7. Consider a closed queuing network with a total of $n = 2$ customers and two processors having rates $\mu_1 = 1$ and $\mu_2 = 2$. 40% of traffic from the first processor is fed back to the same queue. 70% of traffic from the second processor is fed back to itself. Determine the expected number of customers in each station.

8. A sensor network has two processors that wait idly in a *queue A* until called for service by a request. Request arrivals are Poisson with a rate of one in 10 ms (milli second). If there is no idle processor when a request comes in, the

request vanishes with no service. If there is at least one idle processor, the service request picks the processor at the head of *queue A* for work. 40% of the requests need a remote database transaction; the processor from the sensor network chosen for this request accesses the database in a FIFO Markovian *queue B*; average time for each database access is 20 ms. At the end of the database transaction the original request is completed and the processor returns to *queue A*. The remaining 60% of the original requests make the chosen processor go through a Markovian *queue C* for an output device with an average service time of 30 ms, at the end of which, the processor returns to the original *queue A*.

The entire system is a continuous time closed Markovian network of three FIFO queues and two tokens (each token is a processor that goes around the network).

(*a*) Write the complete queuing network diagram. Identify the relative traffic rate at each queue.

(*b*) List every possible joint state for the system. Determine the steady state probability of each such state.

(*c*) Determine the probability that a random request will vanish without getting service, due to no processor being available.

9. An internal revenue service IRS electronic tax filing server services three different tax filing data input lines as follows. The data lines wait in an FIFO waiting line for the server to transfer them to the service queue. The server polls the waiting line queue to see if there is any data line in that queue, at average time intervals of 100 milli seconds (msec). If any data line is waiting, the server picks only one line and places it in its service queue. During the tax season, the data lines in the waiting line always have one tax return to file.

The service queue functions as follows. Each data line needs an average of 40 msec of the server's service time to complete one tax return filing. The server gives piece meal round robin service for the data lines in its service queue, with an average of 10 msec for each piece of service. After one tax return is completely filed, that data line will be placed back in its waiting line. All the time periods above are exponentially distributed with the specified averages.

(a) Develop the Markovian closed queuing network model for the IRS server with two queues. One queue is where the data lines wait for the server to poll them. The other is the round robin service queue. Enter every required numerical parameter in the queuing network diagram.

(b) Evaluate the numerical values of all the joint state probabilities. Do this by a direct method, without using the Convolution Algorithm or MVA.

(c) Determine the average number of tax returns filed through these three lines in one hour.

(d) In order to fend off complaints from people that the data lines do not respond, IRS needs to publish the fraction of time that each data line is in the waiting line for the server to pick up. Determine the ratio of the average time spent in the waiting queue to the total average time spent in the IRS system by a tax line.

10. In an industrial facility, there are M different embedded systems that monitor the status (for the sake of emergency response) of N different but statistically independent and identical manufacturing units. The manufacturing units are virtually shipped around through the FIFO queues of the different embedded systems as follows. When an embedded system is servicing a manufacturing unit, it requests, receives, and processes some particular sensory data. Depending on the results, it then virtually ships the serviced manufacturing unit to one of the M embedded systems, (including itself). This statistically repetitive process goes on endlessly.

In a particular case study, we have $N = 3$ manufacturing units and $M = 3$ embedded monitoring systems. Call the corresponding queues as 1, 2, and 3. The entire system is well approximated to be Markovian as follows. The service rates in the queues are 3, 2, and 4 per second, respectively. 20% of jobs leaving queue 1 are shipped to queue 2 and the remaining to queue 3. 40% of the jobs leaving queue 2 are shipped to queue 1 and the remaining to queue 3. 30% of the jobs leaving queue 3 are shipped to queue 1 and the remaining to queue 2. Homeland Security requires the industry to report on the average rate at which the manufacturing units are examined by each of the three monitoring systems.

(a) Draw the queuing network diagram. Include all the parameter values.

(b) Evaluate the relative throughput in each of the three queues.

(c) Systematically determine the exact throughput in every queue.

(d) Finally, determine the rate at which each manufacturing unit passes through each queue, in order to report these figures to Homeland Security.

Chapter 8

The $G/M/1$ Queue

8.1 Introduction

Consider an unlimited size buffer single server queue with iid exponential service times of rate μ. Interarrival times are iid, but are not necessarily exponential. In the literature, such queues are denoted by $G_I/M/1/\infty$. The subscript I emphasizes that the interarrival times are iid. It is not uncommon to drop the subscript I with the understanding that unless otherwise stated, IATs are iid. We will follow this simpler notation. $G/M/1$ queues appear in applications in which the interarrival times cannot be approximated as memoryless. As an example, packets may arrive periodically and the packet sizes may vary in a way that it can be approximated by an exponential random variable. Erratic arrivals such as with a Pareto IAT and exponential packet sizes also constitutes a $G/M/1$ queue. This chapter studies the $G/M/1/\infty$ queue. Analysis of finite buffer $G/M/1$ queue is simple and is briefly treated. The important application example with Pareto interarrival times is included.

8.2 The Imbedded Markov Chain for $G/M/1/\infty$ Queue

Let X be the random variable corresponding to the iid IATs, with a pdf $f_X(x)$. The arrival rate is the reciprocal of the expected IAT and is denoted by λ. That is,

$$\lambda = \frac{1}{E[X]}. \tag{8.1}$$

At an arbitrary time instant t, the future statistical behavior of the queue depends not only on the number of customers in the system but also on when the most recent arrival occurred. Equivalently, number of customers and the probability distribution of time for the next arrival (starting from the current time instant t), are sufficient to describe the future statistical behavior of the system. The requirement of the time since the previous arrival or the time till the next arrival, arises due to the IAT being *not* memoryless. Therefore, as in the case of the M/G/1 queue of Chapter 5, the stochastic process $N(t)$, the number of customers as a function of the continuous time parameter, is *not* a Markov chain. However, just before every arrival time instant, the time period remaining for the next arrival is zero and there is no uncertainty about it. Therefore, if we observe the system at arrival time instants only, the number of customers (not including the arriving one) is sufficient to describe the future statistical behavior of the system. In between two successive arrivals, only service completions cause changes in the number of customers. Since service times are memoryless, remaining time for service is not required to characterize the future statistical behavior of the system. Thus, the discrete parameter stochastic process corresponding to the sequence of numbers of customers in the system at arrival time instants is a Markov chain. As mentioned above, the arriving customer is not included in the count of the number of customers. Therefore, at arrival time instants, the number of customers can be any nonnegative integer, including zero. Such a Markov chain is called an imbedded or an embedded Markov chain. Note that a different imbedded Markov chain is constructed for an M/G/1 queue in Chapter 5.

Let N_i be the random variable number of customers at the ith arrival time instant. Let K_i be the number of customers who successfully completed service and departed the system, between the arrival time instants of the ith and the $(i + 1)$th customers. Let n_i and k_i be their respective outcomes. After the arrival of the ith customer and before any departure, there are $n_i + 1$ customers in the system, including the ith arrival. Therefore, $0 \le k_i \le n_i + 1$. The recursive relation between the current and the next state random variables is

$$N_{i+1} = N_i + 1 - K_i. \tag{8.2}$$

The outcome variables have a similar relation

$$n_i = n_i + 1 - k_i, \quad k_i = 0, 1, \dots, n_i + 1. \tag{8.3}$$

Now, consider the sequence of departures starting from after the ith arrival has occurred, and before the next, $(i + 1)$th arrival. The departures time instant based on successive iid exponential service times are identical to those of Poisson events, as long as there are customers available in the system for departures. That is, the probability of exactly $k_i < n_i + 1$ departures occurring is the probability of exactly k_i Poisson events occurring over the random time interval X. Therefore,

$$P[K_i = k] = P[k_i \text{ Poisson events with rate } \mu \text{ in } X], \quad k = 0, 1, \dots, n_i. \tag{8.4}$$

It is possible that all the available $n_i + 1$ customers depart and some time is left over before the random time interval X expires. Figure 8.1 illustrates this situation.

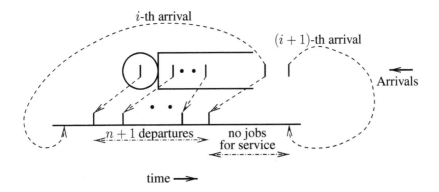

FIGURE 8.1: Illustration of left over time after all departures, during one IAT

That is, if there were more customers available for departing, one or more additional customers may have departed, after the departure of the $n_i + 1$ customers. Therefore,

$$P[K_i = n_i + 1] = P[n_i + 1 \text{ or more Poisson events with rate } \mu \text{ in } X]. \quad (8.5)$$

Let a_k be the probability of exactly k Poisson events during the random time interval X. Also, denote this probability by $P[k \text{ in } X]$. It is evaluated using the mixed form of the theorem of total probability in equation (A.70), as follows.

$$a_k = P[k \text{ in } X] \quad (8.6)$$

$$= \int_0^\infty P[k \text{ in } x] f_X(x) dx \quad (8.7)$$

$$= \int_0^\infty \frac{\exp(-\mu x)(\mu x)^k}{k!} f_X(x) dx. \quad (8.8)$$

The probability of k departures from the G/M/1/∞ queue is a_k, if $k \leq n_i$. Using equation (8.5), the probability of $n_i + 1$ departures from the G/M/1/∞ queue is given by

$$P[n_i + 1 \text{ departures}] = \sum_{j=n_i+1}^{\infty} a_j \qquad (8.9)$$

$$= 1 - \sum_{j=0}^{n_i} a_j. \qquad (8.10)$$

We are now ready to develop the state transition probabilities of the discrete parameter Markov chain corresponding to the G/M/1/∞ queue. Let an observation of the system yield m customers. Under this condition, we are interested in the probability of observing n customers during the next observation time instant. Starting from m customers just before an arrival, up to $m+1$ customers can leave before the next observation. That is, the state can change from m to any in the set $\{m+1, m, \ldots, 0\}$. The next state $n = m + 1$ corresponds to no departures. That is,

$$P[N_{i+1} = m + 1 | N_i = m] = a_0. \qquad (8.11)$$

The next state $n = 0$ corresponds to all the $m+1$ customers departing within X and possibly some time left over. From equation (8.9),

$$P[N_{i+1} = 0 | N_i = m] = \sum_{k=m+1}^{\infty} a_k. \qquad (8.12)$$

For any other n, that is, for $1 \leq n \leq m + 1$, we have $m + 1 - n$ departures. This includes $n = m+1$ used in equation (8.11). The corresponding transition probability is

$$P[N_{i+1} = n | N_i = m] = a_{m+1-n}, \quad n = 0, \ldots, m. \qquad (8.13)$$

The two-dimensional array q of transition probabilities have rows for $m = 0, 1, \ldots, \infty$ and columns for $n = 0, 1, \ldots, \infty$.

$$q = \begin{bmatrix} \left(\sum\limits_{j=1}^{\infty} a_j\right) & a_0 & 0 & \cdots \\ \left(\sum\limits_{j=2}^{\infty} a_j\right) & a_1 & a_0 & 0 \cdots \\ \left(\sum\limits_{j=3}^{\infty} a_j\right) & a_2 & a_1 & a_0 \; 0 \cdots \\ \vdots & & \ddots \\ \left(\sum\limits_{j=m+1}^{\infty} a_j\right) & a_m & a_{m-1} & \cdots \; a_1 \; a_0 \; 0 \cdots \\ \vdots & & & \cdots \cdots \\ & & & \cdots \cdots \end{bmatrix} . \qquad (8.14)$$

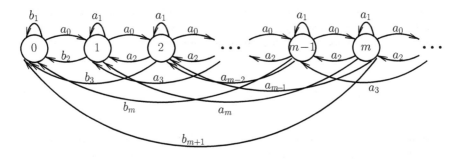

FIGURE 8.2:   State transition diagram for the imbedded Markov chain of the G/M/1/∞ queue

The state transition diagram is shown in Figure 8.2. There is a nonzero probability path from every state to every other state. There is also a single arc from every state to itself. Therefore, the Markov chain is irreducible and aperiodic. Let us assume that the system is stable in which case all the equilibrium state probabilities, p_0, p_1, $p_2, \ldots$ are nonzero. We will derive the condition for stability later. The balance equations are easily written around every state n as follows. The unconditional probability of leaving any state n (including leaving to return to itself in one transition) is p_n. The unconditional probability of entering state n from state m is $p_m q_{mn}$. The unconditional probability of reaching state n from any state is summed and equated to the probability of leaving state n below.

$$p_n = \sum_{m=0}^{\infty} p_m q_{mn}. \tag{8.15}$$

Examining the nth column of the transition probability array in equation (8.14), we have

$$p_n = p_{n-1}a_0 + p_n a_1 + p_{n+1}a_2 + p_{n+2}a_3 + \cdots, \quad n = 1, 2, \ldots . \tag{8.16}$$

For comparison, p_{n+1} evaluates to

$$p_{n+1} = p_n a_0 + p_{n+1}a_1 + p_{n+2}a_2 + p_{n+3}a_3 + \cdots. \tag{8.17}$$

The index of all the states for which the equilibrium probabilities appear in the above two equations are correspondingly increased by one each, position by position, in the equation for p_{n+1}. This suggests the candidate solution

$$p_{n+1} = \alpha p_n, \quad n = 0, 1, 2, \ldots \tag{8.18}$$

for some unknown α satisfying $0 < \alpha < 1$. Indeed, if we use equation (8.18) in equation (8.17), every p_j is replaced by αp_{j-1}. Canceling the common factor α in every term on both sides, we get the equation (8.16). With this procedure, the balance equation (8.16) for every $n = 1, 2, \ldots$ is finally reduced to

$$p_n = \alpha^n p_0 \tag{8.19}$$

$$= \alpha^{n-1} p_1 \tag{8.20}$$

$$= \alpha^{n-1}p_0 a_0 + \alpha^{n-1}p_1 a_1 + \alpha^{n-1}p_2 a_2 + \alpha^{n-1}p_3 a_3 + \cdots, \text{ for } n = 1, 2, \ldots .$$

$$\tag{8.21}$$

Equating the RHS of the two equations (8.20) and (8.21) and canceling α^{n-1} on both sides, we have

$$p_1 = p_0 a_0 + p_1 a_1 + p_2 a_2 + p_3 a_3 + \cdots. \tag{8.22}$$

That is, the use of the candidate solution in equation (8.18) reduces every balance equation for p_n, $n > 1$ to the known balance equation for p_1. Therefore, the candidate solution (8.18) is a valid solution. We can now substitute the corresponding function of α from equation (8.18) for every p_j in equation (8.22) and attempt to solve for α.

8.3 Analysis of the Parameter α

Equation (8.18) leads to

$$p_n = (1 - \alpha)\alpha^n, \quad n = 0, 1, 2, \ldots. \tag{8.23}$$

Using this equation (8.23) in (8.22), we obtain the following equation for α.

$$(1 - \alpha)\alpha = \sum_{j=0}^{\infty} (1 - \alpha)\alpha^j a_j \quad \text{or} \tag{8.24}$$

$$\alpha = \sum_{j=0}^{\infty} \alpha^j a_j. \tag{8.25}$$

The above equation (8.25) can have more than one solution. If we substitute $\alpha = 1$, the RHS evaluates to the sum of all the probabilities a_j which is 1, corresponding to the LHS also. Note that $\alpha = 0$ is *not* a solution since the RHS has the term $a_0 > 0$ with no factor of α in it. Define two functions of α as follows.

$$y_1(\alpha) = \alpha \tag{8.26}$$

$$y_2(\alpha) = \sum_{j=0}^{\infty} \alpha^j a_j. \tag{8.27}$$

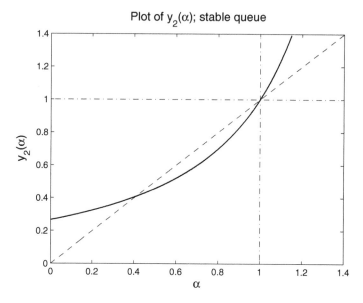

FIGURE 8.3:   Plot of $y_2(\alpha)$ for a stable Markov chain case

For stability of the imbedded Markov chain, $\alpha < 1$ is required to ensure that the sum of probabilities following equation (8.23) is one. Therefore, the solution α should satisfy

$$y_2(\alpha) < 1. \tag{8.28}$$

We have

$$y_2(0) = a_0 > 0 \quad \text{and} \tag{8.29}$$

$$y_2(1) = 1. \tag{8.30}$$

Also $y_2(\alpha)$ has positive terms only with high powers of α. Therefore, as α increases from zero, the derivative of $y_2(\alpha)$ is strictly monotonically increasing. Figures 8.3, 8.4, and 8.5 illustrate the three categories of possible cases. Let the equation $y_2(\alpha) = y_1(\alpha)$ have a solution at $\alpha < 1$. This corresponds to Figure 8.3.

The plot of $y_2(\alpha)$ cuts the plot of $y_1(\alpha)$ at $\alpha < 1$ from above. Since it cuts $y_1(\alpha)$ from above, the derivative of $y_2(\alpha)$ is less than 1 at the point that it cuts the $y_1(\alpha)$ plot. The plot of $y_2(\alpha)$ continues to increase with increasing derivative. It evaluates to 1 for $\alpha = 1$. Therefore, the plot of $y_2(\alpha)$ cuts the plot of $y_1(\alpha)$ at $\alpha = 1$ from below. Thereafter, the RHS shoots up faster than α due to the high degree polynomial in equation (8.25). The conclusion is that if the equation $y_2(\alpha) = y_1(\alpha)$ has a solution at $\alpha < 1$, the derivative of $y_2(\alpha)$ is larger than 1 at $\alpha = 1$.

If equation $y_2(\alpha) = y_1(\alpha)$ has *no* solution at any $\alpha < 1$, the plot of $y_2(\alpha)$ still meets the plot of $y_1(\alpha)$ at $\alpha = 1$. But in this case, the plot of $y_2(\alpha)$ only touches the plot of $y_1(\alpha)$ tangentially at $\alpha = 1$. This is illustrated in Figure 8.4. The derivative of $y_2(\alpha)$ at $\alpha = 1$ is one.

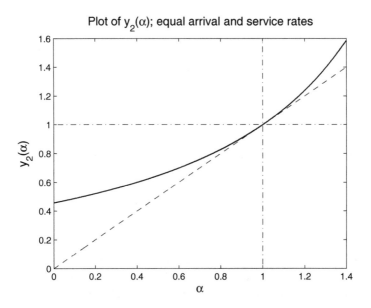

FIGURE 8.4: Plot of $y_{(}\alpha)$ for equal arrival and service rates

In the third possible category of plots, shown in Figure 8.5, there is no solution with $\alpha < 1$ and the plot of $y_2(\alpha)$ cuts the plot of $y_1(\alpha)$ from above at $\alpha = 1$. In this case, the derivative of $y_2(\alpha)$ at $\alpha = 1$ is less than 1.

The conclusion from the above analysis of the three categories is that if there is no solution for the equation $y_2(\alpha) = y_1(\alpha)$ at any $\alpha < 1$, the derivative of $y_2(\alpha)$ evaluated at $\alpha = 1$ is less than or equal to 1. Finally, due to the strict monotonicity of the derivative of $y_2(\alpha)$, note that $y_2(\alpha)$ cannot fluctuate around the plot of $y_1(\alpha)$ and cut it in more than two points. Combining the above arguments, the necessary

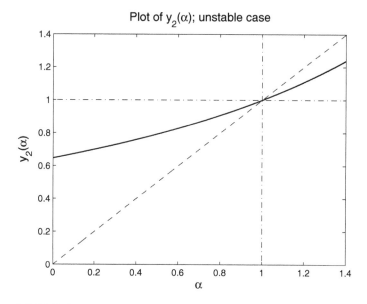

FIGURE 8.5:   Plot of $y_2(\alpha)$ for an unstable Markov chain case

and sufficient condition for the stability of the imbedded Markov chain is that

$$\frac{d}{d\alpha}y_2(\alpha)\Big|_{\alpha=1} > 1. \tag{8.31}$$

An alternative approach to arguing for the same conclusion is to point out that the RHS is a sum of powers of α with strictly positive coefficients. Each component is convex and hence the sum is also a convex function of α; therefore, $y_2(\alpha)$ cannot cut $y_1(\alpha)$ at more than two points.

The definition of $y_2(\alpha)$ uses a_j which are in turn functions of the pdf of the interarrival times X. The following evaluates $y_2(\alpha)$ directly from the pdf of X. Substitute expressions for a_j from equation (8.8) in the RHS of equation (8.25). We have

$$\sum_{j=0}^{\infty}\alpha^j a_j = \sum_{j=0}^{\infty}\alpha^j \int_0^{\infty}\frac{\exp(-\mu x)(\mu x)^j}{j!}f_X(x)dx. \tag{8.32}$$

Interchange the order of summation and integration to obtain

$$\sum_{j=0}^{\infty} \alpha^j a_j = \int \exp(-\mu x) f_X(x) \left(\sum_{j=0}^{\infty} \frac{(\alpha \mu x)^j}{j!} \right) dx. \tag{8.33}$$

Recognize that the summation is the Maclaurin series for the exponential.

$$\sum_{j=0}^{\infty} \alpha^j a_j = \int_0^{\infty} \exp[-\mu x(1 - \alpha)] f_X(x) dx \tag{8.34}$$

The integral above is the Laplace transform of $f_X(x)$ evaluated at $s = \mu x(1 - \alpha)$. Therefore, we have

$$y_2(\alpha) = \sum_{j=0}^{\infty} \alpha^j a_j = \mathcal{L}_X[\mu(1 - \alpha)]. \tag{8.35}$$

Using this in the equation (8.25) to evaluate α, we have

$$\alpha = \mathcal{L}_X[\mu(1 - \alpha)]. \tag{8.36}$$

8.3.1 Stability criterion in terms of the parameters of the queue

In the equation

$$\alpha = \sum_{j=0}^{\infty} \alpha^j a_j = \mathcal{L}_X[\mu(1 - \alpha)], \tag{8.37}$$

a_j is the probability that j but not $j + 1$ or a larger number of service times can be fit into the interarrival random variable X. Let K be the random variable number of service times that can be fit into an interarrival time random variable X. The expected number of service times that can be fit into X is obtained by using the property of $\mathcal{Z}$ transforms, that is

$$E[K] = \frac{d}{d\alpha} \sum_{j=0}^{\infty} \alpha^j a_k \Big|_{\alpha=1}. \tag{8.38}$$

Therefore,

$$E[K] = \frac{d}{d\alpha}\mathcal{L}_X[\mu(1-\alpha)]\Big|_{\alpha=1} \tag{8.39}$$

$$= \frac{d\mathcal{L}_X[\mu(1-\alpha)]}{d[\mu(1-\alpha)]}\frac{d[\mu(1-\alpha)]}{d\alpha}\Big|_{\alpha=1} \tag{8.40}$$

$$= -\mu\frac{d}{ds}\mathcal{L}_X(s)\Big|_{s=0}. \tag{8.41}$$

Therefore, the stability condition reduces to

$$E[K] > 1. \tag{8.42}$$

We know that

$$\frac{d}{ds}\mathcal{L}_X(s) = \frac{d}{ds}\int_0^\infty \exp(-sx)f_X(x)dx \tag{8.43}$$

$$= \frac{d}{ds}\sum_{i=0}^\infty \frac{(-sx)^i}{i!}f_X(x)dx. \tag{8.44}$$

Interchange the order of differentiation and summation to obtain

$$\frac{d}{ds}\mathcal{L}_X(s) = \sum_{i=1}^\infty \int_0^\infty \frac{-(-s)^{i-1}x^i}{(i-1)!}f_X(x)dx. \tag{8.45}$$

Evaluate the above expression at $s = 0$; the first term in the summation does not have the factor s. All other terms have a factor of s and vanish. Therefore,

$$\frac{d}{ds}\mathcal{L}_X(s)\Big|_{s=0} = -\int_0^\infty xf_X(x)dx \tag{8.46}$$

$$= -E[X]. \tag{8.47}$$

The above result is a standard way to evaluate the expectation of a continuous non-negative random variable with the help of the Laplace transform. Using this in equation (8.41), we finally have

$$E[K] = -\mu\left(-E[X]\right) \quad > \quad 1 \tag{8.48}$$

as the stability condition. Equivalently,

$$\mu E[X] > 1 \qquad \text{or} \tag{8.49}$$

$$\mu > \lambda \tag{8.50}$$

as the condition for the stability of the imbedded Markov chain. The final form is the familiar stability condition for the M/M/1/∞ queue and for the imbedded Markov chain of the M/G/1/∞ queue. Even though the condition $\mu > \lambda$ may appear to be intuitively obvious, the confirmation of it comes as a consequence of the original condition $\alpha < 1$.

Example 8.1
   The interarrival time in an M/G/1/∞ queue is the sum of independent exponential random variables with rates $\lambda_1 = \frac{2}{3}$ and $\lambda_2 = 2$ per millisecond. Figures 8.3, 8.4, and 8.5 show the plots of $y_1(\alpha)$ and $y_2(\alpha)$ respectively for each case

1. $\mu = 1$ per millisecond,

2. $\mu = 0.5$ per millisecond, and

3. $\mu = 0.25$ per millisecond.

⧠

8.3.2   Determination of α

   If a given system is stable, the next task in an application is the determination of α. Let us refer to the implicit parameter α of a stable M/G/1∞ queue as "the effective load." Define

$$y(\alpha) = y_1(\alpha) - y_2(\alpha). \tag{8.51}$$

The function $y(\alpha)$ is well behaved. The following is a simple numerical algorithm to evaluate α so that $y(\alpha)$ is close to zero by at least a given δ.

1. Set $\alpha_0 = 0$, $y_0 = y(0)$, $\alpha_1 = 0.5$, $y_1 = y(0.5)$, and $d = 1$.

2. Loop through steps (2a) and (2b) with $i = 2, 3, \ldots$ if error $d > \delta$

   (a)

$$\alpha_{i+1} = \alpha_i - \frac{\alpha_i - \alpha_{i-1}}{y_i - y_{i-1}} y_i \qquad (8.52)$$

   (b)

$$d = |y(\alpha_{i+1})|. \qquad (8.53)$$

   If $d \leq \delta$ stop.

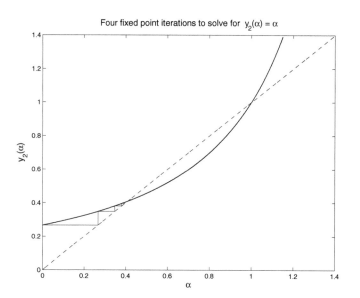

FIGURE 8.6:   Illustration of numerical solution for α

Example 8.2
Figure 8.6 shows a plot with four iterations in the evaluation of α for the case of Example 8.1.   ☐

8.4 Performance Figures in G/M/1/∞ Queue

8.4.1 Expected response time

If the continuous time stochastic process $N(t)$ corresponding to the G/M/1/∞ queue is in equilibrium, evaluation of the expected response time of an arriving customer is simple. This can be carried out with the help of the imbedded Markov chain itself, since the response time of a customer starts at the time instant of its arrival. If there are n customers at the time of arrival of a new customer, the response time of this new customer is the sum of $n + 1$ iid exponential random variables, each with rate μ. That is, the conditional expected response time is

$$E[R|n] = \frac{n+1}{\mu}. \tag{8.54}$$

The unconditional expected response time is

$$E[R] = \frac{1}{\mu} \sum_{i=0}^{\infty} (n+1)(1-\alpha)\alpha^n \tag{8.55}$$

$$= \frac{1}{\mu(1-\alpha)}. \tag{8.56}$$

The final form is obtained with manipulation as is done for the case of the M/M/1/∞ queue in Chapter 3.

8.4.2 Expected number in the system

This is easily obtained with the help of Little's result.

$$E[N] = \lambda E[R] \tag{8.57}$$

$$= \frac{\rho}{1-\alpha}. \tag{8.58}$$

The last expression is obtained by using the expression for $E[R]$ from equation (8.56).

8.5   Finite Buffer G/M/1/k Queue

The transition probability matrix gets modified as follows. The number of rows and columns each range from 0 through k. If the system has k customers at the time of an attempted arrival, the arrival gets lost and does not enter the queue. Thereafter, until the next arrival time instant, there are only k customers, some or all of which can depart. Therefore, the last row of the transition probability matrix is identical to the previous row. The solution for equilibrium probabilities is not too involved. Indeed, is fairly simple to manipulate the equations for the matrix to be transformed to a lower triangular matrix. Every equilibrium state probability p_i of the imbedded Markov chain can be expressed as a linear combination of $p_{i+1} \ldots, p_k$. Therefore, every equilibrium state probability can be expressed as a function of the unknown p_k, which is finally evaluated by equating the sum of all the probabilities to one. The resulting algorithm to compute the equilibrium state probabilities is very simple.

$P[\text{drop}]$ is at the arriving time instant and it is p_k. Therefore, the throughput is

$$E[Y] = \lambda(1 - p_k). \tag{8.59}$$

At the time an arrival occurs, the remaining service time of a customer under service is exponential with μ due to the memorylessness of service times. Therefore, the expected response time $E[R]$ is easily obtained by summing the expected service time of the new arrival and those of all the customers in the system at the time of arrival, as follows.

$$E[R|i] = \frac{i+1}{\mu} \quad \text{and} \tag{8.60}$$

$$E[R] = \frac{1}{\mu} \sum_{i=0}^{k-1} (i+1)p_i. \tag{8.61}$$

Using Little's result, the expected number in the system is given by

$$E[N] = E[Y]E[R]. \tag{8.62}$$

8.6 Pareto Arrivals in a G/M/1/∞ Queue

The Pareto pdf with a finite mean and infinite variance exhibits a heavy tail and can be used to model interarrival times of bursty traffic. Such a pdf is given by

$$f_T(t) = \begin{cases} \left(\frac{\gamma}{\beta}\right)\left(\frac{\beta}{t}\right)^{\gamma+1} & \text{if } t \geq \beta \\ 0 & \text{if } t < \beta \end{cases} \tag{8.63}$$

with $1 < \gamma \leq 2$ and $\beta > 0$. The symbol γ is used in the exponent instead of the α introduced in Chapter 2. This is because α is commonly used to represent the effective load of a G/M/1/∞ queue, as in Section 8.5. The Hurst parameter $H = \frac{3-\gamma}{2}$. We know that

$$\alpha = \int_0^\infty e^{-\mu(1-\alpha)t} f_T(t)dt. \tag{8.64}$$

The above equation (8.64) can be rewritten as

$$\alpha = \int_0^\beta e^{-\mu(1-\alpha)t} f_T(t)dt + \int_\beta^\infty e^{-\mu(1-\alpha)t} f_T(t)dt$$

$$= 0 + \int_\beta^\infty e^{-\mu t + \mu t \alpha} \left(\frac{\gamma}{\beta}\right)\left(\frac{\beta^{\gamma+1}}{t^{\gamma+1}}\right)dt$$

$$= \gamma \beta^\gamma \int_\beta^\infty \frac{e^{-\mu t + \mu t \alpha}}{t^{\gamma+1}}dt. \tag{8.65}$$

The solution to equation (8.65) is not readily apparent. Since β is just the scaling factor, we can set $\beta = 1$. Furthermore, let $x = \mu(1-\alpha)t$. Therefore, $dt = \frac{dx}{\mu(1-\alpha)}$. With this change of variables, the above equation becomes

$$\alpha = \gamma \int_{\mu(1-\alpha)}^\infty \frac{e^{-x}}{\left[\frac{x}{\mu(1-\alpha)}\right]^{\gamma+1}} \frac{dx}{\mu(1-\alpha)}$$

$$= \gamma \left[\mu(1-\alpha)\right]^\gamma \int_{\mu(1-\alpha)}^\infty e^{-x} x^{-\gamma-1} dx. \tag{8.66}$$

On integrating by parts, we have

$$\alpha = \gamma \left[\mu(1-\alpha)\right]^\gamma \left\{\left[\frac{-e^{-x}x^{-\gamma}}{\gamma}\right]_{\mu(1-\alpha)}^\infty - \frac{1}{\gamma}\int_{\mu(1-\alpha)}^\infty e^{-x} x^{-\gamma} dx\right\}$$

$$= \gamma \left[\mu(1-\alpha)\right]^{\gamma} \left\{ \left[\frac{1}{\gamma e^{\mu(1-\alpha)} \left[\mu(1-\alpha)\right]^{\gamma}}\right] - \frac{1}{\gamma} \int_{\mu(1-\alpha)}^{\infty} e^{-x} x^{-\gamma} dx \right\}.$$

$$(8.67)$$

On integrating by parts again, we get

$$\alpha = \gamma \left[\mu(1-\alpha)\right]^{\gamma} \left\{ \frac{1}{\gamma e^{\mu(1-\alpha)} \left[\mu(1-\alpha)\right]^{\gamma}} - \frac{1}{\gamma} \left[\frac{-1}{(\gamma-1)e^x x^{\gamma-1}}\right]_{\mu(1-\alpha)}^{\infty} \right.$$

$$\left. + \frac{1}{\gamma(\gamma-1)} \int_{\mu(1-\alpha)}^{\infty} e^{-x} x^{-\gamma+1} dx \right\}$$

$$= \gamma \left[\mu(1-\alpha)\right]^{\gamma} \left\{ \frac{1}{\gamma e^{\mu(1-\alpha)} \left[\mu(1-\alpha)\right]^{\gamma}} - \frac{1}{\gamma(\gamma-1)e^{\mu(1-\alpha)} \left[\mu(1-\alpha)\right]^{\gamma-1}} \right.$$

$$\left. + \frac{1}{\gamma(\gamma-1)} \int_{\mu(1-\alpha)}^{\infty} e^{-x} x^{-\gamma+1} dx \right\}. \qquad (8.68)$$

We integrate by parts the third time to get

$$\alpha = \gamma \left[\mu(1-\alpha)\right]^{\gamma} \left\{ \frac{1}{\gamma e^{\mu(1-\alpha)} \left[\mu(1-\alpha)\right]^{\gamma}} - \frac{1}{\gamma(\gamma-1)e^{\mu(1-\alpha)} \left[\mu(1-\alpha)\right]^{\gamma-1}} \right.$$

$$+ \left[\frac{-1}{\gamma(\gamma-1)(\gamma-2)e^x x^{\gamma-2}}\right]_{\mu(1-\alpha)}^{\infty}$$

$$\left. - \frac{1}{\gamma(\gamma-1)(\gamma-2)} \int_{\mu(1-\alpha)}^{\infty} e^{-x} x^{-\gamma+2} dx \right\}$$

$$= \gamma \left[\mu(1-\alpha)\right]^{\gamma} \left\{ \frac{1}{\gamma e^{\mu(1-\alpha)} \left[\mu(1-\alpha)\right]^{\gamma}} - \frac{1}{\gamma(\gamma-1)e^{\mu(1-\alpha)} \left[\mu(1-\alpha)\right]^{\gamma-1}} \right.$$

$$+ \frac{1}{\gamma(\gamma-1)(\gamma-2)e^{\mu(1-\alpha)} \left[\mu(1-\alpha)\right]^{\gamma-2}}$$

$$\left. - \frac{1}{\gamma(\gamma-1)(\gamma-2)} \int_{\mu(1-\alpha)}^{\infty} e^{-x} x^{-\gamma+2} dx \right\}$$

$$= \gamma \left[\mu(1-\alpha)\right]^{\gamma} \left\{ \frac{1}{\gamma e^{\mu(1-\alpha)} \left[\mu(1-\alpha)\right]^{\gamma}} - \frac{1}{\gamma(\gamma-1)e^{\mu(1-\alpha)} \left[\mu(1-\alpha)\right]^{\gamma-1}} \right.$$

$$\left. + \frac{1}{\gamma(\gamma-1)(\gamma-2)e^{\mu(1-\alpha)} \left[\mu(1-\alpha)\right]^{\gamma-2}} \right.$$

$$- \frac{1}{\gamma(\gamma-1)(\gamma-2)} \left[\int_0^\infty e^{-x} x^{-\gamma+2} dx \right.$$

$$\left. - \int_0^{\mu(1-\alpha)} e^{-x} x^{-\gamma+2} dx \right] \Bigg\}. \qquad (8.69)$$

Now, $0 \le -\gamma + 2 < 1$. That is, $-\gamma + 2 > -1$. Therefore, the integral terms in equation (8.69) can be expressed as (complete or incomplete) gamma functions. Therefore, we can rewrite equation (8.69) as follows.

$$\alpha = \gamma \left[\mu(1-\alpha) \right]^\gamma$$

$$\left\{ \frac{1}{\gamma e^{\mu(1-\alpha)} \left[\mu(1-\alpha) \right]^\gamma} - \frac{1}{\gamma(\gamma-1) e^{\mu(1-\alpha)} \left[\mu(1-\alpha) \right]^{\gamma-1}} \right.$$

$$+ \frac{1}{\gamma(\gamma-1)(\gamma-2) e^{\mu(1-\alpha)} \left[\mu(1-\alpha) \right]^{\gamma-2}}$$

$$\left. - \frac{1}{\gamma(\gamma-1)(\gamma-2)} \left[\Gamma(-\gamma+3) - \Gamma^*(-\gamma+3, \mu(1-\alpha)) \right] \right\}$$

$$(8.70)$$

where

$$\Gamma^*(-\gamma+3, \mu(1-\alpha)) = \Gamma(-\gamma+3) P(-\gamma+3, \mu(1-\alpha)) \text{ and} \qquad (8.71)$$

$P(-\gamma+3, \mu(1-\alpha))$ is the incomplete gamma function.

Equation (8.70) can be solved numerically to yield the profile of α curves for different values of the Hurst parameter H and the normalized load ρ. The curves are plotted in Figure 8.7[†]. Regardless of the value of H, for low values of ρ, the effective load $\alpha < \rho$. In other words, for low values of ρ, the effective load (α) in the queue by incoming packets is lower than the real load ρ. For $H = 0.5$ and $H = 0.6$, $\alpha < \rho$ over most of the normal operating range of the queue (i.e., $\rho < 0.75$). However, for high values of H, that is, for $H = 0.9$ and $H = 0.99$, $\alpha < \rho$ only for very low values of ρ. As ρ increases, the effective load observed by the incoming traffic is considerably higher than ρ. This implies that a G/M/1/∞ queue with Pareto traffic arrivals saturates at relatively low values of ρ, for high values of H. This is illustrated by examining $E[N]$ as a function of ρ and α. Figure 8.8 plots the expected number of customers as a function of the normalized load ρ for various values of H. The solid line to the extreme right and closest to the ρ axis corresponds to $\rho = \alpha$ or the expected number in an M/M/1/∞ queue. The plots in Figure 8.8 are obtained as

---

[†]Figures 8.7 and 8.8 are reproduced (with copyright permission) from the article G. R. Dattatreya and S. S. Kulkarni, "Performance of communication networks fielding bursty traffic," *Annual Review of Communications*, volume 57, November 2004, pp. 1259–1273.

follows. The expected number of customers (packets) in the system, expressed as a function of α and ρ is given in Section 8.4 as

$$E[N] = \frac{\rho}{1 - \alpha}. \tag{8.72}$$

The values of α corresponding to the values of ρ (over closely spaced intervals, $0 < \rho < 1$) are computed with equation (8.70) for $H = 0.5, 0.6, 0.7, 0.8, 0.9$, and 0.99. Then, for each such computed α, the corresponding expected number of customers is computed with equation (8.72) and plotted. The resulting plots show that for low values of H (that is, for $H = 0.5, 0.6$, and 0.7), the load curves are similar to those observed in an M/M/1/∞ queuing system. For $H = 0.9$, saturation occurs at barely 60–70% of the load. In general, as H increases, the corresponding load threshold at which saturation occurs, diminishes rapidly.

8.7 Exercises

1. A constant bit rate (CBR) data source outputs a packet after every 3 milliseconds. The packet transmission system is a contention-based medium access system with an overall total time period for successful transmission being exponentially distributed with an average of 2 milliseconds. Determine the following performance figures during equilibrium operation of the queuing system.

   (a) Expected response time.

   (b) Expected queue length.

   (c) Probability there is at least one packet in the system immediately after the time instant a packet departs.

2. Repeat Exercise 1 with the following difference. After every time period of 3 milliseconds, at most one packet arrives with a probability 0.8. Packet arrivals during successive time instants separated by 3 milliseconds are iid.

3. Determine the equilibrium state probabilities for a G/M/1/∞ system with a shifted Pareto IAT at customer arrival time instants. For the $\alpha = 1.2$, an expected IAT of 2 milliseconds, and an exponential service time with an expectation of 1 millisecond, compare the expected response times of G/M/1/∞ queues with shifted and unshifted Pareto IATs.

4. Develop an algorithm to evaluate the equilibrium state probabilities of a finite buffer G/M/1/k queue at arrival time instants. Determine the expected response time, the expected number in the system, and the probability that an attempted arrival will be dropped. Apply the results to Exercise (1) with $k = 8$.

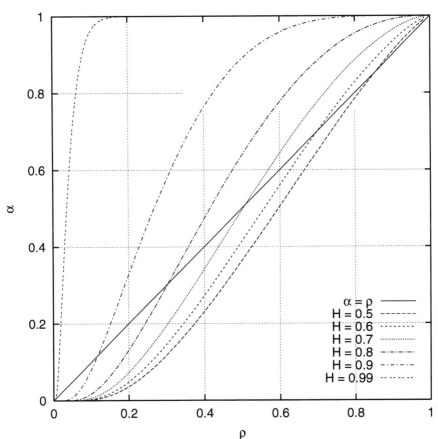

FIGURE 8.7: α versus ρ, single-source Pareto traffic

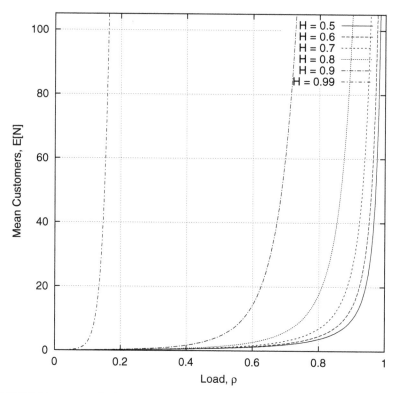

FIGURE 8.8: $E[N]$ versus ρ, G/M/1 queue with single-source Pareto traffic

Chapter 9

Queues with Bursty, MMPP, and Self-Similar Traffic

9.1 Introduction

The intensity of data traffic arriving at a point can be specified in various ways such as bits per second, packets per unit time, ordered pair of ON time for a packet and OFF time between successive packets, or, the total number of bits or packets received over a given large time interval. Unless otherwise specified, there is the implicit notion that these intensity figures do not change from one time interval to the next, and that the quantities in successive intervals are independent, over meaningful ranges of times. The observed traffic in some types of data networks appears to violate this property. Packets may arrive in clusters, with occasional packets present between clusters separated by appreciable time intervals. These occasional packets may not allow us to model the incoming traffic with intermittent time periods of arrivals. Furthermore, the variance in the amount of traffic may not decrease rapidly as the length of the time interval used for averaging. Therefore, averaging the arrivals over a long time interval to include several packet clusters in the interval does not help us in realizing stable values for intensities. Traffic exhibiting such characteristics is referred to as bursty traffic. The two causes of traffic burstiness are (1) unbounded variance, and (2) long range dependence (LRD) in interarrival times, described below.

In classical teletraffic theory, telephone traffic has been modeled traditionally with Poisson call arrivals and exponential service times. Since Poisson processes have elegant analytical properties, they have been employed widely in queuing analysis of telecommunication systems. However, data traffic in some types of data networks such as in the Ethernet depict vastly different statistical characteristics in comparison with voice traffic in telecommunication networks. These patterns conform to the above subjective definition of burstiness. The burstiness spans several time scales, with a high variance in burst sizes and in the time interval between bursts. Furthermore, the sequence of interarrival times of data packets shows strong autocorrelations. The autocorrelation function decays slowly giving rise to what is known as long range dependence (LRD). These traffic characteristics cannot be modeled adequately using Poisson processes. Therefore, researchers have suggested that some cases of network traffic be modeled using processes known as self-similar processes

that capture the properties of burstiness and LRD. Further justification of this suggestion stems from observations on the World Wide Web (WWW) data traffic. Studies
of such data traffic show that the WWW document size distributions, caching algorithms of the web browser and user preferences in following the displayed links have
a significant impact on the nature of the generated data traffic. The super imposition
of many file transfers in a local area network, with the above dynamics influencing
each such transfer, contributes to traffic self-similarity. Statistical analysis of some
variable bit rate (VBR) video sample traffic have also shown considerable burstiness
and LRD.

In this chapter, we develop many properties of burstiness, LRD and self-similarity
from first principles, to gain a comprehensive understanding of the subject. This
chapter is organized as follows. A clear distinction between smooth and bursty traffic
is brought out in Section 9.2. The properties of self-similarity are developed and
a particular self-similar process, the fractional Brownian motion (FBM) process is
studied in Section 9.3. Robert Brown (1773–1858) was a British Botanist who
observed the movement of pollen and fine dust particles and the original Brownian
motion is named in his honor. The driver process of FBM is the fractional Gaussian
noise (FGN) process. The profile of the autocorrelation sequence of the discrete
time FGN process is developed from first principles and the problems in generating
such a process are identified.

FBM is the most commonly employed example of a self-similar process. Its range
includes negative values. There are also additional difficulties in attempts to directly
use self-similar processes as exact models of traffic input to queues. A large number
of traffic streams, each with Pareto IATs, when merged, is known to approximate
self-similarity. Each Pareto IAT can be further approximated as a hyperexponential
random variable. We study a composite traffic source created by merging several iid
substreams, in each of which IATs are hyperexponential and packet sizes are exponential. This composite traffic source is Markovian with a surprisingly large number
of states and provides an excellent model for bursty traffic. This traffic model is
shown to form a closed queuing network in which the service discipline in each
queue is "immediate service." This is an example of a closed queuing network with
state-dependent service rates. An efficient product form solution for the equilibrium
state probabilities of this composite traffic source is developed. The analysis of a
queue input by such traffic is conducted. The equilibrium state probabilities of the
number of packets in such queues is evaluated. The entire analysis and performance
evaluation is computationally efficient. Matrix inversion corresponding to the composite traffic source is not required.

Markov modulated Poisson process (MMPP) is another related model for a bursty
traffic source. In this model, the arrival rate of packets switches between states according to a Markov chain. Analysis of queues input by MMPP is very similar to the
one input by the earlier described composite traffic source with merged substreams.
This analysis is also carried out.

9.2   Distinction between Smooth and Bursty Traffic

Let λ be the arrival rate of traffic (in bytes per unit time). Then, $\lambda\tau$ is the average amount of traffic (in bytes) received in the time interval τ. Let $X_i(\tau)$ be the fluctuation around the mean $\lambda\tau$. Therefore, $X_i(\tau) + \lambda\tau$ represents the amount of traffic received in the ith interval of successive, equal, and nonoverlapping time intervals, each time interval being τ long. We concentrate our attention on $X_i(\tau)$, the variation around the mean, and refer to this variation itself as the traffic. Therefore, in the following discussion, unless otherwise specified, random processes are zero mean.

The quantity $\frac{X_i(\tau)}{\tau}$ is the traffic arrival rate averaged over the ith such interval. We now form larger nonoverlapping time intervals, with each interval made of k such original intervals. Consider the cumulative traffic received over k such successive time intervals. Let $Y_i(k\tau)$ be the traffic received in the ith of such aggregated, larger intervals. Then, $\frac{Y_i(k\tau)}{k\tau}$ is the time average of the traffic rate received in the ith aggregated interval. The dimensions of both $\frac{X_i(\tau)}{\tau}$ and $\frac{Y_i(k\tau)}{k\tau}$ are "bytes per second."

Case 1: Smooth Traffic   Let $X_i(\tau)$ be an independent, identically distributed sequence of random variables indexed by i. The function var denotes the variance of the argument random variable. Let

$$\mathrm{var}[X_i(\tau)] = \sigma^2(\tau). \tag{9.1}$$

$$Y_i(k\tau) = \sum_{j=l}^{k+l-1} X_j(\tau) \text{ for some } l. \tag{9.2}$$

From Probability theory,

$$\mathrm{var}[\frac{X_i(\tau)}{\tau}] = \frac{\sigma^2(\tau)}{\tau^2} \tag{9.3}$$

and

$$\mathrm{var}[Y_i(k\tau)] = k\sigma^2(\tau). \tag{9.4}$$

Then,

$$\mathrm{var}[\frac{Y_i(k\tau)}{k\tau}] = \frac{k\sigma^2(\tau)}{k^2\tau^2}$$

$$= \frac{\sigma^2(\tau)}{k\tau^2}. \tag{9.5}$$

Therefore,

$$\mathrm{var}[\frac{Y_i(k\tau)}{k\tau}] = \frac{\mathrm{var}[\frac{X_i(\tau)}{\tau}]}{k}. \tag{9.6}$$

In the above equation, both $\frac{X_i(\tau)}{\tau}$ and $\frac{Y_i(k\tau)}{k\tau}$ are random variables corresponding to the traffic received per unit time. However, $Y_i(k\tau)$ is the traffic averaged over an interval k times the size of the interval used to average $X_i(\tau)$. Since the amounts of traffic received over successive intervals are assumed to be independent in this case, the fluctuations over the different (smaller) intervals tend to cancel out to quite some extent when considering the traffic aggregated over many such intervals. Hence we observe the $\frac{1}{k}$ type of drop in the variance of $\frac{Y_i(k\tau)}{k\tau}$, in comparison with the variance of $\frac{X_i(\tau)}{\tau}$. This phenomenon is observed widely in practice. That is, as the time period for averaging increases, the averaged (or blurred) observations tend to exhibit smaller variance (smaller by a factor proportional to the linear scale of blurring), and appear smooth. However, if data traffic defies this principle up to long intervals of time averaging, it is said to be bursty. Thus, for bursty data traffic, the variance of the corresponding $\frac{Y_i(k\tau)}{k\tau}$ does not decrease linearly with k, but decreases much more slowly. We deal with such a case of bursty traffic in the following discussion.

Case 2: Bursty Traffic If the components of $\{X_i(\tau)\}$ are statistically correlated (as opposed to being statistically independent) in a particular way, the cancellation of fluctuations can get decelerated as follows. Consider the autocorrelation sequence formed from the sequence $X_i(\tau)$. We denote this by $R_X(k, \tau)$. That is,

$$R_X(k, \tau) = E\left[X_i(\tau)X_{i+k}(\tau)\right], \ k = 0, 1, \ldots. \tag{9.7}$$

If the parameters representing the traffic are invariant to the time index i of the traffic segment, $E[X_i(\tau)X_{i+k}(\tau)]$ is not a function of i. In addition, from equation (9.7),

$$R_X(k, \tau) = R_X(-k, \tau). \tag{9.8}$$

Note that if $\{X_i(\tau)\}$ is an independent sequence,

$$R_X(0, \tau) = \sigma_X^2(\tau) \quad \text{and} \tag{9.9}$$

$$R_X(k, \tau) = 0, \ \forall k \neq 0. \tag{9.10}$$

From elementary probability theory, we know that

$$-\sigma_X^2(\tau) \leq R_X(k, \tau) \leq \sigma_X^2(\tau), \ k = 0, 1, \ldots. \tag{9.11}$$

In some cases of dependent sequences, $R_X(k, \tau)$ may be nonzero up to $k = m$, for a small integer m. In some other cases, $R_X(k, \tau)$ may decay as an exponential function of k. In these two cases, if we average $X_i(\tau)$ over many intervals, the variance diminishes rapidly as the number of intervals used for aggregation increases. On the other hand, for some profiles of $R_X(k, \tau)$, the variance of the data averaged over many intervals can decrease very slowly as demonstrated below. The variance of $\frac{Y_i(k\tau)}{k\tau}$ is evaluated as follows.

$$\text{var}\left[\frac{Y_i(k\tau)}{k\tau}\right] = \frac{1}{k^2\tau^2}\text{var}[Y_i(k\tau)]$$

$$= \frac{1}{k^2 \tau^2} E\left\{ [Y_i(k\tau)]^2 \right\}, \tag{9.12}$$

since $Y_i(k\tau)$ is zero mean.

$$\text{var}\left[\frac{Y_i(k\tau)}{k\tau}\right] = \frac{1}{k^2 \tau^2} E\left\{ \left[\sum_{i=1}^{k} X_i(\tau)\right]^2 \right\} \tag{9.13}$$

$$= \frac{1}{k^2 \tau^2} E\left\{ \left[\sum_{i=1}^{k} X_i(\tau)\right] \left[\sum_{j=1}^{k} X_j(\tau)\right] \right\} \tag{9.14}$$

$$= \frac{1}{k^2 \tau^2} \sum_{j=1}^{k} \sum_{l=1}^{k} E[X_j(\tau) X_l(\tau)] \tag{9.15}$$

$$= \frac{1}{k^2 \tau^2} \sum_{j=1}^{k} \sum_{l=1}^{k} R_X(j - l, \tau) \tag{9.16}$$

For different values of j and l, the structure of $R_X(j - l, \tau)$ is easily visualized with the help of the autocorrelation matrix, as follows. Let $R_X(j - l, \tau)$ be denoted by a_{j-l} for simpler notation. Then, as j and l each vary independently over $1, \cdots, k$, we have the double summation in equation (9.16) is given by the sum of all elements in the $k \times k$ matrix

$$\begin{bmatrix} a_0 & a_1 & \cdot & \cdot & & a_{k-1} \\ a_1 & a_0\ a_1\ a_2 & \cdot\cdot & a_{k-2} \\ a_2 & a_1\ a_0\ a_1 & & a_{k-3} \\ \cdot & \cdot\ \cdot\ \cdot & & \cdot \\ \cdot & \cdot\ \cdot\ \cdot & & \\ a_{k-1} & \cdot\ \cdot\ \cdot & & a_0 \end{bmatrix}. \tag{9.17}$$

The elements on the main diagonal are all a_0. On both the diagonals immediately above and below the main diagonal, each element is a_1. Similarly, on both the diagonals m levels above and below the main diagonal, each element is a_m. The number of elements in each of the two diagonals m levels above and below the main diagonal is $k - m$. The number of times a_0 occurs in the sum of all the elements in the matrix is the number of elements on the main diagonal, that is k times. The number of times a_m occurs in the sum of all the elements in the matrix is $2(k - m)$. Adding all these, the sum of all the elements in the matrix is given by

$$k a_0 + 2 \sum_{m=1}^{k-1} (k - m) a_m. \tag{9.18}$$

Substituting $R_X(m, \tau)$ for a_m, we have

$$\mathrm{var}\left[\frac{Y_i(k\tau)}{k\tau}\right] = \frac{1}{k^2\tau^2}\left[kR_X(0,\tau) + 2\sum_{m=1}^{k-1}(k-m)R_X(m,\tau)\right]$$

$$= \frac{\sigma^2(\tau)}{k\tau^2} + \frac{2}{k^2\tau^2}\sum_{l=1}^{k-1}(k-l)R_X(l,\tau). \qquad (9.19)$$

If the second term (the summation) on the right side of equation (9.19) is zero, then

$$\mathrm{var}\left[\frac{Y_i(k\tau)}{k\tau}\right] = \frac{\sigma^2(\tau)}{k\tau^2} \qquad (9.20)$$

corresponding to the iid sequence $X_i(\tau)$. If $R_X(k, \tau)$ decays rapidly (exponentially), then the second term on the right side of equation (9.19) is also bounded by an exponentially decaying function of k. This set of conditions corresponds to smooth traffic. However, if $R_X(k, \tau)$ are positive and large for $k > 0$, from equation (9.19), we observe that the variance of $\frac{Y_i(k\tau)}{k\tau}$ will be much larger than in the case of smooth traffic. The argument cannot be extended to make $\frac{R_X(k,\tau)}{\sigma^2(\tau)} = 1, \ k > 0$, since this would render $X_i(\tau)$ to be identical and fully correlated for all values of k, with no variations at all. If we want to extend this property for large values of k, then $\frac{R_X(k,\tau)}{\sigma^2(\tau)}$ should decay slowly, for example, as $k^{-\alpha}$ with $0 < \alpha < 1$.

Similarly, we can study the effects and required properties of variations and correlations for an arbitrarily sized window of averaging. That is, instead of examining the statistical properties of the sequence $Y_i(k\tau)$ over a time window of size $k\tau$ with an integer k, we can examine the statistical properties of $Y_i(\delta\tau)$, with a positive real δ. In an abstract model, we can let $\tau \to 0$, resulting in traffic that arrives as a continuous function of time. This is in contrast to the earlier described model in which we studied increments in traffic received over successive, equal time intervals.

9.3 Self-Similar Processes

The above discussion suggests that if $R_X(k, \tau)$ are positive and large for $k > 0$, then

$$\mathrm{var}\left[\frac{Y_i(k\tau)}{k\tau}\right] \gg \frac{1}{k}\mathrm{var}\left[\frac{X_i(\tau)}{\tau}\right]. \qquad (9.21)$$

If this property is realized, the averaged traffic that is received will still exhibit considerable variations (burstiness) over a large range of time scales and will not appear smoother as the time scale increases. These ideas can be quantified using the concepts of self-similar processes originally studied by Benoit B. Mandelbrot in the 1960s.

DEFINITION 9.1   *Let $Z(t)$ be a stochastic process and consider any t_0 and δ, $(\delta > 0)$. If the processes $Z(t_0 + \tau) - Z(t_0)$ and $\delta^{-H}[Z(t_0 + \delta\tau) - Z(t_0)]$ have the same finite joint distributions, we say that the stochastic process $Z(t)$ is self-similar with the parameter H. Mandelbrot's definition is valid for $H \geq 0$.*   ▯

The concept of self-similarity is used by Mandelbrot to describe naturally occurring fractals. Self-similar processes exhibit structural similarities in their statistics over a large number of different time scales. That is, even if the time scale of measurement is changed, the statistics of the process remain similar, (not identical). In this section, we enunciate some of the properties and consequences of the above definition in our special case of data traffic. As mentioned earlier, it is convenient to restrict $Z(t)$ to be a zero mean process. Any required mean value can be added at convenient points of mathematical (and correspondingly physical) transformations. In addition, we consider stationary increments.

9.3.1   Fractional Brownian motion

An example family of self-similar stochastic processes is the fractional Brownian motion (FBM).

DEFINITION 9.2   *$Y(t)$ is an FBM process with parameter $0.5 \leq H < 1$, if the increment $Y(t + t_0) - Y(t_0)$ is a stationary Gaussian process with zero mean and variance t^{2H}. The parameter H is the Hurst parameter introduced in Chapter 2.*   ▯

By stationarity, we mean that $Y(t + t_0) - Y(t_0)$ in the above definition is not a function of t_0. Using the notation $\mathcal{N}(\eta, \sigma^2)$ for a Gaussian random variable with a mean η and variance σ^2, we can express the rate of the FBM averaged over an interval δ as

$$\frac{Y(t + \delta) - Y(t)}{\delta} = \delta^{H-1}\mathcal{N}(0, 1). \tag{9.22}$$

Therefore,

$$\frac{d}{dt}Y(t) = \lim_{\delta \to 0} \frac{Y(t + \delta) - Y(t)}{\delta}$$

$$= \lim_{\delta \to 0} \delta^{H-1}\mathcal{N}(0, 1). \tag{9.23}$$

Since $0.5 \leq H < 1$, $\delta^{H-1} \to \infty$ as $\delta \to 0$. That is, the variance of the instantaneous rate of variation of the FBM is unbounded.

9.3.2   Discrete time fractional Gaussian noise and its properties

The above degeneracy is usually stated as "FBM is not mean square differentiable." However, its increments over any time interval $\delta > 0$ have finite variances. We can construct a time series (or a sequence of Gaussian random variables) corresponding to FBM increments over successive nonoverlapping δ. The increments $V_i(\delta) = a[Y(i\delta) - Y((i-1)\delta)]$ of the FBM process $aY(t)$ have variance $\sigma^2(\delta) = a^2 \delta^{2H}$. Let $a = \frac{1}{\delta}$. The sequence $V_i(\delta)$ constitutes the discrete fractional Gaussian noise (FGN) process. Consider the autocorrelation sequence of $V_i(\delta)$.

$$R_V(k,\delta) = E\left[\left(\frac{Y((k+1)\delta) - Y(k\delta)}{\delta}\right)\left(\frac{Y(\delta) - Y(0)}{\delta}\right)\right]. \qquad (9.24)$$

We make use of the algebraic identity

$$(a-b)(c-d) = \frac{1}{2}\left[(a-d)^2 - (a-c)^2 + (b-c)^2 - (b-d)^2\right].$$

The identity is easy to prove by expanding the RHS. Rewrite equation (9.24) as follows.

$$
\begin{aligned}
R_V&(k,\delta) \\
&= E\left[\frac{1}{2\delta^2}\left((Y((k+1)\delta) - Y(0))^2 - (Y((k+1)\delta) - Y(\delta))^2\right.\right. \\
&\qquad\qquad \left.\left. + (Y(k\delta) - Y(\delta))^2 - (Y(k\delta) - Y(0))^2\right)\right] \\
&= \frac{1}{2\delta^2}\left[\mathrm{var}[Y((k+1)\delta) - Y(0)] - \mathrm{var}[Y((k+1)\delta) - Y(\delta)]\right. \\
&\qquad\qquad \left. + \mathrm{var}[Y(k\delta) - Y(\delta)] + \mathrm{var}[Y(k\delta) - Y(0)]\right] \\
&= \frac{a^2}{2\delta^2}\left[|\delta(k+1)|^{2H} - |\delta k|^{2H} + |\delta(k-1)|^{2H} - |\delta k|^{2H}\right] \\
&= \frac{a^2}{2\delta^{2-2H}}\left[|k+1|^{2H} - 2|k|^{2H} + |k-1|^{2H}\right]. \qquad (9.25)
\end{aligned}
$$

Therefore, the normalized autocorrelation sequence of $V_i(\delta)$ is

$$
\begin{aligned}
r_V&(k,\delta) \\
&= \frac{R_V(k,\delta)}{\mathrm{var}[V_i(\delta)]} \\
&= \frac{\frac{a^2}{2\delta^{2-2H}}\left[|k+1|^{2H} - 2|k|^{2H} + |k-1|^{2H}\right]}{a^2\delta^{2H}} \\
&= \frac{1}{2\delta^2}\left[|k+1|^{2H} - 2|k|^{2H} + |k-1|^{2H}\right]
\end{aligned}
$$

$$\sim \left[\frac{H(2H-1)}{\delta^2} \right] k^{2H-2}, \quad k \to \infty. \tag{9.26}$$

The final limiting form of $r_V(k, \delta)$ in equation (9.26) can be verified by using L'Hospital's rule twice to evaluate the limit of $\frac{\delta^2 r_V(k,\delta)}{H(2H-1)} k^{2H-2}$ as $\frac{1}{k} \to 0$. The normalized autocorrelation coefficients $r_V(k, \delta)$ in equation (9.26) is not infinite summable over $k = 1, 2, \ldots$.

9.3.3 Problems in generation of pure FBM

In the literature, FBM is, almost exclusively, the only self-similar process studied in detail. Most publications in literature on FBM-based self-similar traffic model the cumulatively arriving bursty traffic as a sample path of the continuous time FBM process. Continuous time FGN is the derivative of FBM and forms its driver process. Continuous time FGN has unbounded instantaneous variance. The continuous time FBM process can be discretized over nonoverlapping windows. The increments form an FGN sequence with finite variance. The cumulative addition of successive random variables in such an FGN sequence is a discretized FBM sequence. Many research publications report the realization of bursty traffic through the approximation of continuous time FGN.

In order to satisfy self-similarity, discretized FGN must follow the autocorrelation function specified in equation (9.25) in the previous subsection. Note that as $\delta \to 0$, $r_V(k) = \infty$, $\forall k$, in equation (9.25). Therefore, continuous time FGN is not suitable for generating self-similar traffic. The autocorrelations given in equation (9.25) are nonsummable over the infinite range of k, even for $\delta > 0$.

Markovian approximations to bursty traffic are more likely to lead to exact analysis and practical interpretations. In order to retain the desirable properties of burstiness, traffic models with correlations lasting sufficient time periods should be chosen. Markov modulated Poisson process is one popular class of traffic models. In this family, an independent continuous time Markov chain controls the rate of Poisson packet emissions. Different states of the Markov chain emit packets at different rates.

9.4 Hyperexponential Approximation to Shifted Pareto Interarrival Times

The Pareto random variable is a commonly used one in the family of random variables with heavy tailed distributions. Its probability density function (pdf) is given by

$$f_X(x) = \frac{\alpha}{\beta} \left(\frac{\beta}{y} \right)^{\alpha+1} \tag{9.27}$$

for $y \geq \beta$ and zero otherwise. The parameter β is a positive scale factor and has the units of the random variable. The parameter α controls the tail profile. For $1 < \alpha \leq 2$, the expectation is finite and the variance is infinite, corresponding to the heavy tail requirement. The Pareto pdf can be shifted so that it is nonzero for all positive y, resulting in the random variable Y whose pdf is

$$f_Y(y) = \frac{\alpha}{\beta}\left(\frac{\beta}{y+\beta}\right)^{\alpha+1}, \quad y \geq 0 \text{ and} \tag{9.28}$$

$$= 0, \quad y < 0. \tag{9.29}$$

The complementary cumulative distribution function (ccdf) of Y is given by

$$F_c(y) = P[Y > y] \tag{9.30}$$

$$= \left(\frac{\beta}{y+\beta}\right)^{\alpha}, \quad y \geq 0 \text{ and} \tag{9.31}$$

$$= 0, \quad y < 0. \tag{9.32}$$

The first and second order statistics of this shifted Pareto random variable are

$$E[Y] = \frac{\beta}{\alpha - 1} \quad \text{and} \tag{9.33}$$

$$\text{var}[Y] = \infty \tag{9.34}$$

for $1 < \alpha \leq 2$. A heavy tailed shifted Pareto random variable may be approximated by a weighted sum of exponential pdfs. The resulting pdf is known as a hyperexponential pdf and for large y, it decays as a negative exponential, as y increases. Therefore, it is not really heavy tailed. The advantage of a hyperexponential pdf over a single exponential pdf is the following. The hyperexponential pdf has a steep fall for small values of y corresponding to the high rate components of the hyperexponential pdf. For large values of y, the low rate components of the hyperexponential pdf dominate. This approximates the slower fall off rate of the Pareto pdf profile for large y, while maintaining the exponential property, essential for Markov modeling. The formulation of the optimization criterion and numerical evaluation of the parameters of the approximation problem are not the topics of this chapter. A general suggestion is to minimize the integral of the squared difference between the cumulative distribution functions of the shifted Pareto random variable Y and a candidate hyperexponential random variable. For the remainder of the chapter, we assume that the interarrival time (IAT) random variable X for a single stream of packets (called a packet source) has the following hyperexponential density with m exponential components.

$$f_X(x) = \sum_{i=1}^{m} p_i \alpha_i \exp(-\alpha_i x), \quad x \geq 0 \quad \text{and} \tag{9.35}$$

$$= 0, \quad x < 0. \tag{9.36}$$

The parameters α_i are different from the tail profile parameter α used for the Pareto family above. Without loss of generality the m element set of $\{\alpha_1, \ldots, \alpha_m\}$ may be ordered in some meaningful way such as in an increasing order. This hyperexponential pdf represents the IAT in one of the packet sources. Each packet completely arrives in an instant of time and successive packet arrivals are separated by independent and identically distributed (iid) X.

9.5   Characterization of Merged Packet Sources

Let k iid packet sources be merged to form a composite arrival process. Each component packet source follows the hyperexponential IAT described in the above section. At any time instant, each of the packet sources operates as follows. There is a selected component from the set of m exponential components of the hyperexponential pdf. All the packet sources are competing to emit the next packet, with their respectively chosen rate of the exponential components. Soon after a packet arrives, the next composite IAT is influenced by the following. The most recent arrival was due to a packet emission from one of the sources. This particular source now chooses one of the m exponential components for its next packet emission IAT, with probabilities p_i. All other sources are operating at their current rates. Therefore, the composite packet arrival stream follows a Markov chain. Its characteristics are developed below. This Markov chain is referred to as the environment chain. At any time instant, each packet source is in one of m states, corresponding to the chosen component of its hyperexponential pdf. All the sources that have chosen the same exponential component have some similarity. Therefore, let k_i denote the number of individual packet sources that are in state i meaning that they all have chosen the i-th component of the hyperexponential pdf. Let k denote the m-element vector as

$$\boldsymbol{k} = (k_1, \ldots, k_m). \tag{9.37}$$

Clearly,

$$k_i \geq 0, \quad i = 1, \ldots, m \quad \text{and} \quad \sum_{i=1}^{m} k_i = k, \tag{9.38}$$

where k is the number of individual packet sources. Let $\boldsymbol{v}_i$ be a unit vector representing the i-th exponential component as follows. The vector $\boldsymbol{v}_i$ has zeros at each of the m possible positions, except at position i at which the value is 1. Therefore,

$$\boldsymbol{k} = \sum_{i=1}^{m} k_i \boldsymbol{v}_i. \tag{9.39}$$

The number of possible states in the environment chain is easily evaluated as the number of ways in which k indistinguishable objects can be distributed into m distinguishable bins. Place the k objects and $m-1$ barriers in a line. These $m-1$ barriers separate the k objects into m distinguishable bins. All the possible arrangements can be realized by designating different combinations of the $m-1$ items as barriers and the remaining k items as the objects in a line-up of the $k+m-1$ items. Therefore the number of such combinations is

$$\binom{k+m-1}{k} = \binom{k+m-1}{m-1} \tag{9.40}$$

$$= \frac{(k+m-1)!}{k!\,(m-1)!}. \tag{9.41}$$

As an example, if 25 individual packet sources are merged and if each individual packet source has a 10-component hyperexponential IAT, the number of states in the resulting environment Markov chain of the composite packet source is 52,451,256.

9.6   Product Form Solution for the Traffic Source Markov Chain

In order to specify the behavior of the environment chain, the state transition rates of the chain are required. Their equilibrium probabilities are also useful characteristics. The large number of states motivates a quest for a computationally efficient algorithm to evaluate the equilibrium state probabilities. This section analyzes the environment chain and shows that the equilibrium state probabilities follows a product form of a network of m immediate service queues. A convolution algorithm is developed for an efficient evaluation of the equilibrium probabilities.

Let a particular individual packet source in state i emit the next packet. The rate at which this event occurs is $k_i\alpha_i$, since k_i is the number of individual packet sources in state i, each competing to emit a packet with a rate α_i. Once such a packet is emitted, the source that emitted it then independently chooses the next rate with a probability mass function (pmf) $p_1,\ldots,p_m$ for rates corresponding to $\alpha_1,\ldots,\alpha_m$. If a rate α_j is chosen, the vector state changes from $\boldsymbol{k}$ before the packet emission to $\boldsymbol{k}-\boldsymbol{v}_i+\boldsymbol{v}_j$, after the packet emission. We can imagine these state changes with the help of m bins containing k objects changing their bin occupying configuration. When the above change takes place, an object moves from the i-th bin to the j-th bin. At any instant of time, each of the objects in the i-th bin is attempting to leave the bin with a rate α_i. As the first object leaves, it selects one of the m bins to reenter, with a pmf $p_1,\ldots,p_m$. Thus, the movement of k objects in the system is identical to a closed network of m queues. The service discipline in each of these m queues is "immediate service" with an exponential service time of rate α_i for the bin (or the queue) i. When an object leaves a bin (queue), its selection of the next bin (queue) to reenter is independent of everything else. Such a network of queues is known to possess a product form for its equilibrium state probabilities. The following analysis evaluates the product form solution and establishes this result as well. The object leaving bin i can reenter the same bin i. At every time instant an object leaves a bin, a data packet is emitted by the composite packet source. Since a data packet is emitted even if an object leaves and reenters the same bin, we have that data packets are emitted whenever the source chain changes state, as well as with a particular rate during the time interval that the source chain stays in the same state. The rates of change of states and data packet emissions are evaluated as follows.

Let an individual source in state i emit the next packet. The rate at which this event occurs is $k_i \alpha_i$. The probability that the source that emitted a packet will choose j as its next state is simply p_j. Therefore, the rate of change of state from k to $k - v_i + v_j$ is $p_j k_i \alpha_i$. A data packet is emitted from this environment chain at the time instant of a state change. If $i = j$, the environment does not change state but a data packet is emitted. Therefore, the rate of packet emission during the time the environment chain resides in a state k and before it changes to some other state is $p_i k_i \alpha_i$. During the time the environment chain is in state k, the total rate with which the chain changes to some other state is

$$\sum_{i=1}^{m} k_i \alpha_i (1 - p_i) = \sum_{i=1}^{m} k_i \alpha_i \sum_{\substack{j=1 \\ j \neq i}}^{m} p_j. \tag{9.42}$$

The factor $1 - p_i$ on the left hand side (LHS) is due to the fact that if a packet source in state i emits a packet and reenters state i, the overall environment chain does not change state. Consider the rates of change from state $k - v_i + v_j$ with $j \neq i$ to k. Such a change requires that a packet source at state j emit a packet and that the source change its state to i. This change is possible only if $k_i - 1 \geq 0$ or $k_i \geq 1$. If $i \neq j$ and $k_i \geq 1$, clearly, $k_j < k$. The rate of this event conditioned on the environment chain being in state $k - v_i + v_j$ is

$$p_i (k_j + 1) \alpha_j u(k_i). \tag{9.43}$$

The function $u(k_i)$ is the unit step function defined as

$$u(l) = 1, \text{ if } l \geq 1 \text{ and} \tag{9.44}$$
$$= 0, \text{ otherwise.} \tag{9.45}$$

The factor $u(k_i)$ is used in expression (9.43) to ensure that the rate is zero if $k_i = 0$, since this latter condition renders the state $k - v_i + v_j$ invalid. Let $P[k]$ be the equilibrium probability that the environment chain is in state k. The global balance equation around state k is

$$P[k] \sum_{i=1}^{m} \sum_{\substack{j=1 \\ j \neq i}}^{m} p_j k_i \alpha_i$$

$$= \sum_{\substack{i=1 \\ j \neq i}}^{m} \sum_{j=1}^{m} P[\boldsymbol{k} - \boldsymbol{v}_i + \boldsymbol{v}_j] p_i(k_j + 1) \alpha_j u(k_i). \tag{9.46}$$

The factor $u(k_i)$ on the RHS of the above equation (9.46) is redundant and can be eliminated since $P[\boldsymbol{k} - \boldsymbol{v}_i + \boldsymbol{v}_j] = 0$ if $k_i = 0$. There is one such global balance equation for every possible vector state.

A potential candidate for solution satisfies

$$P[\boldsymbol{k} - \boldsymbol{v}_i + \boldsymbol{v}_j] p_i(k_j + 1) \alpha_j$$

$$= P[\boldsymbol{k}] p_j k_i \alpha_i, \quad \text{for all } j \neq i, \tag{9.47}$$

and for every valid combination of $\boldsymbol{k}$ and $\boldsymbol{k} - \boldsymbol{v}_i + \boldsymbol{v}_j$. Equivalently,

$$P[\boldsymbol{k} - \boldsymbol{v}_i + \boldsymbol{v}_j] = \frac{p_j k_i \alpha_i}{p_i(k_j + 1)\alpha_j} P[\boldsymbol{k}] \tag{9.48}$$

$$= \frac{\frac{p_j}{(k_j+1)\alpha_j}}{\frac{p_i}{k_i \alpha_i}} P[\boldsymbol{k}]. \tag{9.49}$$

This suggests a candidate product form solution

$$P[\boldsymbol{k}] = \frac{1}{h} \prod_{i=1}^{m} \left(\frac{1}{k_i!} \left(\frac{p_i}{\alpha_i} \right)^{k_i} \right). \tag{9.50}$$

The constant h is used to ensure that the sum of the probabilities of the finite state environment chain evaluates to 1. The physical dimension of h is (time^k). The next step is to verify that the above product form solution satisfies the global balance equations for all valid combinations of $\boldsymbol{k}$ and $\boldsymbol{k} \boldsymbol{v}_i + \boldsymbol{v}_j$. If $k_i \geq 1$, we have from the candidate product form solution,

$$P[\boldsymbol{k} - \boldsymbol{v}_i + \boldsymbol{v}_j] = \frac{1}{h} \prod_{i=1}^{m} \left(\frac{1}{k_i!} \left(\frac{p_i}{\alpha_i} \right)^{k_i} \right) \frac{\frac{p_j}{(k_j+1)\alpha_j}}{\frac{p_i}{k_i \alpha_i}}$$

$$= P[\boldsymbol{k}] \frac{p_j k_i \alpha_i}{p_i(k_j + 1)\alpha_j}. \tag{9.51}$$

Using this on the RHS of the global balance equation, the RHS of equation (9.46) evaluates to

$$\sum_{\substack{i=1 \\ j \neq i}}^{m} \sum_{j=1}^{m} P[\boldsymbol{k}] \frac{p_j k_i \alpha_i}{p_i(k_j + 1)\alpha_j} p_i(k_j + 1)\alpha_j. \tag{9.52}$$

Canceling $p_i(k_j+1)\alpha_j$ on the numerator and the denominator, the RHS of the global balance equation (9.46) simplifies to

$$\sum_{\substack{i=1 \\ j \neq i}}^{m} \sum_{j=1}^{m} P[\boldsymbol{k}] k_i \alpha_i, \tag{9.53}$$

which is the LHS of the global balance equation (9.46). This successfully concludes the verification of the validity of the product form solution given in equation (9.50) for the equilibrium state probabilities of the environment Markov chain.

9.6.1 Evaluation of h, the Constant in the Product Form Solution

In order for all the state probabilities of the environment chain to sum to 1, we have

$$h = \sum_{\forall k} \prod_{i=1}^{m} \frac{1}{k_i!} \left(\frac{p_i}{\alpha_i} \right)^{k_i}. \tag{9.54}$$

The approach to evaluate h is the typical decomposition of the sum in the above equation (9.54), resulting in a convolution algorithm for closed queuing networks with state-dependent service rates. Define $h(i, j)$ as the constant for i individual packet sources and for j components in the hyperexponential pdf of the IAT of each packet source. The idea is to develop

$$h = h(k, m) \tag{9.55}$$

with an iterative algorithm which evaluates $h(i, j)$ from smaller values of i and j all the way through $i = k$ and $j = m$.

$$h = h(k, m) \tag{9.56}$$

$$= \sum_{\forall k} \prod_{i=1}^{m} \frac{1}{k_i!} \left(\frac{p_i}{\alpha_i} \right)^{k_i} \tag{9.57}$$

$$= \sum_{j=0}^{k} \sum_{\substack{k \in S(k,m) \\ k_m = j}} \prod_{i=1}^{m} \frac{1}{k_i!} \left(\frac{p_i}{\alpha_i} \right)^{k_i} \tag{9.58}$$

$$= \sum_{j=0}^{k} \frac{1}{j!} \left(\frac{p_m}{\alpha_m} \right)^{j} \sum_{\forall k \in S(k-j,m-1)} \prod_{i=1}^{m-1} \frac{1}{k_i!} \left(\frac{p_i}{\alpha_i} \right)^{k_i} \tag{9.59}$$

$$= \sum_{j=0}^{k} \frac{1}{j!} \left(\frac{p_m}{\alpha_m} \right)^{j} h(k-j, m-1). \tag{9.60}$$

The above iteration starts as follows. If $k = 0$, we have no packet sources and only one state in the environment. Therefore,

$$h(0, j) = 1, j = 1, \ldots m. \tag{9.61}$$

On the other hand, if $m = 1$ all the i objects are in the same bin resulting again in only one state. Therefore,

$$h(i, 1) = \frac{1}{i!} \left(\frac{p_1}{\alpha_1} \right)^i, i = 1, \dots k. \tag{9.62}$$

Note that the convolution algorithm uses a computational decomposition only and does not change the network configuration. Therefore, even though we use only one station for the case of evaluating $h(i, 1)$ in equation (9.62), p_1 should not be changed to 1. The iterations continue with

$$h(i_1, j_1) = \sum_{i=0}^{i_1} \frac{1}{i!} \left(\frac{p_{j_1}}{\alpha_{j_1}} \right)^j h(i_1 - i, j_1 - 1) \tag{9.63}$$

up to and including $i_1 = k$ and $j_1 = m$. The algorithm generates a matrix with k rows and m columns. The top row and the leftmost column are filled with the help of equations (9.61) and (9.62), respectively. Filling any entry at the current position (i_1, j_1) in the matrix requires all the elements up to and including row i_1 of the column to the left of the current entry. The complexity of the algorithm is $O(k^2 m)$. This concludes the computationally efficient evaluation of the normalization constant h. If we need all the equilibrium state probabilities, the convolution algorithm to evaluate h is redundant for the following reason. All the unnormalized equilibrium state probabilities evaluated through the use of equation (9.50) without the factor $\frac{1}{h}$ will sum to h.

9.7   Joint Markov Chain for the Traffic Source and Queue Length

The topic of this section is the analysis of an FIFO queue that is fed by a Markovian data traffic of the type discussed in the previous section. We can be a little more general and consider the following Markov chain for the packet sources. Consider a continuous parameter irreducible Markov chain with l states and in equilibrium. The states are numbered $1, \dots, l$ for convenience. This Markov chain controls the generation of data packets to be fed into the queue; it is called the environment chain, as its special case is, in the previous section. Whenever the environment chain changes its state, it emits a data packet into the queue. In addition, during a time interval that the environment chain is residing in a state, and before it changes to any other state, it generates data packets with iid exponential IAT. The rate of such IATs are, of course, a function of the state of the environment, in general. Clearly, the environment Markov chain developed in the previous section for data packet generation due to merged streams is a special case of this general environment chain. The only differences may be that the state transition rates of the previous environment chain follows a particular structure. Data packets require iid exponential service time with a rate μ. Let b_{ii} be the cumulative rate of packet generation when the environment is in state i. This cumulative rate has the following components. Let $a_{ii} = b_{ii} q_{ii}$ be the rate of packet generation while the environment chain is in state i, not including any rate caused by the chain changing its state. In keeping with the properties of the composite traffic source developed in the previous section, we assume that $a_{ii} > 0$, $i = 1, \ldots, l$. Let $a_{ij} = b_{ii} q_{ij}$ be the rate with which the environment changes its state from state i to state j, $j \neq i$. As a consequence, $b_{ii} q_{ij}$ is the additional rate of packet generation when the environment chain is in state i, since it emits a packet whenever it changes its state to j. The motivation for this terminology is now clear; each row of the matrix $Q = [q_{ij}]$ is a pmf and the entire matrix Q is a stochastic matrix. Note that $q_{ii} > 0$, $i = 1, \ldots, l$. The reason for emphasizing this is that in the case of the transition rates of a continuous parameter Markov chain, the diagonal entries are restricted to be zero. In particular, for the environment chain of the previous section, $q_{ii} > 0$ for every i. The entries b_{ij} are defined to be zeros, if $j \neq i$. This completes the definition of a matrix $B = [b_{ij}]$ with strictly positive entries on the main diagonal and entries of zeros everywhere else. Define a normalized matrix by dividing all its entries of B by the packet service rate μ, as follows.

$$C = \frac{1}{\mu} B. \tag{9.64}$$

We also have the following.

$$A = BQ \quad \text{and} \tag{9.65}$$
$$\frac{1}{\mu} A = CQ. \tag{9.66}$$

The joint system of the environment and the number of packets in the queue is a Markov chain. Let the state of this joint chain be denoted by (j, n) corresponding to j being the state of the environment and n, the number of packets in the queue; $j = 1, \ldots, l$ and $n = 0, 1, \ldots,$. Let $P_{j,n}$ be the equilibrium probability of state (j, n). The following are the state transition rates. The symbol $(., .) \rightarrow (., .)$ denotes the transition rate from the state specified on the left side of the arrow to the state specified on the right side of the arrow.

$$(i, n) \rightarrow (j, n + 1) = a_{ij}, \quad i = 1, \ldots l; j = 1, \ldots, l;$$
$$\text{and} \quad n = 0, \ldots, \tag{9.67}$$
$$(i, n + 1) \rightarrow (i, n) = \mu, \quad i = 1, \ldots l; n = 0, \ldots. \tag{9.68}$$

All other transition rates are zeros. The following develops the global balance equation around each of the states. Each LHS corresponds to the unconditional rate of the chain leaving a particular state. This is obtained by multiplying the equilibrium probability of the state in question by the sum of all outgoing transition rates from the state. The RHS of each equation corresponds to the unconditional rate of entering the state corresponding to the state on the LHS. This is obtained by summing the product of the equilibrium probability of a state from which there is a transition to the state on the LHS and the rate of the corresponding transition. Balance around state $(j, 0)$. There is only one state $(j, 1)$ from which there is a transition to state $(j, 0)$. We have

$$P_{j,0} \sum_{i=1}^{l} a_{ji} = P_{j,1}\, \mu. \tag{9.69}$$

Balance around state $(j, n+1)$, $n \geq 0$. There are transitions from the state $(j, n+1)$, $i = 1, \ldots, l$ to each of the states $(i, n+2)$, with rates a_{ji}, correspondingly. There is one more transition from the state $(j, n+1)$, to the state (j, n), with a rate μ. There is a transition from each of the states (i, n) to the state $(j, n+1)$, $i = 1, \ldots, l$ with rates a_{ij}, correspondingly. There is a transition from the state $(j, n+2)$ to the state $(j, n+1)$, with a rate μ. We have

$$P_{j,n+1}\left(\mu + \sum_{i=1}^{l} a_{ji}\right) = \sum_{i=1}^{l} P_{i,n} a_{ij} + P_{j,n+2}\mu, \tag{9.70}$$

for $j = 1, \ldots, l$ and $n \geq 0$. Normalize all the equations by dividing each by μ. Substitute $c_{ii}q_{ij}$ for $\frac{a_{ij}}{\mu}$, $i = 1, \ldots, l$ and $j = 1, \ldots, l$. We have, for $n = 0$, from equation (9.69),

$$P_{j,0} \sum_{i=1}^{l} \frac{a_{ji}}{\mu} = P_{j,1} \quad \text{or} \tag{9.71}$$

$$P_{j,0} \sum_{i=1}^{l} c_{jj}q_{ji} = P_{j,1} \quad \text{or} \tag{9.72}$$

$$P_{j,0} c_{jj} = P_{j,1} \quad \text{or} \tag{9.73}$$

$$P_{j,1} = P_{j,0} c_{jj}, \quad j = 1, \ldots, l. \tag{9.74}$$

Similarly, the equations obtained by balancing around states with the number of packets in the queue $n > 0$ are manipulated. From equation (9.70), we have

$$P_{j,n+2} = P_{j,n+1}\left(1 + \sum_{i=1}^{l} \frac{a_{ji}}{\mu}\right) - \sum_{i=1}^{l} P_{i,n} \frac{a_{ij}}{\mu} \tag{9.75}$$

$$= P_{j,n+1}\left(1 + \sum_{i=1}^{l} c_{jj}q_{ji}\right) - \sum_{i=1}^{l} P_{i,n} c_{ii}q_{ij} \tag{9.76}$$

$$= P_{j,n+1}(1 + c_{jj}) - \sum_{i=1}^{l} P_{i,n} c_{ii}q_{ij} \tag{9.77}$$

for $j = 1, \ldots, l$ and $n \geq 0$. The above equations can be represented in compact matrix form, with the help of the following notation. Let P_n be a row vector

$$P_n = [P_{1,n} \ldots P_{l,n}], \quad n \geq 0 \tag{9.78}$$

and I, the identity matrix. We have

$$P_1 = P_0 C \tag{9.79}$$
$$P_{n+2} = P_{n+1}(I + C) - P_n C Q, \quad n \geq 0. \tag{9.80}$$

The above equations can be used to recursively generate the sequence of vectors, $\{P_1, P_2, \ldots\}$ starting from P_0. Note that P_1 is a matrix multiple of P_0, followed by P_2 being a matrix linear combination of P_0 and P_1, etc. Therefore, each P_n is eventually a matrix multiple of P_0.

The joint Markov chain of the environment and the queue is irreducible. We know from the theory of Markov chains that there exists a strictly positive solution for the equilibrium probabilities to the balance equations which is unique except for a single normalization factor. If the system is stable, the normalization factor is uniquely determined by

$$\sum_{j=1}^{l} \sum_{n=0}^{\infty} P_{j,n} = 1. \tag{9.81}$$

If the system is not stable, the only solution that allows convergence of the sum of all the probabilities requires all of them to be zero. In this case, of course, the probabilities cannot sum to one. If we find a strictly positive solution for the equilibrium probabilities such that the sum of all the probabilities converges to one, then that is the only solution.

If the system is stable, we have additional equations based on the equilibrium state probabilities of the environment chain. Let the row vector

$$S = [s_1 \ldots s_l] \tag{9.82}$$

be the known equilibrium state probabilities of the environment chain. The matrix CQ is the known matrix of the state transition rates of the l (finite) state continuous parameter Markov chain. The quantities q_{ii} can be ignored in the state transition diagram of the environment Markov chain, since a continuous parameter Markov chain shows a state transition only when the state changes to some other state; a state change back to itself does not show any change in the timed sequence of states. However, the parameters q_{ii} play a role in emitting a packet whenever the state changes back to itself. Therefore they should not be completely eliminated from consideration. The equilibrium state probabilities of the environment chain satisfies the following matrix balance equation.

$$SC = SCQ. \tag{9.83}$$

It is easy to see that the effects of q_{ii} cancel on both sides of the above equation (9.83). Together with the condition that

$$\sum_{j=1}^{l} s_j = 1, \tag{9.84}$$

the matrix balance equation (9.83) uniquely determines S. If the environment chain satisfies the conditions of the merged packet sources with each individual packet source possessing iid hyperexponential pdf, S is obtained from the product form results of the previous section. In any case, we assume that S is known. The environment chain functions independently. The function of the queue is affected by the behavior of the environment chain. If we sum the joint probabilities of queue occupancies, we recover the marginal equilibrium probability of the state of the environment chain. That is,

$$\sum_{n=0}^{\infty} P_{i,n} = s_i, i = 1, \ldots, l. \tag{9.85}$$

In matrix form this is equivalent to

$$\sum_{n=0}^{\infty} P_n = S. \tag{9.86}$$

9.8   Evaluation of Equilibrium State Probabilities

The following principles and results from the matrix theory are helpful.

DEFINITION 9.3   *A matrix is said to be positive if all its entries are strictly positive.   A nonnegative matrix is similarly defined. Let A and B be matrices of identical sizes.   If every entry of A is strictly less than the corresponding entry of B we denote it with*

$$A < B. \tag{9.87}$$

Similar notation is also used for loose inequality.   A positive diagonal matrix has strictly positive entries on its main diagonal and zero entries everywhere else.   ∎

DEFINITION 9.4   *A square matrix A is said to be convergent if*

$$\lim_{n \to \infty} \boldsymbol{A}^n = \boldsymbol{0}. \tag{9.88}$$

☐

LEMMA 9.1
If the matrix $\boldsymbol{A}$ is convergent, the matrix $(\boldsymbol{I} - \boldsymbol{A})$ is invertible and the inverse is given by

$$(\boldsymbol{I} - \boldsymbol{A})^{-1} = \sum_{n=0}^{\infty} \boldsymbol{A}^n. \tag{9.89}$$

Proof
The proof is very simple. Since $\boldsymbol{A}$ is convergent, we know that $\boldsymbol{A}^n$ is finite for every n, including as $n \to \infty$. Consider

$$(\boldsymbol{I} - \boldsymbol{A}) \sum_{i=0}^{n} \boldsymbol{A}^i = \sum_{i=0}^{n} \boldsymbol{A}^i - \sum_{i=0}^{n} \boldsymbol{A}^{i+1} \tag{9.90}$$

$$= \boldsymbol{I} + \sum_{i=1}^{n} \boldsymbol{A}^n - \sum_{i=1}^{n+1} \boldsymbol{A}^n \tag{9.91}$$

$$= \boldsymbol{I} - \boldsymbol{A}^{n+1}. \tag{9.92}$$

Taking limits as $n \to \infty$ on both sides, we have

$$(\boldsymbol{I} - \boldsymbol{A}) \sum_{i=0}^{\infty} \boldsymbol{A}^i = \boldsymbol{I} \lim_{n \to \infty} \boldsymbol{A}^{n+1} \tag{9.93}$$

$$= \boldsymbol{I}. \tag{9.94}$$

Therefore,

$$\sum_{i=0}^{\infty} \boldsymbol{A}^i = (\boldsymbol{I} - \boldsymbol{A})^{-1}. \tag{9.95}$$

☐

In order to evaluate the equilibrium state probabilities of the joint Markov chain of the environment and the queue length, we seek a solution of the form

$$P_n = S(I - R)R^n, \quad n = 0\dots \tag{9.96}$$

with nonnegative and convergent matrix R that also results in a nonnegative $S(I - R)$. If such a matrix R exists, equation (9.96) is the unique solution for the equilibrium probabilities of the joint Markov chain of the environment and the number of packets in the queue. The task at hand is to develop an algorithm for evaluating a such a matrix R, if it exists, or show that such a matrix does not exist. Substitute the candidate solution from equation (9.96) in the balance equations. We need R to satisfy

$$S(I - R)R = S(I - R)C \quad \text{and} \tag{9.97}$$

$$S(I - R)R^{n+2} = S(I - R)R^{n+1}(I + C) - S(I - R)R^n CQ, \quad n \geq 0. \tag{9.98}$$

Rearranging equation (9.98), we need R to satisfy

$$S(I - R)R^n \left(R^2 - R(I + C) + CQ \right) = 0. \tag{9.99}$$

We can attempt to obtain a matrix R that satisfies

$$R^2 - R(I + C) + CQ = 0 \tag{9.100}$$

in addition to earlier specified requirements. So far, we have used the balance equations connecting P_{n+2} and other probability vectors, with $n \geq 0$ only. Expand the first balance equation (9.97) above. We have

$$SR - SR^2 = SC - SRC \tag{9.101}$$

$$= SCQ - SRC \tag{9.102}$$

since we know that $SC = SCQ$. Rearranging equation (9.102), we have

$$S\left(R^2 - R(I+C) + CQ\right) = 0 \qquad (9.103)$$

verifying that if R satisfies the quadratic equation (9.100), then it also satisfies the remaining balance equation (9.97). In an attempt to develop an algorithm to evaluate R, rearrange the required equation (9.100) for R as

$$R = (R^2 + CQ)(I + C)^{-1}. \qquad (9.104)$$

The matrix R is required to be nonnegative and convergent. We can initiate a computational procedure with $R_{(0)} = 0$ to begin with, use it on the RHS of the equation (9.104) and evaluate the LHS as its next matrix in an iterative procedure. Clearly, the components of R will remain nonnegative. Let us examine the behavior of such an iterative procedure is defined below.

$$R_{(0)} = 0 \qquad (9.105)$$

$$R_{(n)} = (R_{(n-1)}^2 + CQ)(I + C)^{-1}, \quad n = 1, \ldots. \qquad (9.106)$$

9.8.1   Analysis of the sequence $R_{(n)}$

LEMMA 9.2
The sequence $\{R_{(n)}\}$ is monotonically nondecreasing.

Proof
The proof is by induction. We know that

$$R_{(1)} = CQ(I + C)^{-1} \geq R_{(0)} = 0. \qquad (9.107)$$

Assume that $R_{(n)} \geq R_{(n-1)}$. Denote the entries of $R_{(n)}^2$ by $\left(R_{(n)}^2\right)_{ij}$ and evaluate them.

$$\left(R_{(n)}^2\right)_{ij} = \sum_{k=1}^{m} \left(R_{(n)}\right)_{ik} \left(R_{(n)}\right)_{kj} \qquad (9.108)$$

$$\geq \left(R_{(n-1)}\right)_{ik} \left(R_{(n-1)}\right)_{kj} \qquad (9.109)$$

simply because all the corresponding entries are nonnegative and nondecreasing, and because the inequality is preserved after addition and multiplication. Therefore, we have

$$R_{(n)}^2 \geq R_{(n-1)}^2. \tag{9.110}$$

Now, it is easy to simplify $R_{(n+1)} - R_{(n)}$ as

$$R_{(n+1)} - R_{(n)} = (R_{(n+1)}^2 - R_{(n)}^2)((I + C)^{-1} \tag{9.111}$$

$$\geq 0 \tag{9.112}$$

thus showing that the monotonically nondecreasing property carries on for every as n to $n + 1$.   ☐

LEMMA 9.3
The sequence is $R_{(n)}$ is bounded from above.

Proof
Again, proof is by induction.

$$R_{(1)} = CQ(I + C)^{-1} \tag{9.113}$$

$$SR_{(1)} = SC(I + C)^{-1} \tag{9.114}$$

$$< S. \tag{9.115}$$

Equation (9.114) above follows due to $SCQ = SC$. In our application system, S is the row vector of equilibrium probabilities of an irreducible finite state chain and hence has strictly positive entries. Also, the matrix C is a positive diagonal matrix. Now let

$$SR_{(n)} < S. \tag{9.116}$$

Then,

$$SR_{(n)}^2 = SR_{(n)}R_{(n)} \tag{9.117}$$

$$< SR_{(n)} \tag{9.118}$$

$$< S. \tag{9.119}$$

Use this in the evaluation of $SR_{(n+1)}$.

$$SR_{(n+1)} = S(R_{(n)}^2 + CQ)(I+C)^{-1} \tag{9.120}$$

$$< S(I+C)(I+C)^{-1} \tag{9.121}$$

$$< S \tag{9.122}$$

thus proving that

$$SR_{(n)} < S \quad \text{for every } n \geq 1. \tag{9.123}$$

Now, every entry in S is strictly positive. Therefore, in the evaluation of $SR_{(n)}$, every entry in $R_{(n)}$ contributes to the sum. Since every entry in $R_{(n)}$ is nonnegative, this effectively establishes a bound on every entry in $R_{(n)}$. The following is the algebraic elaboration of the same argument.

$$s_{\min} = \min\{s_1, \ldots, s_m\} \tag{9.124}$$

denotes the minimum entry in S. At this point, we are interested in establishing any (finite) bound for $R_{(n)}$. Starting from the componentwise inequalities in $SR_{(n)} < S$, we can reduce the values on the LHS and increase the values on the RHS

$$\sum_{i=1}^m s_i(R_{(n)})_{ij} < S \quad \text{or} \tag{9.125}$$

$$s_{\min} \sum_{i=1}^m (R_{(n)})_{ij} < 1 \quad \text{or} \tag{9.126}$$

$$s_{\min}(\boldsymbol{R}_{(n)})_{ij} < 1 \quad \text{or} \tag{9.127}$$

$$(\boldsymbol{R}_{(n)})_{ij} < \frac{1}{s_{\min}} \quad \text{or} \tag{9.128}$$

$$\boldsymbol{R}_{(n)} < \frac{1}{s_{\min}}. \tag{9.129}$$

The last inequality bounds every entry of the matrix $\boldsymbol{R}_{(n)}$ by the quantity on the RHS. □

We have shown that the sequence of matrices $\{\boldsymbol{R}_{(n)}\}$ is monotonically nondecreasing and bounded from above by a finite constant. From the dominated theorem of convergence in the theory of sequences, the above establishes the following result.

LEMMA 9.4

The sequence of matrices $\{\boldsymbol{R}_{(n)}\}$ is a convergent sequence. Denote the limiting matrix by $\boldsymbol{R}$. We have

$$\lim_{n \to \infty} \boldsymbol{R}_{(n)} = \boldsymbol{R}. \tag{9.130}$$

Together with the inequality (9.123), that is,

$$\boldsymbol{SR}_{(n)} < \boldsymbol{S}, \tag{9.131}$$

we have

$$\boldsymbol{SR} \leq \boldsymbol{S}. \tag{9.132}$$

The strict inequality in (9.131) is replaced by the loose inequality in the above (9.132) for the following reason. As the index n of the sequence $\{\boldsymbol{R}_{(n)}\}$ progresses, the strict inequality of (9.131) is true for every n. However, it is not clear if the difference between the corresponding elements of $\boldsymbol{S}$ and $\boldsymbol{SR}_{(n)}$ can or cannot be made as small as desired by making n sufficiently large. That is, it is not clear if the strict inequality is maintained in the limit as n tends to infinity. Therefore, all we can say from the above arguments is that

$$\boldsymbol{S}(\boldsymbol{I} - \boldsymbol{R}) \geq 0. \tag{9.133}$$

The book by Marcel Neuts listed in the Short Bibliography treats queues input by a more general class of Markovian arrivals than the one we have at hand. Neuts shows that the algorithm in equations (9.105) and (9.106) produces a sequence of $R_{(n)}$ that converges to what is known as the "minimal nonnegative solution" R and that R satisfies the additional property

$$S(I - R) > 0. \qquad (9.134)$$

We state it below as a theorem, for our special case, without proof (of the convergent property of R).

THEOREM 9.1
The sequence of matrices, $\{R_{(n)}\}$, generated in equations (9.105) and (9.106), satisfies the following properties.

1. *Every matrix $R_{(n)} \geq 0$, $n = 0, \ldots$.*

2. *The sequence $\{R_{(n)}\}$ converges to a limiting matrix R.*

3. *The limiting matrix R is a convergent matrix. That is*

$$\lim_{n \to \infty} R^n = 0 \quad and \qquad (9.135)$$

$$(I - R)^{-1} = \sum_{n=0}^{\infty} R^n. \qquad (9.136)$$

4. *The vector $S(I - R)$ is strictly positive.*   ⬜

9.9 Queues with MMPP Traffic and Their Performance

The environment emitting the packets is different in this system. The environment is a finite chain with l states and transitions rates $c_{ii}q_{ij}\mu$ from state i to state j, as in the earlier case. However, packets are not emitted when the environment chain changes state. Therefore, $q_{ii} = 0$, since there is no event that signal a transition from state i back to itself. The equilibrium probability row vector S follows $SC = SCQ$. The environment does emit packets in a Poisson stream with rate $d_{ii}\mu$ as long as the environment chain is in state l. D is a diagonal matrix with entries d_{ii}. When the environment chain changes state, the rate of Poisson packet arrivals changes.

The resulting matrix balance equations are

$$P_1 = P_0[D + C(I - Q)] \tag{9.137}$$

$$P_{n+2} = P_{n+1}[I + D + C(I - Q)] + P_n D, \quad n \ge 0. \tag{9.138}$$

As in the earlier case, seek a solution of the form

$$P_n = S(I - R)R \tag{9.139}$$

with a nonnegative and convergent R which should also lead to

$$I - R > 0. \tag{9.140}$$

Following the earlier approach, substituting the candidate solution in the balance equations (9.137) and (9.138), we obtain

$$S(I - R)R^n \left(R^2 - R\left(I + D + C(I - Q) + D \right) \right) = 0. \tag{9.141}$$

We can further restrict the candidate solution to satisfy

$$R^2 - R\left(I + D + C(I - Q) + D \right) = 0. \tag{9.142}$$

The above class of problems is included in the book by Marcel Neuts (listed in the Short Bibliography and referenced earlier). The algorithm proposed and proved there to obtain the minimal nonnegative solution for R is

$$R_{(0)} = 0 \tag{9.143}$$

$$R_{(n+1)} = (R_{(n)}^2 + D)\left(I + D + C(I - Q) + D \right)^{-1}, \quad n = 0, 1, \dots. \tag{9.144}$$

In this case of MMPP, inverting the matrix

$$I + D + C(I - Q) + D \tag{9.145}$$

restricts the number of states of the environment chain that the computational procedure can handle.

9.10   Performance Figures

The simple mathematical structure of the resulting equilibrium state probabilities in both of the different cases of the environment Markov chain leads to easy evaluation of performance figures. Some of these are suggested in the exercises.

9.11   Conclusion

Poisson traffic with a constant rate is considered to be smooth since the number of arrivals averaged over even reasonably short time periods tends to be close to its expectation. As the time period of averaging increases, the variance of the number of arrivals decreases inversely proportional to the time of averaging. Data traffic patterns in which the amounts of traffic received in successive constant time periods are positively correlated and in which these correlations persist and do not decay exponentially tend to be bursty. Self-similar traffic is known to be a limiting case of burstiness, in some sense. Merging a large number of independent traffic sources in which each source exhibits a heavy tailed distribution for interarrival time is known to result in a composite traffic source with properties close to self-similarity. Such an aggregation of individual traffic sources results in long range dependence. It is easy to see this cause-effect relationship, as follows. Among the k individual traffic sources, at any instant of time, each source will emit a data packet, after some time. These times for packet emission are not memoryless since all the interarrival times are heavy tailed. Soon after a particular source emits a packet, it implicitly resets its timer to start a new independent heavy tailed interval for its next packet emission. However, all other sources are still in the process of elapsing their respective times for their next packet emission. Since these time intervals are heavy tailed, the dependency also intuitively lasts for longer time intervals.

Fractional Brownian motion (FBM) is the most understood and most useful self-similar process. FBM being a Gaussian process with fluctuations on both sides of the zero is not particularly suitable for traffic modeling. The derivative of the FBM is the continuous fractional Gaussian noise (FGN) and has infinite instantaneous variance. The increments of the FBM over successive nonoverlapping intervals is called the discrete time FGN. The autocorrelation sequence of the discrete time FGN is not infinite summable.

A Markovian bursty data traffic model with a large number of states is developed as follows. Let successive packets in a data packet stream be separated by an m component hyperexponential interarrival times. The hyperexponential pdf approximates a heavy tailed pdf. Let k independent sources of such packet streams be merged. This merged traffic approximates self-similar traffic. In exact representation, the merged packet traffic results in a Markov chain with a very large number of states. This Markov chain is elegantly analyzed by first showing that it satisfies a product form of a closed network of m state dependent queues and then evaluating the equilibrium state probabilities with an efficient algorithm.

The behavior of a single Markovian queue with such composite data traffic is analyzed. The analysis of a single FIFO queue input by an MMPP is similar to that input by the composite large Markovian bursty traffic. Its results are briefly pointed out.

9.12   Exercises

1. Develop the expressions for the important performance figures of the two Markovian bursty traffic models studied in this chapter.

2. A two state environment Markov chain generates exponential size data packets. The rate of packet generation is controlled by the state of the environment. As long as the environment is in state 1, no packets are generated. If the state of the environment is 2, packets are generated at the rate of 1 per ms. In addition, a packet is generated at every time instant when the state of the environment changes. The average time the environment stays in state 1 is 2 ms, and in state 2, it is 3 ms. Packets enter an FIFO queue buffer with unlimited waiting line.

   (a) What is the maximum average service time below which the system is stable?

   (b) Numerically determine the R matrix for the case of the normalized load $\rho = 0.7$.

   (c) Compute and plot the expected response time in the queue as a function of the average service time, for the range of $0.1 < \rho < 0.9$.

3. Repeat Exercise 2 for the case when there are no packet arrivals at the time instants of state changes in the environment chain.

4. Four iid traffic substreams are merged and fed to an FIFO queue. The IAT between packets in each substream is hyperexponential with rates of 1, 2, and 3 per ms, respectively. Their corresponding mixing probabilities are 0.1, 0.3, and 0.6. All the packets require iid exponential service time with a rate μ. Solve the following with the help of computer programs.

   (a) Develop the state space and the corresponding state transition rates of the packet arrival system.

   (b) Determine the equilibrium state probabilities of the packet arrival chain withe the help of two different techniques.

      i. The traditional method of matrix inversion
      ii. The convolution algorithm for the product form solution

   (c) Determine the minimum μ above which the queue is stable.

   (d) Let ρ be the normalized load of the queue, which is a function of μ. Plot the expected number in the queue over $0.1 < \rho < 0.9$.

   (e) Compare the plot of the expected number in the above exercises with that of an M/M/1/∞ queue.

   (f) Plot the ratio of the expected numbers in the above two Exercises.

5. Investigate the problem of fitting a hyperexponential pdf for a shifted Pareto IAT. Recall the following about the Fourier series expansion of a periodic function. The coefficients of the different harmonics are not changed if we try to fit a finite number of harmonics for the original periodic function. Attempt to formulate an optimization problem to fit a hyperexponential pdf to a shifted Pareto pdf with a similar property. That is the rates of the exponential functions should be independent of the number of exponential functions used for the hyperexponential approximation. If this is successful, we can find such "optimal rates" of exponential functions one after another and stop after some number of components. For a given number of components with a given set of rates of exponential functions, solve the problem of determination of the corresponding mixing probabilities.

6. This chapter has introduced closed queuing networks with immediate service, a category of networks with stated-dependent service rates. These principles are useful in the channel allocation problem of cognitive radio networks in which multiple groups of users intelligently share a common set of radio channels.

   Each of a set of N channels can be in one of several functionalities.

   (a) Channel under testing to determine quality. There are two categories of usable channels. High (H) quality, and acceptable (A) quality. Channels required to be tested go through an FIFO queue. Each test takes an exponential amount of time. On testing, if a channel is found to be in one of two quality states, it is moved to the corresponding idle queue. If the channel quality is found to be unacceptable, it is moved back to the testing queue for testing again, when it gets its turn in the FIFO testing waiting line again.

(b) If the quality testing is successfully complete, a channel is sent to one of the two idle (H or A) queues, in each of which, channels wait in an FIFO queue for allocation to a user.

(c) When a request is made for a particular type (H or A) of channel, if the idle queue for that type of channel has at least one channel, the channel at the head of the queue is allocated. If not, the request disappears. Requests for a particular type of channel allocation come in after iid exponential times with a particular rate.

(d) There are two categories of users: primary (P) and secondary (S). Therefore, there are four categories of channels being used. The four combinations are the two types of usable channel qualities and the two types of users. The two different qualities use different bit rates for transmission and therefore have different average service times, even if the packet sizes are the same. Primary users have higher priority and therefore can hold onto the chancel for longer durations. Secondary users are required to use an allocated for shorter duration so they can squeeze in some communication inbetween the requirements of the primary users.

(e) Once a channel is released by the user, it is either sent for testing to the quality testing queue or to the corresponding idle queue, based on the recommendation of the user that used it for the most recent connection.

Include additional interesting conditions that may allow the primary users to have a higher priority than the secondary users. Develop the Markovian queuing network diagram and include the necessary interconnections. Indicate which interconnections in the queuing network are necessary and why other interconnections do not exist. Indicate the type of service in each queue. Note that the service discipline in queues in which channels are used for data communication is immediate service. Supply some meaningful physical values for rates and switching probabilities. Develop the algorithm for the evaluation of equilibrium state probabilities and performance figures. Evaluate the probability that a primary user finds no free channel when it needs one.

7. Investigate other ways of organizing the operation of a cognitive radio network. As one example, let there be N_c number of channels and N_p number of primary users. Let the number of secondary users be uncertain, but assume some statistically regular way in which secondary users request channels.

8. Prove that the equilibrium number of customers in an M/G/∞ queue is a Poisson pmf. Guess the parameter of this Poisson distribution before deriving it. Investigate whether or not a closed queuing network in which one or more

stations have immediate service but with nonexponential service times has a product form solution. Any and all other FIFO queues in the network have memoryless service times. Note that a product form for the equilibrium state probabilities by itself does not imply that the continuous time stochastic chain of the network's vector state must be Markov.

Chapter 10

Analysis of Fluid Flow Models

10.1 Introduction

We have studied several Markov chain models of queuing systems to represent and analyze computer network performance problems. In these models, packets have been assumed to appear instantaneously. The departure time instant of a packet from a queue is considered to be the time instant when the entire packet including the last bit has just completed leaving the system. In the case of the simplest M/M/1/∞ queue in equilibrium, departure time instants are shown to be Poisson. In reality, data packets begin to flow out of the system when the first bit is serviced and continues to flow out for a nonzero amount of time until the last bit has departed. This is easily visualized in the case of a transmitter whose purpose is to move the packet from the system to the surroundings. If we have a sequence of queues, such as the output of the transmitter being fed to a remote receiver, the data packets arriving into the receiver also take a nonzero amount of time for arrival. That is, a packet starts arriving when the first bit starts arriving and continues until the last bit has completed arriving. As mentioned above, if we mark the end of the arrival time interval as the time instant of the packet arrival, the arrival time instants have been shown to be a Poisson stream, if the arrivals came from the departures of a previous M/M/1/∞ queue under equilibrium.

In some practical systems, the server need not wait for all of the packet to start servicing it. If the server is free at the time a packet starts arriving, or if the server becomes available to service a packet midway through its arrival time interval, the server can start servicing the packet before it has completed its entire arrival time interval. Such data arrival and departures are henceforth referred to as fluid arrivals and departures. In the case of a single server, the total service time for a packet is usually modeled as a time interval that is proportional to the total time for the complete arrival of the packet. In some systems, the total time for service may be less than the total time of arrival. An illustrative example is that of a high speed transmitter which can pump out a packet on an outgoing datalink at a rate higher than the rate at which the packet flowed into the transmitter queue. In a particular application example, let the transmitter (server) start acting on (servicing) a packet only after it has completely arrived. Then the effect of higher fluid service rate in comparison with the fluid arrival rate is easily visualized as less time for servicing a packet than its fluid arrival time interval. The rate of flowing in here is not the number of packets arriving over a unit time interval; it is the rate at which the bits of a packet flow in within a packet. In such a system, the average inactive time interval between the end of a packet arrival and the start of the next packet arrival is less than the corresponding time interval at the output. Consider such a system which is empty at some point and a packet starts flowing in. The transmitter cannot function at its full rate simply because bits are not flowing in at a rate that it can transmit. Neither can it predict the perfect time delay after which it should start transmitting so as to complete the transmission exactly at the time instant that the packet arrival completes. So, what is the purpose of having a high speed transmitter? There are two reasons. The first is that if there are packets that have completed arrival, the transmitter can pump it out at its high rate without having to slow down in the middle for the arrival to catch up. The second reason is that fluid packets may be able to simultaneously arrive from different sources and multiplexed into the buffer. Then it may be necessary to transmit fluid bits at a rate higher than the fluid arrival rate of one of the arrival streams.

If the fluid transmission rate is lower than fluid arrival rate, we have what is called a "leaky bucket." Such a system may be used to "regulate" traffic. This effectively stretches packets so that if a burst of packets arrived over a short time period, the output is pumped slowly resulting in smoothing out the fluctuations in short time arrival rates. The simplest fluid flow system is such a leaky bucket which drains fluid bits at a constant rate. The input is a two state Markov chain in which no fluid is input during one of the states and fluid is pumped at a higher rate than transmission rate in the other state. The next section analyzes such a system.

10.2   Leaky Bucket with Two State ON-OFF Input

The Markovian fluid input process has two states, ON and OFF. Let the random variable corresponding to the OFF state be 1 and that for the ON state, 2. During the ON state, 2, the environment pumps bits at a bit rate of γ. Of course, during the OFF state, state 1, the environment does not pump bits at all, that is, it pumps with a rate of zero. At any time instant the environment is in the OFF state, the time required to switch over to the ON state is exponentially distributed with rate α. Similarly, during the ON state, the environment will switch over to the OFF state after an exponential time with a rate β. This leads to the following equilibrium probabilities for the environment Markov chain pumping fluid into the buffer.

$$p_1 = \frac{\beta}{\alpha + \beta} \quad \text{and} \tag{10.1}$$

$$p_2 = \frac{\alpha}{\alpha + \beta}. \tag{10.2}$$

We refer to the fluid input system as the Markov chain or simply the chain. The fluid flows into a buffer, and it is drained or transmitted out by the transmitter. The transmitter empties the bits at a constant rate of η bits per unit time, provided the buffer has bits to transmit. Let $x(t)$ be the real variable amount of bits in the buffer at any time instant t. Let $X(t)$ be the corresponding random process. The objective is to evaluate the equilibrium probability distribution of the random variable X, provided that the system is stable. The condition for stability is intuitively seen as the requirement that the overall average rate of pumping in is less than the capacity of the transmitter to pump out. This is easily evaluated as follows. The ON and OFF states strictly alternate. The average amount of fluid pumped in during one ON time period is $\frac{\gamma}{\beta}$, over an average time period of $\frac{1}{\beta}$. This is followed by an OFF time period with lasting an average time of $\frac{1}{\alpha}$. Therefore, the overall average pumping-in rate is

$$\frac{\frac{\gamma}{\beta}}{\frac{1}{\beta} + \frac{1}{\alpha}} \tag{10.3}$$

per unit time. The capacity to transmit bits out of the buffer is η bits per unit time. Therefore the condition for stability is given by

$$\frac{\frac{\gamma}{\beta}}{\frac{1}{\beta} + \frac{1}{\alpha}} < \eta \quad \text{or} \tag{10.4}$$

$$\frac{\alpha\gamma}{\alpha + \beta} < \eta. \tag{10.5}$$

Within the class of stable systems, if the transmission rate η is higher than the pumping-in rate γ, the buffer will be empty all the time. The transmitter will function to drain the incoming bits. Since the incoming bit rate is less than the transmitter's capacity, the transmitter works at a lower rate of γ and empties the bits as they come into the buffer. This is a very simple case in which the buffer content is always zero. Therefore, we assume $\eta > \gamma$. In this case, as the bits flow in, the transmitter drains at a lower rate and a portion of the bits flowing in accumulate in the buffer. When the system switches to the state zero, the bits stop flowing in but the transmitter continues to drain the bits at its capacity.

10.2.1 Development of differential equations for buffer content

In the nondegenerate case being studied, $\gamma > \eta$, the buffer content increases by a constant rate of $\gamma - \eta > 0$ when the state of the fluid input process is ON. The buffer content decreases with rate η during the OFF state, provided there is some fluid (bits) to drain. The randomness in the fluid amount is a consequence of the randomness in the ON-OFF process only.

Let $F_i(X \leq x, t)$ be the joint probability that the state is $i \in \{1, 2\}$ and that the buffer content is at most x at time instant t. Consider the time interval $[t, t + dt]$. Let

$$dt = dt_1 + dt_2 \tag{10.6}$$

where a state change, if any during dt, takes place at some $t + dt_1$. Given that the state of the chain at t is 1, the probability of no state change in the environment is $(1 - \alpha dt)$. Under this condition, the buffer simply drains ηdt amount of bits. On the other hand, if the state is 2 at t, a state change to state 1 can take place in dt with a probability βdt. In this case, the amount of fluid (bits) change from the original amount x for the duration dt_1 is positive and given by $(\gamma - \eta)dt_1$. During the following infinitesimal time interval dt_2, the buffer content decreases by ηdt. Therefore, over dt, the net change in x is $\gamma dt_1 - \eta dt$. The probability of the state of the chain being 1 and that $X \leq x$ at $t + dt$ is evaluated by considering different possibilities at t and the changes that need to take place in order to reach the desired condition. We have

$$F_1(x, t + dt) = F_1(x + \eta dt, t)(1 - \alpha dt) + F_2(x - \gamma dt_1 + \eta dt, t)\beta dt. \tag{10.7}$$

Rearranging, we have

$$\frac{F_1(x, t + dt) - F_1(x + \eta dt, t)}{dt}$$

$$= -\alpha F_1(x + \eta dt, t) + \beta F_2(x - \gamma dt_1 + \eta dt, t). \tag{10.8}$$

Add and subtract $F_1(x, t)$ in the numerator of the LHS of the above equation (10.8). This results in

$$\frac{F_1(x, t + dt) - F_1(x, t)}{dt} + \frac{F_1(x, t) - F_1(x + \eta dt, t)}{dt}$$

$$= -\alpha F_1(x + \eta dt, t) + F_2(x - \gamma dt_1 + \eta dt, t)\beta. \tag{10.9}$$

As $dt \to \infty$, the first ratio clearly evaluates to the partial derivative $\frac{\partial F_1(x, t)}{dt}$. To evaluate the limit of the second ratio, note that at any time instant that the state is

1, there is no fluid flow into the buffer and the transmitter drains at a rate of η. Therefore, when the state is 1,

$$\frac{dx}{dt} = -\eta \quad \text{or} \tag{10.10}$$

$$\eta dt = -dx \quad \text{and} \tag{10.11}$$

$$dt = -\frac{dx}{\eta}. \tag{10.12}$$

Using these in equation (10.9), we have

$$\frac{\partial F_1(x, t)}{\partial t} - \eta \frac{F_1(x, t) - F_1(x - dx, t)}{dx}$$

$$= -\alpha F_1(x + \eta dt, t) + \beta F_1(x - \gamma dt_1 + \eta dt, t). \tag{10.13}$$

Evaluating the limits, we obtain the following partial differential equation

$$\frac{\partial F_1(x, t)}{\partial t} - \eta \frac{\partial F_1(x, t)}{\partial x} = -\alpha F_1(x, t) + \beta F_2(x, t). \tag{10.14}$$

We are interested in the equilibrium cdf, that is under the condition that the cdf $F_i(x, t)$ that does not vary with time. If such a solution is possible,

$$\frac{\partial F_i(x, t)}{\partial t} = 0 \tag{10.15}$$

and the parameter t in $F_i(x, t)$ need not be explicitly written since $F_i(x, t)$ does not vary with time. The derivatives of $F_i(x)$ wrt x are not any more partial, again due to only one independent variable x. Using these simplifications and rearranging, we have

$$\frac{dF_1(x)}{dx} = \frac{\alpha}{\eta} F_1(x) - \frac{\beta}{\eta} F_2(x). \tag{10.16}$$

The above equation (10.16) is dimensionally correct. The rate η is in number of bits per unit time and x is in bits. The rates α and β are simply in "per unit time." The development of a similar differential equation for the joint probability of the state of the chain being 2 and $X \leq x$ at the time instant $t + dt$ is similarly carried out. If the state is 2 at t and it does not change over the next dt, the change in the fluid amount is $(\gamma - \eta)dt$. If the state at t is 1 and it changes to 2 after dt_1, the change in fluid amount over $dt > dt_1$ is $\gamma dt_1 - \eta dt$. We have

$$F_2(x, t + dt) = F_2(x - \gamma dt + \eta dt, t)(1 - \beta dt) + F_1(x - \gamma dt_1 + \eta dt, t)\alpha dt,$$
(10.17)

or,

$$\frac{F_2(x, t + dt) - F_2(x - \gamma dt + \eta dt, t)}{dt}$$

$$= -\beta F_2(x - \gamma dt + \eta dt, t) + \alpha F_1(x - \gamma dt_1 + \eta dt, t).$$
(10.18)

To evaluate the limits as $dt \to \infty$, add and subtract $F_2(x, t)$ to the numerator of the ratio on the LHS of the above equation (10.18).

$$\frac{F_2(x, t + dt) - F_2(x, t)}{dt} + \frac{F_2(x, t) - F_2(x - \gamma dt + \eta dt, t)}{dt}$$

$$= \alpha F_1(x - \gamma dt_1 + \eta dt, t) - \beta F_2(x - \gamma dt + \eta dt, t).$$
(10.19)

The limit of the first ratio on the LHS of (10.19) evaluates to $\frac{\partial F_2(x, t)}{dt}$. In order to evaluate the limit of the second ratio, observe that in state 2, the rate of increase of fluid is

$$\frac{dx}{dt} = \gamma - \eta \quad \text{or}$$
(10.20)

$$(\gamma - \eta)dt = dx \quad \text{and}$$
(10.21)

$$dt = \frac{dx}{\gamma - \eta}.$$
(10.22)

Using these in equation (10.19), simplifying, and carrying out the limit in the remaining parts of the equation, we have

$$\frac{\partial F_2(x, t)}{\partial t} + (\gamma - \eta)\frac{dF_2(x, t)}{\partial x} = \alpha F_1(x, t) - \beta F_2(x, t).$$
(10.23)

As in the earlier case, we are interested in the equilibrium cdf, that is under the condition that the cdf $F_i(x, t)$ that does not vary with time. If such a solution is possible,

$$\frac{\partial F_2(x, t)}{\partial t} = 0 \tag{10.24}$$

and the parameter t in $F_i(x, t)$ need not be explicitly written since $F_i(x, t)$ do not vary with time. Using these simplifications and rearranging, we have

$$\frac{dF_2(x)}{dx} = \frac{\alpha}{\gamma - \eta} F_1(x) - \frac{\beta}{\gamma - \eta} F_2(x). \tag{10.25}$$

The two final equations connecting $F_1(x)$ and $F_2(x)$ are

$$\frac{dF_1(x)}{dx} = \frac{\alpha}{\eta} F_1(x) - \frac{\beta}{\eta} F_2(x) \quad \text{and} \tag{10.26}$$

$$\frac{dF_2(x)}{dx} = \frac{\alpha}{\gamma - \eta} F_1(x) - \frac{\beta}{\gamma - \eta} F_2(x). \tag{10.27}$$

We finally have a set of two coupled linear first order ordinary differential equations with constant coefficients. They are differential equations due to the presence of derivatives. They are coupled since each cannot be separately solved. They are linear, since, if we can find two solutions $y_i(x)$ and $z_i(x)$ for $F_i(x)$, then $ay_i(x)+bz_i(x)$ is also a solution for $F_i(x)$. Similar comments hold for linearly combining multiple individual sets of solutions. The differential equations are "ordinary" since there are no partial derivatives and all the derivatives are with respect to the same independent variable x. They have constant (but different) coefficients multiplying all the functions $F_i(x)$ and their derivatives. We are required to solve the equations and produce $F_1(x)$ and $F_2(x)$ as functions of x for solutions. Examining the equations, we see that the functional dependency on x of $F_i(x)$ and their derivatives must be the same if the equations (10.26) and (10.27) are to hold for all x. This provides a hint that any solution for $F_1(x)$ and $F_2(x)$ must have a variation with respect to x of the form

$$F_i(x) = \exp(vx). \tag{10.28}$$

Note that the same form of variation wrt x is used for both $i = 1$ and $i = 2$, that is, the same v. Substituting this form into the original differential equation allows us to verify its validity, and more importantly, to evaluate the unknown constant v.

When we substitute the equation (10.28) in the original differential equations, the functional variation $\exp(-vx)$ cancels out and we get algebraic equations for the unknown v. We may get multiple values for v, each of which satisfies the set of algebraic equations. In this case, the general solution will be a linear combination of all such solutions. These constants are evaluated if enough initial conditions are known about the nature of the system described by the differential equations. In our case, this additional information is that $F_i(x)$ are joint cdfs. Therefore,

$$\lim_{x \to \infty} F_1(x) = p_1 = \frac{\beta}{\alpha + \beta} \quad \text{and} \tag{10.29}$$

$$\lim_{x \to \infty} F_2(x) = p_2 = \frac{\alpha}{\alpha + \beta}. \tag{10.30}$$

Other conditions such as conservation of throughput at the flow-in and flow-out points are also initial conditions.

Recall that the entire derivation has been carried out for $x > 0$, so that the transmitter drains the buffer with its full capacity. In the final solution for $F_i(x)$, we do know that $F_i(X) = 0$ for $x < 0$. Therefore, $F_i(0)$ will automatically give us the joint probability of the the environment's chain being in state i and the buffer being empty.

The above general method is better illustrated with a numerical example in which the clutter due to parameters α, β, γ, and η is eliminated without changing the structure of the differential equations. This allows us to concentrate on the solution approach.

Example 10.1

A lone teenage customer is enjoying the wireless access point in an Internet cafe all for his own laptop computer on a lazy Saturday afternoon. The cafe has installed numerous wireless devices to monitor their equipment. It is not clear why the cafe did not use Ethernet connections for at least their non-mobile equipment. These wireless devices do not use the Internet access point but generate electromagnetic noise that interferes with data communication between the laptop and the access point. Therefore, the laptop transmitter uses a smaller bit transmission rate than the rate of input bits into the transmitter buffer, to combat noise. Packets come into its buffer for transmission at the rate of 1000 packets per second. The average number of bits in a packet is 500. The bit rate with which a packet flows into the buffer 1.5 Mbps (megabits per second). The bit transmission rate of the transmitter is 1 Mbps. Successive packets do not flow in continuously as there is a time period for acknowledgment followed by a possible delay for the next packet to start flowing in. State the approximations necessary to model this as a simple Markovian fluid flow system. Determine the equilibrium cdf of the number of bits left over in the transmitter buffer. If the transmitter

expends 10 mW of power during the time it is transmitting bits and 2 mW when it is not, evaluate the average power consumption by the transmitter.

Solution
The number of bits in packets is approximated as a continuous random variable with an iid exponential distribution. Time intervals of OFF periods between successive packets coming into the buffer are also modeled as id exponential random variables. This is consistent with the given condition that successive packets do not arrive with zero gap of time period between them.

The average ON time of an incoming packet is

$$\frac{1}{\beta} = \frac{500 \text{ bits}}{1.5 \text{ Mbps}} \quad \text{or} \tag{10.31}$$

$$\beta = 3 \text{ per ms.} \tag{10.32}$$

The packet arrival rate is the reciprocal of the average time between the starting points of two successive packets. Therefore, the average OFF time is the reciprocal of the packet arrival rate minus the average ON time. That is,

$$\frac{1}{\alpha} = \left(1 - \frac{1}{3}\right) \text{ ms} \quad \text{or} \tag{10.33}$$

$$\alpha = 1.5 \text{ per ms.} \tag{10.34}$$

The arriving bit rate within a packet is $\gamma = 1.5$ Mbps or 1.5 kilo bits per millisecond. The bit transmission rate is $\eta = 1$ Mbps or 1 kilo bits per millisecond. With these, we have time in milliseconds and the amount of bits (fluid) in kilo bits The required parameters in the differential equations are

$$\frac{\alpha}{\eta} = 1.5 \tag{10.35}$$

$$\frac{\beta}{\eta} = 3 \tag{10.36}$$

$$\frac{\alpha}{\gamma - \eta} = 3 \quad \text{and} \tag{10.37}$$

$$\frac{\beta}{\gamma - \eta} = 6. \tag{10.38}$$

Using these in the differential equations, we have

$$F_1' = 1.5F_1 - 3F_2 \quad \text{and} \tag{10.39}$$

$$F_2' = 3F_1 - 6F_2. \tag{10.40}$$

In the above, the common argument x of the functions is omitted for simplicity. Also, the prime superscript denotes the derivative wrt x. These differential equations are represented in matrix notation as

$$\boldsymbol{F}' = \boldsymbol{A}\boldsymbol{F}. \tag{10.41}$$

The matrix $\boldsymbol{A}$ contains the parameters.

$$\boldsymbol{A} = \begin{bmatrix} 1.5 & -3 \\ 3 & -6 \end{bmatrix}. \tag{10.42}$$

We seek a solution of the form

$$\boldsymbol{F} = \boldsymbol{B}\exp(vx) \tag{10.43}$$

where $\boldsymbol{B}$ is an unknown column vector and v is an unknown value. The above form for the solution uses a constant multiplied by the exponential function for each unknown function $F_i(x)$. The constants may turn out to be different for $F_1(x)$ and $F_2(x)$ but the exponential function $\exp(vx)$ is common to both the functions. Substituting the candidate solution in the vector differential equation (10.41), we have

$$v\boldsymbol{B}\exp(vx) = \boldsymbol{A}\boldsymbol{B}\exp(vx), \tag{10.44}$$

$$v\boldsymbol{B} = \boldsymbol{A}\boldsymbol{B} \quad \text{or} \tag{10.45}$$

$$(\boldsymbol{A} - v\boldsymbol{I})\boldsymbol{B} = \boldsymbol{0}. \tag{10.46}$$

We now clearly see that the problem of solving the differential equations has been reduced to solving the algebraic problem of determining v and $\boldsymbol{B}$ in equation (10.46). The quantity v is called the eigenvalue of the matrix $\boldsymbol{A}$ and the vector $\boldsymbol{B}$ is called the eigenvector corresponding to the eigenvalue. There may be multiple eigenvalues and corresponding multiple eigenvectors. Equation (10.46) has a nonzero solution for $\boldsymbol{B}$ only if the determinant of $\boldsymbol{A} - v\boldsymbol{I}$,

$$\begin{vmatrix} 1.5 - v & -3 \\ 3 & -6 - v \end{vmatrix} = (v - 1.5)(v + 6) + 9 = 0. \tag{10.47}$$

Solving the quadratic equation for v, we have $v = 0$ or $v = -4.5$. For $v = 0$, the corresponding eigenvector $\boldsymbol{B}$ is determined by substituting $v = 0$ in equation (10.46) and solving the set of linear simultaneous equations for b_1 and b_2. The RHS of the matrix equation (10.46) is a column vector of zeros. There are two consequences of this. The first is that any equation can be expressed as a linear combination of all others. The second is that we will not be able to obtain unique values for b_1 and b_2. In this case of only two unknowns, we obtain

$$1.5b_1 - 3.0b_2 = 0 \quad \text{or} \tag{10.48}$$

$$b_2 = \frac{1}{2}b_1. \tag{10.49}$$

Since we will be using the two solutions with the different v values in a linear combination, one of the values for b_1 and b_2 can be chosen arbitrarily (but nonzero), for each different case of v. For the case of $v = 0$, let $b_2 = 1$ so that $b_1 = 2$.

For the eigenvalue $v = -4.5$, the eigenvector $\boldsymbol{B}$ is given by

$$6b_1 - 3b_2 = 0 \quad \text{or} \tag{10.50}$$

$$b_2 = 2b_1. \tag{10.51}$$

Let $b_1 = 1$ and $b_2 = 2$ for this case of $v = -4.5$. The general solution given by the linear combination

$$\boldsymbol{F} = c_1 \begin{bmatrix} 2 \\ 1 \end{bmatrix} + c_2 \begin{bmatrix} 1 \\ 2 \end{bmatrix} \exp(-4.5x). \tag{10.52}$$

There is no exponential function of x multiplying the first column vector, since the first eigenvalue is 0. How do we evaluate c_1 and c_2 for our particular problem? We do it with the help of the so called "initial conditions" for the differential equations, known about the system. We know that each of $F_1(x)$ and $F_2(x)$ is a joint cdf. The marginal cdf of the buffer content X is simply the sum of $F_1(x)$ and $F_2(x)$. Adding these functions with their unknown constants, we have

$$F_X(x) = F_1(x) + F_2(x) \tag{10.53}$$

$$= 3c_1 + 3c_2 \exp(-4.5x). \tag{10.54}$$

The unknown constant c_1 is easily evaluated by using the fact that the cdf $F_X(x)$ tends to 1 as x tends to infinity. We obtain $c_1 = \frac{1}{3}$. To evaluate c_2, equate the known throughput flowing into the buffer to the throughput flowing out of the transmitter; the latter is a function of $F_X(x)$ and this facilitates the evaluation of c_2. The throughput flowing in is simply the rate of incoming bits while a packet is being pumped in multiplied by the probability that a packet is flowing in. This is given by

$$E[Y_{\text{in}}] = \frac{\gamma\alpha}{\alpha + \beta} \tag{10.55}$$

$$= \frac{1.5 \times 1.5}{1.5 + 3} \tag{10.56}$$

$$= \frac{1}{2}. \tag{10.57}$$

The throughput flowing out of the transmitter is η whenever the transmitter is transmitting bits. This occurs with a probability of $[1 - F_X(0)]$. Therefore,

$$E[Y_{\text{out}}] = \eta[1 - F_X(0)] \tag{10.58}$$

$$= 1 \times [1 - 3c_1 - 3c_2 \exp(0)] \tag{10.59}$$

$$= -3c_2. \tag{10.60}$$

Equating $E[Y_{\text{in}}]$ and $E[Y_{\text{out}}]$, we have

$$\frac{1}{2} = -3c_2 \quad \text{or} \tag{10.61}$$

$$c_2 = -\frac{1}{6}. \tag{10.62}$$

Putting them all together, we have

$$\boldsymbol{F}(x) = \begin{bmatrix} \frac{2}{3} \\ \frac{1}{3} \end{bmatrix} - \begin{bmatrix} \frac{1}{6} \\ \frac{2}{6} \end{bmatrix} \exp(-4.5x). \tag{10.63}$$

The marginal cumulative distribution of the buffer content only is given by

$$F_X(x) = 1 - \frac{1}{2}\exp(-4.5x). \tag{10.64}$$

This is the required cdf of the number of bits left over in the buffer. The probability that the buffer is empty is

$$F_X(0) = \tfrac{1}{2}. \tag{10.65}$$

The conditional pdf of the buffer content given that the it is not empty is

$$f_X(x|X > 0) = \frac{d}{dx}F_X(x|X > 0) \tag{10.66}$$

$$= \frac{d}{dx}\frac{P[0 < X \le x]}{P[X = 0]} \tag{10.67}$$

$$= \frac{d}{dx}\frac{F_X(x) - P[X = 0]}{P[X = 0]} \tag{10.68}$$

$$= \frac{d}{dx}\frac{\frac{1}{2} - \frac{1}{2}\exp(-4.5x)}{\frac{1}{2}} \tag{10.69}$$

$$= 4.5\exp(-4.5x) \tag{10.70}$$

which is seen as a valid pdf. The expected buffer content is evaluated by using the theorem of total expectation as

$$E[X] = E[X|X > 0]P[X > 0] + E[X|X = 0]P[X = 0] \qquad (10.71)$$

$$= \frac{1}{4.5} \times \frac{1}{2} \qquad (10.72)$$

$$= \frac{1}{9} \text{ kilo bits.} \qquad (10.73)$$

The physical dimension is supplied in the above final answer as it has been identified to be kilo bits earlier. From the above performance figures, the transmitter is transmitting bits half the time and is quiet the rest. Therefore, the average power consumption is the simple average of 10 mW and 2 mW, that is 6 mW.

10.2.2   Stability condition

In general the solutions for v can be complex numbers. The system is stable if at least one of the solutions for v has a negative real part. If not, the exponential function will be monotonically increasing for all of the positive x domain. Let us establish this for the general set of parameters. The determinant equation to determine v is

$$\begin{vmatrix} \frac{\alpha}{\eta} - v & -\frac{\beta}{\eta} \\ \frac{\alpha}{\gamma - \eta} & -\frac{\beta}{\gamma - \eta} - v \end{vmatrix} = 0. \qquad (10.74)$$

Evaluating the determinant and simplifying, we obtain

$$v^2 \eta(\gamma - \eta) + v[\eta\beta - \alpha(\gamma - \eta)] = 0 \qquad (10.75)$$

the solutions for which are $v = 0$ and

$$v = \frac{\alpha(\gamma - \eta) - \eta\beta}{\eta(\gamma - \eta)} \qquad (10.76)$$

$$= \frac{\alpha}{\eta} - \frac{\beta}{\gamma - \eta}. \qquad (10.77)$$

We have two conclusions from the above. The first is that one of the two solutions for v is always zero, so that the cdf has only one exponential variation as x varies. The original condition for stability intuitively developed in equation (10.5) is identical to the nonzero solution for v in equation (10.77) being strictly negative. Therefore, stability and $v \leq 0$ are equivalent.

10.3   Little's Result for Fluid Flow Systems

The result developed in this section is applicable to any stable fluid flow system and not just for the two state fluid input system of Section 10.2. Consider a fluid buffer system with an overall fluid input rate (wrt time) of $E[Y_{in}]$. Let the system be stable so that $E[Y_{in}]$ equals the rate $E[Y_{out}]$ of the fluid transmitted or drained out of the system. Let $E[X]$ be the expected amount of fluid in the buffer. We can associate a response time for every vanishingly small (infinitesimal) amount of fluid dx. Start observing the system at time zero. Let $g(t)$ be a sample function of the cumulative amount of fluid that has flowed in up to time t starting from time instant zero. Let $h(t)$ be a sample function of the cumulative amount of fluid that has flowed out of the system, up to time t from the starting time instant of zero.

The function $g(t)$ is monotonically nondecreasing since fluid can only flow-in in nonnegative increments over any time interval. Similarly, $h(t)$ is monotonically nondecreasing. The amount of fluid that has so far departed the system cannot be more than the amount of fluid that has been input up to that time instant. Therefore,

$$g(t) \geq h(t). \tag{10.78}$$

Figure 10.1 shows an illustrative time plot of fluid flow-in and flow-out functions. The plots are for a system more general than a fluid flow system whose input and output rate are controlled by a discrete state Markov chain. This is seen in the non-linear rise of fluid amount entering the system over some segments of time. If the rates are constants over different segments of the time variable, the rates would be constant over each such segments. Had such been the case, the amount of fluid received (and drained) would be made of broken straight line segments. This nonlinear changes are used in the plots merely to show the generality of the Little's result. In Figure 10.1, there is no confusion about which segments correspond to $g(t)$ and which segments to $h(t)$, since, $h(t) \leq g(t)$. The amount of fluid remaining in the system at time instant t is

$$x(t) = g(t) - h(t), \tag{10.79}$$

the height of the ordinate segment intercepting the top and bottom curves. The fluid flow-in rate, averaged up to time instant t is

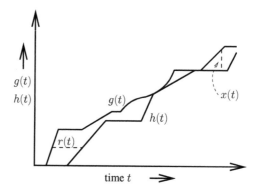

FIGURE 10.1: Amount of fluid as a function of time to develop Little's result

$$y(t) = \frac{1}{t} \int_{\tau=0}^{t} g(\tau).$$ (10.80)

The time averaged amount of fluid remaining in the buffer, averaged from the time instant zero to t, is denoted by $\bar{x}(t)$ and given by

$$\bar{x}(t) = \frac{1}{t} \int_{\tau=0}^{t} x(\tau).$$ (10.81)

Let the fluid-flow system be FIFO in the first and simple case, in the sense that the FIFO property applies to every vanishingly small amount of fluid entering the system. Then the response time of every fluid element dx entering the system around the time instant t is the length of the abscissa drawn from $g(t)$ to up to the point that the abscissa intersects the curve $h(\cdot)$. Denote this response time by $r(t)$ representing the response time of the fluid element entering the system at t. This is illustrated by studying the inverse functions of $g(t)$ and $h(t)$. Let u represent the nondecreasing amount fluid that flows as t increases. Figure 10.2 shows the plots of time taken for a given amount of fluid to flow-in, $w(u)$, and flow out, $z(u)$.

$$w(u) = \text{time taken for total amount } u \text{ of fluid to flow in}$$ (10.82)

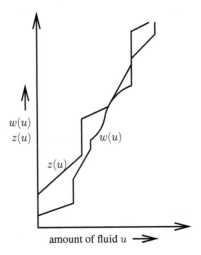

amount of fluid u ⟹

FIGURE 10.2: Time as a function of amount of fluid to develop Little's result

$$z(u) = \text{time taken for total amount } u \text{ of fluid to flow out} \qquad (10.83)$$

$$z(u) \geq w(u). \qquad (10.84)$$

Both these functions are strictly monotonically increasing and can have jump discontinuities. Indeed, they do, if the rates of flow are controlled be a discrete state Markov chain. When the fluid flow-in stops for a time period, the time taken for the flowed in fluid to increase jumps up by the length of the time segment during which no fluid flows in. In order for the functions $w(u)$ and $z(u)$ to be uniquely defined, they are defined to be left continuous, to reflect the reality that time progresses in the positive direction only. That is,

$$\lim_{|\epsilon| \to 0} w(u - |\epsilon|) = w(u) \quad and \qquad (10.85)$$

$$\lim_{|\epsilon| \to 0} z(u - |\epsilon|) = z(u). \qquad (10.86)$$

These definitions around discontinuities do not change the integrals enclosed by the two curves, to be evaluated in two different ways. Now, the response time of the fluid element that enters the system after u amount of fluid has entered is easily represented by

$$r(u) = z(u) - w(u), \tag{10.87}$$

the length of the ordinate intercepted by the curves $w(u)$ and $r(u)$.

Now, Little's result is developed by simply evaluating the integral enclosed by the two curves in two different ways and equating them. As in the development of the original Little's result for queues represented by discrete state Markov chains in Section 4.7, we assume that the system is stable and that the instantaneous difference $h(t) - g(t)$ is finite with probability one so that the effect of this difference vanishes when we average the integrals over either $t \to \infty$ or $u \to \infty$. For stable Markovian systems, we have seen that this is true (with probability one and in the means square sense), in Section 4.6. Therefore, if the sample functions $g(t)$ and $h(t)$ satisfy this condition, evaluate the time average amount of fluid in the system over an infinite time interval and equate it to the expected value of the equilibrium random variable X. We have

$$E[X] = \lim_{t \to \infty} \frac{1}{t} \int_{\tau=0}^{\infty} [g(\tau) - h(\tau)] d\tau. \tag{10.88}$$

Similarly, evaluate the average of response times of all the fluid elements entering after u amount of fluid has entered. Equate this to the expected response time of a random fluid element entering the system. We have

$$E[R] = \lim_{u \to \infty} \frac{1}{u} \int_{v=0}^{\infty} [w(v) - z(v)] du. \tag{10.89}$$

The variable v in the above equation (10.89) is the dummy variable of integration. Now, $u(t)$ in the above equation (10.89) is the amount of fluid that has flowed in up to time t which is given by

$$u(t) = g(t) \tag{10.90}$$

and as $t \to \infty$, so does u. Take the ratio of the two equations for $E[X]$ and $E[R]$. We have

$$\frac{E[X]}{E[R]} = \frac{\lim\limits_{t\to\infty} \frac{1}{t} \int\limits_{\tau=0}^{\infty} [g(\tau) - h(\tau)]d\tau}{\lim\limits_{u\to\infty} \frac{1}{u} \int\limits_{v=0}^{\infty} [w(v) - z(v)]du} \tag{10.91}$$

$$= \lim\limits_{t\to\infty} \frac{g(t)}{t} \frac{\int\limits_{\tau=0}^{\infty} [g(\tau) - h(\tau)]d\tau}{\int\limits_{v=0}^{\infty} [w(v) - z(v)]du}. \tag{10.92}$$

As noted earlier, the integrals in the numerator and denominator are the same since they are the areas enclosed by the same curves. They both tend to infinity with only a finite difference between them (with probability one) as time tends to infinity. Therefore, we have

$$\frac{E[X]}{E[R]} = \lim\limits_{t\to\infty} \frac{g(t)}{t} \tag{10.93}$$

$$= E[Y],$$

resulting in our familiar Little's result

$$E[X] = E[Y]E[R]. \tag{10.94}$$

Let all the fluid elements dx be statistically identical at the entering point. The fluid element departing the system just after a particular amount u departed at a time instant $z(u)$ in Figure 10.2 can be considered to be statistically the same as the fluid element that entered just after u amount of fluid entered the system, that is, just after a time $w(u)$. These interchanges of fluid elements are causal in the sense, that the fluid element leaving the system is interchanged for one that has already entered the system. This points out that the Little's result is valid for non-FIFO fluid systems, in the same way that it is valid for queues with discrete customers. If a fluid system is composed of two isolated systems in which fluid elements entering at two different points are never in the same chamber, then, the Little's result should be applied differently to the two isolated systems. In such an example, all the fluid elements are not statistically identical.

10.4   Output Process of Buffer Fed by Two State ON-OFF chain

If $\gamma \leq \eta$, the output process is exactly the same as the input process and the buffer content is always zero. The following assumes the interesting case of $\gamma > \eta$. The output process, that is the transmitted fluid is either flowing with a rate η bits per unit time or no fluid is flowing out. The latter is the same as fluid flow output with rate zero. It is possible for the input state to be 1 (OFF) and the output flowing to drain any remaining fluid in the buffer. However, whenever the output flow rate is zero, the input state must be OFF or 1. At any time instant the output rate is zero, the time for the output to start flowing is the same as the remaining time for the input chain to change to state 2, which is an exponential random variable with rate α. Therefore, the OFF time periods of the output process is exponential with rate α. The time interval corresponding to a continuous flow out, or the ON times, is more difficult to characterize.

A simplification arises when we note that as long as the input process is ON, the buffer content can only be increasing, and never stay constant or decrease. Indeed, the rate of increase is $\gamma - \eta$ and this lasts for an exponential time period with a rate β. At the end of an input flow ON-time period, the amount of fluid increase (during the most recent ON time) is exponential with an average of $\gamma - \eta\beta$ fluid bits. We can now consider the ON period of the output flow to be composed of alternating time segments during which the buffer content increases and decreases. When an output flow ON time period starts, the input state must also have been just turned ON. Over the next exponential time period with an average of $\frac{1}{\beta}$ the buffer content increases by one "random fluid unit," with an average of $\gamma - \eta\beta$ fluid bits. When the input process turns OFF, the buffer content empties these "random fluid units" with a constant rate of η, until all of the buffer content is emptied or until the input process is turned ON again, whichever occurs first.

The above description allows us to construct an interesting Markov chain corresponding to the number of "random fluid units" the buffer has at any time instant. The discrete state of such a Markov chain changes only when the number of such "random fluid units" increases or decreases by one. The state transition diagram for such a Markov chain is shown in Figure 10.3. The state is an ordered pair (m, n) with $m \in \{1, 2\}$ corresponding to the state of the fluid input process Markov chain. The nonnegative integer n represents the number of integer "random fluid units," last seen by the buffer. The expression "last seen by the buffer" indicates that the number changes only when the content completes increasing or decreasing the number by one; recall that the amount of fluid is really a continuous variable and it continuously changes as long as there is some fluid in the buffer. In the state $(1, 0)$ of this composite Markov chain, the buffer content is zero and the input state is 1 (OFF). The only way the state can change is when the input state changes to 2 (ON), and the composite state change is to the state $(2, 0)$. When the input state reverts to 1 (OFF), the buffer content is exactly one random fluid unit so that the composite state changes to

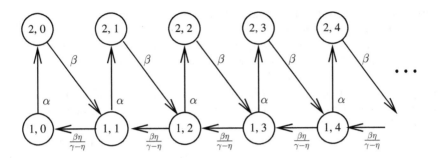

FIGURE 10.3: State transition diagram of the equivalent Markov chain for the buffer content fed by a two state ON-OFF fluid input

(1, 1). Whenever the state is $(1, n)$, the buffer is draining fluid at a continuous rate of η. Since each "random fluid unit" is made of exponentially distributed fluid content with an average of $\frac{\gamma-\eta}{\beta}$ fluid bits, the rate at which the buffer is emptying "random fluid units" is $\frac{\beta\eta}{\gamma-\eta}$. During the time periods that the composite state is $(2, n)$ existing "random fluid units" are not being drained. The buffer is merely transmitting the η portion of the γ rate with which the input process is pumping and this difference in the incoming rate can only cause an increase (by one) in the number of "random fluid units," when the input process changes to state 1 or OFF. This interpretation of the fluid flow system allows a simpler solution to the problem of characterizing the busy period of the fluid transmitter. Suppose we consider the condition that during a busy time period of the fluid transmitter, the system received exactly k "random fluid units" before completely emptying. We know from Section 3.11 that for the standard M/M/1/∞ queue with λ and μ as arrival and service rates, the Laplace transform of the conditional busy time is

$$\mathcal{L}_B(s|k) = \left(\frac{\lambda+\mu}{s+\lambda+\mu}\right)^{2k+1} \tag{10.95}$$

where $k = 0, 1, 2, \ldots$ is the number of additional arrivals during the busy time, once the system gets busy with a first arrival. We know that the probability of the number of these additional arrivals being k is given by

$$P[k] = \frac{(2k)!}{k!(k+1)!} \frac{\lambda^k \mu^{k+1}}{(s+\lambda)^k (s+\mu)^{k+1}} \tag{10.96}$$

from equation (3.158), Section 3.11. We need to make a few modifications to the above conditional transform. Of course we should replace the λ and μ by α and

$\frac{\beta\eta}{\gamma-\eta}$, respectively. The reason is that α is the rate at which the time interval for the start of the next arrival of the "random time unit" is progressing. The rate $\frac{\beta\eta}{\gamma-\eta}$ is the rate at which "random fluid units" are being emptied, whenever, the transmitter is doing nothing other than transmitting existing amount of fluid in the buffer. We need an additional modification. During this entire time interval, there are $k+1$ iid exponentially distributed random time intervals during which the input process is pumping in extra "random fluid units" and the transmitter is disabled from transmitting existing buffer content, in favor of draining part of the input currently flowing in. Each of these $k+1$ additional time periods is exponential with rate β. The Laplace transform can be finally expressed in an infinite series form with the help of the theorem of total probabilities, as the integer index of summation k increases from 0 to ∞. The infinite sum can be expressed in a closed form expression with the help of an identity, also developed in Section 3.11 given in equation (3.192). The following is a slightly modified version of that identity.

$$\sum_{k=0}^{\infty} \frac{(2k)!a^{k+1}}{k!(k+1)!} = \frac{1-\sqrt{1-4a}}{4}. \qquad (10.97)$$

Details are left out for Exercise 4.

10.5 General Fluid Flow Model and its Analysis

The environment feeding fluid bits into the buffer is a continuous time stable Markov chain with states $0, 1, 2, \ldots$ (possibly infinite number of states). The rate of transition from state i to state j is α_{ij}. As usual, we use $\alpha_{ii} = 0$ for convenience. The equilibrium state probabilities of this chain are s_0, s_1, s_2, $\ldots$, respectively. The random process $X(t)$ denotes the amount of fluid left in the buffer at time instant t. Its outcome is $x(t)$. When the chain is in state i, the environment is pumping fluid bits at a rate of $\gamma_i \geq 0$ bits per unit time. In the same state, the transmitter has a capacity to drain bits at a rate of $\eta_i \geq 0$. Thus the transmission capacity is also a function of the state of the environment chain. The actual rate of draining the fluid can be different from the capacity to drain. It depends on whether or not the buffer has any fluid to drain, in addition to the fluid being pumped in. If $\gamma_i \geq \eta_i$, the rate of draining in state i is the same as its capacity to drain, η_i. However, if $\gamma_i < \eta_i$, and if the buffer has no fluid left to drain, the rate of draining is simply the rate of fluid input into the buffer, that is γ_i itself. On the other hand, if $\gamma_i < \eta_i$ and the buffer has a nonzero amount of fluid to drain, the rate of draining is the capacity of draining, that is, η_i. If $\gamma_i > \eta_i$, the amount of fluid increases by a rate $\gamma_i - \eta_i$ whenever the state of the environment is i. If $\gamma_i < \eta_i$, the amount of fluid does not decrease whenever the state of the environment is i. If $x(t) = 0$ and the state of the chain is i with $\gamma_i < \eta_i$ the transmitter adjusts its rate of draining to γ_i, which is less than its capacity. It is possible to translate $\{\gamma_i, \eta_i\}$ to ignore the portions of rates of pumping in and out that do not contribute to change in bugger content. We prefer not to do this in order to preserve the original throughput.

The random process $X(t)$ is of continuous state, except that, in general,

$$P[X(t) = 0] > 0 \qquad (10.98)$$

so that $X(t)$ does have a discrete component. Let $N(t)$ denote the discrete state of the environment chain. The joint random process of $\{X(t), N(t)\}$ is Markov due to the following reason. Given the state at t to be $X(t) = x(t)$ and $N(t) = n(t)$, the future behavior of $X(t)$ depends only on $x(t)$ and the behavior of the Markov chain $N(t)$.

Let $X(t) > 0$. We are interested in the probability that $X < x$ at time $t+dt$ and the state of the environment chain is i. Denote this probability by the cdf $F_i(x, t + dt)$. This combination of x and i at $t+dt$ can result from a variety of combinations of the buffer content and state at t, as follows. Let $j \neq i$ at t and let $dt = dt_1 + dt_2$ with positive infinitesimals dt_1 and dt_2. Let the state of the chain change from j to i at $t+dt_1$. The increase in buffer content from t till $t+dt_1$ is at the rate $(\gamma_j - \eta_j)$. From $t + dt_1$ till $t + dt$, the rate of increase in the buffer content is $(\gamma_i - \eta_i)$. One way for the buffer content to be $\leq x$ and the state i at time instant $t + dt$ is for the system to be at state j and $\left(x - (\gamma_j - \eta_j)dt_1 - (\gamma_i - \eta_i)dt_2 \right)$ at time t and the chain's state change to i at $t+dt_1$. Alternatively, the system can be at state i and $\left(x - (\gamma_i - \eta_i)dt \right)$ followed by no change in the chain's state during dt. The probability of change from state j to state i in dt is $\alpha_{ji}dt$. The probability of no change from state i during dt is $(1 - \sum_{j=0}^{\infty} \alpha_{ij}dt)$. The total probability $F_i(x, t + dt)$ is obtained by using the above quantities and the theorem of total probability.

$$F_i[x, t + dt] = \sum_{j=0}^{\infty} \alpha_{ji}dt F_j[x - (\gamma_j - \eta_j)dt_1 - (\gamma_i - \eta_i)dt_2, t]$$

$$+ \left(1 - \sum_{j=0}^{\infty} \alpha_{ij}dt \right) F_i[x - (\gamma_i - \eta_i)dt, t]. \qquad (10.99)$$

In both the above summations, $j \neq i$ is effectively realized due to $\alpha_{ii} = 0$. Rearranging and dividing by dt, we have

$$\frac{F_i[x, t + dt] - F_i[x - (\gamma_i - \eta_i)dt, t]}{dt}$$

$$= \sum_{j=0}^{\infty} \Big(\alpha_{ji} F_j [x - (\gamma_j - \eta_j)dt_1 - (\gamma_i - \eta_i)dt_2, \ t]$$

$$- \alpha_{ij} F_i [x - (\gamma_i - \eta_i)dt, \ t] \Big) \tag{10.100}$$

Add and subtract $F_i(x,t)$ in the numerator of the LHS of the above equation (10.100).

$$\frac{F_i[x, \ t+dt] - F_i(x,t)}{dt} + \frac{F_i(x,t) - F_i[x - (\gamma_i - \eta_i)dt, \ t]}{dt}$$

$$= \sum_{j=0}^{\infty} \Big(\alpha_{ji} F_j [x - (\gamma_j - \eta_j)dt_1 - (\gamma_i - \eta_i)dt_2, \ t]$$

$$- \alpha_{ij} F_i [x - (\gamma_i - \eta_i)dt, \ t] \Big). \tag{10.101}$$

As $dt \to \infty$, the first ratio on the LHS of equation (10.101) evaluates to $\frac{\partial F_i[x,t]}{\partial t}$. To evaluate the second ratio, observe the following. When the environment is in state i and we have $x > 0$ at t, the rate of increase of fluid content

$$\frac{dx}{dt} = \gamma_i - \eta_i \quad \text{or} \tag{10.102}$$

$$(\gamma_i - \eta_i)dt = dx \quad \text{and} \tag{10.103}$$

$$dt = \frac{dx}{\gamma_i - \eta_i}. \tag{10.104}$$

Using these in the above equation, we have

$$\frac{\partial F_i[x, \ t]}{\partial t} + (\gamma_i - \eta_i) \frac{F_i[x, \ t] - F_i[x - dx, \ t]}{dx}$$

$$= \sum_{j=0}^{\infty} \Big(\alpha_{ji} F_j [x - (\gamma_j - \eta_j)dt_1 - (\gamma_i - \eta_i)dt_2, \ t] - \alpha_{ij} F_i [x - (\gamma_i - \eta_i)dt, \ ] \Big). \tag{10.105}$$

Letting the other infinitesimals tend to zero, we have

$$\frac{\partial F_i[x, \ t]}{\partial t} + (\gamma_i - \eta_i) \frac{dF_i(x, \ t)}{dx} = \sum_{j=0}^{\infty} \Big(\alpha_{ji} F_j(x, \ t) - \alpha_{ij} F_i(x, \ t) \Big), i = 0, 1, \ldots.$$

$$(10.106)$$

Once again, we are interested in equilibrium distribution of $F_i(x,t)$. Therefore,

$$\frac{\partial F_i[x,\ t]}{\partial t} = 0 \qquad (10.107)$$

and we are left with a set of coupled linear ordinary differential equations with constant coefficients. If we have a finite number of states in the Markov chain controlling the fluid input and output rates, the resulting differential equations can be solved by the eigenvalue eigenvector method as in the case of the two state Markov chain environment, studied in Section 10.2. If the number of states of the environment Markov chain is unlimited, the eigenvalue eigenvector method is not directly applicable. The equations will then need to be manipulated in ways that are specific to the nature of γ_i, η_i, and α_{ij}. An important simple special case of infinite state environment is dealt with in the next section.

10.6 Leaky Bucket Fed by M/M/1/∞ Queue Output

The output of an M/M/1/∞ queue can be considered to be an ON-OFF fluid flow system with fluid flow output at a constant rate during all of the service time of a packet. The output flow rate when the M/M/1/∞ queue is empty is zero. Let this flow output process form an ON-OFF input flow process to another system for us to study. First of all, we need to characterize the Markov chain of this flow-in process. Even though this is an ON-OFF flow-in process, it turns out that it is not a two state Markov process. While this statement may be surprising at a cursory glance, we have already proved it Section 3.11; the time period during which an equilibrium M/M/1/∞ queue remains busy is not exponential. The only Markovian system associated with this input process is the infinite state Markov chain corresponding to the state of the M/M/1/∞ queue. An appropriate system to study in this context is the following. We have the Markov chain of the M/M/1/∞ queue that supplies data to the fluid buffer system. The M/M/1/∞ system itself has a packet arrival rate of λ packets per unit time and a packet service rate of μ per unit time. As usual, denote $\frac{\lambda}{\mu}$ by ρ. Whenever the queue is busy, it pumps in data at the rate of γ bits per unit time. The average service time for a packet is $\frac{1}{\mu}$ so that the average number of fluid bits in a packet is $\frac{\gamma}{\mu}$. The fluid transmitter drains at a constant rate of η bits per unit time whenever the buffer content is nonzero. If η, the capacity to drain is larger than γ the input rate of pumping, the output process is identical to the input process and there is nothing more to analyze. Therefore, assume that $\eta < \gamma$ so that the leaky bucket is draining fluid bits at the same rate of η bits per unit time whenever the input queue is busy as well as whenever the leaky bucket buffer is nonempty. The throughput of the M/M/1/∞ queue is $\frac{\lambda\gamma}{\mu}$ bits per unit time. Therefore, the stability condition for the fluid buffer is that

$$\eta > \frac{\lambda\gamma}{\mu}. \tag{10.108}$$

We assume that the stability condition is satisfied.

The differential equations for the equilibrium buffer content X are obtained by the specialization of the general case and reduce to

$$-\eta F_0' = \mu F_1 - \lambda F_0 \quad \text{and} \tag{10.109}$$

$$(\gamma - \eta)F_i' = \lambda F_{(i-1)} + \mu F_{(i+1)} - (\lambda + \mu)F_i, \quad i \geq 1 \tag{10.110}$$

where i is the state of the M/M/1/∞ queue whose output forms the fluid input process. We seek solutions of the form

$$F_i(x) = a_i \exp(-vx) \tag{10.111}$$

where the set $\{v, \{1, a_1, a_2, a_3, \dots\}\}$ is one solution. We need to obtain as many different sets of solutions as there may be and use a linear combination of all the solutions. Note that a_0 in the above sequence $\{a_i\}$ is preset to 1. By using known properties about the system, we should develop expressions for all the parameters of the final solution in terms of the known system parameters, λ, μ, γ, and η. Note that equation (10.111) uses $(-vx)$ instead of (vx) used in earlier treatment; this is due to the fact that the cdf cannot be exponentially increasing without bounds. Substituting equation (10.111) into the differential equations (10.109) and (10.110), we obtain

$$\eta v = \mu a_1 - \lambda \quad \text{and} \tag{10.112}$$

$$-(\gamma - \eta)va_i = \lambda a_{i-1} + \mu a_{i+1} - (\lambda + \mu)a_i, \quad i \geq 1. \tag{10.113}$$

We know that $v = 0$ is always a possible solution since its substitution into the above equations (10.112) and (10.113) result in the balance equations for the Markov chain of the fluid-input system, except that the quantities a_i are not required to sum to 1 and also that a_0 has been chosen to be 1. Using the results for the equilibrium state probabilities of the M/M/1/∞ queue, we have one solution for the algebraic equations to be

$$\{v, \{1, a_1, a_2, a_3, \dots\}\} = \{0, \{1, \rho, \rho^2, \rho^3, \dots\}\}. \qquad (10.114)$$

For all the $v \neq 0$ cases, we have the following. From equation (10.112)

$$v = \frac{\mu a_1 - \lambda}{\eta}. \qquad (10.115)$$

Add all the equations of the form (10.113) for $i = 1, 2, 3 \dots$ and rearrange. We obtain

$$(\gamma - \eta)v \sum_{i=1}^{\infty} a_i = \mu a_1 - \lambda. \qquad (10.116)$$

The RHS of equations (10.112) and (10.116) are equal. Therefore, equating their LHS, we find

$$(\gamma - \eta)v \sum_{i=1}^{\infty} a_i = \eta v \quad \text{or} \qquad (10.117)$$

$$\sum_{i=1}^{\infty} a_i = \frac{\eta}{\gamma - \eta}. \qquad (10.118)$$

Let us seek a solution of the form

$$a_i = a_1 r^{i-1}, \quad i = 1, 2 \dots. \qquad (10.119)$$

We need to find every possible value of r which is accepted by the equations and the corresponding sequence of $\{a_i\}$ for each r. Summing all the terms of the above sequence $\{a_1, a_2, a_3 \dots\}$, we have

$$\sum_{i=1}^{\infty} a_i = \frac{a_1}{1 - r}. \qquad (10.120)$$

$$(10.121)$$

Comparing equations (10.118) and (10.120), we have

$$a_1 = \frac{(1-r)\eta}{\gamma - \eta}. \tag{10.122}$$

Substituting for a_1 from equation (10.122) in equation (10.115) and simplifying, we obtain

$$v = \frac{(1-r)\mu}{\gamma - \eta} - \frac{\lambda}{\eta} \quad \text{or} \tag{10.123}$$

$$\lambda + \mu - (\gamma - \eta)v = \frac{r\eta\mu + \gamma\lambda}{\eta}. \tag{10.124}$$

Now, rearrange equation (10.113) to

$$\mu a_{i+1} - [\lambda + \mu - (\gamma - \eta)v]a_i + \lambda a_{i-1} = 0, \quad i \geq 1. \tag{10.125}$$

Using equation (10.124) in (10.125), we have

$$\mu a_{i+1} - \frac{r\eta\mu + \gamma\lambda}{\eta}a_i + \lambda a_{i-1} = 0, \quad i = 1, 2, \ldots. \tag{10.126}$$

Now, use the general form of one solution proposed in equation (10.119) in the above equation (10.126).

$$\mu a_1 r^i - \frac{r\eta\mu + \gamma\lambda}{\eta}a_1 r^{i-1} + \lambda a_1 r^{i-2} = 0, \quad i = 2, 3, \ldots. \tag{10.127}$$

The reason for not including $i = 1$ in the above equation (10.127) is that we still do not know the relation between a_1 and $a_0 = 1$. Cancel the common factor $a_1 r^{i-2}$. We obtain the quadratic equation

$$\mu r^2 - \frac{r\eta\mu + \gamma\lambda}{\eta}r + \lambda = 0. \tag{10.128}$$

The quadratic equation can have at most two different roots giving us a possible maximum of two more sets of solutions (in addition to the set corresponding to $v = 0$). So, there are at most two solutions (in addition to $v = 0$). Manipulating the quadratic equation (10.128), we find that the quadratic terms cancel and it indeed simplifies to a simple equation in r whose solution is given by

$$r = \frac{\eta}{\gamma}. \tag{10.129}$$

Using this solution, the other unknowns a_1 and v are easily evaluated to be

$$a_1 = \frac{\eta}{\gamma} = r \quad \text{and} \tag{10.130}$$

$$v = \frac{\mu}{\gamma} - \frac{\lambda}{\eta}. \tag{10.131}$$

Comparing the above with the stability condition in equation (10.108), we find that $v > 0$. The complete sequence of $\{a_i\}$ now evaluate to

$$a_i = r^i, \quad i = 0, 1, 2, \ldots. \tag{10.132}$$

$$= \left(\frac{\eta}{\gamma}\right)^i, \quad i = 0, 1, 2, \ldots. \tag{10.133}$$

The solution for $F_i(x)$ for this case of v is

$$F_i(x) = \left(\frac{\eta}{\gamma}\right)^i \exp\left[-\left(\frac{\mu}{\gamma} - \frac{\lambda}{\eta}\right)x\right] i = 0, 1, \ldots. \tag{10.134}$$

The general solution is obtained as a linear combination of the first solution with $v = 0$ resulting from equation (10.114) and the above in equation (10.134). The resulting general solution is

$$F_i(x) = c_1 \rho^i + c_2 \left(\frac{\eta}{\gamma}\right)^i \exp\left[-\left(\frac{\mu}{\gamma} - \frac{\lambda}{\eta}\right)x\right] \tag{10.135}$$

where c_1 and c_2 are the unknown constants to be determined from the initial conditions of the system. As $x \to \infty$, we know that

$$F_i(\infty) = (1 - \rho)\rho^i. \tag{10.136}$$

This leads to

$$c_1 = 1 - \rho. \tag{10.137}$$

The marginal cdf $F_X(x)$ is obtained by summing all the $F_i(x)$ and is given by

$$F_X(x) = 1 + c_2 \frac{1}{1 - \frac{\eta}{\gamma}} \exp\left[-\left(\frac{\mu}{\gamma} - \frac{\lambda}{\eta}\right)x\right] \tag{10.138}$$

$$= 1 + c_2 \frac{\gamma}{\gamma - \eta} \exp\left[-\left(\frac{\mu}{\gamma} - \frac{\lambda}{\eta}\right)x\right]. \tag{10.139}$$

The M/M/1/∞ system is busy for a fraction $\frac{\lambda}{\mu}$ of time, during which bits are pumped in at a rate of γ. Therefore, throughput observed entering the fluid flow system is

$$E[Y_{in}] = \frac{\lambda\gamma}{\mu}. \tag{10.140}$$

The throughput observed at the fluid transmitter output is at a rate of η whenever $X > 0$. The fraction of time when the transmitter is actively draining fluid is given $1 - F_X(0)$. Substituting expressions for the required quantities, we have

$$E[Y_{out}] = \eta\left(1 - 1 - c_2 \frac{\gamma}{\gamma - \eta}\right) \tag{10.141}$$

$$= -c_2 \frac{\eta\gamma}{\gamma - \eta}. \tag{10.142}$$

Equating $E[Y_{in}]$ and $E[Y_{out}]$ we obtain

$$\frac{\lambda\gamma}{\mu} = -c_2 \frac{\eta\gamma}{\gamma - \eta} \quad \text{or} \tag{10.143}$$

$$c_2 = -\frac{\lambda(\gamma - \eta)}{\mu\eta}. \tag{10.144}$$

Substituting the value for c_2 in $F_X(x)$ and simplifying, we finally have

$$F_i(x) = (1 - \rho)\rho^i - \frac{\lambda}{\mu}\left(\frac{\eta}{\gamma}\right)^{i-1} \exp\left[-\frac{\mu\eta - \lambda\gamma}{\gamma\eta}x\right]$$

$$i = 0, 1, \ldots \quad \text{and} \quad (10.145)$$

$$F_X(x) = 1 - \frac{\lambda\gamma}{\mu\eta} \exp\left[\frac{\mu\eta - \lambda\gamma}{\gamma\eta} x\right]. \quad (10.146)$$

Operating on these functions, we also obtain

$$P[X > 0] = \frac{\lambda\gamma}{\mu\eta} < 1 \quad \text{(from stability condition)} \quad (10.147)$$

$$f_X[x|X > 0] = \frac{\mu\eta - \lambda\gamma}{\gamma\eta} \exp\left[\frac{\mu\eta - \lambda\gamma}{\gamma\eta} x\right], \quad \text{and} \quad (10.148)$$

$$E[X] = \frac{\lambda}{\mu} \frac{\gamma^2}{\mu\eta - \lambda\gamma}. \quad (10.149)$$

Example 10.2
In Example 10.1, consider each ON state as pumping in a packet over a continuous time. We had an exponential OFF time period between two such successive fluid bursts. Instead, let such packets come out of a previous M/M/1/∞ queue. That is, the fluid input system in this present example is similar to that in is Example 10.1 with the following exception. The fluid input chain is the output of a previous M/M/1/∞ queue as opposed to being a two state chain. Compare the expected values of the equilibrium fluid content in the buffer for Example 10.1 and the present example.

Solution
The packet arrival rate is $\lambda = 1$ per ms. Average packet service time $\frac{1}{\mu} = \frac{1}{\beta} = \frac{1}{3}$ ms. Bit rate in an arriving packet $\gamma = 1.5$ Mbps. Bit rate of the leaky bucket $\eta = 1$Mbps. Substituting this in equation (10.149), we obtain

$$E[X] = \frac{3.375}{9} \text{ kilo bits.} \quad (10.150)$$

The expected fluid amount in Example 10.1 is $\frac{1}{9}$ kilo bits. We see that the expected fluid amount in the case of the buffer fed by an M/M/1/∞ queue is more than three times that for the case of the buffer fed by a two state chain. One reason for this difference is that the two state input process allows the buffer time to drain between successive bursts of input which is not always the case with the input flowing from the output of the M/M/1/∞ queue. □

10.7   Exercises

1. In the two state ON-OFF fluid flow input and constant rate fluid transmission system, evaluate the average time period for which a continuous transmission lasts. Do not use its Laplace transform.

2. In Example 10.1, the access point has additional facilities to monitor the quality of the wireless channel and change the bit transmission rate to suit the quality. During a reasonably long time period, the transmitter keeps switching between two rates, 1 Mbps and 2 Mbps. The average time duration of transmission with 1 Mbps lasts for 10 ms and the average duration of transmission with 2.048 Mbps lasts for 15 ms. Again, approximate this to retain the Markovian nature and determine the cdf of buffer content and average off times between two transmission streams.

3. Consider optimizing the performance of the system similar to the one in Example 10.1. Suppose we know that the bit error rate at one particular transmission rate. Erroneous packets need retransmission. Also, we can increase the transmission power to combat noise. However, this increases the battery consumption. Let the battery power be a constant plus a term proportional to transmission power. Study this problem and investigate the relative effects of power increase versus transmission rate decrease for reliable communication over the noisy channel.

4. Complete the derivation of a closed form expression for the Laplace transform for the busy time period of the transmitter in the case of the two state ON-OFF input and constant rate transmission fluid flow system. Use the numerical figures of Example 10.1 and determine the values of the Laplace transform for $s = 0$, and a few other positive values. Use these numerical figures to investigate the feasibility of a function of the form

$$\mathcal{L}(s) = \frac{\psi}{\psi + s} \tag{10.151}$$

to represent the Laplace transform of the busy time. Hence show that the time periods of continuous output flow in our two state input system is not an exponential random variable.

5. Up to three simultaneous transport connections may be active at a router. Each transport connections feeds data packets for a time duration all of which can be approximated to be a fluid flow at a constant bit rate during the time period of the transport connection. Each transport connection lasts for an average of 1 second and pumps in data at a rate of 1 Mbps for its duration. The average

OFF time between successive ON times of each of the three possible connections is 2 seconds. The three possible connections appear from three different datalinks and are iid. The router drains data at a constant rate of 2 Mbps, provided its buffer has data and/or receiving data to be transmitted. Evaluate the equilibrium statistics of the buffer content.

6. In the above problem, let there be two identical outgoing links. At least one outgoing link is active all the time. Two outgoing links are active for an average continuous time duration of 3 seconds and not active for an average time duration of 2 seconds. Evaluate the statistics of the router buffer content in this case. Of course, the entire system is a Markovian fluid flow system.

7. Develop the state transition diagram of the joint Markov chain for the output of an M/M/1/∞ queue feeding fluid bits into a constant rate leaky bucket. The state is an ordered pair of the number of packets in the M/M/1/∞ queue and the random number of "integer fluid units." The latter quantity, the integer random number of fluid bits increases by one when the buffer content is increasing and the environment completes pumping a full fluid packet. It attempts to decrease by one when the environment is not pumping in and the leaky bucket successfully completes pumping out the equivalent of one full fluid packet. Solve for the equilibrium state probabilities of this Markov chain and obtain an expression for the cdf of the fluid buffer content. Compare this answer with that developed in Section 10.6.

8. Chapter 9 developed a Markov chain with a large number of states by merging several iid substreams each with hyperexponential IATs. In the course of analyzing that Markov chain of a nonfluid packet source, Chapter 9 introduced closed queuing networks with stated-dependent (immediate service) service rates. A corresponding convolution algorithm to develop the equilibrium state probabilities is also developed there. The packets arrived instantaneously in such a traffic model.

Investigate the above model, but with fluid packet arrival. Each subsource has ON times that are iid exponential and OFF times that are iid hyperexponential. Multiple fluid flows from multiple substreams are allowed.

Appendix A

Review of Probability Theory

A.1   Random Experiment

A *random experiment* consists of choosing, at random, an element from a known set of elements. Each possible element is referred to as an *outcome*. The exact outcome chosen cannot be predicted or determined with certainty, prior to the selection. However, if a sequence of such experiments is conducted, the relative frequencies of occurrences of the different outcomes tends to follow some *statistical regularity*.

Reasons for the inability to exactly predict the outcome to be chosen in a random experiment can be many. For instance, the mechanism for selecting the exact element may be hidden or unknown to the experimenter or the experimenting device. The entire set of possible outcomes is known as the sample space and is denoted by S. Subsets of the sample space S are known as *events*. In a random experiment, if an outcome a occurs, then any event containing a also occurs. What we mean by the statement "event A occurred" is that one outcome in the set of outcomes A, occurred.

In order to illustrate the terms defined above, consider a simple example of a random experiment in which a six-sided die is rolled. This is clearly a random experiment since we cannot predict exactly which numbered face will be on top after rolling. There are six possible outcomes and the sample space is $S = \{1, 2, 3, 4, 5, 6\}$. An example of an event, A, is finding an even number after a roll, and so $A = \{2, 4, 6\}$ in this case. It is useful to construct a probabilistic model for a random experiment, which allows us to determine the chance or probability of a particular outcome or event. Probabilistic models are valuable when long sequences of repetitions of a random experiment exhibit patterns.

A.2   Axioms of Probability

The probability value of a possible event from a sample space satisfies certain properties or axioms. These axioms are useful in proving and deriving many interesting results. Let A and B be two events from the sample space S. Let their probabilities be denoted by $P[A]$ and $P[B]$, respectively. The assigned probabilities, $P[A]$ and $P[B]$ are required to satisfy the following three axioms:

1. $P[A] \geq 0$ for every $A \subset \mathcal{S}$.

2. $P[\mathcal{S}] = 1$.

3. If A and B are mutually exclusive (i.e., either A can occur or B can occur, but not both at the same time), then $P[A \cup B] = P[A] + P[B]$. This is also extended to the union of an infinite sequence of mutually exclusive events. That is, if an infinite sequence of events e_1, e_2, ... are mutually exclusive,

$$P[e_1 \cup e_2 \cup \cdots] = P[e_1] + P[e_2] + \cdots. \qquad (A.1)$$

This extension of the axioms is known as the infinite additivity axiom.

The symbol $\cup$ denotes the set theoretic union. In other words, $P[A \cup B]$ may be read as $P[A$ or $B]$.

The meaning of the term statistical regularity mentioned above is the following. If a random experiment is conducted a large number of times, say n times, and if outcomes of these experiments are not influenced by one another, the number of times an event A occurs, $n_A \approx nP[A]$. That is, the relative frequency of the occurrence of an event and the probability of the event are approximately equal for large n. The axiomatic theory of probability is not concerned with the assignment of probabilities to the outcomes of a random experiment. In many application areas, some fundamental assumptions about the randomness of the underlying physical phenomenon can be made. These correspond to simple and intuitive assignment of probability values to events that may be hidden from the eventual observations. The observable outcomes of a practical random experiment are the results (functions) of such hidden compound experiments. The axiomatic probability theory helps us to evaluate the probability values of the outcomes of the observable random experiment, starting from the assumed probability values of outcomes of the simpler hidden experiments.

A.2.1   Some useful results

Following are some simple consequences of the axioms of probability.

THEOREM A.1

1. $P[A] \leq 1$ *for every* $A \subset \mathcal{S}$.

2. $P[\overline{A}] = 1 - P[A]$.

3. $P[\emptyset] = 0$. *The null event is the empty set denoted be* $\emptyset$ *and has zero probability.*

4. $P[A \cup B] = P[A] + P[B] - P[A \cap B]$.

5. If $A \subseteq B$, then $P[A] \le P[B]$. ▯

The symbol $\emptyset$ above denotes the null set, also known as the impossible event. The symbol $\cap$ denotes the set intersection operator. The expression $P[A \cap B]$ is also read as $P[A$ and $B]$. The symbols $+$ and $\cdot$ are also used to denote set theoretic union and intersection, respectively. In addition, sometimes $A \cdot B$ is written as AB when there is no confusion. The bar above an event, e.g., $\bar{A}$ denotes the set theoretic complement, with respect to S. That it, $\bar{A}$ contains all the elements in S except for all those in A.

A.2.2 Conditional probability and statistical independence

In some cases, the probability of an event is influenced (either increased or decreased) by the probability of another event. Representation and study of the influence of an occurred event on the occurrence of subsequent events is facilitated by defining *conditional probabilities*.

DEFINITION A.1 *The conditional probability, $P[C|D]$ (read as the probability of event C given event D) is defined as*

$$P[C|D] = \frac{P[C \cap D]}{P[D]},\tag{A.2}$$

when $P[D] \ne 0$. The conditional probability, $P[C|D]$ is the probability that the event C will occur, given that the event D has occurred. ▯

Although $P[C|D]$ is not defined if $P[D] = 0$, we know that $P[C \cap D] = 0$ if $P[D] = 0$. Therefore, it is convenient to define both $P[C|D]P[D]$ and $P[D]P[C|D]$ as zeros. The occurrence of a particular event may or may not influence the probability of another particular event occurring. It is useful to recognize if two given events do, or, do not, influence the occurrence of each other.

DEFINITION A.2 *Two events A and B are said to be statistically independent (or independent) if $P[A \cap B] = P[A]P[B]$.* ▯

If events C and D are independent and $P[D] > 0$, the conditional probability $p[C \mid D]$ evaluates to $P[C]$. The extension of the concept of independence to many events requires careful attention.

DEFINITION A.3 *All the events in a set of events $A_1, \cdots, A_k$ are said to be mutually independent if the probability of the joint occurrence of every subset of these events evaluates to the product of probabilities of the all the* *events in the subset under consideration.*   ▢

It is a straightforward matter to verify that the conditional probability definition satisfies the axioms of probability. That is, we have

THEOREM A.2

1. $P[C|D] \geq 0,$

2. $P[S|D] = 1,$

3. *if* $C \cap E = \emptyset,$ *then* $P[(C \cup E)|D] = P[C|D] + P[E|D].$ ▢

In the above Theorem A.2, C, D, and E are arbitrary events and $P[D] > 0$.

A.3   Random Variable

In general, the sample space can consist of arbitrary outcomes. For example, in a simple random experiment in which a coin is tossed, the outcomes are either the head or the tail of the coin. However, we frequently encounter random experiments in which the possible outcomes are real numbers. The key point is that the outcome of a random experiment need not be a real number, or even a number for that matter. In order to deal with different types of outcomes, and operations on outcomes, the idea of a random variable is introduced.

DEFINITION A.4   *A random variable is a function that maps every outcome of a sample space to a unique real number.*   ▢

Thus, the values taken by a random variable are all real numbers, and the transformation is a means of giving a numerical value to an outcome.

Example A.1
A random variable that has only two outcomes in its sample space called a Bernoulli random variable, named after Jacob Bernoulli (1654–1705). A random variable that has more than two, but a finite number of outcomes is

known as a generalized Bernoulli random variable. Consider a random experiment in which a coin is tossed twice in a row. The outcome of each toss is either a head (H) or a tail (T). The sample space, $\mathcal{S} = \{HH, HT, TH, TT\}$. Define the random variable X as the total number of heads in the two coin tosses. Thus, X assigns each outcome of this random experiment to one of the values in the set $\{0, 1, 2\}$. For instance, the outcome HH has a corresponding value of $x = 2$. If the probability all outcomes in $\mathcal{S}$ are equal, $P[X = 2] = P[HH] = 0.25$, $P[X = 1] = P[HT] + P[TH] = 0.5$, and $P[X = 0] = P[TT] = 0.25$. ⬜

The random variable in Example A.1 has a finite set of outcomes, and the probabilities of individual outcomes of the random variable are nonzero. However, this is not always the case. For example, suppose we conduct a random experiment in which we measure the height of every person that walks into a classroom on a college campus. Let Y be the random variable representing the maximum height among them. Clearly this is a random experiment, since we cannot predict with certainty what value Y will have. Moreover, the range of Y is a real set that we will assume to be in the set $[1.20, 2.20]$ meters. This set is not countable. It is possible for the probability of every specific height value to be zero and yet for $P[1.5 \text{ meter} < Y < 1.7 \text{ meter}] > 0$. To accommodate such "distributed" probability, we make use of the cumulative distribution function defined below.

A.3.1   Cumulative distribution function

DEFINITION A.5   *The cumulative distribution function (cdf) of a random variable is*

$$F_X(x) = P[X \le x], \quad -\infty < x < \infty. \tag{A.3}$$

⬜

The symbol X represents the random variable and x represents the real valued argument. Note that $F_X(x)$ is defined for every finite x even if some intervals over x are impossible events. We know that if $A \subseteq B$, then $P[A] \le P[B]$. As a consequence, the following properties of the cdf are easy to prove.

THEOREM A.3

1. *$F_X(x)$ is a nondecreasing function of x.*

2. $F_X(-\infty) = 0$.

3. $F_X(\infty) = 1$.

4. $F_X(x)$ is a continuous from the right. That is, $F_X(x^+)$ defined as

$$F_X(x^+) = \lim_{\epsilon \to 0} F_X(x + |\epsilon|) \qquad (A.4)$$

exists and evaluates to $F_X(x)$ for every x. ▯

Example A.2
A biased die has six faces numbered 0 through 5 with probabilities of occurrence corresponding to 0.25, 0.1, 0.3, 0.18, 0.05, and 0.12, respectively. Such a die is called biased due to the unequal probabilities of occurrences of its different faces. Let X be the random variable corresponding to the number on the face that shows up in a toss of the die. Determine the cdf of X. ▯

Solution
The cdf is obtained by adding successive probabilities starting from 0. That is, if $i \leq x < i + 1$,

$$F_X(x) = \sum_{k=0}^{i} P[X = k]. \qquad (A.5)$$

▯

In the above example, as the argument x increases, the event $X \leq x$ includes a larger set of outcomes. As x crosses from $x < 0$ to $x = 0$, the outcome 0, occurring with a nonzero probability leads to a jump discontinuity in $F_X(x)$ at $x = 0$ (and also at $x = 1, 2, 3, 4, 5$). That is, $P[X < x] = 0$ but $P[X \leq 0] = 0.25$. Thus, the loose inequality in $F_X(x) = P[X \leq x]$ leads to the property, mentioned above , that $F_X(x)$ is a right continuous function. But, in the above example, the left limit,

$$\lim_{\epsilon \to 0} F_X(0 - |\epsilon|) \qquad (A.6)$$

and the right limit

$$\lim_{\epsilon \to 0} F_X(0 + |\epsilon|) \qquad (A.7)$$

are not equal.

A.3.2   Discrete random variables and the probability mass function

Random variables are classified into three categories, discrete, continuous, and mixed.

DEFINITION A.6 *A discrete random variable is one with nonzero probabilities for a countable set of outcome values only. That is, the probability of any event not containing one or more of the above outcome values is zero.* ⬚

The cdf of a discrete random variable has discontinuities at a countable set of values. The above Example A.2 on page 402 of the biased die is an example of a discrete random variable. In general, the set of outcomes of a discrete random variable, each with a nonzero probability, can have a countably infinite number of elements. As an example, consider a random variable that selects every positive integer with a nonzero probability given by

$$P[X = k] = p(1 - p)^{k-1}, \ k = 1, 2, \ldots, \tag{A.8}$$

where p is a probability value. This random variable is called a geometric random variable. The definition of a discrete random variable allows for a discrete random variable to take on fractional (i.e., noninteger) values as outcomes with nonzero probabilities. However, most discrete random variables that we will encounter have only integer outcome values with nonzero probabilities. Many of these discrete random variables are further limited to only natural numbers, i.e., $\{0, 1, 2, \ldots, \}$. Unless otherwise specified, it is assumed that any outcome of a discrete random variable that is not a natural number, occurs with probability zero. An alternative approach to characterizing a discrete random variable is through the definition of the *probability mass function* (pmf), denoted as $P_X(k)$ (or P_k or p_k, if there is no ambiguity). The probability mass function is simply the probability values for every outcome. For a nonnegative integer random variable, it is

$$p_k = P_X(k) = P[X = k], \ k = 0, 1, 2, \ldots. \tag{A.9}$$

A.3.3 Continuous random variables and the probability density function

The second category of random variables is the *continuous random variable*, which has a continuous cdf. Indeed, the cdf of a continuous random variable is continuous everywhere. Therefore

$$P[X = x] = P[X \le x] - P[X < x] = 0 \tag{A.10}$$

since $F_X(x) = P[X \le x]$ is continuous at every x. A very useful approach to characterizing a continuous random variable is through the definition of the *probability density function* (pdf), developed as follows. Consider the change in the cdf of X over an infinitesimal interval of its argument

$$P[x < X \le x + dx] = F_X(x + dx) - F_X(x). \tag{A.11}$$

DEFINITION A.7   *The probability density function of a continuous random variable X is*

$$f_X(x) = \lim_{dx \to 0} \frac{P[x < X \le x + dx]}{dx} \tag{A.12}$$

$$= \frac{dF_X(x)}{dx}. \tag{A.13}$$

□

The density function is commonly denoted by $f_X(x)$ as above, or by $p_X(x)$. Since $F_X(x)$ is continuous for a continuous random variable, the left limit and the right limit exist for $f_X(x)$, although they may be unequal. If the limits are unequal, the density will have finite jump discontinuities. Since the cdf is monotonically nondecreasing, the density function is positive and,

$$\int_\infty^\infty f_X(x)dx = 1. \tag{A.14}$$

A.3.4   Mixed random variables

The third category of random variables is the mixed type. Such a mixed random variable has well defined nonzero values of $\frac{dF_x(x)}{dx}$ over at least one nonzero interval. In addition, the mixed random variable has at least one specific outcome value with a nonzero probability. Thus, the mixed random variable is a "mixture" of a continuous and a discrete random variables. Hence, the cdf of a mixed random has a countable set of discontinuities, as well as at least one segment over which the cdf is continuous. A practical example of mixed random variables occurs in queuing systems.. Consider the time interval a customer spends in the waiting line, before getting service from a bank teller. Time is modeled as a continuous variable, the waiting time random variable has a continuous part. However, at least occasionally, a customer may find a teller to be free to immediately serve a customer as the customer enters the bank. That is, there is a nonzero probability of this occurring. Thus the waiting time random variable has a continuous part and a discrete part and hence, it is of the mixed type.

Example A.3

A random variable X has $P[X \le a] = 0$ and $P[X > b] = 0$, with $b > a$. In the interval $(a, b]$, the probability that any event $(c, d]$ satisfying $a < x \le d \le b$ occurs is proportional to the length of the segment $d - c$. The latter property is referred to as the *uniform distribution*. Evaluate the density function of this random variable.

□

Solution
Clearly X is a continuous random variable since $P[X = x] = 0$ for each point in $-\infty < x < \infty$. Since $P[X < a] = 0$ and $P[X = a] = 0$, $F_X(a) = 0$. Since $P[X > b] = 0$, $F_X(b) = 1$. Now, $P[X \le x] = \alpha(x - a)$, where α is a proportionality constant. So, $P[X \le b] = \alpha(b - a) = 1$. Therefore, $\alpha = \frac{1}{b-a}$.

$$F_X(x) = \frac{x-a}{b-a}, \quad x \in [a, b], \tag{A.15}$$

$$f_X(x) = \frac{dF_X(x)}{dx}, \tag{A.16}$$

$$= \frac{1}{b-a}, \quad x \in (a, b), \tag{A.17}$$

$$f_X(x) = \begin{cases} 0, & x < a \\ 0, & x > b. \end{cases} \tag{A.18}$$

Note that the above specification of $f_X(x)$ does not include $x = a$ and $x = b$, at which there are jump discontinuities. The density values at these points can be specified to be left continuous or right continuous, without affecting the original problem specification. ☐

A.4 Conditional pmf and Conditional pdf

The probability mass function maps the outcomes to probability values. Hence the conditional pmf, conditioned on event A is written as

$$P_X[X = k|A] = \frac{P[k \cap A]}{P[A]}, \tag{A.19}$$

if $P[A] \ne 0$, where X is a discrete random variable and k are the discrete outcomes.

Example A.4
In the biased die random experiment of Example A.2, on page 402, consider the following situation. The die is thrown and the outcome is known to be a prime number. What is the conditional pmf given this information? ☐

Solution

$$P[X = k \mid K \text{ is prime}] = \frac{P[(X = k) \cap (X \in \{1, 2, 3, 5\})]}{P[X \in \{1, 2, 3, 5\}]} \tag{A.20}$$

$$= 0, \quad \text{for } k = 0, 4, \qquad\qquad (A.21)$$

$$= \frac{P[X = k]}{0.7}, \quad \text{for } k \in \{1, 2, 3, 5\}. \qquad (A.22)$$

□

If X is a continuous random variable, $P[X \in A|B]$ is defined only if $P[B] \neq 0$. But the event B can be a single outcome of another continuous random variable, such as the the event $Y = y$, in which case $P[Y = y] = 0$ and the corresponding conditional probability $P[X \in A \mid Y = y]$ is undefined. To extend the concept of conditional probabilities to continuous random variables, we develop the of conditional density. Let X and Y be continuous random variables. Consider,

$$P[x < X \leq x + dx, y < Y \leq y + dy], \qquad (A.23)$$

which is called the joint probability of the two random variables X and Y being in the rectangular infinitesimal neighborhood defined by $(x, x + dx]$, and $(y, y + dy]$.

DEFINITION A.8   *The function*

$$f_{XY}(x, y) = \lim_{dy \to 0} \lim_{dx \to 0} \frac{P[x < X \leq x + dx, y < Y \leq y + dy]}{dx \, dy}, \quad (A.24)$$

is called the joint density *of the ordered pair of random variables* (X, Y), *at the ordered pair of outcomes* (x, y). *The functions,* $f_X(x)$ *and* $f_Y(y)$ *are called* marginal densities.

□

The conditional probability

$$P[x < X \leq x + dx \mid y < Y \leq y + dy] \qquad (A.25)$$

$$= \frac{P[x < X \leq x + dx, y < Y \leq y + dy]}{P[y < Y \leq y + dy]}. \qquad (A.26)$$

Consider

$$\lim_{dx \to 0} \lim_{dy \to 0} \frac{P[x < X \leq x + dx \mid y < Y \leq y + dy]}{dx} \qquad (A.27)$$

$$= \lim_{dx \to 0} \lim_{dy \to 0} \frac{\left(\frac{P[x < X \leq x + dx, y < Y \leq y + dy]}{dx \, dy} \right)}{\left(\frac{P[y < Y \leq y + dy]}{dy} \right)} \qquad (A.28)$$

$$= \frac{f_{XY}(x,y)}{f_Y(y)}, \tag{A.29}$$

if $f_Y(y) \neq 0$.

DEFINITION A.9 $\frac{f_{XY}(x,y)}{f_Y(y)}$ *is defined as the conditional density of X under the condition that y is the outcome of the random variable Y. It is defined for all y at which $f_Y(y) \neq 0$. It is denoted by $f_X(x|y)$ or $f_X(x|Y=y)$.* ▯

Note that this definition is valid in spite of $P[Y = y] = 0$, as long as $f_Y(y) \neq 0$. Instead of the condition being on a different random variable from X, applications arise in which the condition is an event of the random variable X, such as $X \in A$ for some event A. If this situation arises,

$$f_X(x|X \in A) = \frac{d}{dx} \frac{P[X \leq x, X \in A]}{P[X \in A]}. \tag{A.30}$$

It is straightforward to verify the following property.

THEOREM A.4
Conditional densities satisfy all the properties of a pdf. ▯

A.5 Expectation, Variance, and Moments

In the previous section, we studied how the behavior of a random variable can be represented using the cdf or pdf functions. In many cases, however, we are only interested in summary information about a random variable. The simplest number representing information about a random variable is the *expected value*, which is also know by other names, such as the *mean*, the average, the centroid, and the first moment.

DEFINITION A.10 *The expected value of a continuous random variable, X, is defined as*

$$E[X] = \int_{-\infty}^{\infty} x f_X(x) dx. \tag{A.31}$$

If X is a discrete random variable, the expected value or expectation of X is defined as

$$E[X] = \sum_{\forall k} x_k P[X = x_k].$$ (A.32)

☐

Notice that in the case of a continuous random variable, we make use of the pdf of the random variable and integrate for computing the expectation. In the case of a discrete random variable, this pdf is replaced by the pmf of the random variable and the integral by the sum. It is straightforward to obtain the expectation of a mixed random variable, one with a continuous and a discrete part.

Example A.5

A discrete random variable N has the sample space of all natural numbers. We know that

$$P[N = 0] = 0.1,$$

$$P[N = i] = \frac{a}{b^i}, \quad \text{for } i > 0,$$ (A.33)

and that $E[N] = 3$. Determine a and b. ☐

Solution

$$\sum_{i=0}^{\infty} P(N = i) = 0.1 + \sum_{i=1}^{\infty} \frac{a}{b^i}$$ (A.34)

$$= 0.1 + \frac{a}{b} \sum_{i=0}^{\infty} \left(\frac{1}{b}\right)^i$$ (A.35)

$$= 0.1 + \frac{a}{b} \frac{1}{1 - \frac{1}{b}}, \quad b > 1$$ (A.36)

$$= 0.1 + \frac{a}{b - 1}$$ (A.37)

$$= 1.$$ (A.38)

$$E[N] = a \sum_{i=1}^{\infty} i \left(\frac{1}{b}\right)^i$$ (A.39)

$$= a \sum_{i=0}^{\infty} i \left(\frac{1}{b}\right)^i \tag{A.40}$$

$$= \frac{a}{b} \sum_{i=0}^{\infty} i \left(\frac{1}{b}\right)^{i-1}. \tag{A.41}$$

Let $\frac{1}{b} = x$. We have

$$E[N] = \frac{a}{b} \sum_{i=0}^{\infty} i x^{i-1} \tag{A.42}$$

$$= \frac{a}{b} \sum_{i=0}^{\infty} \frac{d}{dx} x^i \tag{A.43}$$

$$= \frac{a}{b} \frac{d}{dx} \sum_{i=0}^{\infty} x^i \tag{A.44}$$

$$= \frac{a}{b} \frac{d}{dx} \frac{1}{1-x} \tag{A.45}$$

$$= \frac{a}{b} \frac{1}{(1-x)^2} \tag{A.46}$$

$$= a \frac{\frac{1}{b}}{\left(1 - \frac{1}{b}\right)^2}$$

$$= \frac{ab}{(b-1)^2}. \tag{A.47}$$

Substituting the given values, we have

$$\frac{a}{b-1} = 0.9 \quad \text{and} \tag{A.48}$$

$$\frac{ab}{(b-1)^2} = 3. \tag{A.49}$$

Divide one by the other.

$$\frac{b-1}{b} = \frac{0.9}{3}$$
$$= 0.3. \tag{A.50}$$
$$b = \frac{10}{7}.$$

$$a = 0.9\,(b-1)$$
$$= \frac{27}{70}.$$

⬜

It is important to understand that the above definition of the expectation in equations (A.31) and (A.32) is *not* a special case of the definition of $E[g(X)]$ where $g(X)$ is a function of the random variable X. Indeed, if $g(x)$ is a well defined function of x, then $g(X)$ is a random variable with its own cdf and its expectation follows Definition (A.10). The evaluation of $E[g(X)]$ is an interesting problem and it is dealt with in Theorem A.13. on page 427.

DEFINITION A.11   *The nth moment of a continuous random variable, X, is defined as*

$$\mathcal{M}(n) = \int_{-\infty}^{\infty} x^n f_X(x)dx. \tag{A.51}$$

If X is a discrete random variable, then the nth moment is given by

$$\mathcal{M}(n) = \sum_{\forall k} x_k^n P[X = x_k]. \tag{A.52}$$

⬜

It is clear by this definition that the mean of a random variable is identical to the first moment. We can also calculate the moments centered around the mean or first moment of the random variable. These moments are referred to as *central moments* and are defined below.

DEFINITION A.12

$$\mathcal{M}_c(n) = \int_{-\infty}^{\infty} (x - E[X])^n f_X(x). \tag{A.53}$$

If X is a discrete random variable, then

$$\mathcal{M}_c(n) = \sum_{\forall k} (x_k - E[X])^n P[X = x_k]. \tag{A.54}$$

⬜

The second central moment of a random variable has a special significance, and is referred to as the *variance* of that random variable. The variance is an important indicator of the extent to which the occurrences of outcomes of a random variable deviate from the mean. Commonly used notation for the variance of a random variable X include $\text{var}[X]$ and σ_X^2. The positive square root of the variance is known as the standard deviation.

Example A.6
Evaluate the mean and variance of a single throw of the biased die experiment of Example A.2. 􀀀

Solution
Let the random variable be K.

$$E[K] = 0 \times 0.25 + 1 \times 0.1 + 2 \times 0.3 + 3 \times 0.18$$
$$+4 \times 0.05 + 5 \times 0.12$$
$$= 2.04. \tag{A.55}$$

Using the mean obtained above, we have

$$\text{var}[K] = 0.25(-2.04)^2 + 0.1(-1.04)^2 + 0.3(0.04)^2$$
$$+0.18(0.96)^2 + 0.05(1.96)^2 + 0.12(2.96)^2 \tag{A.56}$$

$$= 2.5584. \tag{A.57}$$

􀀀

A.5.1   Conditional expectation

In section A.4, the notion of conditional probability was introduced. In the previous section, the expectation of a random variable was defined. A natural progression would be to establish the expectation of a random variable under a specified condition. Therefore, in this section we present the conditional expectation of a random variable. Building on the definition of expectation and conditional probability, it is clear that the conditional expectation of a continuous random variable, X, conditioned on Y should follow

DEFINITION A.13

$$E[X|Y = y] = \int_{-\infty}^{\infty} x f_X(x|Y = y) dx. \tag{A.58}$$

If X is a discrete random variable, then

$$E[X|Y=y] = \sum_{\forall k} x_k P[X = x_k|Y = y]. \tag{A.59}$$

□

A.6 Theorems Connecting Conditional and Marginal Functions

We will start with probability masses to develop the theorem of total probability. The results can be extended to densities and expectations. Let K and M be discrete random variables taking all possible integer values, with k and m being their corresponding outcome variables. The marginal probability $P[K = k]$ can be obtained by summing the joint probabilities $P[K = k, \ M = m]$ over all possible outcomes m. That is,

$$P[K=k] = \sum_{m=-\infty}^{\infty} P[K=k, \ M=m]. \tag{A.60}$$

Note that the argument of the summation above is nonzero only for m satisfying $P[M = m] > 0$. From the definition of conditional probability, the joint probability can be expressed as the product of corresponding conditional probability and conditioning probability as follows.

$$P[K=k, \ M=m] = P[K=k|M=m]P[M=m], \tag{A.61}$$

for each m for which $P[M = m] \neq 0$. Let $P[K = k|M = m]P[M = m]$ be defined as zero if $P[M = m] = 0$. Using equation(A.61) in the earlier summation of equation (A.60), we have

THEOREM A.5 Total probability
Let K and M are discrete random variables with the set of integers as the sample space each. Then $P[K = k, \ M = m] = 0$ for that m.

$$P[K=k] = \sum_{m=-\infty}^{\infty} P[K=k|M=m]P[M=m]. \tag{A.62}$$

□

We can derive the equivalent of the theorem of total probability for continuous random variables, by simply recognizing that the probability of a random variable X being in the infinitesimal interval $(x, \ x + dx]$ is the product of the density and the infinitesimal interval, as follows.

$$P[x < X \le x + dx] = f_X(x)dx. \tag{A.63}$$

Using the above equation (A.63) and the arguments used in deriving the theorem of total probability, we have,

$$f_X(x)dx = P[x < X \le x + dx] \tag{A.64}$$

$$= \sum_{\forall dy} P[x < X \le x + dx, \ y < Y \le y + dy]$$

$$= \sum_{\forall dy} \left(P[x < X \le x + dx | y < Y \le y + dy] \right.$$

$$\left. \frac{P[y < Y \le y + dy]}{dy} dy \right). \tag{A.65}$$

In the above, as $dy \to 0$, the summation becomes an integral. Also, the condition $y < Y \le y + dy$ becomes $Y = y$ and the quantity $\frac{P[y<Y\le y+dy]}{dy}$ becomes $f_Y(y)$. Note that although $P[Y = y] = 0$, since y is a continuous random variable, $Y = y$ is not an impossible event. Indeed, when we conduct a random experiment corresponding to a continuous random variable, we do observe a particular y whose probability was 0. There is nothing inconsistent about actually realizing an outcome whose probability is zero, in a random experiment. Indeed, the probability of every outcome of a continuous random variable is zero. Yet, when a random experiment is conducted, we are guaranteed that one such outcome will occur. Therefore, we have

$$f_X(x)dx = \int_{y=-\infty}^{\infty} P[x < X \le x + dx | Y = y] f_Y(y) dy \tag{A.66}$$

$$= \int_{y=-\infty}^{\infty} f_X(x|Y = y) dx f_Y(y) dy. \tag{A.67}$$

Again, the integral above should be carried out over the range of y for which $f_X(x|Y = y)$ is defined, which is the range of y over which $f_Y(y)$ is nonzero. However, as long as the integrand is recognized as 0 for all y for which $f_Y(y) = 0$, the integral can be carried out over $y \in (-\infty, \ \infty)$. Canceling dx on both sides, we have

THEOREM A.6 Total density

$$f_X(x) = \int_{y=-\infty}^{\infty} f_X(x|Y=y)f_Y(y)dy. \tag{A.68}$$

▯

Mixed forms of the above theorems straightforward to develop. They are

$$f_X(x) = \sum_{\forall k} f_X(x|K=k)P[K=k] \quad \text{and} \tag{A.69}$$

$$P[K=k] = \int_{y=-\infty}^{\infty} P[K=k|Y=y]f_Y(y)dy. \tag{A.70}$$

In each of the above equations (A.69) and (A.70), one random variable is continuous and the other is discrete. That is, each of the random variables by itself is not mixed.

Consider $f_X(x|Y=y)$. This is the density function of the random variable X under the condition that Y was observed to take on the outcome y. If we leave the random variable Y as the condition in the conditional density, instead of letting Y take the outcome y, we get $f_X(x|Y)$. Notice that this density is a random variable! That is, for every x, we get a random variable. Suppose we take the expectation of X under the condition of the random variable Y, as

$$E[X|Y] = \int_{x=-\infty}^{\infty} x f_X(x|Y)dx. \tag{A.71}$$

$E[X|Y]$ is also a random variable, a deterministic function of the random variable Y. And we can evaluate the expectation of $E[X|Y]$ as

$$E\Big(E[X|Y]\Big) = \int_{y=-\infty}^{\infty} \left(\int_{x=-\infty}^{\infty} x f_X(x|Y=y)dx \right) f_Y(y)dy \tag{A.72}$$

$$= \int_{x=-\infty}^{\infty} \int_{y=-\infty}^{\infty} x f_{XY}(x,y)dy\,dx \tag{A.73}$$

$$= \int_{x=-\infty}^{\infty} x f_X(x)dx \tag{A.74}$$

$$= E[X].\tag{A.75}$$

Thus, we have the useful

THEOREM A.7 Total expectation

$$E[X] = E\Big(E[X|Y]\Big).\tag{A.76}$$

◻

If we have one or both of X and Y as discrete random variables, the above theorem of total expectation can be derived by properly using probability values and summations instead of integrals. Another important observation is that to use the theorem of total expectation, we do not need to be concerned about the range of y for which the $P[Y = y] = 0$ (in the discrete case) or $f_Y(y) = 0$ (in the continuous case). The expectations automatically take care of such singularities.

A.7   Sums of Random Variables

A.7.1   Sum of two discrete random variables

Let K and L be random variables, the sample space for each being the set of all (positive and negative) integers. Let $M = K + L$.

$$P[M = m] = P[K + L = m]\tag{A.77}$$

$$= \sum_{k=-\infty}^{\infty} P[K = k, L = m - k]$$

$$= \sum_{k=-\infty}^{\infty} P[L = m - k|K = k]P[K = k].\tag{A.78}$$

Note that the last expression corresponds to the theorem of total probability. If K and L are independent, the above expression for the pmf of the sum can be simplified. In this case, the condition $K = k$ is irrelevant in the above conditional probability. Hence, we have

THEOREM A.8

For two independent integer valued random variables M and K,

$$P[M = m] = \sum_{k=-\infty}^{\infty} P[L = m - k]P[K = k]. \tag{A.79}$$

The above sum is called the convolution sum.   ◻

If the sample space of K or L is a limited range of integers, further simplification is possible. For example, let K and L be nonnegative integer random variables. In such a case, $P[K = k]$ is zero for $k < 0$ and $P[L = m - k]$ is 0 for $k > m$. Therefore,

$$P[M = m] = \sum_{k=0}^{m} P[L = m - k]P[K = k]. \tag{A.80}$$

A.7.2   Sum of two continuous random variables

Let X and Y be continuous random variables and let $Z = X + Y$. For a given z, the outcomes x and y can vary as follows. One of x and y, say x can be any value and then y is required satisfy $y = z - x$. The pdf of Z is derived below, with the help of the theorem of total density.

$$f_Z(z) = \int_{x=-\infty}^{\infty} f_Z(z|X = x)f_X(x)dx. \tag{A.81}$$

In the above equation (A.81), given the outcome x for X, in order for Z to take on the outcome z, Y is required to take on the outcome $z - x$. Therefore, $f_Z(z|X = x)$ in the above is the same as $f_Y(z - x|X = x)$. Substituting the latter for the former in the equation (A.81), we obtain

$$f_Z(z) = \int_{x=-\infty}^{\infty} f_Y(z - x|X = x)f_X(x)dx. \tag{A.82}$$

If X and Y are independent, a further simplification ensues:

THEOREM A.9

For two independent continuous random variables X and Y and $Z = X + Y$,

$$f_Z(z) = \int_{x=-\infty}^{\infty} f_Y(z - x)f_X(x)dx. \tag{A.83}$$

The right hand side (RHS) in equation (A.83) is called the convolution integral. ⬚

In addition to independence, if X and Y are nonnegative, $f_X(x) = 0$ for $x < 0$ and $f_Y(z - x) = 0$ for $x > z$ and

$$f_Z(z) = \int_{x=0}^{z} f_Y(z - x) f_X(x) dx. \tag{A.84}$$

An alternative approach to deriving the density of the sum of two continuous random variables is to consider the cdf of Z which can be obtained by double integrating the joint density $f_{XY}(x, y)$ over the region $-\infty < y \leq z - x$ and $-\infty < x < \infty$.

Example A.7
Obtain the pmf and cdf of the sum of the numbers that show up when two independent and identically distributed (iid) biased dice of Example A.2 on page 402 are tossed. ⬚

Solution
Since the maximum outcome of each die is 5, we have

$$P[M = m] = \sum_{k=0}^{\min\{m, 5\}} P[L = m - k] P[K = k], \quad m = 0, \cdots, 10. \tag{A.85}$$

Substituting the values the probabilities of outcomes in the single die throwing experiment of Example A.2, we have $P[M = 0]$ through $P[M = 10]$ given by 0.0625, 0.05, 0.16, 0.15, 0.151 0.178, 0.0864, 0.09, 0.0457, 0.012, and 0.0144, respectively. The pmf is plotted in Figure A.1, and the cdf in Figure A.2. ⬚

A.8 Bayes' Theorem

Bayes' theorem is a useful and powerful result that relates conditional probabilities of random variables. Thomas Bayes (1702–1761) was a British mathematician. We shall first develop Bayes' theorem for two events A and B. Consider,

$$P[A|B] = \frac{P[A \cap B]}{P[B]} \tag{A.86}$$

$$= \frac{P[B|A]P[A]}{P[B]}. \tag{A.87}$$

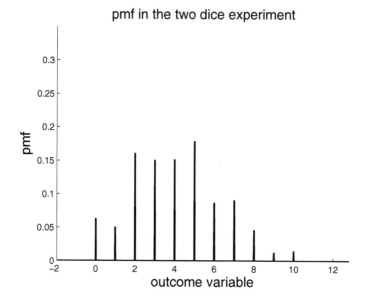

FIGURE A.1:   pmf in the two dice tossing experiment

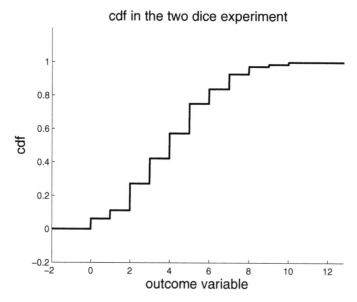

FIGURE A.2:   cdf in the two dice tossing experiment

In the above equation (A.87), $P[A]$ is called the *a priori* or the prior probability. It is the probability of the event A *before* the random experiment resulting in the event B is conducted. The quantity $P[A \mid B]$ is called the *a posteriori* or the posterior probability. It is the probability of the event A after observing the event B.

A partition *partition* of the sample space S is a set of mutually exclusive events whose union is S itself. Using the theorem of total probability for $P[B]$ in equation (A.87) produces the following result.

THEOREM A.10
Bayes' theorem for a discrete partition:

$$P[A_j|B] = \frac{P[B|A_j]P[A_j]}{\sum\limits_{i=1}^{n} P[B|A_i]P[A_i]}, \quad for\ any\ j \in \{1, \cdots, n\}. \qquad (A.88)$$

☐

A simple application of Bayes' theorem is elegantly demonstrated in the following famous puzzle.

Example A.8 Bertrand's box paradox
Joseph Louis Francois Bertrand (1822–1900) was a French mathematician. There are three identical looking boxes. In one of them, there are two gold coins. In another, two silver coins. In the third, a gold and a silver coin. A box is chosen at random and one of the two coins is picked from it, at random, without finding out about the other coin. The picked coin is found to be gold. What is the probability that the other coin in the same box is also gold? ☐

Solution
The reason for this problem being called a paradox, although an apparent one, is that one can jump to the conclusion that the other coin in the chosen box is gold or silver, with equal probability. If we actually conduct a large number of iid experiments, the observed frequency of the "other coin" being gold turns out to be not close to half. However, the resolution of the apparent paradox is simple, if we systematically apply the principles of probability, as follows.

Let C_1 be the random variable for the first pick of the coin from a box, and C_2, for the second pick. Let the outcomes of gold correspond to 1 and that of silver, to 0. Let B be the random variable corresponding to the box chosen. The sample space of $B = \{0, 1, 2\}$, where each of the numbers 0, 1, and 2 corresponds to the possible number of gold coins in the box. Now,

$$P[C_2 = 1 \mid C_1 = 1] = P[B = 2 \mid C_1 = 1] \qquad (A.89)$$

$$= \frac{P[C_1 = 1 \mid B = 2]P[B = 2]}{\sum_{i=0}^{2} P[C_1 = 1|B = i]P[B = i]}. \tag{A.90}$$

The RHS of equation (A.90) is the result of applying the Bayes' theorem to the RHS of equation (A.90). Substituting numerical values, we have

$$P[C_2 = 1 \mid C_1 = 1] = \frac{1 \times \frac{1}{3}}{(0 \times \frac{1}{3}) + (\frac{1}{2} \times \frac{1}{3}) + (1 \times \frac{1}{3})} \tag{A.91}$$

$$= \frac{2}{3}. \tag{A.92}$$

One can also use simple intuition and the following subjective argument to point out that the probability in question is larger than $\frac{1}{2}$. After all, if the first coin picked turns out to be gold, it immediately increases the chance that the box selected has *both* its coins gold! Therefore, there is a higher than even chance, *a posteriori*, that the second coin is also gold. ⬜

Bayes' theorem may be applied to problems in which we have a combination of discrete and continuous random variables. For instance, we can use the theorem of total probability for finding the conditional pmf. Then we obtain

THEOREM A.11
Bayes' theorem for a continuous conditioning random variable:

$$P[K = k|X = x] = \frac{f_X(x|K = k)P[K = k]}{\sum_{\forall i} f_X(x|K = i)P[K = i])}. \tag{A.93}$$

⬜

Equation (A.93) is extensively used in digital communication. Using the theorem of total density for finding the conditional pdf, Bayes' theorem takes the following form.

THEOREM A.12
Bayes' theorem for the a posteriori density:

$$f_X(x|Y = y) = \frac{f_Y(y|X = x)f_X(x)}{\int_{-\infty}^{\infty} f_Y(y|X = z)f_X(z)dz}. \tag{A.94}$$

⬜

A.9 Function of a Random Variable

Let the the real valued function y of a real valued variable x be uniquely defined by $y = g(x)$. That is, for every given value of x there is a uniquely specified value of y. If x is considered as the outcome of a random variable X, the function $g(x)$ induces a transformed random variable $Y = g(X)$. The random experiment corresponding to the random variable Y is easily described as follows. Conduct the random experiment to generate the outcome x of X. Find the corresponding value of y from the transformation $y = g(x)$. Then y is the outcome of Y. If the cdf of X is known, the determination of the pdf, pmf, or cdf of the new random variable Y is very useful.

The cases of discrete functions are dealt with first. Among the continuous functions, a strictly monotonically increasing function is the simplest and dealt with next. Strictly monotonically decreasing functions require a little modification and are treated next. In the very general case, the random variable may possess some discrete points for outcomes with nonzero probability and a continuous part. The function may map to constants over segments of the real line as well as increase and decrease over other segments. Although the case of increasing and decreasing functions are commonly encountered, the very general case is not commonly encountered. However, regardless of how complicated a function of a random variable is, the expectation of the function can be directly evaluated without evaluating the pdf, pmf, or the cdf of the function of the random variable.

A.9.1 Discrete function of a random variable

A.9.1.1 Discrete function of a discrete random variable

Let the sample space of a random variable X be $\{x_1, \cdots, x_n, \cdots, \}$ and let $y = g(x)$ be the transformation. Note that the corresponding random variable Y is discrete even if $y = g(x)$ is a continuous function. If X is discrete, x_i maps to y_i for every i and if $y_i \neq y_j$ for every $i \neq j$, then the pmf of Y is given by

$$P[Y = y_i] = P[X = x_i]. \tag{A.95}$$

Now, consider a transformation $y = g(x)$ in which two or more different x_i values can map to the same y_j. That is, given a y_j, the inverse transformation may not be unique. Let the set a_j contain all and only those values of x_i that map to y_j. Then, the pmf of Y is easily written as

$$P[Y = y_j] = P[X \in a_j] = \sum_{\forall x_i \in a_j} P[X = x_i]. \tag{A.96}$$

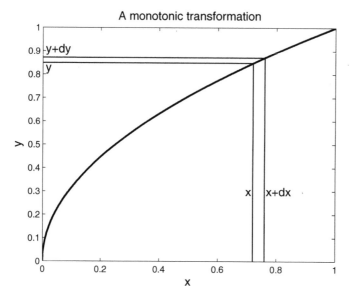

FIGURE A.3: A monotonic transformation of a random variable

A.9.1.2 Discrete function of a continuous random variable

In this case, the above transformation $y = g(x)$ results in each a_j being composed of segments of the real line x. Therefore,

$$P[Y = y_j] = \int_{x \in a_j} f_X(x)dx. \tag{A.97}$$

A.9.2 Strictly monotonically increasing function

Let X be a continuous random variable and $y = g(x)$ be defined for all x over which the pdf $f_X(x)$ is nonzero and let $g(x)$ be strictly monotonically increasing in that region. Let $x = h(y)$ be the inverse function. Due to the monotonicity of $g(x)$, the function $h(y)$ is also uniquely defined in its region. Figure A.3 illustrates this.

Consider an infinitesimal strip along the real line y between y and $y + dy$ with a positive dy. The probability of Y being in this strip is the same as the probability of X being in the strip bounded by $x = h(y)$ and $x + dx = h(y + dy)$. The quantity dx is positive since dy is positive and $y = g(x)$ is strictly monotonically increasing. Therefore,

$$P[y < Y \le y + dy] = P[x < h(y) \le x + dx] \tag{A.98}$$

can be expressed as

$$f_Y(y)dy = f_X(h(y))dx \quad \text{and} \tag{A.99}$$

$$f_Y(y) = f_Y(y) \frac{dx}{dy} \tag{A.100}$$

$$= f_Y(y) \frac{dh(y)}{dy}. \tag{A.101}$$

The reason for substituting $\frac{dh(y)}{dy}$ in place of $\frac{dx}{dy}$ is that the final result should be expressed as a function of y only.

A.9.3 Strictly monotonically decreasing function

Now, if $g(x)$ is strictly monotonically decreasing, the only change in the above arguments is that for $dy > 0$, we know that $dx < 0$. Therefore, equation (A.98) changes to

$$P[y < Y \le y + dy] = P[x + dx < h(y) \le x]. \tag{A.102}$$

We know that $dy > 0$ since we simply consider varying the independent variable y from a lower value to to a higher value. Therefore,

$$f_Y(y) = f_Y(y) \left| \frac{dx}{dy} \right| \tag{A.103}$$

$$= f_Y(y) \left| \frac{d}{dy} h(y) \right| \tag{A.104}$$

takes care of both the cases of strictly monotonic functions.

A.9.4 The general case of a function of a random variable

In general, the function $y = g(x)$ can increase and decrease. In such a case, the real line of y should be split into segments such that in each segment, the function is strictly monotonic. If $g(x)$ is a constant b over a segment of the real line x, $P[Y = b]$ can be nonzero, even if X is a continuous random variable. Irrespective of the nature of $g(x)$, a very important result facilitates the evaluation of the direct expectation of a function of a random variable.

Let u, v, and w are integer parameters. Let X be a random variable with a continuous part and a discrete part that take values $a_1, a_2, \cdots, a_m$ where m need not be finite. Let

$$P[X = a_i] = p_i, \quad i = 1, \cdots, u \text{ and} \tag{A.105}$$

$$\sum_{i=1}^{m} p_i = p. \tag{A.106}$$

Let $f(x)$ be the function representing the continuous part of X. Note that $f(x)$ is positive and must integrate to $1 - p$. Therefore $f(x)$ is not a valid pdf by itself. But,

$$P[x < X \le x + dx] = f(x)dx \text{ if } a_i \notin (x, \ x + dx] \text{ is true for all } i = 1, \cdots, m \text{ and}$$
$$\text{(A.107)}$$
$$P[x < X \le x + dx] = f(x)dx + p_j, \text{ if } a_j \in (x, \ x + dx]. \qquad \text{(A.108)}$$

Consider $y = g(x)$, a uniquely defined function for every x. The function $g(x)$ may tend to positive or negative infinity at specified discrete points of the real line x. But we exclude the such points from being any of the set $\{a_1, \cdots a_m\}$. This ensures that the random variable Y takes finite values with probability 1. That is, the transformation of the random variable, $g(X)$ is very general, but not pathological. The first task is to identify the set of points on the real line y each of which is an outcome of Y with nonzero probability. Clearly, $y = g(a_i)$, $i = 1, \cdots m$ are such points. It is possible for two or more distinct a_i values mapping to the same value. That is, $g(a_i) = g(a_j)$ is possible even if $i \ne j$. Considering all this, let $b_1, \cdots, b_k$ be the real numbers such that for every $i = 1, \cdots, m$,

$$g(a_i) = b_j \text{ for some } j. \qquad \text{(A.109)}$$

However, $b_1, \cdots, b_v$ are not the only points on the real line y which are outcomes of Y with nonzero probabilities. There may be segments of the real line x over which the function $g(x)$ is constant. The function $f(x)$ integrated over each such segment can produce a nonzero probability. Including all these points, let the totality of all the points, each of which is an outcome of Y with nonzero probability be $c_1, \cdots, c_n$. Let

$$P[Y = c_i] = q_i, \ i = 1, \cdots, n. \qquad \text{(A.110)}$$

Again, n can be infinite. Figure A.4 shows such a transformation $g(x)$. Now consider only those portions of the real line x over which there are no discrete points with nonzero probability for X and there is no segment for which $g(x)$ is a constant. Over each segment of the subset of x under consideration now, $g(x)$ is either increasing with $\frac{dy}{dx} = \frac{dg(x)}{dx} > 0$ or $g(x)$ is decreasing with $\frac{dy}{dx} = \frac{dg(x)}{dx} < 0$. This excludes single points at each of which $\frac{dg(x)}{dx} = 0$ as well. Let the resulting subset of the real line x be represented by a set of several segments $R = \{r_1, \cdots, r_m\}$ over each of which $\frac{dg(x)}{dx} > 0$ and a set of several segments $S = \{s_1, \cdots, s_n\}$ over each of which $\frac{dg(x)}{dx} < 0$.

For a given value of y in the subset of the real line under consideration, there may be several, k, values of x satisfying $g(x_i) = y$, $i = 1, \cdots, k$. Denote these different functions by $y = g_i(x_i)$. Denote each solution for x from $g_i(x)$ by the inverse transformation $h_i(y)$. That is, if $g(x_i) = y$, then $h_i(y) = x_i$. Some of these values may be in R and others in S. Nevertheless, the probability of Y being in the strip between y and $y + dy$ is given by

$$P[y < Y \le y + dy] = \sum_{i=1}^{k} P[X \in \text{ strip bounded by } x_i \text{ and } x_i + dx]. \quad \text{(A.111)}$$

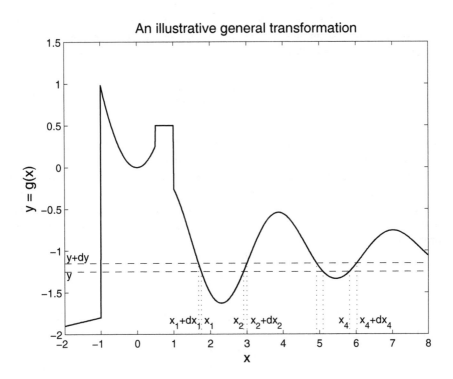

FIGURE A.4: Inverse function of the random variable has multiple roots

The peculiar notation is because dx can be positive or negative. In either case, we know that

$$P[y < Y \le y + dy] = \sum_{i=1}^{k} f(h_i(y))|dx| \qquad (A.112)$$

$$\xi(y)dy = \sum_{i=1}^{k} f(h_i(y))|dx| \qquad (A.113)$$

where $\xi(y)$ is the continuous part of the density function of Y. In order for the left hand side (LHS) of the above equation (A.113) to be a probability, dy is required to be positive. This just implies that we are varying the independent variable y in an increasing fashion. This allows us to express

$$\xi(y) = \sum_{i=1}^{k} \frac{f(h_i(y))}{\left|\frac{dg_i(x_i)}{dx_i}\right|} \qquad (A.114)$$

where $\frac{dg_i(x_i)}{dx_i}$ is expressed as a function of x. This is the continuous part. The discrete part, pmf, is given by $\{a_i\}$ with probabilities p_i.

The summary conclusion is the following. If the random variable X has discrete component at $x = a_i$ with a probability p_i, The random variable Y has a discrete part at $g(a_i)$ with a probability p_i. If the random variable has only a continuous part in $x \in (u, v)$ and $g(x)$ is a constant w for $x \in (u, v)$, this contributes a discrete probability value of

$$\int_u^v f_X(x)dx \qquad (A.115)$$

for Y at $y = w$. If $g(x)$ is strictly monotonic over an interval $x \in (s, t)$, this contributes

$$\frac{f_X\left(g^{-1}(y)\right)}{\left|\frac{dg(x)}{dx}\right|} \qquad (A.116)$$

(expressed as a function of y) to the continuous part of the pdf of Y. All the contributions due to all the parts are added to get the final continuous part pdf and the discrete part pmf of Y.

The above arguments are useful to evaluate the expectation of the random variable Y. The discrete part at $x = a_i$ with a probability p_i contributes $g(a_i)p_i$ to the expectation. The continuous part in $x \in (u, v)$ with $g(x)$ is a constant w for $x \in (u, v)$, contributes

$$w \int_u^v f_X(x)dx = \int_u^v g(x)f_X(x)dx \qquad (A.117)$$

to the expectation. Each segment of x over which $g(x)$ is monotonic contributes

$$\int y \frac{f_X\left(g^{-1}(y)\right)}{\left|\frac{dg(x)}{dx}\right|} dy = \int_s^t g(x) f_X(x)|dx| \tag{A.118}$$

since $y = g(x)$, $dg(x) = dy$, and dy is required to be positive in the integration on the LHS of the above equation (A.118. The quantity $|dx|$ is similarly recognized as dx itself, since dx is positive while the integration is carried out on the RHS of the above equation. Thus, we have the following important result.

THEOREM A.13
Let Y be a random variable, a function of X such that $y = g(x)$ is uniquely specified for every x. If X is a continuous random variable, we have

$$E[Y] = \int_{x=-\infty}^{\infty} g(x) f_X(x) dx. \tag{A.119}$$

If X is a discrete random variable, we have

$$E[Y] = \sum_{i=0}^{\infty} g(i) P[X = i]. \tag{A.120}$$

Let X have a continuous part and a discrete part with outcomes $a_1, \cdots, a_n$ possessing nonzero probabilities $p_1 \cdots, p_n$, respectively. The parameter n can be finite or infinite. Let $p = \sum_{i=1}^{n} p_i$. Let $f(x)$ be the nonnegative function of x representing the probability density portion of X. That is,

$$P[x < X \le x + dx] = f(x) dx \tag{A.121}$$

if $(x, \ x + dx]$ includes none of a_j and

$$P[x < X \le x + dx] = f(x) dx + p_j, \ \text{if } a_j \in (x, \ x + dx]. \tag{A.122}$$

Note that

$$\int_{-\infty}^{\infty} f(x) dx = 1 - p. \tag{A.123}$$

Then we have

$$E[Y] = \sum_{i=1}^{n} g(a_i) p_i + \int_{-\infty}^{\infty} g(x) f(x) dx. \tag{A.124}$$

□

A.10   The Laplace Transform $\mathcal{L}$

An equivalent way to represent all the properties of a nonnegative continuous random variable is the Laplace transform $\mathcal{L}_X(s)$ of the pdf of X. It is named after Pierre-Simon Laplace (1749–1827). It is a function of a complex variable s. Some properties of combinations of random variables, especially sums of independent random variables, are easily developed using the Laplace transform. The Laplace transform is usually defined for functions that are more general than the pdf of a nonnegative continuous random variable. Our interest is more restricted and the following definition reflects it.

DEFINITION A.14   *The Laplace transform of a continuous nonnegative random variable X is represented by $\mathcal{L}_X(s)$ and is defined as*

$$\mathcal{L}_X(s) = \int_0^\infty f_X(x)e^{-sx}dx = E[e^{-sX}] \qquad (A.125)$$

where s is a complex variable.   ⬜

It is easy to show that such a transformation exists for every s with a positive real part. Furthermore, the representation is unique in the sense that given a transform $\mathcal{L}_X(s)$, the corresponding density $f_X(x)$ can be completely recovered from $\mathcal{L}_X(s)$. This result is not proved here.

Example A.9

Evaluate the Laplace transform of an exponentially distributed   random variable X with a rate μ.   ⬜

Solution

$$f_X(x) = \begin{cases} \mu e^{-\mu x}, & x \geq 0 \\ 0, & x < 0. \end{cases} \qquad (A.126)$$

$$\mathcal{L}_X(s) = \int_0^\infty e^{-sx}\mu e^{-\mu x}dx \qquad (A.127)$$

$$= \mu \int_0^\infty e^{-(\mu+s)x}dx \qquad (A.128)$$

$$= \frac{\mu}{-(\mu+s)}\left[e^{-(\mu+s)x}\right]_0^\infty. \qquad (A.129)$$

For every s whose real part is larger than $-\mu$,

$$\lim_{x \to \infty} e^{-(\mu+s)x} = 0. \tag{A.130}$$

Therefore,

$$\mathcal{L}_X(s) = \frac{\mu}{\mu + s}, \tag{A.131}$$

if X is exponential with rate μ. Conversely, if $\mathcal{L}_Y(s) = \frac{\alpha}{\alpha+s}$, we know from unique-ness that

$$f_Y(y) = \begin{cases} \alpha e^{-\alpha y}, & y \geq 0 \\ 0, & y < 0. \end{cases} \tag{A.132}$$

$\square$

The most common use of Laplace transforms in probability theory is in the addition of two independent random variables. Let X and Y be continuous nonnegative random variables. Let $Z = X + Y$.

$$\mathcal{L}_Z(s) = E[e^{-sZ}] \tag{A.133}$$

$$= E[e^{-s(X+Y)}] \tag{A.134}$$

$$= \int_0^\infty \int_0^\infty e^{-s(x+y)} f_{X,Y}(x, y) dx dy. \tag{A.135}$$

In the above, $f_{X,Y}(x, y)$ is the joint density of the two random variables, also written as $f_{XY}(x, y)$ and $f(x, y)$ when there is no ambiguity.

$$P[(x < X \leq x + dx) \text{ and } (y < Y \leq y + dy)]$$

$$= f_{X,Y}(x, y) dx dy. \tag{A.136}$$

If X and Y are independent, we know (from probability theory, or from a little thought on the above equation), $f_{X,Y}(x, y) = f_X(x) f_Y(y)$. Therefore, if X and Y are independent,

$$\mathcal{L}_Z(s) = \int_0^\infty \int_0^\infty e^{-sx} e^{-sy} f_X(x) f_Y(y) dx dy \tag{A.137}$$

$$= \left[\int_0^\infty e^{-sx} f_X(x)dx \right] \left[\int_0^\infty e^{-sy} f_Y(y)dy \right]. \qquad \text{(A.138)}$$

That is,

$$\mathcal{L}_Z(s) = \mathcal{L}_X(s)\mathcal{L}_Y(s). \qquad \text{(A.139)}$$

This general result is stated as a theorem below.

THEOREM A.14
The Laplace transform of the sum of two independent continuous nonnegative random variables is the product of their individual Laplace transforms. ⬜

A.11   The $\mathcal{Z}$ Transform

The $\mathcal{Z}$ transform is defined for a discrete random variable X whose sample space is a subset of the set of natural numbers. The transform is a function of the entire pmf sequence of the random variable. In general, the $\mathcal{Z}$ transform is defined for sequences whose domain is the entire set of all negative and nonnegative integers. Also, unlike the pmf sequence, a general sequence for which the $\mathcal{Z}$ transform can be defined can also take on negative values and need not sum to one. However, our interest will be limited to the domain of nonnegative integers and pmf sequences which are nonnegative and sum to 1. In this sense, our definition of the $\mathcal{Z}$ transform is a restricted one. As a consequence, some important properties of the $\mathcal{Z}$ transform are simpler to develop. The uses of the $\mathcal{Z}$ transform are in the manipulation of the interaction of discrete random variables, similar to the uses of the Laplace transforms of continuous random variables.

DEFINITION A.15   *Let X be a random variable with a sample space of integers $0, 1, \cdots$, and denote $P[X = i]$ by p_i. The $\mathcal{Z}$ transform of X is denoted by $\mathcal{Z}_X(z)$ and defined by*

$$\mathcal{Z}_X(z) = \sum_{i=0}^{\infty} p_i z^i \qquad \text{(A.140)}$$

where z is a complex variable, $r(\cos\theta + \sqrt{-1}\sin\theta)$, with $r \geq 0$. Since $\sum_{i=0}^{\infty} |p_i| = 1$ the infinite series $\mathcal{Z}_X(z)$ converges for all $|r| < 1$. Therefore, the above definition of $\mathcal{Z}_X(z)$ is restricted for the cases of $|r| < 1$. ⬜

If the domain of a discrete random variable is a proper subset of the set of natural numbers, the above definition is nevertheless applicable by substituting zeros for the probabilities of impossible outcomes. Some important properties of the $\mathcal{Z}_X(z)$ are established below.

THEOREM A.15

The $\mathcal{Z}$ transform of a random variable is unique. That is, given a $\mathcal{Z}_X(z)$, the pmf of X can be completely recovered.

Proof

Note that

$$\mathcal{Z}_X(z) = p_0 + p_1 z + p_2 z^2 + \cdots + p_i z^i \cdots . \tag{A.141}$$

If $\mathcal{Z}_X(z)$ is differentiated i times, all the terms with indices $j < i$ in the above series will vanish; the i-th term will remain with no factor of z. All the terms with indices $j > i$ will be present with a factor of z^k, $k \geq 1$. Therefore, the quantity p_i alone can be recovered by evaluating the differentiated function at $z = 0$. Formally,

$$p_0 = \mathcal{Z}_X(0) \tag{A.142}$$

$$p_1 = \frac{d\mathcal{Z}_X(z)}{dz} \text{ evaluated at } z = 0 \tag{A.143}$$

$$\vdots$$

$$p_i = \frac{1}{i!} \frac{d^i \mathcal{Z}_X(z)}{dz^i} \text{ evaluated at } z = 0 \tag{A.144}$$

$$\vdots$$

$\square$

If a discrete random variable is modified by adding or subtracting an integer, another random variable results. If the resulting random variable does not have any negative number as its outcome, the definition and properties of the $\mathcal{Z}$ transform hold. It is easy to show the following.

THEOREM A.16

Let X be a discrete random variable and $Y = X + 1$. Then

$$\mathcal{Z}_Y(z) = z\mathcal{Z}_X(z). \tag{A.145}$$

Similarly, if $P[X = 0] = 0$ and if $W = X - 1$, we have

$$\mathcal{Z}_W(z) = z^{-1}\mathcal{Z}_X(z). \tag{A.146}$$

The following theorem is also easy to establish.

THEOREM A.17
Let X be a discrete random variable. Then,

$$E[X] = \frac{d\mathcal{Z}_X(z)}{dz} \text{ evaluated at } z = 1 \text{ and} \qquad \text{(A.147)}$$

$$E[X(X-1)] = \frac{d^2\mathcal{Z}_X(z)}{dz^2} \text{ evaluated at } z = 1. \qquad \text{(A.148)}$$

Finally, consider W, the sum of two independent discrete random variables X and Y. The $\mathcal{Z}$ transform of W can be obtained as the product of the $\mathcal{Z}$ transforms of X and Y as the following theorem shows.

THEOREM A.18
If X and Y are independent discrete random variables and if $W = X + Y$,

$$\mathcal{Z}_W(z) = \mathcal{Z}_X(z)\mathcal{Z}_Y(z). \qquad \text{(A.149)}$$

Proof
By definition,

$$\mathcal{Z}_W(z) = E[z^W] \qquad \text{(A.150)}$$

$$= E[z^{X+Y}] \qquad \text{(A.151)}$$

$$= E[z^X z^Y]. \qquad \text{(A.152)}$$

In the above, z^X is a random variable, a function of X alone; similarly, z^Y is a function of Y alone. Since X and Y are independent, the random variables z^X and z^Y are also not influenced by one another; that is, they are independent. Therefore, continuing from the above equation, we have

$$\mathcal{Z}_W(z) = E[z^X z^Y] \qquad \text{(A.153)}$$

$$= E[z^X]E[z^Y] \qquad \text{(A.154)}$$

$$= \mathcal{Z}_X(z)\mathcal{Z}_Y(z) \qquad\qquad \text{(A.155)}$$

which proves the theorem. ⬜

Example A.10
Evaluate the mean and variance of the sum of the numbers resulting in the two biased die experiment of Example A.7. ⬜

Solution
Let the random variables corresponding to the two throws of the die be X and Y. Let the sum be W.

$$\mathcal{Z}_X(z) = 0.25 + 0.1z + 0.3z^2 + 0.18z^3 + 0.05z^4 + 0.12z^5 \qquad \text{(A.156)}$$

$$\mathcal{Z}_Y(z) = 0.25 + 0.1z + 0.3z^2 + 0.18z^3 + 0.05z^4 + 0.12z^5 \qquad \text{(A.157)}$$

$$\mathcal{Z}_W(z) = (0.25 + 0.1z + 0.3z^2 + 0.18z^3 + 0.05z^4 + 0.12z^5)^2 \qquad \text{(A.158)}$$

In order to evaluate the expectation, differentiate once.

$$\frac{d\mathcal{Z}_W(z)}{dz} = 2(0.25 + 0.1z + 0.3z^2 + 0.18z^3 + 0.05z^4 + 0.12z^5)$$

$$\times (0.1 + 0.6z + 0.54z^2 + 0.2z^3 + 0.6z^4). \qquad \text{(A.159)}$$

Evaluate the above derivative at $z = 1$ to obtain

$$E[W] = 2 \times 1 \times (0.1 + 0.6 + 0.54 + 0.2 + 0.6) \qquad \text{(A.160)}$$
$$= 2 \times 2.04 = 4.08. \qquad \text{(A.161)}$$

In order to evaluate the variance, differentiate $\mathcal{Z}_W(z)$ twice.

$$\frac{d^2\mathcal{Z}_W(z)}{dz^2} = 2(0.1 + 0.6z + 0.54z^2 + 0.2z^3 + 0.6z^4)^2$$

$$+ 2(0.25 + 0.1z + 0.3z^2 + 0.18z^3 + 0.05z^4 + 0.12z^5)$$

$$\times (0.6 + 1.08z + 0.6z^2 + 2.4z^3). \qquad \text{(A.162)}$$

Evaluate the above second derivative to obtain

$$E[W(W-1)] = 2 \times (2.04)^2$$

$$+2 \times 1 \times (0.6 + 1.08 + 0.6 + 2.4) \tag{A.163}$$

$$= 2 \times (2.04)^2 + 9.36 \tag{A.164}$$

$$E[W^2] - E[W] = 2 \times (2.04)^2 + 9.36 \tag{A.165}$$

$$\text{Var}[W] = E[W^2] - (E[W])^2 \tag{A.166}$$

$$= E[W] + 2 \times (2.04)^2 + 9.36 - (E[W])^2 \tag{A.167}$$

$$= 2.04 + 9.36 - (2.04)^2 \tag{A.168}$$

$$= 7.3184. \tag{A.169}$$

$$\square$$

A.12 Exercises

1. The instructor of a class announces that the numerical score in a midterm test, approximated as a real number, has a triangular density function spread between 30 and 95. The density function peaks at 80, and a score of 70 is a pass. A student only knows his/her performance in terms of a pass/fail result. At the end of the semester, the top 10% of the students are awarded a scholarship.

   (a) Determine the peak value of the density function.

   (b) Determine the mean and variance of the score.

   (c) Given that a student passed, what is the probability that he/she will be awarded a scholarship?

2. Evaluate the mean and variance of the sum of two iid biased-dice random experiment in Example (A.7), without using the $\mathcal{Z}$ transform.

3. A simple a microprocessor-based control system has three interrupting devices A, B, and C. The microprocessor checks for interrupts frequently, once every 10 milliseconds (msec). The device A has priority over the other two devices, and B has priority over C. This means that if all the devices are interrupting, only A is serviced. If only B and C are interrupting, only B will be served. If only C is interrupting, it will be served. The devices A, B, and C generate

interrupts statistically independently with probabilities of 0.1, 0.4, and 0.6, respectively. Their respective interrupt service times are 5, 3, and 2 msecs. Unserviced interrupts are lost. There is no queuing at all.

Determine each of the probabilities with which the microprocessor services A, B, or C after it checks. Also determine the average time spent on interrupt service during a 10 msec time period.

4. The function $G_X(x) = 1 - F_X(x)$ is called the complementary cumulative distribution function (ccdf) and also by the name of the tail distribution function. It is also commonly denoted by $F_c(x)$ when the random variable under consideration is obvious. Prove that the expectation of a nonnegative random variable is the integral of its ccdf over the nonnegative real line.

5. Prove that the expectation of the sum of two random variables is the sum of their individual expectations. Do not assume that the two random variables are independent. Do this for the two cases of continuous and discrete random variables.

6. Prove that the variance of the sum of two independent random variables is the sum of the variances of the individual random variables.

7. From the *Parade* weekly news magazine. Consider a TV game show in which the host shows the participant three identical doors and tells her that behind one of them is a sports car and behind the others are a goat each. The participant should try to guess the door with the car. The participant picks one. The host opens a different door that shows a goat. The host then gives a chance for the participant to switch the choice to the remaining door. The question is, at that time, what are the probabilities of finding the car in each of the two closed doors? This will help the participant to determine if she should switch the doors if given a chance.

Remember that any time anyone has to choose between two or more identical choices (to the knowledge of the person making the choice), one is picked "at random."

8. This problem is based on a fictional story titled "The curious prisoner and the warden." There were three prisoners A, B, and C, in different cells. They knew that one of them had already been chosen at random to be executed the next morning. Prisoner A went to the warden and said "I know you are not allowed to tell me which one of us will be executed. But I do know that one of the other two will *not* be executed. Will you please tell me which of the other two will not be executed?" The warden reflected for a moment and obliged the prisoner A with a true answer. Did this change A's calculation of the probability that he would be executed? And according to A's calculations, what is the probability that the other candidate (other than the survivor as disclosed by the warden) would be executed?

Instead of checking with the warden, let us say that A found a true document that he was not supposed to have access to. And let us say that the document implied that a particular prisoner from $\{B,\ C\}$ will be alive following the next day. Now repeat the same calculations as above and compare.

9. Prove the Markov inequality. That is, for any nonnegative random variable X, with an expectation η and for any $\alpha > 0$, show that

$$P[X \geq \alpha] \leq \frac{\eta}{\alpha}. \qquad \text{(A.170)}$$

10. Prove the Chebyshev inequality. That is, for any random variable with an expectation of η and variance of σ^2, and for any $\epsilon > 0$, show that

$$P[|X - \eta| \geq \epsilon] \leq \frac{\sigma^2}{\epsilon^2}. \qquad \text{(A.171)}$$

This is named after Pafnuty Chebyshev (1821–1894), a Russian mathematician.

Index

Milton Keynes UK
Ingram Content Group UK Ltd.
UKHW021902071024
449327UK00021B/1602